D0120384

To War with Wellington

Also by Peter Snow

Leila's Hijack War
Hussein, a Biography
Battlefield Britain (with Dan Snow)
Twentieth Century Battlefields (with Dan Snow)

To War with Wellington

From the Peninsula to Waterloo

PETER SNOW

JOHN MURRAY

First published in Great Britain in 2010 by John Murray (Publishers)
An Hachette UK Company

1

© Peter Snow 2010

The right of Peter Snow to be identified as the Author of the Work has been asserted by him in accordance with the Copyright, Designs and Patents Act 1988.

All rights reserved. Apart from any use permitted under UK copyright law no part of this publication may be reproduced, stored in a retrieval system, or transmitted, in any form or by any means without the prior written permission of the publisher, nor be otherwise circulated in any form of binding or cover other than that in which it is published and without a similar condition being imposed on the subsequent purchaser.

A CIP catalogue record for this title is available from the British Library

ISBN 978-1-84854-103-0

Endpapers: *Battle of Talavera* 1809, courtesy of the Council of the National Army Museum

Typeset in Bembo by Servis Filmsetting Ltd, Stockport, Cheshire

Printed and bound by Clays Ltd, St Ives plc

John Murray policy is to use papers that are natural, renewable and recyclable products and made from wood grown in sustainable forests. The logging and manufacturing processes are expected to conform to the environmental regulations of the country of origin.

John Murray (Publishers)
338 Euston Road
London NW1 3BH

www.johnmurray.co.uk

To my wife, Ann, and Margaret, my sister-in-law, for their constant inspiration

Contents

List of Illustrations		ix
List of Maps		xi
	Introduction	1
1.	First foothold	7
	Mondego Bay, August 1808	
2.	You must have bribed Junot	23
	Vimeiro, August 1808	
3.	Scum of the earth	35
	Oporto, 1809	
4.	The obstinate old Gentleman	54
	Talavera, 1809	
5.	Damned with might and main	71
	Retreat, 1809	
6.	Unpardonable butchery	82
	The Côa and Bussaco, 1810	
7.	A dangerous hour for England	101
	Fuentes d'Oñoro, 1811	
8.	Now, lads, for the breach	122
	Ciudad Rodrigo, 1812	
9.	The town's our own. Hurrah!	138
	Badajoz, 1812	
10.	*Marmont est perdu*	155
	Salamanca, 1812	
11.	One step forward, two steps back	168
	Madrid and Burgos, 1812	
12.	I saw them fall like a pack of cards	184
	Vitoria, 1813	

CONTENTS

13. The finger of God is upon me   201
    Pyrenees, 1813
14. Extraordinary news   218
    Southern France, 1813–1814
15. In the Elysian Fields   234
    Paris and Vienna, 1814–1815
16. Duchess, you may give your ball   246
    Brussels, 1815
17. Blücher has had a damn good hiding   260
    Quatre-Bras, 16 June 1815
18. Hard pounding   276
    Waterloo, morning 18 June 1815
19. Now, Maitland, now's your time!   292
    Waterloo, afternoon 18 June 1815
20. See the Conquering Hero Comes   310
    Aftermath

    Author's Note   319
    Notes   323
    Bibliography   353
    Illustration credits   361
    Index   367

Illustrations

1. Arthur Wellesley 1804
2. Wellesley's army lands in Portugal 1808
3. Wellesley's crossing of the Douro 1809
4. August Schaumann
5. Jonathan Leach
6. Recruiting for Wellington's army
7. Robert Craufurd
8. Sir Thomas Picton
9. Battle of Bussaco 1810
10. Fred Ponsonby
11. Rowland Hill
12. Ned Costello
13. Battle of Fuentes d'Oñoro 1811
14. Crossing the River Guadiana 1811
15. Crossing the River Tagus 1811
16. The siege of Ciudad Rodrigo 1812
17. The morning after the storming of Ciudad Rodrigo
18. Storming the castle at Badajoz 1812
19. Primitive surgery
20. Harry Smith
21. Juana María de los Dolores de León, wife of Harry Smith
22. A caricature of Wellington's army on the march
23. Major General Edward Pakenham
24. Battle of Salamanca 1812
25. Battle of Vitoria 1813
26. Wellington and his ADC Fitzroy Somerset
27. Rees Gronow
28. Battle of the Nivelle 1813

29. Kitty, Duchess of Wellington
30. Harriette Wilson
31. Mademoiselle George
32. Cartoon of Wellington
33. Battle of Waterloo
34. French cuirassiers charge British infantry at Waterloo
35. Sergeant Ewart seizes a French Eagle at Waterloo
36. The British Guards at Waterloo.
37. A Frenchman revives Fred Ponsonby after Waterloo
38. Wellington visits the wounded Lord Uxbridge after Waterloo
39. Napoleon Bonaparte at the time of his first abdication in 1814
40. The Waterloo banquet of 1836

Maps

1. Wellington's Peninsular War   6
2. The Battle of Roliça   16
3. The Battle of Vimeiro (1)   22
4. The Battle of Vimeiro (2)   22
5. Central Portugal   45
6. The Battle of Oporto   47
7. The Battle of Talavera   59
8. The Battle of Bussaco   92
9. The Battle of Fuentes d'Oñoro (1)   108
10. The Battle of Fuentes d'Oñoro (2)   112
11. The Siege of Ciudad Rodrigo   127
12. The Siege of Badajoz   139
13. The Battle of Salamanca   159
14. The Battle of Vitoria   190
15. The Siege of San Sebastián   205
16. 1813–14 Campaign   208
17. 15–18 June 1815   249
18. The Battle of Waterloo: Morning   278
19. The Battle of Waterloo: 4.00–6.00 p.m.   293
20. The Battle of Waterloo: 7.30–8.00 p.m.   302

Introduction

ONE MIDWINTER DAY, in January 1786, during a gap in the seemingly interminable wars between Britain and France, a shy Irish teenager was sent off to a French school to learn to be a soldier. His father had died and his mother had almost despaired of him. 'I don't know what I shall do with my awkward son Arthur,' she grumbled. His father had been an Irish earl, part of that curious Protestant minority known as the Anglo-Irish. They had tried to make something of Arthur by sending him to Eton. But that had been hopeless. The boy was lonely and idle. Just about all he could do was play the violin. He came fifty-fourth out of seventy-nine boys in the fourth form. So when he was seventeen Arthur's exasperated mother sent him off to the French equestrian school at Angers. The only thing to do with the feckless younger son of an aristocratic family was to try and make him a soldier. France was the place you learned to be a man in those days, and Angers might just give him the skills and the fibre to survive in the army.

The school in France did a lot more than that. The young Arthur Wesley – the family name would be changed to Wellesley by his ambitious elder brother, Richard – emerged from Angers after just one year's study of horsemanship, fencing and the humanities with a new self-assurance. He was to build on the knowledge and skills he had gained in France to confront French armies on the battlefield and eventually to destroy the French Emperor Napoleon himself. And Arthur Wellesley would become the Duke of Wellington. This book is the story of how this once unpromising boy led one of the most successful military enterprises in British history through seven years of struggle, from its first small-scale landing in Portugal to the battlefield of Waterloo. It is the story of how this withdrawn but single-minded soldier turned a band of men he described as the 'scum of the earth' into one of the world's finest armies, and how together they helped defeat Napoleon.

The men we meet in these pages were as varied an assortment of characters as ever went to war, from brutish scoundrels to the thoughtful and humane. Wellington was a military genius, his personality a curious mix of aloof intolerance, dry wit and an occasional flash of humanity. It was astonishing how a man so arrogant, so class conscious and so insensitive could become such a national hero by the time he was forty-five. Wellington was to go on, after Waterloo, to dominate British public life for decades, as a conservative prime minister and an opponent of electoral reform. But the reason he remained a legendary figure until the day he died was the debt that Britain and Europe owed him for undermining and finally defeating Napoleon Bonaparte.

Wellington was, above all, a lucky man. Lucky in that he escaped death so often when many of his senior colleagues and aides were killed or wounded around him. But lucky too in the great advantage the privilege of aristocracy gave him in launching his career. It was an oddity of the age that it wasn't merit but money and connections that won promotion in the army. His brother Richard, well on the way to high office in London, was to play a vital part in Arthur's career in the years between his return from Angers and the launch of the great adventure in Portugal.

Arthur Wellesley came back from Angers a superb horseman, speaking fluent French and with the glint of ambition in his eye. He duly took his turn to be MP for Trim and, with Richard's help, bought his way to the rank of lieutenant colonel by 1793. Yet when he proposed marriage to the daughter of Lord Longford, Kitty Pakenham, Longford judged him a fellow of such little promise that he made her reject him. Arthur, his pride dented, set his heart on active service. He gave away his violin and set off to join the war against revolutionary France as a commander in the Netherlands just as Napoleon Bonaparte, only thirteen weeks younger than him, became commander of the French artillery at Toulon. In the years after the Revolution of 1789, France had guillotined its aristocrats and was at war with its neighbours. It wouldn't be long before, under Napoleon, it evolved into a rampant imperial power bent on dominating the whole of Europe.

Then in 1796 Arthur's career took a turn that was to give him a decisive boost. His regiment – the 33rd Yorkshire West Riding, later to become the Duke of Wellington's – was posted to India. And by a lucky coincidence his brother Richard was appointed governor general of India a year later. Richard promptly named the fourth of his five brothers, Henry, his private secretary and vowed to do what he could to further the career of Arthur, who had preceded him to the subcontinent as an army colonel. In 1799 Richard (who became Marquess Wellesley at the end of that year) ordered the invasion of the southern state of Mysore on the ground that its ruler Tippoo Sultan was too close to the French. Arthur Wellesley took Tippoo's capital Seringapatam by storm on 4 May.

By the summer of 1803 Arthur, now a major general, was commanding the British force of 7,000 that confronted the 44,000-strong army of the Maratha states at Assaye 200 miles north-east of Bombay. He scored a masterly victory. Looking for a way to fight the Marathas on favourable ground, he spotted two villages either side of a river. Rightly guessing that the river would be fordable there, he led his army across and with his Indian troops outflanked and defeated his opponents. One of Arthur's young lieutenants wrote: 'The general was in the thick of the action the whole time and had a horse killed under him. No man could have shown a better example to the troops than he did. I never saw a man so cool and collected as he was.'

By mid-December Arthur had defeated the Marathas again at Argaum. He returned from India in 1805 an accomplished field commander. He had discovered the vital importance of intelligence in establishing the whereabouts and strength of his enemy. He had learned how to use the terrain and understood the importance of keeping his men supplied however unforgiving the countryside. He had seen the value of leading by example and making brisk decisions. He came home determined to fight Napoleon, by now Emperor of France, master of most of Europe and a major threat to Britain. The struggle between the British and French empires for world hegemony was reaching its height. Arthur trusted that his record would propel him to high command. But in the eyes of his military rivals he was still – as Napoleon put it later – only a 'sepoy general'. The man who had made his name commanding Indian forces so skilfully still had to prove he could lead a substantial British force in the war against the French Empire in Europe.

Arthur Wellesley also came home with a reputation as a bit of a ladies' man. He had had one particularly close relationship with the wife of one of his captains. Still smarting at the way his proposal of marriage had been rejected ten years before, he proposed to Kitty again. This time his increased stature induced Lord Longford to change his mind, and Kitty accepted. They married in April 1806. It was a sad mistake on both sides. As time went on, she became deeply introverted and self-absorbed, quite unable to play the wife to someone as renowned and sexually eligible as Arthur. Even before he married her, he let slip the telling aside that he now found that she had grown ugly, and he later told a great friend that that he had been 'a damned fool' to marry someone like Kitty. 'I was not the least in love with her.'

Wellesley saw some active service in Germany and Denmark in the next two years. But the opportunity that was to change his life – and the course of history – came in 1808. He was sent with a modest force to open a new front against Napoleon on the west coast of Portugal. The men he brought with him were not only about to take the first firm step on Britain's road to Waterloo. They were also to launch a literary revolution. This was the first campaign in history to give rise to a rich tide of eyewitness accounts by those who fought it. In the post-war years a generation of new readers, with an appetite for stories about what they called the Great War, proved an attractive market for memoirs about the conflict. Growing literacy in early Victorian Britain inspired soldiers, from generals down to privates, to record their accounts of what had happened. Wellington himself wrote copious letters and despatches.

Everything from the fighting itself to the camaraderie and skulduggery of camp life and the mischief the men got up to in the local villages is revealed in these first-hand accounts by those who were there. Some wrote journals at the time, when their memories were fresh – men like George Simmons, who kept three notebooks in his hat. Others, like Rifleman Benjamin Harris, recounted their stories

4

months or even years afterwards. Many exaggerate British prowess and downplay that of the French. But all bring the horror, the suffering, the hopes and the fears of the soldiers alive in strikingly modern language. The men who landed in the Iberian Peninsula with Wellesley were about to make a contribution to the human story of warfare in a detail and a variety that the world had never seen before.

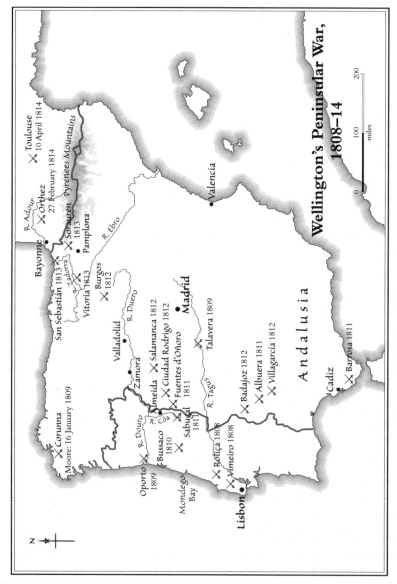

Wellington's Peninsular War

I

First foothold

Mondego Bay, August 1808

I T TOOK THE best part of two weeks to unload the ships. The weather wasn't the problem. It was fine – hot and sticky by day, crisp and clear at night. The snag was the swell piling in across 3,000 miles of open Atlantic on to Portugal's unprotected coast. The lumpy transport vessels rolled so much on anchor that the yards at times almost touched the water. Captain Jonathan Leach, a young rifleman who had had to wait six days for the order to disembark, complained that the motion had 'caused some awful breakages amongst our wine glasses'.

It was 1 August 1808, the height of summer. George Landmann, an ambitious young engineer, was on the deck of his ship as she slipped into Mondego Bay to join the other seventy British transports and warships bobbing about. Suddenly the boredom of walking around the deck was 'exchanged for a scene of the utmost activity'. Landmann's cabin floor was covered in trunks, hats, boots, blankets, greatcoats, saddles and bridles. People were shouting, 'What do you think I ought to take with me?' or 'Do you think we shall be many days away from the ship?' Officers told their servants to assemble their kit. The servants were 'tumbling down the companionway' and knocking each other over, upon which the most 'expressive epithets were exchanged'. Landmann decided to take as little as possible, and left his greatcoat behind. He was to regret it. He was soon back on deck using his spyglass to look for vessels to take people ashore. The bay was buzzing with activity as boats braved the surf to get men, guns and horses on to the beach. His ship was a mile and a half off-shore; most of the others were further in and he could see a busy ferry service going on.

Charles Leslie and his regiment – the 29th of Foot – transferred into flat-bottomed boats soon after midday. But reaching the beach in the breaking rollers was a dangerous operation. 'Several boats were upset and one containing a part of our grenadiers lost arms and everything and the men narrowly escaped with their lives.' James Hale, from Gloucester, had earned himself a bounty of ten guineas twelve months earlier by signing up for seven years as an ordinary private. He and his 9th Regiment of Foot braved the surf on 2 August and they landed in style. The Portuguese, who by now were persuaded that the British troops had come not to invade their country but to rescue it from the French, decided to give them a dry landing. They 'came running into the water, above their knees, to carry us out of the boats . . . and young women came flocking around about us with their aprons full of fruit'. Hale and his comrades all landed without getting their feet wet, but 'one boat load . . . was upset by the violence of the heavy swell, in crossing the bar at the mouth of the River Mondego and unfortunately several soldiers and sailors were drowned'. It wasn't unusual in those days for soldiers to be unable to swim.

The landing at Mondego Bay under Lieutenant General Sir Arthur Wellesley was Britain's first tentative move in what would develop into a grand design to undermine Napoleon. It was the beginning of seven exhausting years of fighting on land that would bring out the best and the worst in a band of young British men. It would have its moments of gallantry and glory but mostly it was downright savage. Many of those who scrambled ashore that August hadn't yet reached their late teens: few were more than thirty. Some were inspired by patriotism, the chance to join the mighty struggle to throw Napoleon out of Europe. Most were there for the adventure and the plunder and the chance to kill a few Frenchmen. Very few would survive the coming battles unscathed: most would die or suffer wounds that would leave them limbless or scarred for life. And disease, heat, cold and thirst would take an even greater toll than battle.

The small force of 9,000 men which landed with Wellesley was largely untried. Napoleon's massive army had subdued most of Europe with victories as spectacular as Austerlitz, Jena and Friedland over the Austrians, Prussians and Russians. Compared to the French, the British soldiers piling on to the beach were novices. Few had fought in any major land campaign: if they had, they had been largely unsuccessful. Britain's army had been neglected since the glorious days of Plassey and Quebec half a century earlier. The money had been spent on the Royal Navy, making Britain the strongest sea-power in the world. The army had played only a small part in the fight with Napoleon so far. But Wellesley's force of 9,000 men would grow to 90,000 by the end of 1813 and play a decisive role in redrawing the map of Europe. It would plant a host of unforgettable names – of people as well as battles – in the annals of military history. And their leader, Arthur Wellesley, the reluctant choice of some of his masters in London in August 1808, would by 1815 become the world's most admired soldier.

Wellesley was watching his troops struggling ashore. He too cursed the swell, but if he was to disembark within reach of his objective, Lisbon, which was occupied by the French, the landing had to be on Portugal's 'Iron Coast', as he called it. There was simply no shelter for a hundred miles north of the Portuguese capital. He was standing on the deck of the fleet's flagship, HMS *Donegal*. By an irony she had been captured from the French during their unsuccessful attempt to invade Wellesley's native Ireland only a decade earlier.

Wellesley was still only thirty-nine, but he had come a long way from the diffident little boy with the violin. He was a slim, wiry man with sharp blue eyes and a pronounced nose. He had a habit of looking down it at people he despised. He radiated not warmth but confidence and command. He abhorred ostentation, dressing more often than not in smart but simple civilian clothes. He had no time for fools, and even with those he trusted he was reluctant to delegate authority. He was doing exactly what he wanted to do: going off to fight the French. Typically, he believed he was the obvious man for the job. If anyone could beat Napoleon and his marshals, he could. He told a friend: 'I am not afraid of them [the French] as everyone else seems to be.'

A month earlier Wellesley's boss, Lord Castlereagh, the Secretary of State for War, had given him command of an army with a challenging new mission. Napoleon, now master of Europe, who had seized Spain and Portugal the previous year, was subjecting the two countries to a cruel and ruthless occupation. He sat his own brother

Joseph, a deeply inadequate and unappealing man, on the Spanish throne and imposed a repressive military rule on Portugal. Both nations rose in popular revolt against France. But if the rebels were to do any significant damage to Napoleon, they would need outside support. They soon found an ally in Britain, whose Royal Navy had been using Portuguese ports in its blockade of the French Empire but had now lost access to them. With Portugal in French hands only Swedish ports remained open to British ships. There was a compelling case for Britain to take the war with Napoleon to the Iberian Peninsula. On 30 June 1808 Castlereagh told Wellesley he would be given 14,000 troops 'to be deployed under your orders in counteracting the designs of the enemy and in affording to the Spanish and Portuguese nations every possible aid to throwing off the yoke of France'. It was a major opportunity for Wellesley. He believed that British troops, well led, could be more than a match for the French. But it was a formidable challenge. Few of the men he commanded had fought with him before. The officers and ordinary soldiers he would mould into his formidable Peninsular Army were no band of brothers – yet. He had only a few trusted friends with him from the beginning.

One was his old comrade Rowland Hill, a major general, a dependable soldier and a kind and generous leader. The men he commanded affectionately called him 'Daddy'. George Bell, one of Hill's junior officers, referred to him as 'our kind, good and amiable soldier-in-chief . . . with his honest, benevolent face'. Wellesley, who had got to know Hill in the Netherlands campaign, wrote: 'I rejoice extremely at the prospect before me of serving again with you.' Another early member of what would become a close-knit team was Lord James Henry Fitzroy Somerset, a bright but still largely untried youth of nineteen. He had been strongly recommended to Wellesley as 'an active and intelligent fellow' by his friend the Duke of Richmond. Fitzroy Somerset would be Wellesley's chief aide de camp from that day on the deck of the *Donegal* to Waterloo seven years later.

But Wellesley's hopes were to suffer one early setback. The government in London began to contemplate the implications of landing a force on the continent to capture Lisbon, and decided that to dislodge Napoleon's General Junot and his army a larger force would be needed. And that called for a more senior commander than Wellesley, who was still a very junior lieutenant general. Wellesley sailed south, unaware that a hot debate raged in London between his supporters, Castlereagh and the Foreign Secretary George Canning, and the Duke of York, the Army Commander in Chief (and second son of King George III), who favoured other generals such as Sir John Moore. Moore was senior to Wellesley and had also enjoyed a distinguished military career. He was respected for his sponsorship and training of the rifle regiments which were fast being recognised as the elite units in the British army.

Two days after he set foot on the beach at Mondego Bay, Arthur Wellesley was seen by one of his staff heading south on horseback looking very crestfallen. It was not surprising. He had just received another despatch from Castlereagh, which had him struggling to swallow his resentment. It informed him that far from commanding the army to be landed in the Peninsula, he would be number three in the pecking order. 'His Majesty has been pleased to entrust the command of his troops serving on the coast of Spain and Portugal to Lt Gen Sir Hew Dalrymple with Lt Gen Sir Harry Burrard second in command.' Castlereagh, no doubt guessing that Wellesley would be deeply upset, went on to urge his protégé to make the most of his command 'with every expedition that circumstances will permit' without awaiting the arrival of the more senior generals. Wellesley was dismayed by the prospect of no longer being in charge. His view, as he explained to his subordinates, was 'I didn't know what the words "second in command" meant . . . I alone commanded the army.' And yet here he was being instructed to take orders from at least two generals, Dalrymple and Burrard, with singularly undistinguished military careers. He wrote a private letter to his friend the Duke of Richmond expressing his strong sense of injured pride. 'I hope I shall have beaten Junot before they arrive, and then they can do as they please with me.'

The landing at Mondego Bay was just about complete by the end of the first week of August. George Landmann had made it ashore, but he had been soaked to the skin when a wave broke over his boat. 'Fortunately we did not capsize, and . . . a vast concourse of the people who had been watching our movements with great anxiety rushed into the sea and seizing our boat by the gunwales on each side dragged it . . . high and dry.' Norbert Landsheit, a German cavalryman in British service, was a sergeant in the small cavalry detachment of 200 light dragoons Wellesley had brought with him. He had a nervous time landing his horses: 'One punt capsized upon the surf, but no lives were lost, because the horses, sometimes swimming, sometimes wading, carried their riders ashore.' And there weren't just men with their guns and horses scrambling ashore: there were women and children too. It was a tradition of the British army that a handful of wives were permitted to travel with each regiment. They helped with the washing, sewing and cooking, and in return they were allowed to sleep with their husbands. Wellesley decreed that women would get half a man's ration each day 'and the children a quarter: but no spirits or wine will be issued to women or children'. The wives who came counted themselves lucky: each one who travelled had to endure fierce competition at the port of departure. Those left behind knew there was a good chance they would never see their husbands again.

Wellesley had chosen his landing spot well. He had a remarkable knack for judging the topography and the timing of any move forward – skills he was to perfect in the years that led to Waterloo. He had chosen Mondego Bay when he learned it was free of French troops. He also knew it was overlooked by a fort which some Portuguese rebels had secured and handed over to a small force of British marines. Once ashore, his men began to march. Even the rawest recruits in the army had marched before. But that was back home. Very few had marched in temperatures over 30 degrees centigrade. One of the youngest and newest was a young Scot, Thomas Todd. He had joined the army only after trying and failing to make a name for himself as an actor – he had been hissed off the stage at his first performance in Edinburgh. He and his comrades in the Highland Light Infantry, the 71st Regiment of Foot, marched for twelve miles 'up to the knees in sand which caused us to suffer much from thirst. We lost four men of our regiment who died from thirst. We buried them where they fell.' Todd later discovered a remedy for thirst. 'I put a small pebble into my mouth and sucked it.' It was no mean feat to tramp down that coast in the searing heat. Jonathan Leach said the sand was 'hot enough almost to have dressed a beefsteak'. Each man had a big load to carry, a rucksack and seventy rounds of shot as well as the heavy firearm itself. Many were soon floundering. And it didn't take long for the bright uniforms, red for the infantry, dark green for the riflemen and mainly blue for the small force of cavalry, to be caked in dust. The proud regiments rapidly became almost indistinguishable. George Landmann found himself riding beside one senior officer whose red coat looked no different in all the dust from his own bright-blue one.

The sandy terrain was part of the penalty Wellesley had to pay for keeping his men close to the shore: he had decided, wisely, to stay within reach of his fleet so that further reinforcements could join him easily. He had been reinforced by a brigade under General Spencer on 6 August, and was now marching on Lisbon. He had some 14,000 men – enough, he reckoned, to defeat Junot in battle whether the French commander chose to wait for the British near Lisbon or race north to meet them. The sooner the battle took place the better. Wellesley was determined to strike before he was superseded.

Wellesley may have been confident of his own leadership and even of the ability of his largely untried army, but he was fast becoming disillusioned by his new Spanish and Portuguese allies. The Spanish had promised to send a force to support him. There was no sign of it. He was promised 5,000 Portuguese troops but he told London the Portuguese were 'afraid of the French' and were unable to feed their own troops – let alone keep their promise to feed the British army and its horses. And as if this wasn't enough Wellesley railed at his own British supply line, run by the so-called Commissary General. Wellesley had become obsessive about supply in India: his painstaking orchestration of his army's logistics there had been an essential element of his success. 'If I had rice and bullocks [for transport],' he told a friend, 'I had men, and if I had men I knew I could beat the enemy.' He now made typically detailed demands of those who ran his supply line, the commissariat: 'a quantity equal to three days' consumption for 10,000 men must be carried if possible on the backs of mules . . . viz two bags or 224lbs on each mule; this will require 130 mules.' But a few days later he was complaining to London that 'I have had the greatest difficulty in organising my commissariat for the march, and that department is very incompetent. The existence of the army depends upon it, and yet the people who manage it are incapable of managing anything out of a counting house.'

As they marched south, the British soldiers had their first taste of how the French treated the Portuguese. Junot's invasion of Portugal had been barbaric. French troops had barnstormed their way through the countryside with no regard for the inhabitants. The scale of the destruction was shocking. Houses were stripped, furniture burned, food looted. In one abandoned village, plundered by the French, there 'were a great many wine stores that had been broken open . . . In a large wine cask we found a French soldier, drowned . . .' The looting, slaughter and burning provoked bitter resentment. Hatred of the French in Portugal and Spain became so intense that few Frenchmen were safe if they were caught alone away from their units. Wellesley was determined his army should not fall into the same trap. In his view Junot's treatment of the population was not just brutal and dishonourable: it was foolish. Wellesley knew that his army's success would depend on local goodwill. In contrast to the French, he imposed a ruthless regime of punishment for those who failed to respect local property. A good lashing was the usual punishment, but the worst offenders were hanged. This didn't endear him to his soldiers, whose first impression of their new leader was that he was devoid of warmth and humanity.

The men marched on, struggling with the heat and discomfort. Only the small force of cavalry – the 20th Light Dragoons – were all on horseback, though some infantry officers had their own mounts, anything from spirited stallions to stubborn mules. Buying a horse, if you could afford one, was seen as the only sure way to survive a gruelling campaign. The trouble was you could end up with a dud. George Landmann thought he had a good deal when he bought a pony off a brother officer, but it turned out to be hopelessly lethargic: much of the time he had to walk in front of it, dragging it along by the bridle. The horses could be a menace if the men were sleeping among them at night in the open: occasionally they would break their tethers and go charging around out of control. If you wanted to avoid being trampled, the best place to sleep was under a wagon.

Even so, several times horses came so near the wagon Landmann was sleeping under that he had to jump up 'throwing my arms about and shaking my blanket in their faces'. And at night there was the cold to contend with. Landmann soon realised his mistake in leaving his greatcoat on the ship. He couldn't sleep. He wrote in his journal that the ground was so wet with dew that 'I remained shivering until the bugle sounded the hour for morning parade about three o'clock.'

Wellesley was now hastening south, and his fast-developing intelligence network of scouts and local Portuguese spies told him that Junot's army was split. When the French general heard of the landing, he urgently recalled a brigade – around 3,000 men – under General Loison which he had sent off to eastern Portugal. He directed it north to join another force under General Delaborde about thirty miles north of Lisbon. The two of them were ordered to try and block Wellesley's advance on the Portuguese capital. With Loison still hours away, Delaborde had just 4,000 troops facing Wellesley's approaching army of some 14,000. He was heavily outnumbered. But Delaborde had a good eye for the ground and he selected a position in and behind the village of Roliça. It was to be the scene of the first battle between Britain and France in the Peninsular War.

Wellesley and his generals could see Roliça three miles away at the far end of a valley. The village was on the valley floor, and behind it the land rose very sharply with deep ravines offering tortuous access to a plateau at the top. Delaborde's plan – a brave one – was to make a show of defending the village, then to withdraw to the powerful hilltop position behind it and some 500 feet above it. Wellesley knew that, although he had the advantage of numbers, the terrain was against him, and he did not know yet how well his men would fight. Nor, to be fair, did his men know just how good Wellesley would be at conducting the battle. 'Many of us,' wrote Landmann later, 'totally ignorant of our commander's military skill, advanced towards the enemy anxiously looking for a sign' of his competence. They did not have long to wait.

Wellesley divided his attacking force into three. He sent one group in a great wide sweep along the ridge to the left to swoop down on the village from the east and despatched another group including

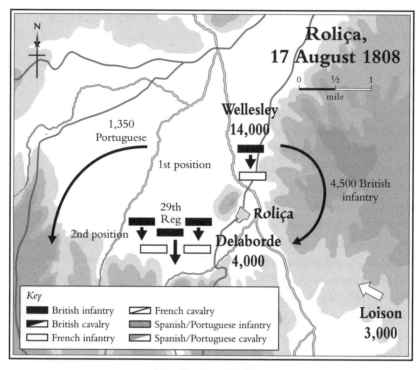

Key

■ British infantry	▨ French cavalry
◤ British cavalry	▨ Spanish/Portuguese infantry
□ French infantry	▨ Spanish/Portuguese cavalry

The Battle of Roliça

some light cavalry to outflank the French on the right. He himself led the main force of infantry right up the centre of the valley. The key formation in his main force was the battalion. He had fifteen of them as well as some Portuguese troops. Each battalion had, on paper, around a thousand men, in practice much less. George Landmann watched one battalion coming up to take its place in the move forward – the 1st Battalion of the 29th Regiment (1/29th for short) – with its band playing a country dance. In the British army the regiment, which could consist of one or more battalions, was the essential focus of loyalty. Each regiment was fiercely proud of its own county or regional base. The 1/29th was from Worcestershire, and its commanding officer Lieutenant Colonel George Lake was at its head on a fine charger seventeen hands high, light brown, with a very long tail. Lake was dressed in an 'entirely new suit, his hair was powdered . . . his cocked hat placed on his head square to the front'. 'Colonel,' said Landmann, 'you are dressed as if you were going to be received by the king.' 'Egad, sir,' replied Lake, 'if I am killed today I mean to die like a gentleman.'

Each of the battalions had small groups of skirmishers who fought ahead of them and on their flanks. Their task was to probe and harry the enemy, taking pot-shots at individual Frenchmen with their Baker rifles. Designed by Ezekiel Baker a decade earlier, the new weapon's rifled barrel gave it longer range but made it a little slower to load than the smoothbore musket. As the army advanced on Roliça, the riflemen, like Jonathan Leach in the dark-green uniform of the 95th Regiment, were out ahead needling the French front line. The superior range of their rifles allowed them to blunt the impetus of an enemy advance by picking off men in exposed positions on the other side. They targeted French skirmishers like themselves, and attempted to disrupt the neat pattern of advancing infantry columns.

Each rifleman darted from one bit of cover to another loading his weapon just like a musket, which was what most other soldiers carried. It took him thirty seconds to grab a cartridge from his pouch, bite away the musket ball attached to the end of it and hold it in his mouth, pouring some of the powder from the ripped-open cartridge on to the pan. Then he poured the rest of the powder down the barrel, shoved the one-ounce lead ball on top of it and rammed it in with the now empty cartridge paper. When he pulled the trigger, a flint would snap forward, causing a spark as it hit the metal frizzen and igniting the powder in the tray. The flash travelled through a small hole into the breech and exploded the powder, sending the shot spinning along the rifled barrel. The ball would be propelled more than three times as far as its counterpart in the smooth-bore barrel of the ordinary infantryman's musket. Compared to the rifle's range of some 300 yards, a ball fired from a musket would be virtually spent after as little as eighty yards. But a musket ball striking at short range did dreadful damage to human tissue. It expanded as it entered the body and caused catastrophic wounds. Muskets were faster to load: there was no rifling to impede the ball and cartridge as they were stuffed down the barrel. A dab hand with a musket could get a shot off in twenty seconds, ten seconds faster than a rifle. But, the musket's effective range being so short, even the deftest of soldiers would be lucky to get off more than one lethal shot at an enemy charging straight at him.

Benjamin Harris was a Dorset shepherd who had joined the rifle-men because he 'fell so in love with their smart, dashing and devil-may-care appearance'. He was now in combat with the 95th Rifles for the first time. He was sent off with Jonathan Leach's company to tackle the French skirmishers. 'All was action with us Rifles . . . and the barrel of my piece was so hot from continual firing that I could hardly bear to touch it.' For many soldiers in Wellesley's army, such as Benjamin Harris and Thomas Todd, this was their first experience of battle and of the ghastly punishment dealt out by musket ball, sword and bayonet. Each of them had to confront that dreaded moment of self-doubt. Would they have the skill and the courage to tackle an enemy soldier intent on killing them? Once they were in the mêlée the doubt quickly vanished. For the first time they were fighting for their lives and that induced in almost everyone a fierce determination to kill in order to survive.

During a break in the fighting Leach took a moment to accept a swig of wine from a brother officer's canteen. A musket ball passed through the canteen and severely wounded its owner. The canteen was shattered and Leach's face was 'splashed thoroughly with wine'. He felt a blow, 'which cut my mouth and spun me round like a top. For a few moments I concluded I was wounded.' But it was his friend who had got the worst of it: he was out of action for weeks.

While the riflemen were trying to confuse the enemy, Wellesley's next task was to deliver his infantry – with their muskets – to within killing distance of the main French lines. They approached their enemy in column but, well before they reached them, they would fan out into lines in order to bring as many of their muskets to bear on the French as possible. A few hundred men in one or two ranks in line abreast could utterly destroy an enemy if they held their formation and their fire till they were at point-blank range, as little as thirty yards. But that required supreme coolness and discip-line. Everything would depend on how well drilled Wellesley's footsoldiers would be under fire, compared with the French.

The first phase of the battle passed fairly quickly. Delaborde, still without Loison's reinforcement, had already decided not to make a major stand in the village but to retire to his second position on the escarpment overlooking it. Before the British could engage the whole enemy line at close quarters, the French pulled back to the hillside. This was when the real struggle began. Jonathan Leach found the heat suffocating. 'Every mouthful of air was such as is inhaled when looking into the oven.' The French fought hard to defend the steep windy paths trailing down the hill in front of them. Lake's battalion, the 1/29th, found itself ahead of the rest of Wellesley's force and plunged deep into the French line.

Landmann's impression was that the 29th had actually chosen 'the steepest and most difficult ravine'. They were drowned in heavy musketry fire, which killed sixty men from the special grenadier company, the fittest and strongest element in the battalion. Traditionally they had been the men picked to throw grenades, which were now long out of use. They were elite troops whom Wellesley could ill afford to lose. 'Poor Lake was killed at the commencement near the foot of the heights while riding at the head of his regiment and his horse was also killed it would appear at the same time; for when I saw them they were very near to each other . . . Thus died the Honourable George Lake "like a gentleman".' The leaderless 29th owed a lot at that moment to Wellesley's old friend Major General Rowland Hill. Harris watched him gallop across, rally the troops and lead them in a charge. 'Few men could have conducted the business with more coolness and quietude of manner, under such a storm of balls as he was exposed to.'

Wellesley too was seldom far behind the front line. He knew that in a fast-moving battle command and control were the most critical features of leadership. And the surest way of communicating orders was for the commander to deliver them to subordinate commanders in person. He was never still, his telescope at his eye, members of his staff, like Fitzroy Somerset, frantically trying to keep up with him as they cantered from unit to unit. Wellesley was able to relieve pressure on the 29th only when his troops' superior numbers prevailed and the British managed to scale the hill, obliging the French to retire. The 29th had lost 300 men and their colours. In the despatch Wellesley wrote to London that night, he implied that Lake had been foolish to launch his attack without waiting for other units to join him. He reported that they had 'attacked with the utmost impetuosity, and reached the enemy before those whose attacks were to be made on their flanks'. But in a rare show of feeling Wellesley wrote a very sympathetic letter to Lake's brother-in-law, a Mr R. Borough: 'However acute may be the sensations which it may at first occasion, it must in the end be satisfactory to the family of such a man as Col Lake to know that he was respected and loved by the whole army . . .'

Others grieved that day. Benjamin Harris, the Dorset shepherd, had been standing beside a man called Joseph Cochan who suddenly fell dead with a bullet through his brain. He was one of the few men who had been accompanied by his wife, and Harris had the painful task of taking her to where her husband's body lay on the battlefield. She dissolved in tears at the sight of his disfigured face, and Harris was so sorry for her he offered later to marry her. 'She had, however, received too great a shock on the occasion of her husband's death to think of marrying another soldier,' and she soon went home to England.

The next day Landmann was appalled to see a Portuguese woman about to crack open the skull of a badly wounded French soldier so that she could rob him. His hand was on his sword to try and stop her when another soldier suddenly leaped out of the thicket, shouted at her that she was not a woman but a devil, put his rifle to her head and blew half of it off. 'Bravo!' shouted Landmann, and he then watched as the man 'carefully untied the woman's apron which was thickly filled with watches, rings, valuables of all kinds'. The man scooped them up, 'darted from the spot and disappeared among the bushes casting at me a ferocious glance'.

Roliça was a savage little overture to the long Peninsular campaign that was to follow. The British had narrowly won. Wellesley's casualties were 500 to Delaborde's 700. Wellesley later reckoned Roliça was 'one of our most important affairs . . . it was terrible hard work . . . our men fought monstrous well'. Both armies had now got the measure of each other. The British quickly realised that even with overwhelming numbers no battle with the French was going to be a walkover. And those French soldiers who had hoped that the British had forgotten how to fight on land were disappointed.

Jean Andoche Junot believed that the French were invincible. He was Napoleon's commander in Portugal and a man who acted more on impulse than cool calculation. Even before he had a full report on the fierce fight at Roliça, he was already on his way north to fight Wellesley. He didn't yet know that Sir Arthur was about to be reinforced by 4,000 men landing further down the Portuguese coast. Utterly confident of victory, Junot marched boldly north without even taking all his available troops with him. He left 6,000 of his 20,000 men to guard Lisbon.

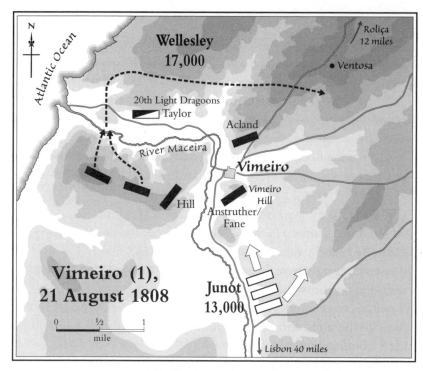

The Battle of Vimero (1)

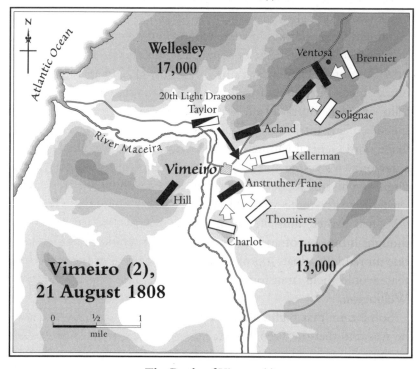

The Battle of Vimero (2)

2

You must have bribed Junot

Vimeiro, August 1808

WELLESLEY WAS DETERMINED not to lose momentum in his drive south. He wrote to Castlereagh saying he hoped to defeat the French, although he warned the government that he probably would not destroy them altogether 'for want of cavalry'. He still had only 200 horsemen. On his map he had ringed the village of Vimeiro – twelve miles south of Roliça. It was a short distance from a beach where reinforcements could land, and had clearly defensible ridges running north and west from the village. Just the place to consolidate and build up strength before advancing on Lisbon.

But Wellesley's spell as an independent commander was about to come to an end. Three days after Roliça, General Sir Harry Burrard, appointed by London as his superior, turned up with reinforcements in the frigate HMS *Brazen*, in the bay off Vimeiro. It was the evening of 20 August. Wellesley, with his army now at Vimeiro, took a boat out to meet Burrard and told him he was planning to advance the following day. Burrard told Wellesley he was deeply unhappy with the idea of any further move on Lisbon, and certainly none should be made until General Moore's army of some 20,000 extra troops, only a day or two's sailing away, could join Sir Arthur's force. Wellesley, disguising his impatience, asked Burrard if he wanted to come ashore. Burrard, a fifty-three-year-old veteran in the twilight of his career, who had earned himself the nickname 'Betty' because his troops thought him a bit of an old woman, said he would prefer to spend one more night afloat. It proved to be one of those strokes of fortune that would help transform Wellesley into the future Duke of Wellington.

Some time that night, after Wellesley had stepped back on shore, he was told that the French were advancing. He must have thanked his luck that Burrard was not ashore, because a cavalry patrol early the following morning led by Sergeant Norbert Landsheit reported that the French were within an hour or two of his front line, clearly seeking a battle. After listening to Landsheit's account Wellesley 'gave his orders in a calm, clear and cheerful voice . . . "Now Gentlemen, go to your stations but let there be no noise made – no sounding of bugles or beating of drums. Get your men quickly under arms and desire all outposts to be on the alert."'

Wellesley surveyed the ground with care. From the village of Vimeiro ran two ridges – one north, one west. Most of Wellesley's troops were bivouacking on the western ridge, facing south, the direction from which he expected the French to attack him. His left was just in front of the village, on Vimeiro Hill, whose gentle slopes rise some 150 feet above the valley. He placed about 5,000 of his most trusted troops – with a row of guns – just behind the brow of the hill: the French wouldn't see them until they were almost upon them. Ahead of these units on the forward slope of Vimeiro Hill and in the undergrowth below he scattered his light troops, the skirmishers, mainly riflemen. Captain Jonathan Leach was among them, with Benjamin Harris in his company, and so was Lieutenant Colonel Sydney Beckwith, leading two companies of the 1st Battalion the 95th Regiment (1/95th). Beckwith had landed from the ships with his 200 men only the night before. He was about to embark on the first of many engagements that were to make him one of the great commanders in the Peninsula, and his regiment – the Rifles – the one most feared by the French.

Leach was out front on picket duty in a pine wood when 'a cloud of light troops, supported by heavy columns of infantry, entered the wood, and assailing the pickets with great impetuosity, obliged us to fall back . . .'. Harris was in the middle of so much firing and smoke that all he could see was the red flash of his rifle in the cloud of smoke that enveloped him. 'The Rifles, as usual, were pretty busy in this battle. The French, in great numbers, came steadily down upon us, and we pelted away upon them like a shower of leaden hail.' They darted from one piece of cover to the next, 'firing one moment, jumping up and running for it the next; and, when we could see before us, we observed the cannon balls making a lane through the enemy's columns as they advanced, huzzaing and shouting like madmen'.

The British guns, which created such havoc among the French, were on the crown of Vimeiro Hill in the hands of Lieutenant Colonel Robe of the Royal Artillery. His gun teams worked tirelessly to make every shot count as the French, in massed columns – thirty men wide by forty-two deep – pushed back the British riflemen by sheer weight of numbers and advanced up the hill with their own light troops probing towards the guns. Robe ordered his men to fire alternate shots: first, roundshot – great heavy cast-iron balls that could shatter whole files of men at several hundred yards – and then canister or case, which sprayed a whole bag of musket balls like a giant shotgun over a wide circle at much shorter range. And they were firing a new type of ammunition as well: the shell, invented only recently by William Shrapnel. It was a hollow roundshot stuffed with musket balls and carrying a further charge within it that caused it to explode on or above the ground, killing or wounding anyone unprotected and within reach. Shrapnel shells were to play a lethal role in conflicts from then on.

But the vigorous artillery fire did not stop the French. Robe shouted to Landmann that he was lucky to have a horse, as some of the French were yards away and would soon be upon them. But when Landmann suggested he get a horse himself, Robe replied, 'No no. I'll neither leave my guns nor my gunners.' The French could not yet see the main British infantry lines waiting concealed behind the guns. By now the French columns – thousands of men in close formation – were close enough for the British to hear shouts of 'En avant, mes amis!' and 'Vive l'Empereur!' French drums sounded the *pas de charge* and their pace quickened. The regiment directly ahead of the advancing French was the 50th, known as the Dirty Half-Hundred after the black flashes on their uniforms. As the French came over the brow of the hill, Landmann saw the commanding officer of the 50th, Colonel Walker, advance his troops to the crest, 'where he gave the words "Ready, present! And let every man fire when he has taken his aim."' The result was 'destruction and carnage'.

The effect of some 800 men in two ranks firing their muskets from very close range ravaged the approaching French columns. 'I received them in line,' Wellesley remarked later, 'which they were not accustomed to.' Caught before they were able to fan out into long lines abreast where each man could bring his musket to bear, the French were utterly outgunned. Only some thirty men in the front rank of each column were able to fire their weapons at the redcoats who sprang up suddenly from the dead ground just beyond the brow of the hill. And as the French columns hesitated and crumpled, the men of the 50th charged them with their bayonets, yelling and stabbing at the enemy soldiers. The column had proved to be Napoleon's most successful infantry formation in his battles in central Europe and Italy. A great solid mass of tightly packed French footsoldiers, rank after rank of them, had smashed through enemy defences by concentrating force on a particular point. But now the French columns were faced with long, thin red lines of footsoldiers who stood their ground, and every one of them discharged his musket at point-blank range. Landmann watched as the entire French force turned around and ran, 'every man throwing away his arms and accoutrements as also his knapsack, cap and, in short, everything that could have obstructed speed'. A force that had advanced proudly just minutes earlier, a dense mass of 5,000 men, disintegrated. It was 'like an immense flock of sheep scampering away from the much-dreaded shepherd's dog'.

Wellesley had been watching all this, mobile as ever on horseback, from the eastern ridge. It was quickly apparent to him that Junot had thrown only part of his army at Vimeiro Hill itself, and that he was planning to deliver the second prong of his attack not on the western ridge where Wellesley had placed his troops the night before, but on its twin the other side of Vimeiro – the eastern ridge. Junot had despatched two whole brigades under General Jean-Baptiste Solignac and General Antoine-François Brennier in a great sweep around to the east of Vimeiro. They were aiming for the village of Ventosa on the eastern ridge to threaten Wellesley's rear. It was a classic tactic: outflank the enemy if you can and make him face two ways at once. At Vimeiro it met two snags. First, Wellesley was ready for it. The moment he saw the great cloud of dust early that morning indicating that Junot was heading round his east side and not towards his troops on the western ridge, he ordered a brisk move by half his army. He left the trusted Hill with some 5,000 troops on the western ridge and shifted all his other units to the eastern ridge to meet any attack Junot made on it.

Junot's second problem was that the ground his flanking units would have to cover to approach the eastern ridge was hilly and broken. It would be a hard grind, difficult enough for one large force to traverse and maintain cohesion. And Junot took the further risk of dividing this force in two – sending the two brigades off separately but telling their commanders to synchronise their attack on Ventosa. This way he created two weaknesses that would prove fatal to his plans: he concentrated too few troops on the pivot of Wellesley's deployment – Vimeiro Hill – and he landed his staff with a communications nightmare. They were unable to co-ordinate the movements of the three groups, which soon became separated in rough country.

The main battle was still raging at Vimeiro Hill. Junot had not yet exhausted his attempts to defeat the British there. Around 2,000 French grenadiers, massed this time in even narrower columns, advanced over the same ground and suffered the same fate. Robe's shrapnel cut swathes through them as they approached. At the finish they were again caught in that tight vulnerable formation before they could expand into line and even fewer of their muskets could be brought to bear on the British. They were shattered.

Junot threw two further attacks at Vimeiro Hill, which suffered the same fate. Then, heavily bruised by these setbacks, he chose a slightly different approach for his next attempt to break through. Where the hill fell away to the north there was a valley that ran up behind it towards the church in the village. He sent two further battalions of grenadiers under General Kellerman to smash their way up this hollow. But they marched straight into an even more murderous killing zone. They found themselves trapped – as they advanced – between the British troops on Vimeiro Hill and a brigade that Wellesley had placed on the other side of the valley. The village was at the top of the valley, and the British were there too. Charles Leslie watched a 'party of the 43rd light infantry stealing out of the village and moving behind a wall . . . they opened a fire at the moment when the enemy came in contact . . . the French had been allowed to come in close, then our gallant fellows, suddenly springing up, rapidly poured on them two or three volleys with great precision, and rushing on, charged with the bayonet'. At the end of this phase of the battle Landmann saw the ground in front of Vimeiro Hill 'seriously scattered over with killed, wounded, arms, drums, caps, knapsacks, canteens, dead horses, and ammunition wagons . . . and, where an attempt had been made to deploy to form a line, the dead and dying were in some places . . . lying in heaps three or four men in height'. It was at this moment that Wellesley ordered the 200 horsemen of the 20th Light Dragoons under Colonel Taylor to make the first cavalry charge of the Peninsular War. Wellesley knew that well-timed cavalry charges against a fleeing enemy could wreak havoc. This would be the first test for the horsemen he had brought with him. Landmann described Colonel Taylor as 'a particularly handsome fellow' on a 'fine prancing horse'. He saw Taylor tying a handkerchief round a wound in his thigh and urged him to get it dressed. 'I am just going to make a charge,' replied Taylor. 'If I survive I shall have plenty of leisure for tending to this trifle. If I fall I shall have spared myself some unnecessary trouble and pain.'

Sergeant Landsheit was one of the horsemen who heard Wellesley shout, 'Now, 20th, now!' while 'his staff clapped their hands and gave us a cheer'. Very quickly Landsheit and the 20th were in among the French cavalry 'cutting and hacking, and upsetting men and horses . . . till they broke and fled in every direction'. The dragoons then turned on the infantry, their sabres flashing and slicing at the fleeing footsoldiers 'till our white leather breeches, our hands, arms and swords were all besmeared with blood'. They raced on as the French gave way all around them and suddenly found they had 'rushed into an enclosure, where to a man we well nigh perished' because the enemy 'hastened to take advantage of our blunder' by immediately closing the door. The 20th's 'blunder' was to allow a successful charge to turn into a reckless pursuit. They simply went too far. Their initial advantage in numbers and momentum was lost once they were deep into the enemy's ranks and they found themselves surrounded. They were rescued only by the sudden arrival of the 50th, who had pursued the French down the hill and on to the flatter ground below.

The Rifles too were involved in the pursuit, firing at every Frenchman in sight. Some ran out of ammunition; William Brotherwood ended up ramming his razor down his barrel and loosing it off instead. The exhausted cavalry returned, having lost at least a third of their number killed or wounded. Among the dead was Colonel Taylor, who had been killed after he was surrounded and refused to be taken prisoner. Harris, who had fallen over when the British dragoons rushed past, was lucky not to have died beneath their onrushing hooves. He saw Taylor leading the charge and observed that he 'bore himself like a hero with his sword waving in the air . . . dashing upon the enemy, and hewing and slashing at them in tremendous style'. He noticed that the colonel did not return. As he got up, he saw he had been lying beside a dying Frenchman. He raised the soldier's head and gave him a swig from his water flask. One of his companions, a man named Mullins, 'damned me for a fool for my pains. "Better knock out his brains Harris . . . he has done us mischief enough."'

The charge of the 20th at Vimeiro was the first of a number of cavalry actions over the next seven years – including at Waterloo – in which rash over-enthusiasm led to needless losses. For Wellington this failure of his cavalry became an obsession. 'They gallop at everything,' he said later, 'and never consider their situation.'

Although Junot's troops had been heartily repulsed at Vimeiro Hill, the French general still had a chance of turning Wellesley's flank at Ventosa. The trouble was that the two flanking brigades he had sent northwards lost touch with each other and failed to attack together. Moreover they did not know of the dreadful carnage that had resulted from French columns meeting British lines on Vimeiro Hill. The same was now to happen to them at Ventosa, at the northeastern edge of the battle. The first wave of three French battalions in column under Solignac clambered to the top of a hill where they were suddenly confronted by two long British lines. Thomas Todd was in one of them. He was still a comparative novice, and on entering his first lethal combat he felt a 'breathless sensation' come over him. But one look along the British line was enough to strengthen him. 'The steady determined scowl of my companions assured my heart and gave me determination. How unlike the noisy

advance of the French! . . . They came upon us crying and shouting
to the very point of our bayonets. Our awful silence and determined
advance they could not stand. They put about and fled without much
resistance.'

The seventeen-year-old William Lawrence was one of those
involved in the fighting at Ventosa. Back in Bryant's Piddle in Dorset
he had been a ploughboy until his father apprenticed him to a builder
who bullied him so much that he ran away. After several escapades
Lawrence enlisted with the 40th Regiment of Foot, which now
found itself pursuing Solignac. He and his comrades advanced with
British guns 'still playing over our heads until we got within a short
distance of the enemy'. They drove the French back only after some
'very severe fighting well kept up for some time on both sides'.

After a few minutes of welcome rest the British switched their
attention to the second attack by Brennier's brigade, which was
caught in a crossfire between a number of British units including the
29th, which had taken such punishment at Roliça. So fierce was the
fire that the French did not press home their attack and retired east-
wards. The Battle of Vimeiro was over. The French had been
thwarted on all fronts. They had lost around 1,500 men – twice as
many as the British. It was a rude shock for the French Emperor and
for the prestige of his army. They were not in the habit of being
defeated on land. Only in Egypt at Aboukir seven years earlier and in
a minor engagement at Maida in Italy in 1806 had a British army
humbled a land army of post-revolutionary France.

Wellesley was now, not surprisingly, eager for a general pursuit of
an utterly demoralised enemy. But he was now sharply reminded that
he was not in charge. Sir Harry Burrard had finally landed from HMS
Brazen to take command. Wellesley urgently put the case to him for
a quick pursuit. 'Sir Harry, now is your time to advance. The enemy
are completely beaten, and we shall be in Lisbon in three days.'
Burrard replied that he thought a great deal had been achieved 'very
much to the credit of the troops', but he did not think it advisable to
move off the ground in pursuit of the enemy. Wellesley riposted that
the troops were 'perfectly ready to advance'. They had 'plenty of
provisions ready cooked in their haversacks, and plenty of ammunition'. But Burrard was adamant. It may have been his natural caution.

It may have been jealousy. He was certainly deeply distrustful of a man he saw as a headstrong general trying to go too far too fast. Wellesley emerged from his meeting with Burrard angry and disappointed. He 'turned his horse's head and, with a cold and contemptuous bitterness, said aloud to his ADC "You may think about dinner for there is nothing more for soldiers to do this day."' The news spread quickly among the troops. They had been eager to exploit their victory. Now they were ordered to halt, wrote James Hale, 'in the midst of our glory' and, as his men murmured impatiently, Wellesley rode up and down saying, 'I have nothing to do with it: I have no command.'

On the battlefield lay thousands of dead and wounded. Todd witnessed the 'horrible' sight of the 'peasantry prowling about more ferocious than the beasts and birds of prey, finishing the work of death and carrying away whatever they thought worthy of their grasp'. The Portuguese took their revenge on the French who had plundered and laid waste their villages. 'No fallen Frenchman that showed the least sign of life was spared.' The peasants even seemed to revel in 'mangling the dead bodies . . . my sickened fancy felt the same as if it were witnessing a feast of cannibals'.

Looting the dead wasn't just the preserve of the Portuguese. Harris used his bayonet to rip open the lining of one dead Frenchman's coat and helped himself to a fistful of coins. Leslie 'picked up a bill for several hundred francs payable in Paris'. Landsheit had just turned over a dead Frenchman and taken his watch and three Spanish dollars when a badly wounded French grenadier took a shot at him. Landsheit saw he was wounded and shouted that he would spare him if he put aside his weapon. When the Frenchman started to take aim at him again, Landsheit 'gave him a rap with my sword which put an end to all his pugnacious propensities'. Looting of the dead or even of the wounded was widespread and too common to incur a penalty. But sometimes people overstepped the mark. After a later battle a British soldier couldn't get a valuable ring off the finger of one of his own dead countrymen, so he slashed off the finger with his knife. He was spotted and earned himself a court martial and 500 lashes.

Another wretched aftershock of battle was the plight of the wounded. Adam Neale, one of Wellesley's army surgeons, witnessed scenes that would become commonplace in the Peninsula as the fighting intensified. Scores of wounded lay on the ground or, if they were lucky, on makeshift tables in what passed as field hospitals. Many awaited their turn for the crude remedy of amputation that was preferable to the lethal spread of gangrene from a musket wound. Neale did what he could to lessen the pain of those who were in the greatest agony. 'To several, a simple inspection of their wounds, with a few words of consolation, or perhaps a little opium, was all that could be done or recommended. Of these brave men the balls had pierced organs essentially connected with life, and in such cases prudence equally forbids the rash interposition of unavailing art and the useless indulgence of delusive hope . . .'

The final episode in Wellesley's first, short summer campaign was a controversial ceasefire negotiation that threatened to deliver a fatal blow to his career. The so-called Convention of Cintra was signed nine days after the battle – on 30 August 1808. Its terms caused astonishment and uproar in London. It appeared that Wellesley and his superiors, Burrard and Lieutenant General Sir Hew Dalrymple, who arrived on 22 August, had agreed to a very generous deal for the enemy they had just defeated. The French would evacuate Lisbon, but they would be repatriated to France in British ships and could take with them all their weapons and even the loot they had amassed during their occupation of Portugal. There was such an outcry that Wellesley and the other two generals who had signed the Convention were recalled to appear before a court of inquiry in London later that year.

Wellesley arrived back in London on 4 October. 'I don't know whether I am to be hanged, drawn and quartered, or roasted alive,' he wrote with mock nervousness to his brother Richard. He put a bold face on it, trusting to the reputation he had now established for himself with his victory at Vimeiro. But he and his family had to endure a whole barrage of insults. His most vocal political opponents were the Radical MP and rich brewer Samuel Whitbread and the journalist William Cobbett, whose radical views had won him a wide following. They delighted in the humbling of Wellesley and what Cobbett called his 'damned infernal' family, which Cobbett believed far too influential.

Press cartoonists had a field day. Wellesley and his two superiors were ridiculed and lampooned. Byron added a special line to his poem *Childe Harold*: 'Britannia sickens, Cintra, at thy name.' The Whig opposition, whose dovish attitude to Napoleon gave them serious doubts about taking the war to Portugal anyway, lambasted Wellesley and his Tory backers. For his part, Wellesley tried to distance himself from the agreement. He claimed that it was the other two generals who had agreed on detailed clauses like the one that allowed the French to keep what they called 'their possessions'. He told Castlereagh privately that he would like to have made the French generals 'disgorge the church plate they had stolen'. But he told the court of inquiry that he agreed with the Convention's main principle that the French should be allowed to evacuate Portugal. Therefore 'I did not think it proper to refuse to sign the paper on account of my disagreement on the details.' It wasn't until 22 December that the whole damaging controversy was finally resolved with the clearing of the three generals by the court of inquiry. The court took refuge in whitewash and pronounced all three of them blameless. Wellesley was lucky: it was a curious lapse on his part. He may have been exasperated by Burrard and Dalrymple, but he should never have agreed to such lax terms.

Cintra apart, Wellesley had left Lisbon for home with some relief. Constrained by generals senior to him, he would have found it intolerable to stay in the Peninsula any longer. He had written to Castlereagh on 30 August: 'I feel an earnest desire to quit the army. I have been too successful with this army ever to serve with it in a subordinate situation . . .' Once the court of inquiry was out of the way, he scored well with the British public and parliament. He received an effusive vote of thanks in the Lords. Vimeiro was seen, rightly, as a significant victory and a striking humiliation for the French. A delighted Duke of Richmond wrote to his friend: 'You must have bribed him [Junot] to attack you when he did!' The unfortunate Junot soldiered on until his volatile nature got the better of him, and he committed suicide by throwing himself out of a window in 1813.

Wellesley's lightning military campaign had been a stunning success. He left behind him an army in the Peninsula which for the most part admired him but hardly loved him. He showed none of the obvious humanity of commanders like Hill and Beckwith. But the men knew that, although Wellesley might regard them with disdain, he provided what they needed – confident leadership and tireless concern for their needs. His deft switching of the units at Vimeiro, his use of dead ground, his obsession with supplies and his tireless presence in all areas of the battlefield marked him out already as an exceptional commander.

3

Scum of the earth

Oporto, 1809

WELLESLEY'S PRIVATE LIFE that winter was as troubled as his public image. His marriage to Kitty Pakenham began to show strains. It was partly his fault. Sensitivity and warmth were qualities he showed only on rare occasions in his long life. But these were the very feelings his gentle, affectionate wife longed for. She obviously adored, almost worshipped him. This irritated him and prompted him to be increasingly cold with her. She complained to her relations that he was neglecting her and as time went on she retreated more and more into self-pity. She made things worse by lending her younger brother, Henry Pakenham, money to pay off a gambling debt. Wellesley was incensed and never forgave her.

It wasn't long before he strayed into other relationships, one of them with the notorious Harriette Wilson, a London courtesan, whose vitality and sexual charms won her many friends in high places. Whether or not they actually slept together, he later admitted they were close. He revealed he had given her money when she was in debt. And he was not as embarrassed as her other clients when she chose to tell all. Twenty years later, when the publisher of Harriette's planned autobiography tried to blackmail him, the Duke of Wellington was widely reputed to have fired back, in effect, if not in actual words, 'Publish and be damned.' She published accounts of several conversations she said she had had with him, including his farewell as he left for the Peninsula later in 1809. 'He called to take a hasty leave of me a few hours before his departure. "I am off to Spain directly," he said. I know not how it was but I grew melancholy . . . I saw him there perhaps for the last time in my life . . . I burst into tears . . . kissing my eyes, he said "God bless you" and hurried away.'

There was already the whiff of scandal around the Wellesley family.

Charlotte, the wife of Arthur Wellesley's younger brother William, was cavorting with one of Arthur's senior military colleagues, and suddenly sparked a blazing public scandal by running off with him. He was Lieutenant General Henry Paget, fast establishing himself as Britain's most promising cavalry commander. He had been out to Portugal just after Vimeiro and stayed at Wellesley's house for two days in Lisbon. In a letter to his father, Lord Uxbridge, Paget wrote that he admired Wellesley: 'I had during that time an opportunity of observing that he [Wellesley] possesses much method and arrangement. He is besides the luckiest dog upon earth, for it is by a sort of miracle . . . that he has been able to do this by himself.' He went on to say he regretted that, because he was senior to Wellesley on the list of generals, he could hardly take part in the Peninsular Campaign if Wellesley was to command it. 'I feel it is a real misfortune to me as a soldier that I am above him on the list for I think there is a good chance of its cutting me from all service.' When Arthur Wellesley learned that Paget had eloped with his sister-in-law, he was scandalised. One newspaper reported that he punched Paget in the stomach. Charlotte eventually married Paget in 1810, and by 1815 Arthur, then Duke of Wellington, and Henry Paget, then Lord Uxbridge, were sufficiently reconciled to form a winning partnership at Waterloo.

Wellesley was now back in a job he had had before he went to Portugal – the Tory government's Chief Secretary for Ireland. But his mind was never far from events in the Peninsula where prospects for Britain and its allies had taken a severe turn for the worse. In November 1808 Napoleon decided to visit the Peninsula himself. Exasperated by the French loss of Portugal and by his brother Joseph's failure to entrench his rule in Spain and stamp out the Spanish rebellion, he led a massively reinforced French army against Spanish resistance forces. He defeated and scattered the rebels wherever he went. Britain's response was to despatch the army, which Wellesley had commanded, into Spain under the command of Lieutenant General Sir John Moore. Moore was one of the few generals Wellesley respected, but his campaign was a near-disaster. He scored some early successes in December against a few isolated French units. But, seeing his army outnumbered by a force led by Napoleon, he opted for withdrawal. After three weeks of wretched and debilitating retreat, Moore's army reached Corunna in north-west Spain. Napoleon went home, leaving Marshal Soult to finish off Moore. Only Moore's tactical skill and exemplary leadership managed to foil Soult's attempt to eliminate his army. Although Moore himself was fatally wounded, most of the British force escaped. They scrambled aboard a fleet of ships in Corunna harbour and made it safely back to Britain. The core units of Britain's fast-maturing army thus survived to fight another day. But the army's departure left the Portuguese with only a small British force to protect Lisbon. They appealed urgently to London to help them boost the size of Portugal's own army and said they wanted Wellesley to lead it.

The British government was in a quandary. Successive Tory administrations had opposed French expansion – from the one led by William Pitt the Younger that began the fight against revolutionary France in the 1790s to the current government of Lord Portland. The Whigs, mainly in opposition, frequently questioned the need for war and highlighted its cost. The most radical had supported the French Revolution and called for peace with Napoleon. The war's main proponents were George Canning, the energetic Foreign Secretary, and the War Secretary Lord Castlereagh, Canning's ally but at the same time his fiercely ambitious political rival. Wellesley's greatest supporter in the cabinet in the past had been Castlereagh, but now it was Canning who pushed for him to be sent to help the Portuguese while Castlereagh briefly opposed the scheme. He hadn't turned against Wellington but felt it might be the wrong moment to switch commanders. The outcome, on 15 February 1809, was that Canning persuaded his colleagues to send out a junior and much less distinguished officer, Major General William Carr Beresford, to command the newly emerging Portuguese army. It turned out to be an inspired appointment. Marshal Beresford, as he now became, had only one eye, a poor military record and a reputation for obstinacy. But over the next few years he was to hone the Portuguese troops into a well-drilled fighting force which provided Wellesley with valuable extra manpower.

In those early weeks of 1809 Wellesley was anxious to keep his profile high and to fortify those in cabinet who wanted to use the Portuguese and Spanish revolts to weaken Napoleon. He believed that, if wisely exploited, the Peninsula could do much to drain Napoleon's strength. French occupation of the Iberian Peninsula was tying down nearly 200,000 troops. Wellesley now launched an important initiative that was to help secure his return to the battle-field. He sent Castlereagh a memorandum on 7 March emphasising the key importance to the Spanish resistance and to the very survival of Portugal of a reinforced British presence in Lisbon. 'The British force employed in Portugal should . . . not be less than 30,000 men, of which number 4000 or 5000 should be cavalry, and there should be a large body of artillery.' He indicated that such a force would be enough to resist a French force of up to 100,000 men. He added that British reinforcements should include 'some companies of British riflemen'. This analysis was enough to shift Castlereagh back in support of a new Wellesley mission to Portugal. That same month Marshal Soult, one of Napoleon's most trusty and experienced commanders, who had chased Moore to Corunna, swooped down from north-west Spain and made Oporto his headquarters. France's seizure of Portugal's second city and its harbour, vital to the Royal Navy, swung the rest of the British cabinet into line behind the mission.

On 2 April 1809 Wellesley was ordered back to Portugal. His demands for more cavalry, artillery and riflemen were endorsed by the government. The troops' high level of training and superior weapons would greatly enhance his strength. With these new units he acquired the core of the balanced force that would allow him to prise the Peninsula from Napoleon's grasp. And with them would come unprecedented numbers of highly literate and perceptive people determined to record their experiences. Like Wellesley himself they would tell the story of the triumphs and the setbacks, the joys and the horrors of their military crusade all the way to Waterloo. Some, like James Hale, Thomas Todd and Jonathan Leach, had already fought with him at Vimeiro. But a crowd of fresh story-tellers, also eager to record their memories, embarked in ships on Britain's south coast over the next few weeks.

They came from different parts of Britain's massively unequal society of the early nineteenth century. It was a society in which the rich were fabulously wealthy and the poor frequently destitute. The rich were mostly synonymous with the aristocracy, who ran the country and unashamedly protected their privileges. They dispensed favours on the basis of family connection rather than merit. Advancement – including promotion in the forces – depended on patronage or cash or both. The poor were without privilege and, since they had no vote, they had no power to change things. All they could do was look for the best chance of earning money to secure a livelihood for their families. The army offered one avenue for enrichment through the meagre but regular pay it promised and through the opportunity it afforded for plunder. It also offered adventure and even glory to those who regarded fighting Napoleon as a heroic struggle for Britain's survival. And, inevitably, the new Peninsular expedition attracted every extreme of human character, from men of sensitivity and honour to those to whom brutality and indifference to suffering were second nature.

Fred Ponsonby was a keen horseman, to whom a life spent in the cavalry seemed the obvious, natural career. He was twenty-six years old, a bluff, clubbable fellow with a large and prominent chin. The second son of the Earl of Bessborough, he was anchored comfortably in the aristocracy. The Bessboroughs – like the Wellesleys – had estates in Ireland, and Fred Ponsonby and Arthur Wellesley would become close friends in the Peninsula. Ponsonby's mother, Harriet, was the sister of Georgiana, Duchess of Devonshire. Both women dabbled in gambling and it washed off on Fred Ponsonby, who occasionally had to appeal to his mother to pay off his billiard debts. He would write and thank her: 'you have saved me out of a great scrape, and I hope you will not have reason to distrust me . . . in the future'. His sister was the notorious Lady Caroline Lamb. Fred called her Caro for short. As moody and unpredictable as he was buoyant and uncomplicated, she was attractive, a brilliant conversationalist and a natural prey for Lord Byron, who had a passionate affair with her. She famously described Byron as 'mad, bad and dangerous to know'. By the summer of 1809 Ponsonby was a major, ready to embark with his regiment, the 23rd Light Dragoons, and hungry for his first piece of action.

William Tomkinson was another cavalryman. The nineteen-year-old son of a prosperous landowner in Cheshire, Tomkinson had grown up with horses and was to end up a lieutenant colonel. But in

1809 he was a raw young cavalry officer. He distinguished himself by having such a boisterous horse that it kicked overboard the second mate of the ship that was to take them both to Portugal. 'The man fell the whole height of the vessel, there being no water near the quay at which we embarked, from the tide being out. He was left behind sick at Falmouth.'

There were Irishmen and Scots in plenty, a reflection of the poverty of their countries. Ned Costello, an eighteen-year-old from Dublin with more than his share of Irish wit and good humour, was attracted by the bounty of eighteen guineas he was paid on joining up. He soon found himself recruiting other young Irishmen at a guinea or two commission each time. He ended up in the 1st Battalion of the 95th Rifles under Colonel Beckwith. One artful young Irishman earned himself no fewer than four bounties by signing up with four separate regiments and narrowly escaped being arrested for desertion each time. A Scot, Joseph Donaldson, was only sixteen when he joined up in Aberdeen. His parents were distraught at the thought of him going off to fight a war in some strange country, but he defied them and proudly embarked with the 94th Scots Brigade. His enthusiasm waned when just about everyone aboard became seasick as soon as they left port.

Colonel Sydney Beckwith had fought with Wellesley at Vimeiro. His small band of light infantry in the 1/95th had deeply impressed Wellesley, who was now Britain's Commander in Chief in the Peninsula. He had seen what invaluable sharpshooters they were with their long-range rifles, and he asked London to make it an urgent priority to get them to join him in Portugal as soon as possible. Beckwith had gone on after Vimeiro to follow Sir John Moore to Corunna. He and the handful of riflemen who had been shipped home were now stood by for the Peninsula again. But this time – following Wellesley's request – a large battalion of around 1,100 of the Rifles would embark. Beckwith was aged thirty-seven, and popular with his men, who relished his humanity and understanding. They contrasted him very favourably with their brigade commander, the man who was to command all the light infantry troops with Wellesley, Brigadier General Robert Craufurd.

Craufurd was known as 'Black Bob', because however well he

shaved he always had a swarthy chin. He was a hard taskmaster, free with punishment, and he bullied those he didn't like. He came from an old Ayrshire family with a tradition of lawless feuding with its rivals, the Kennedies. Harshness and a quick temper were in Craufurd's blood. He was forty-five when he arrived in the Peninsula, after half a lifetime of military experience. He had joined up at fifteen, observed Frederick the Great's military manoeuvres, enjoyed a distinguished career fighting in India ten years before Wellesley, led a unit of light troops in the disastrous expedition to Buenos Aires in 1807 and commanded the Light Brigade under Sir John Moore in 1808–9. Benjamin Harris, who served with Wellesley at Vimeiro, came to dislike Black Bob's 'sternness' during the Corunna campaign. At one stage he was told that if he, Harris, didn't do one rather routine job better, Craufurd would 'hang him'. In 1800 Robert Craufurd married Mary Holland, and remained her devoted husband until his death. One of Black Bob's most redeeming qualities was his love for his wife, which he frequently expressed in letters to her from the Peninsula. 'The affection is always there,' he wrote in one letter to her, 'as warm and immutable in its nature as the sun itself, though sometimes covered by a cloud.' He talked of retiring from the army to be with her, and at one stage insisted to Wellesley that he had to go home and spend some time with Mary.

Jonathan Leach, another rifleman, veteran of Vimeiro, quickly came to hate his brigade commander. In a letter home he called Craufurd 'a damned tyrant and a great blackguard'. And George Simmons, whose motive for joining up was largely about earning enough to help the other less gifted members of his family, often found himself the object of Craufurd's sharp tongue. Simmons made an entry in one of the three small notebooks he carried in his hat nearly every day, and wrote frequent letters. On the 'long-wished-for day' in May 1809 when he embarked, he wrote home: 'This, my dear parents, is the happiest day of my life; and I hope, if I come where there is an opportunity of showing courage, your son will not disgrace the name of a British soldier.'

Quite separate from the infantry and the cavalry were the commissaries, whose job was supply. And Wellesley had already shown how obsessive he was about food for his men and forage for his horses.

August Schaumann was a commissary officer. He too had struggled ashore in the breakers before Vimeiro. Because he was from Hanover he had the right to join the British regiment recruited exclusively in that city – the King's German Legion, which had been founded in 1803. Refugees from those parts of Germany overrun by Napoleon owed a special allegiance to Britain's King George III, who was also Elector of Hanover. They formed a rapidly growing military force which was much valued by Wellington. Schaumann's childhood in Hanover had been deeply unhappy and it was easy for him to opt for a life of adventure. He had stayed on in the Peninsula after Wellesley went home, and he spent the winter struggling to arrange sustenance for Moore's army as it retreated to Corunna. He complained that the 'duties of a war commissary are the most laborious in the field', but he made the most of his spare time. His childlike appearance belied the mischievous delight he took in the good life. He had a voracious appetite for food and women.

All these, and tens of thousands like them, were men born into that narrow window of history that would allow them to fight with Wellington. He didn't know all of them. But they knew him. They called him 'Old Nosey' after his most distinctive feature. Over the next five or six years they would grow not so much to love him as to trust him because his judgement was nearly always right. Two years later George Simmons was to write in one of his small notebooks: 'Wherever he is, confidence of success is the result. The French own it that, next to Bonaparte, he is the captain of Europe.'

One person Wellesley was to get to know very well was a bright young Scots officer who climbed aboard the warship *Surveillante* with him on 14 April for the voyage to Lisbon. His name was Alexander Gordon. An old colleague had recommended him to Wellesley as a very 'active, intelligent' staff officer. It wasn't long before Gordon became one of his close aides. There was one quality that all the members of what Wellesley called his 'family' of top staff officers shared: high birth. Gordon, like another early recruit to the family, Fitzroy Somerset, had impeccable aristocratic connections: his brother was Lord Aberdeen, who became a diplomat and later Prime Minister. Wellesley didn't think twice about including his own family among his top aides. He was an unashamed Tory, a believer in class and privilege. For him, aristocrats were born to lead, and people from the lower classes and from the ranks were unfit to be officers. Edward 'Ned' Pakenham, Kitty's brother, was an intimate member of his staff and later an inspired commander of the 3rd Division. Wellesley made no secret of his contempt for 'rankers', men from the other ranks promoted to be officers. 'If there is to be any influence in the disposal of military patronage, in aid of military merit, can there be any in our army so legitimate as that of family connection, fortune, and influence in the country?' And years later, after all his campaigns were over, he observed: 'I have never known an officer promoted from the ranks turn out well . . . they cannot stand drink.' One man from the lowest ranks, Rifleman Benjamin Harris, also preferred his officers to be aristocrats: 'I know from experience that in our army the men like best to be officered by gentlemen, men whose education has rendered them more kind in manners than your coarse officer, sprung from obscure origin and whose style is brutal and overbearing.' Wellesley personified the aristocratic arrogance that made the British army one of the most conservative in Europe. France and Prussia had long abandoned the practice of buying commissions, and merit was the essential criterion for promotion in their armies. The odd contradiction in Wellesley was that, traditionalist though he was, he abhorred incompetence and was constantly frustrated by his powerlessness to promote or sack an officer on grounds of merit.

The *Surveillante* spent a boisterous first night at sea. Her captain thought it so dangerous that he sent a message for Wellesley to put his boots on and come on deck where he would be safer if the worst happened. Wellesley sent back that he was very happy in his cabin and preferred to swim, if he had to, without his boots on. The weather soon perked up and Wellesley was in Lisbon a week later on 22 April. He had seen the Portuguese capital before. Many of his soldiers had not. It was not the exotic paradise they had expected. 'As seen on the far off horizon, Lisbon looks like a city of palaces. How cruelly the result disappoints you,' remarked cavalryman George Farmer, who had earned his spurs chasing illegal whisky stills in Ireland. 'Narrow streets choked up with filth of the most horrid kind, miserable wretches crowding about . . . a thousand symptoms besides

of indolence and squalor and national character utterly degraded . . .'
And even three years later, long after its liberation, Portugal still presented an unappealing picture to newcomers from Britain like Private
William Wheeler: 'What an ignorant, priest ridden, dirty, lousy set of
poor devils are the Portuguese. Without seeing them it is impossible
to conceive there exist a people in Europe so debased.'

No doubt these were partly the naive first impressions of newcomers who had expected better, but Portugal had suffered dreadfully and was to be devastated by several years of further fighting. And
this country was to be Wellesley's closest ally in the war against
Napoleon. All he could do was work with what he had, the still-
primitive Portuguese army now being urgently drilled and trained by
William Beresford. Its support would be vital, outnumbered as
Wellesley was in the Peninsula by the French. His plan was to inte-
grate the Portuguese units into his army and march north to try and
throw the French out of Oporto. He would have liked to push east
immediately into Spain to link up with Spanish forces eager for a
battle with the French. But that would have to wait. He didn't think
it wise to leave Portugal with the French 'in possession of a part
of this country that is very fertile in resources and of the town of
Oporto'. Oporto, 150 miles north of Lisbon, was powerfully placed
on the north bank of the wide and fast-flowing River Douro, which
flowed from the heart of Spain into the Atlantic.

For many of Wellesley's troops the long march up from Lisbon
was their first taste of real campaigning. The last day's march, in particular, was a dreadful ordeal. They toiled for twenty-five miles under
a scorching sun and amid clouds of dust. The road was narrow and
there was little or no water on the way. Their feet were sore and their
knapsacks seemed to become heavier and heavier. But marching was
the only way the ordinary footsoldier could travel. The distances they
had to cover and the fierce extremes of the Peninsular climate made
it a harsh challenge. Only a few officers could afford a mount. Most
men marched on foot for days, carrying all their heavy gear. 'The
weight each man had to carry was tremendous in addition to heavy
knapsacks: there were their muskets and accoutrements, seventy
rounds of ammunition, a blanket, a mess kettle and wooden canteen.'
John Dobbs, an Irishman from Dublin, also had what he called a 'tin

Central Portugal

tot', a small container which he and his mates packed with their knife and fork. 'The tot was in constant requisition: on getting up it was paraded with water to wash my mouth; at breakfast it answered for a teacup, on the march for drinking out of, at dinner for soup, after dinner, for rum, punch or wine.'

Wellesley's new army had its first clash with the French just south of Oporto. On 10 and 11 May his cavalry and footsoldiers came up against a 4,000-strong advance guard of French infantry and some cavalry. William Tomkinson was riding with the light dragoons, who were ideally equipped to tackle scouting and other challenges on the fringes of the main action as their horses and swords were less weighty than the ones carried by the heavy cavalry. They quickly scattered the French cavalry outposts on 10 May, but on the 11th Tomkinson was part of a squadron charging massed ranks of infantry. He suddenly found himself unable to hold his reins as both his arms

45

were disabled by musket fire. Within moments his horse ran on to a French bayonet, turned away and galloped off. It passed under a low vine tree that hit Tomkinson on the head and knocked him to the ground. Soon after he had recovered consciousness some allied German infantry came up 'and began to plunder me . . .'. Another British soldier approached and managed to persuade the Germans to stop, and Tomkinson was finally rescued from the battlefield by a surgeon who cut off his clothes and dressed his wounds. He had one musket shot in the neck, and two others in each arm as well as a bayonet wound. He spent several days in pain, but the wounds healed and what a surgeon thought was a musket ball buried in his left arm turned out to be a button torn away from his chest and embedded in his flesh.

Tomkinson was one of nearly a hundred British casualties that day; the French lost 250 and withdrew across the river. Wellesley was thankful for something else too: his Portuguese troops had fought well. He was to draw great satisfaction over the next year or two from the speed with which his Portuguese allies developed their forces under British guidance. The new battalions of Portuguese light troops, the Caçadores, in particular would soon be recognised as some of the most impressive fighters in Europe. But acclaim wasn't universal. The normally generous Ned Costello, who fought beside them in many battles, said the Portuguese were 'the dirtiest and noisiest brutes I ever came across . . . during the whole of the Peninsular War, or at least the time they were with us, I never knew them to perform a gallant act'. George Simmons began with a low opinion of Portugal. Its people were 'dirty in the extreme . . . their houses . . . stink worse than an English pigsty'. And 'their dancing was too indelicate to give pleasure . . . I blessed my stars I was an Englishman.' But Simmons was soon impressed by the increasing confidence of the Portuguese soldiers and within two years he described them as 'fighting like lions'.

With all his troops now back on the north side of the Douro, Marshal Soult had the bridge of boats, the only remaining link between the two banks, blown up. All ferries and other boats of any size were under guard on the north bank. He reckoned he was now so strongly placed in Oporto that he could afford to relax. He

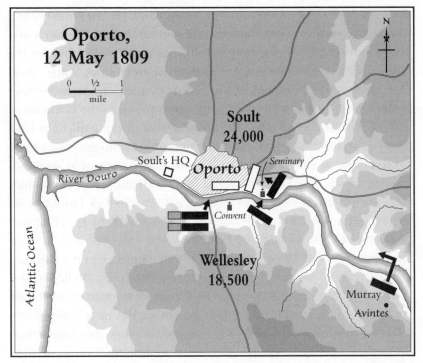

The Battle of Oporto

thought Wellesley was sure to try to cross the Douro near its mouth, where the banks were low. The French marshal, who lived in a fine villa facing west towards the sea, was confident that he would spot any boats Wellesley brought in from the sea, so he glanced only cursorily at the much more difficult stretches of river upstream: Wellesley would be unlikely to try crossing up there; besides it would take him some days to prepare a crossing and French patrols would be sure to spot him. At nightfall on 11 May, as Soult looked through his window to the west, he could see no sign of British activity. He spent the night working on his despatches and then went to bed, leaving his staff to enjoy a leisurely breakfast.

Soult had spectacularly underestimated his adversary. Wellesley was up early, telescope in hand, climbing a hill on the south side of the river. The garden of a convent commanded a superb view of the upper reach of the river. His troops had advanced during the night and were now all concealed behind the brow of the hill he was

47

standing on. They were minutes away from the river, but they couldn't be seen by the French on the other side.

Wellesley scanned the opposite bank and noticed little sign of activity. The further he looked upstream the more deserted it looked. One of his scouts, Colonel Waters, reported that a Portuguese sympathiser, who was a barber in Oporto, had crossed the river in a small skiff to tell the British that there was a way they could cross. He pointed out four barges, which normally carried local wine across the river, tucked under the northern bank and apparently unguarded. The barber also told Waters that a French patrol passed the barges every half-hour. So the colonel invited a small group of local peasants to join him in the skiff, waited for one of those thirty-minute windows and crossed to the other side. Between them they then ferried the barges across without being seen by the French.

Wellesley, whose keen eye had spotted a walled seminary on the other side seemingly unmanned, was delighted when he heard about the boats. 'Well, let the men cross,' he said. And, loaded with thirty men each, first one boat and then a second slipped unobserved across the river. At the same time Wellesley moved three batteries of artillery, eighteen guns, to the top of the hill he was standing on so that they could target the expected French attack on the seminary opposite. For a full hour while Wellesley and his staff stood anxiously watching, the troops crossed the river, climbed to the seminary and secured it. Then the French attacked. Thomas Bunbury was a young British officer with a Portuguese unit that occupied the seminary. 'The advancing French made a great noise when marching – every party having a drummer thumping away with all his might and against these poor devils of drummers our fire was principally directed. We shot several and our opponents did not seem to get on well without them.' It was Bunbury's first time under fire. 'Being a giddy harebrained fellow, I do not suppose that I reflected at all upon the matter. It seemed to me capital fun.'

At 11.30 a.m. after two and a half hours' sleep Soult was awakened by an ADC bursting into his villa shouting that the British had crossed the river. It had taken sixty minutes for the French to spot them. One story has it that the redcoated soldiers in the boats were taken for Swiss infantrymen in the French army on their way to take a swim. By the time Soult had dressed and leaped on his horse issuing a flurry of orders, a big battle was under way. French guns were pounding the 600 British troops who had managed to cross the Douro and secure the seminary. French units attacking it were immediately targeted with shrapnel shells from Wellesley's guns across the river. The French counter-attack faltered and Soult decided to reinforce the assault with troops who had been guarding the foreshore and harbour in Oporto itself. No sooner were the quays clear of French troops than crowds of Portuguese raced out of their houses waving and cheering and a fleet of boats set out for the south bank to pick up Wellesley's main force which had gathered there. It wasn't long before British troops were pouring across and into the city: the French were now under attack from the front and from behind.

Soult's position was hopeless. He had no choice but to follow his men as they fled the way they had come only six weeks earlier. British troops swept through the city as women waved white hand-kerchiefs from the balconies. There were cheers and shouts of 'Viva Ingleses!' and local people started stripping the French dead and wounded. Charles Leslie watched the 'splendid view' of the French fleeing. 'They made no fight – every man seemed to be running for his life – and threw away their knapsacks and arms, so that we had only the trouble of making prisoners every instant, all begging for quarter and surrendering with great good humour.' By teatime Wellesley was in Soult's villa tucking into the lunch the French mar-shal had left uneaten. He then wrote an account of his successful day, telling Castlereagh that the French 'retired in the utmost confusion . . . leaving behind them five pieces of cannon, eight tumbrils of ammunition and many prisoners'. Wellesley's masterly surprise attack had cost him only twenty-three soldiers killed. He was disappointed that in the five days in which his men chased Soult's army to the Spanish frontier they failed to surround and destroy it altogether. But when Soult finally dragged himself into Galicia, he had lost around 4,000 men, scores of them at the hands of Portuguese peasants. The ever observant commissary August Schaumann watched what he called the 'indescribable cruelties' inflicted on 'the French soldiers who fell into their clutches . . . In addition to nailing them up alive on barn doors, they had also stripped many of them, emasculated them, and then placed their amputated members in their mouths – a ghastly sight!'

Within weeks of arriving in Portugal Wellesley's young soldiers were experiencing the full horror of war. In their own fighting with the French they had escaped with light casualties. But for many it was their first sight of the hideous wounds inflicted by musket, sabre and roundshot and their first encounter with the crudeness of the army's medical resources. Tomkinson was one of the luckier ones. He had only a button embedded in his arm. If he had had a musket ball lodged there the army surgeon might well have urged amputation as the surest way of avoiding infection and death. Tomkinson later remarked that British surgeons were more likely to amputate than the French were. The French, he reckoned, 'run great risks with a man's life in hopes of saving a limb, from knowing that a soldier without a leg or an arm is incapable of service and probably a burthen on the state'. There were cases of soldiers who rejected advice to have a limb removed and survived. Amputation without anaesthetic caused agony unimaginable today. For some it was bearable only after a large draught of alcohol, usually rum. Sergeant Thomas Jackson drank almost a pint of rum before having his leg amputated later in the war: 'In an instant it raised up my spirits to an invincible courage.' He still found the tightness of the tourniquet and the sawing of the bone almost unbearable. Instruments became progressively blunter during a busy day. Opium was available but was of little use in reducing pain during an operation. In extreme cold pain might be deadened, and fainting in the middle of an operation was often a blessed relief. But usually the best that surgeons could do was to give the patient something to bite on as well as a good drink. It was to be another forty years before chloroform became the first primitive anaesthetic.

Wellesley did what he could to alleviate the pain of the wounded. He would visit them and talk to them in hospital: he recognised the importance of ensuring that the surgeons had the best means of doing their job. He appreciated that medical care was an important service that his men had a right to expect, just as he believed that an army that was poorly fed and watered would not perform at its best. His despatches are full of demands of his own commissary staff and his allies for a constant supply of food for his soldiers and forage for his horses. All supplies from local people should be properly accounted and paid for, he said. He abhorred the fact that so many of his men stooped to plundering farmers and householders for their needs.

His undisguised disgust at the conduct of some of his men became an obsession, prompting him to send home a rather schizophrenic message. On the one hand he praised his soldiers for their courage. Immediately after Oporto, he wrote to Castlereagh in his formal despatch: 'I cannot say too much in favour of the officers and troops.' And yet just two weeks later he wrote privately that his men were a 'rabble . . . they plunder in all directions'. And a fortnight later: 'it is impossible to describe to you the irregularities and outrages committed by the troops'. He gave an example of this thieving, which he said was terrible and gave him 'the greatest concern'. He said 'they have plundered the people of bullocks among other property'. He said he understood that they did this in order 'to sell them to the people again'. He sent a request to the Portuguese authorities to 'issue a proclamation forbidding the people . . . to purchase anything from the soldiers of the British army'.

His revulsion for plunder had already led him to order summary execution for men caught looting. Ever since Wellesley had first set foot in Portugal he had learned an essential lesson. He had seen how savagely the Spanish and Portuguese rebels treated any Frenchman they laid hands on. The British army was in the Peninsula to liberate the people from Napoleon, not to substitute British oppression for French. He was to maintain his rigid regime of outlawing plunder right through into southern France. On one occasion, convinced of the guilt of two soldiers, he told his Provost Marshal to report back to him within ten minutes that they had both been hanged.

There were small, albeit infrequent glimpses of humanity amid the ruthlessness. Three men were led before him who had been caught looting and he ordered them hanged where all the troops could see them. The next morning three bodies were seen hanging from a tree. But the Commander in Chief's staff, in a moment of kindness, had let the three miscreants go and strung up three corpses from the hospital in their place. Wellesley found out later but, when asked if he was angry, he said he hadn't really wished them dead and was very glad their lives had been spared.

But Wellesley's concern went deeper than a principled disapproval of misconduct. The fact was that he had in general a pretty low opinion of his men. He may have been right about many of them, but his habit of tarring them all with the same brush was one of the least appealing features of his character. His most telling remark was one he made to friends long after he had retired from campaigning. He said his army was 'composed of the scum of the earth – the mere scum of the earth . . . English soldiers are fellows who have enlisted for the drink – that is the plain fact – they have all enlisted for drink.' He then, to his credit, went on to say, 'It is really wonderful that we should have made them the fine fellows they are.' But the sweeping, all-inclusive nature of his contempt is revealing. He seemed not to acknowledge the hugely varied intake of humanity that his army represented. Of course there were crooks and villains. There were many who felt they sometimes had no alternative to stealing food in order to survive. But there were others, as countless eyewitness accounts bear out, who found the savagery of military life and the conduct of some of their comrades deeply offensive. And those of them who encountered it, mainly in the higher ranks in the army, found Wellesley's ill-concealed contempt for his men offensive too.

Many years later Napoleon in exile remarked that English soldiers, who were as brave as any in the world, would have responded better if they had been driven by what he called 'the stimulus of honour . . . instead of the lash'. He would have encouraged rivalry in the ranks and would have promoted people on merit rather than on the basis of their financial or family status. Wellesley, in contrast, particularly in this early stage of the campaign, believed in securing his men's respect by enforced discipline as much as by inspiring leadership. And as for promoting on merit, he was hamstrung by the British tradition of denying to the commander in the field the right to appoint the best men to the top jobs. That right remained with Whitehall throughout the campaign: Wellington could attempt to influence the selection of his officers; he could not choose them himself.

But he knew how much his men mattered to him, rascals though they might be. He spent hours superintending the detail of their supply arrangements and was incensed when the essential needs of his men were not met. He didn't often show emotion but he was ready to go to great lengths to ensure that the wounded were well cared for. After one encounter he heard that some wounded men whom he had ordered to be housed in officers' quarters were actually having to sleep in the open air in rough conditions. He rode thirty miles to see what had happened, and found that his orders had been disobeyed. He had the men moved inside and brought all the officers before a court martial. He also reduced the hospital deductions from the men's pay. A private soldier would now have a penny less deducted for being sick. Of his twelve-pence daily pay the stoppage would now be nine pence instead of ten.*

Strategically, Wellesley had good reason to be pleased with his progress so far. Within a month of arriving in Lisbon he had once again thrown the French out of Portugal at little cost. He had again defeated the most professional land army in Europe, humiliating another of Napoleon's top commanders. After Wellesley's successes in the summer of the year before, Napoleon had told his men, 'Soldiers, I need you. The presence of the hideous leopard contaminates the country of Spain and Portugal. The leopard will flee in terror at your approach.' The Emperor had then come to the Peninsula himself and expelled the army of Sir John Moore. But now the leopard was back in the person of Wellesley and, far from fleeing, the British commander was on the attack – swinging his army around to the east. He believed he could now afford to take the fight with Napoleon into Spain. 'The ball is now at my foot,' he wrote. 'And I hope I shall have strength enough to give it a good kick.'

---

* A penny was not to be sniffed at in those days. According to the Bank of England's online inflation calculator goods costing one pound in 1809 would have cost around sixty pounds in 2009. See www.bankofengland.co.uk/education/inflation. But historical comparisons of inflation can be notoriously misleading. A better guide is purchasing power: in Britain a penny in 1809 would buy you a half-pint of beer and three pence some bread and cheese. In the Peninsula prices varied greatly – depending on supply. George Simmons (pp. 183–4) complains at one stage, 'Every article of food is enormously dear: bread is 1 shilling [12 pence] a pound, butter 4 shillings a pound . . .'

4

The obstinate old Gentleman

Talavera, 1809

WELLESLEY KNEW THAT an advance into Spain would prompt the various French armies Napoleon had posted there to unite against him in a force that would outnumber his. The French could put a total of 50,000 in the field, Wellesley had fewer than 20,000. But he had reinforcements on the way. A fresh regiment of badly needed cavalry, the 23rd Light Dragoons, would soon arrive in Lisbon. Major Fred Ponsonby was one of them. His mother, Harriet, Countess of Bessborough, had been 'quite giddy' when Fred first joined up and she worried about the danger he might face on some 'odious expedition'. But now he was old enough to look after himself.

Wellesley wrote to Ponsonby's commanding officer with his usual attention to detail: 'I am particularly anxious that your horses should join the army in a condition for service.' He instructed him to make sure he had plenty of spare shoes and nails for the horses; he should also carefully watch the balance of the horses' diet so that they got used to eating more 'barley or Indian corn or straw', which were likely to be in better supply than oats.

When the 23rd arrived, noted Ponsonby, 'our great anxiety was to get to the army for an action which we generally expected . . . In passing over the wild country near Villa Vellia, I was with the Advanced Guard and saw a wolf feeding upon the carcase of a horse in the road. I fired my pistol at him but without effect.' When he reached the army in bivouac, Ponsonby and his commanding officer 'dined with [Wellesley] with whom I was scarcely acquainted'. Fred rapidly formed a close relationship with Wellesley. He was rather more hot headed than his composed Commander in Chief, but both had a strong association with Ireland. Fred's father, like Wellesley's, was an Irish peer and both had a passion for hunting. This very British love of the chase was pursued exuberantly by Arthur Wellesley. It was his only real relaxation apart from the dinner parties he held mainly with his immediate staff. It wasn't long before he built up a formidable pack of hounds and a stable of fine horses. Once, later in the campaign, he was preparing for a battle when 'a brace of greyhounds in pursuit of a hare, passed close to him . . . the instant he observed them, he gave the "view hallo" and went after them at full speed to the utter astonishment' of his companions.

Wellesley keenly awaited the arrival of Robert Craufurd's riflemen, who he knew would play a key role in any early battle. But they had hit a snag. Appalling weather in the English Channel had held them up for the best part of two weeks off the Isle of Wight. Jonathan Leach, veteran of Vimeiro, who had returned to Britain after retreating with Moore to Corunna, was among them. They had a lot of time to while away and Leach remarked that he and his mates made 'several excursions' to places in the area. 'We all agreed that the women of the Isle of Wight were particularly handsome.' They finally arrived in Lisbon at the end of June and Leach and the other officers spent four days 'purchasing horses, donkeys . . . cigars and various other odds and ends indispensable in campaigning'. They too found the Portuguese capital full of an 'accumulation of disgusting filth' and were glad to be ordered up the River Tagus in flat-bottomed boats to join Wellesley as soon as possible. After twenty-four hours spent cooped up in the boats, the men went ashore to bivouac on the river bank. 'All the frogs in the Peninsula had assembled . . . to welcome us to Portugal; for such an eternal croaking I never heard before or since. It failed, however, to spoil our night's rest, as sleep the previous night had been quite out of the question, owing to our being constrained to sit upright in the boats.'

Once they were on the move Leach's roving eye was soon active. He and his friends chatted up some young women behind the iron gratings of a convent. All they could see was that the nuns were blessed with 'sparkling black eyes . . . the rest was left to the imagination'. After a while they managed to do a sort of trade. The women smuggled preserved fruits and other delicacies out of the convent, and in return 'little notes and love letters, written in villainously bad

Portuguese, were transmitted . . . to them . . . Two of them who were heartily tired of their unnatural prison declared to myself and brother-officer, that they were ready to make their escape . . . and to share our fortunes . . .' Leach reflected that the young nuns must have been heroines to take the risk of being 'buried alive' or 'broiled on a gridiron' if they were discovered.

Although these valuable troops were still well over 150 miles' march away, Wellesley had one other major reinforcement to count on. He had a new ally, Gregorio García de la Cuesta, who commanded a force of some 20,000 just inside Spain. It was part of the new Spanish army still struggling to reorganise itself under a chaotic revolutionary Spanish government, which had broken away from its old alliance with France. The army was to prove no match for Napoleonic France in nearly every engagement it entered into. Wellesley had every hope that, provided that he and Cuesta could meet up and fight together, they would be more than a match for any army that marched against them. Napoleon's brother Joseph, the nominal King of Spain, had a large force around Madrid, and another army under Marshal Claude Perrin Victor was heading west with only 22,000 men. Wellesley believed that if he and Cuesta could catch Victor on his own, they would score a major victory.

Cuesta was nearly seventy years old, stubborn and highly impatient. He had lost 10,000 men in an earlier battle with Victor (at Medellín), where he himself had been trampled underfoot by his own retreating cavalry. He now wanted to get his revenge on Victor on his own. Wellesley sent Cuesta several messages urging him to wait for the British army to join him, but received no reply. 'I can only say the obstinacy of this old gentleman is throwing out of our hands the finest game that any armies ever had, and that we shall repent that we did not cut off Victor . . .' Finally on 10 July Wellesley managed to catch up with Cuesta. The meeting was not successful, partly because Wellesley arrived very late thanks to a forty-five-mile ride on horseback with poor guides. Even so, he wrote afterwards, 'the General received me well, and was very attentive to me, but I had no conversation with him as he declined to speak French and I cannot talk Spanish'. However Wellesley did manage through an interpreter to persuade Cuesta to agree to unite the two armies at a spot on the Tagus a few miles west of Talavera, a large Spanish town strategically placed on the main road between Madrid and Portugal. If the British and Spanish could scatter the French here, they would be only 120 miles from Madrid.

Wellesley was deeply unimpressed by his new Spanish ally. Cuesta's command post, in which he trundled around issuing orders, was a huge coach drawn by nine mules, and to mount his own horse he needed four large men to hoist him into the saddle. Wellesley would no doubt have ignored such eccentricities had he been able to count on Cuesta as he was able to count on another elderly general, Marshal Blücher, at Waterloo six years later. But Cuesta was no Blücher. He was very reluctant to engage in any joint action with the British. Only after persistent pressure from Wellesley was he persuaded to agree to a co-ordinated assault on Victor's approaching army on the morning of 23 July. They would both attack the French from different directions at the same time.

But when the British moved into position and stood poised for the big attack, there was no sign of the Spanish. Charles Leslie and thousands of other infantrymen were under arms before 3 a.m. but they 'moved forward only a short distance when we were halted, and the men kept standing under arms . . . we were kept for hours in a miserable state of suspense, all being hungry, and no one having anything to eat'. Victor was able to retire safely and wait for more French forces to move up to join him. The opportunity had been lost.

Wellesley tracked down Cuesta and found him sitting on some cushions outside his carriage. He asked him what on earth was going on. The old man told him that his army was tired and that he had not reconnoitred the ground sufficiently. Somehow Wellesley managed to contain his anger, but he was never to forgive Cuesta. The rumour got around – and even reached Wellesley's wife Kitty back home – that Cuesta had refused to move because it was a Sunday. Wellesley denied that Cuesta had ever given that excuse, but he was furious that such a chance had been missed. Long afterwards he told friends that if Cuesta 'had fought when I wanted him at Talavera, I have no hesitation in saying that it would have been as great a battle as Waterloo and would have cleared Spain of the French'. He was, typically, overstating it – he enjoyed the occasional burst of hyperbole. But certainly, if the French and British armies had attacked before Victor could have been reinforced, Wellesley and Cuesta would have had an immense advantage in numbers. The next day Wellesley reported to London: 'I find General Cuesta more and more impracticable [sic] every day. It is impossible to do business with him, and very uncertain that any operation will succeed in which he has any concern.'

But even worse was to come. The following day, 25 July, having tried and failed to persuade Wellesley to join him, Cuesta took his army off on his own in pursuit of Victor. The result was nearly disastrous. He ran into a newly reinforced French army: Victor had been joined by two other large forces and had 50,000 men ready to fight Cuesta's 30,000. Cuesta turned round and retreated, smarting at Wellesley's refusal to follow him. Finally on 27 July Cuesta returned with his army and reluctantly agreed to line up his men alongside Wellesley's. Both armies took up battle positions facing east across the Portina brook which runs down to the River Tagus at Talavera. Wellesley would have his battle with the French, but the odds were now much less sharply tilted in his favour.

The army Wellesley drew up at Talavera was divided into four clearly defined units, a structure that would remain the pattern all the way to Waterloo: first there were divisions of some 5,000 or 6,000 men, each commanded by a general, usually a major general. Divisions, in turn, would divide up into two or three brigades of 1,500 to 2,000 men each, commanded by a brigadier or major general. Each brigade was subdivided into two, three, sometimes four battalions, of between 500 and 1,000 men each. The battalion, commanded by a lieutenant colonel, was the unit for which men's loyalty was fiercest, with its regimental roots in a local community back home. The battalion in turn was split into around ten companies of up to a hundred men. As battles were fought and men fell, these units would sometimes shrink to frighteningly small sizes. But however battered they became, they offered a framework of command at their four different levels, from division down to company, within which the men could put their hard-learned battlefield drills into effect. And the experience of each bloody combat enhanced the mutual comradeship of the survivors and helped motivate them to outdo each other in stamina and courage.

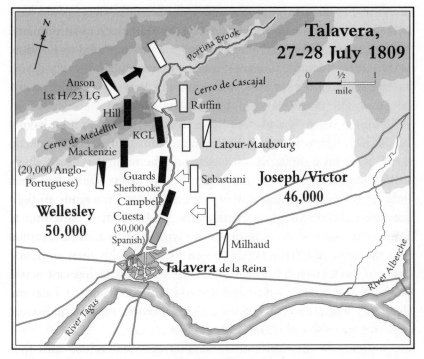

The Battle of Talavera

Early on the 27th, as his men covered Cuesta's retreat, Wellesley narrowly escaped being killed or captured. He was up at the top of a tower well out in front of the main British force scanning the ground ahead with his telescope – as he often did. Suddenly a group of French *tirailleurs* (skirmishers or sharpshooters) managed to filter through some woods and nearly reached the foot of the tower. Wellesley heard some shots as his own infantry spotted them. He raced down the stairs and out into the courtyard, where he leaped on his horse and galloped away in the nick of time – pursued by French musket fire. This was one of many occasions in Arthur Wellesley's career when the course of British history ran the risk of being upset by a stray shot – but he always escaped unscathed.

Later that day Wellesley surveyed the landscape on which the two armies were drawn up. It was harsh and unforgiving. The Portina brook, which at the height of the searing Spanish summer was no more than a trickle of water, formed the front line between the

British and French. It ran down from the north, first through a ravine between two hills and then across an open plain to the Tagus two miles away. Wellesley stood on one of the hills, the Cerro de Medellín, slightly higher than the one opposite, the Cerro de Cascajal, from which Marshal Victor could command the view from the other side. Between them the broken ground, dotted with olive trees, sloped down sharply on either side of the brook. The battle would be fought across this ravine and further south across the brook as it flowed through the flatter country down to the Tagus.

Wellesley suffered from one major weakness. He still didn't have his light troops, the riflemen, with him. They were hurrying to meet him, spurred on by the impatient and irrepressible Robert Craufurd. But they would not arrive until the day after the battle. Wellesley did have the men of Charles Leslie's 29th Infantry Regiment who had fought so well at Roliça and Vimeiro. He placed them under command of the doughty General Rowland Hill on the Cerro de Medellín, urging Hill to keep most of his men behind the hill on the reverse slope where the French could not see them. In the centre he put a powerful division under General Sherbrooke. It had two Guards battalions in its front line. And over on the right on the flat plain, William Lawrence's 40th Infantry Regiment and John Cooper's 7th Fusiliers were part of another division under Brigadier General Alexander Campbell. Fred Ponsonby and other officers in the 23rd Light Dragoons held their horsemen ready behind the centre of Wellesley's long line of regiments, ready to charge off and support any unit that got into trouble. The British ranks were a sea of colour – mainly of redcoated infantry and the odd blue flash of cavalry. The French massed the other side of the brook, dressed mainly in blue. Holding the ground between the British right and the Tagus were Cuesta's Spanish in uniforms of every imaginable colour. They were now held in widespread contempt by Wellesley and his army. Wellesley wrote later that the Spanish 'are, in general, the most incapable of useful exertion of all the nations I have known'. Leslie, looking across at the Spanish from the Cerro de Medellín, said the Spanish presented the most 'motley and grotesque appearance . . . their equipments of the most inferior description'. They were 'deficient in discipline and regular organisation'. Even so, he said he recognised that 'the men were remarkably fine, possessing the most essential qualities to make good soldiers, being individually brave'. Fusilier Cooper had unreserved contempt for the Spanish who were close to him in the front line. They were, he said, 'a motley crowd', and General Cuesta was 'a worthless wretch'.

By the evening of the 27th it was clear to everyone that a battle was inevitable. There had been a lot of French artillery fire all day. 'A battery was opened upon us,' Fred Ponsonby wrote. 'I must confess the sensation was by no means pleasant when the shots came whizzing by us and some came plunging into our columns. I felt very considerable pleasure when we retired out of this fire, the first I had ever experienced.' Among the British ranks most men lay down to avoid presenting an obvious target and by evening all was quiet. The night was very dark and gloomy, and because the French were so close Leslie and his comrades on the top of and behind the Cerro de Medellín kept their weapons in their hands.

The French noticed that there appeared to be only a few British soldiers on the Cerro hill, and they launched the first of several attacks on it after dark. As Leslie recorded, 'About nine o'clock there opened a tremendous fire on the top of the hill.' The French infantry then charged up it and swept through two battalions of the King's German Legion who were on the hill's exposed forward slope. They were snoozing after an exhausting day's marching and the shock of seeing the French racing towards them was too much for them: they could do nothing to stop them. Within minutes 146 out of the 557 men of one KGL battalion had been killed or wounded. 'It was evident that the troops placed on the hill had been surprised.' Within seconds the French were on top of the hill, and Hill himself was nearly captured. He had sped up to the crest to see what was going on and suddenly found himself surrounded. Someone seized his reins and would have grabbed the general himself had not Leslie and his comrades in the 29th at that moment surged up the hill, rescued him and pushed the French troops down again. 'We could see the French column moving up across our front, their drums beating the charge, and we could hear their officers giving orders and encouraging their men: "En avant, Francais! En avant, mes enfants!"' Hill had only narrowly escaped. A staff officer beside him was killed.

At this critical juncture there had been a brief and uncharacteristic lapse of command on the part of Wellesley. He appears to have decided that he had time to go and visit the Spanish troops on his far right. It was unusual for him to let his grasp slacken at vital moments in a battle, but whatever the reason he was not there to give the orders that he was normally so insistent on issuing himself. If it hadn't been for the quick response of the 29th, the French might have established themselves on the Cerro and completely dominated the battlefield the following morning. Leslie was unclear how the 29th had got 'so gloriously into the fight', but they had saved Wellesley deep embarrassment right at the start of the battle. Schaumann, the commissary, was further back behind the front line during the crisis, but he credits Hill with regaining possession of the ground 'by means of a bayonet charge . . . this combat proved very costly to both sides'.

Wherever he had been, Wellesley soon made up for his absence. He reappeared and spent the rest of the night wrapped up in a blanket on the top of the hill. He slept only fitfully, frequently waking and asking what time it was. From then on he remained in complete control of the battle. It was a nervous night for everyone – particularly the Spanish, who ran amok at around midnight. A sudden exchange of musket fire threw them into a panic. A whole section of their front line, believing the French were attacking in force, turned tail and ran back to the rear. There they found themselves among the British baggage train which they promptly began to loot. Cuesta was so furious at the conduct of his troops that he ordered 200 men to be picked out and executed by firing squad the following morning. Wellesley interceded with him to get the number reduced to twenty-five.

On the French side Marshal Victor was in command, even though Napoleon's brother Joseph was there. Victor had had a distinguished career and was able to boast that he had been a fellow gunner with Napoleon Bonaparte at the siege of Toulon sixteen years earlier. He enjoyed a special position and that gave him the whip hand in the French hierarchy at Talavera. No one felt confident enough to dissuade him when he called for another attack on the now heavily reinforced Cerro at dawn.

As the light slowly crept over the two hills that faced each other only 200 yards apart, the British began to discern the strength of the

French force Victor had mustered against them. No fewer than twenty-four guns faced them at close range and thousands upon thousands of French footsoldiers in their already grimy blue uniforms waited for the order to advance. 'In the first place,' observed Leslie, 'immediately below us was formed a heavy solid column on the bank of the ravine . . . with field batteries on both flanks, and the guns already pointed towards us . . . our front showed an extended line only two deep.' Once again Wellesley had ordered his men to deploy in line against the attacking French columns. Troops in a line, with every musket facing forward unobstructed, could concentrate lethal fire on the ground directly in front of them. Wellesley knew the risks: the line had no depth. If enemy cavalry charged troops spread out in a thin line, they could cause havoc. Everything would then depend on how fast the men in line could form a defensive square to foil the oncoming horsemen.

At 5 a.m. a single shot rang out from the French guns and the batteries opened up. But Wellesley had provided for this. As the French footsoldiers began their slog across the ravine and up the hillside, he ordered his men to fall back behind the brow of the hill, where they could shelter from the guns and lie in wait for the infantry. Leslie remembered, 'we were ordered to lie down flat on the ground. The shot flew thick and fast but it went principally over us, the guns being much too much elevated.' On came the French up the hill but they could see nothing until they had reached 'pretty close to us, when our Brigadier General, Richard Stewart, said "Now, 29th! Now is your time!" We instantly sprang to our feet, gave three tremendous cheers, and immediately opened our fire, giving them several well-directed volleys, which they gallantly returned . . .' Leslie and the others in two lines were able to fire all their 400 muskets unobstructed. The French, by contrast, in massed columns of sixty men wide by thirty deep could bring only some 120 muskets to bear in their front two ranks. The soldiers behind were unable to fire for fear of hitting the men in front of them. The exchange of musket fire left the French badly depleted and the survivors confused and hesitant.

The redcoats then got the order to charge: with bayonets clipped on to the barrels of their muskets, they launched themselves at the stalled French column. 'In we went, a wall of stout hearts and bristling steel. The French did not fancy such close quarters. The moment we made the rush they began to waver and then went to the right about.' The whole of the 48th Regiment now joined the charge of the 29th. Most of the French ran for it, but occasionally one or two turned to fire a shot. 'We, however, kept dashing on, and drove them all headlong right before us down the hill into their own lines again. We kept following them up, firing, running, and cheering.' In the space of just forty minutes in that narrow valley between the two hills the French lost 1,300 men. Just as the rout was complete, Hill was hit by a musket ball in the back of the neck. Fortunately it wasn't serious, and he was out of action for only two days. Charles Leslie was wounded too. 'At about 7 o'clock I received a ball in the side of my thigh, about three inches above the right knee. In quitting the field I passed near Sir Arthur Wellesley . . . he looked at me, seeing the blood streaming down my white trousers but he said nothing.' The French commander ordered his men back up the Cerro, but again they were pushed back.

Utterly exhausted, the French and the British enjoyed a moment of truce along the line of the brook. Some collected the dead and wounded. All drank greedily. Even if it was running with blood, as eyewitnesses report, the water was a blessed relief. The men's mouths were parched and hot from biting off the tops of powder cartridges. The two sides even chatted to each other across the brook. It was unusual for this kind of contact to occur during a battle – but it did at Talavera. More often such conversations took place between pickets or sentries when all was quiet. Jonathan Leach recalled that the French were courteous and 'gentlemanly to a degree . . . once in a thick fog a small patrol of ours suddenly found themselves close to a superior force of French cavalry, and instantly retired but in the hurry one of our dragoons dropped his cloak'. A French dragoon then came 'riding up to within a short distance, dropped the captured cloak on the ground and rode away making signs to the English dragoon, who had lost it, to pick it up'. Sometimes the two sides actually did business. On one river front line, the British sentries would 'put some coppers in a mess tin, give it a rattle to draw the attention of the [French] sentry', then one of the British 'stepped down to the water, gave his tin another rattle, placed it on the centre big stone calling out

"Cognac" and retired . . . it was returned in the evening full of brandy (not likely of the best quality)'.

Back on the Talavera battlefield any fraternisation was soon forgotten. Wellesley suddenly had his attention drawn to his extreme left. In the valley to the north of him a large French infantry force was assembling and beginning to threaten his exposed left flank. Unless he moved against them fast, they could assault the north side of the Cerro hill. He sent orders to General Anson's brigade, which included Fred Ponsonby's 23rd Light Dragoons, to stop the French in their tracks. It was to be Ponsonby's first cavalry charge. Under the command of Colonel Seymour, the horsemen trotted off. The moment the French foot regiments saw the approach of the 23rd's blue jackets faced with red, they formed squares. This was the well-tried infantry response to an attack by cavalry. The footsoldiers packed together in a tight square four ranks deep, facing out. The back two ranks stood with muskets aimed, the front two ranks knelt with bayonets tilted up at a 45-degree angle: it was almost unknown for a horse to plunge willingly into this wall of steel blades. No mounted man's sabre could reach through it. Only a lancer could hope that his nine-foot-long weapon would pierce enemy flesh. The square was a formidable defence against cavalry, a sort of giant hedgehog. The 23rd's pace quickened, 460 men packed tight together – only a few inches of space between the riders – with 450 men of the 1st Hussars a little behind. The trot became a canter, the canter a gallop. Sabres down to the horizontal. 'Charge!'

'An ear-splitting yell arose from our own and the Spanish armies, cheering them on.' August Schaumann witnessed it from the top of the hill. 'When the trumpeters blew the charge, a cloud of dust arose, and in a moment an indescribable and terrible scene was enacted.' With the front rank of the French square just 100 yards away, a hollow ravine suddenly yawned in front of the horsemen. It was far too late for them to stop: the first man to reach it managed to clear it. He turned round and frantically tried to signal to those behind to wheel round. Again, too late. Some cleared the large ditch, some fell, some collided with others – there was utter chaos, loose horses running in all directions. Most of the 1st Hussars managed to swerve away. But the 23rd lost half their number almost immediately, and more moments later to the fusillade that met them from the square drawn up just in front of them. They were down to 160 horsemen, led on by Ponsonby, one of the few surviving officers. Galloping wildly forward, they skirted the square and plunged deep into squadrons of French cavalry beyond. William Napier, the soldier historian, who fought in the Peninsula, described the charge of the 23rd. 'Major Frederick Ponsonby, a hardy soldier, rallied all who came up and passing through . . . a fire from both sides, fell with inexpressible violence upon a brigade of French *chasseurs* in the rear.' To spectators, such as August Schaumann on the Cerro, they disappeared into the fog of battle. 'All we could see was here and there a riderless horse appearing through the smoke, and dashing across the battlefield. Meanwhile the furious though unsuccessful attack, which revealed the true mettle of the English cavalry, had so startled the French that they not only ceased storming the hill, but a portion of their cavalry took flight.'

Ponsonby somehow fought his way out of the mêlée and back across the ditch, with what was left of his regiment. He wrote home to his mother: 'We had the pleasing amusement of charging five solid squares with a ditch in their front. After losing 180 [men] and 222 horses we found it was not so agreeable and that Frenchmen don't always run away when they see British cavalry, and so off we set, and my horse never went so fast in its life.' Ponsonby's sister Lady Caroline Lamb was so shocked when she heard the news of his escape, she wrote to their mother: 'Good God how dreadful it is to have him there [in Spain], and what you must suffer if I feel so miserable and anxious.'

Ponsonby concluded that the effect of the cavalry action, 'though it proved so fatal to the 23rd dragoons, was to relieve us of any advance upon our left'. And it did indeed do that: the French move to outflank Wellesley in the plain beyond the Cerro was foiled, and Wellesley could move the exhausted remnants of the 23rd to reinforce his centre and right where the battle was already at its height. He was grateful to the 23rd but irritated as well. Once again, in his judgement, his cavalry had gone far too far and risked the safety of his army by losing so many of their number in just a few minutes. He was putting together a mental dossier of how his cavalry failed to control their ardour. There was Taylor at Vimeiro: now here were Ponsonby and the other officers of the 23rd at Talavera. He began to have growing doubts about what he saw as their recklessness. This made him reluctant to use his cavalry to exploit a collapsing enemy and perhaps prevented him from winning more sweeping victories than he actually did.*

In the early afternoon with the sun beating down and the temperature over 30 degrees, the men in the centre and at the right-hand end of Wellesley's line prepared to receive the main French assault. They had been under destructive gunfire for some time. Even though most of them were lying down, many had been torn apart by the French roundshot or had their limbs smashed by explosive shells. During the worst of the cannonade the only movement came from the men shifting mutilated corpses to the rear. The rest lay still, waiting for the inevitable tramp of the columns of blue straight towards them across the brook. Schaumann, safely behind the lines, found the noise terrifying. 'The thunder of the artillery, combined with the whizzing and whistling of the shot in such an attack, resembles a most dreadful storm, in which flashes of lightning and claps of thunder follow one another in quick succession, and cause the very earth, not to mention the heart in one's breast, to shake and quiver . . . A Spanish powder magazine blew up . . . and with it a gunner was flung aloft, and sailed through the air with arms and legs outstretched like a frog.'

Then the French guns went silent and the assault began. John Cooper's fusiliers were over on the right near the Spanish: 'The enemy were massing for attack. The death cloud was gathering blackness and soon burst with fury.' Cooper saw several columns begin to move towards him. One of them 'called out "Espanholas", wishing us to believe they were Spaniards. Our captain thought they were Spaniards, and ordered us not to fire. But they soon convinced us who they were by a rattling volley.' Then British cannon came into play. First at long range they fired roundshot. One six-pound iron ball could cut a man in half at eight hundred yards. Shrapnel exploded at long range too and scattered deadly fragments over a

* This was almost certainly true of Vitoria in 1813 – see p. 196.

wide area. But at this short range, two hundred yards or less, it was canister that was the most destructive ammunition against advancing infantry. Each shot unleashed a fast-widening circle of musket balls with deadly effect at point-blank range. And behind the guns were the long lines of British infantry who now rose to their feet. They staggered for a moment under the French fire, but Cooper saw his commanding officer spring from his horse and seize one of the colours, shouting, 'Come on Fusiliers!' ''Twas enough. On rushed the Fusiliers and 53rd regiment and delivered such a fire that in a few minutes the enemy melted away.'

Once again the overwhelming firepower of British line against French column paid off. This French attack alone cost Victor and Joseph up to 700 men. Wellesley watched from the top of the Cerro. So far all was going well. But the main French attack now hit Wellesley's centre, and this was where Victor concentrated his greatest strength. Here were his best troops, veterans of Napoleon's victories in eastern Europe. They hugely outnumbered the British troops in front of them and the men of the King's German Legion who had survived the battering they had that morning. Now the French advanced in a vast mass to the beat of their drums. But once again they were in column not in line. Wellesley's men, each regiment in two thin red lines, could bring all their muskets to bear, and they waited till the French were only sixty yards away before they fired. Some of the British didn't wait to fire: the two Guards battalions went straight into a bayonet charge. The French turned and ran.

But this was where triumph nearly led to disaster. The Guards, with the Germans alongside them, chased after the French across the Portina brook and several hundred yards beyond. The further they went, the more their lines broke up in chaos and the French guns began to pound their exposed flanks. The French, who had broken before the guardsmen's charge, now rallied and forced them back. Within a few minutes the Germans had lost 1,000 men, the Guards 600. Worse than that, fresh French infantry poured into the gap the Guards had left in the British line: Wellesley's entire position was now under dire threat. And it was only his cool judgement and swift grasp of command that saved the day. In his account of the battle he reported that the Guards had 'advanced too far' and that he had ordered the 48th (Northamptonshire) Regiment to move from the top of the hill, where he himself was, to plug the gap. They had around a thousand yards to cover to get there. Every second counted. Two other battalions under General Mackenzie were rushed up. The three battalions quickly formed up in line – leaving gaps to allow the retreating Guards to filter through to safety in the rear. Moments later the French were upon them, and they fought a desperate battle to stop the line being broken. Mackenzie himself was killed but his men, with the 48th beside them, fought for every inch of ground, and the line held. By evening it was the French who retired from the field, leaving Wellesley to claim the victory.

Talavera was, Wellesley boasted, 'a great and glorious victory over more than double our numbers, which has proved to the French that they are not the first military nation in the world'. It was true that the 20,000 British had borne almost the whole force of the attacks by 46,000 French, while the Spanish for the most part looked on. Wellesley's men had killed or wounded 7,250 Frenchman, many of them veterans of Napoleon's triumphs at Austerlitz and Jena. But the Emperor still had well over 100,000 men available to fight in the Peninsula. Wellesley had lost 5,300 of his far smaller British force, and his victory did not in the end put him any closer to Madrid. He himself had escaped being wounded when a bullet scraped his shoulder and made a hole in his coat. In London the battle prompted plenty of doubters, but the government delighted Wellesley's admirers by pronouncing him a viscount. Since he was not available to choose a title, his brother William plumped for Wellington, in Somerset, 'a town', he said, 'not far from Wellesley'. 'Wellington . . .' – Arthur Wellesley toyed with the name for a moment, then nodded: 'Exactly right!'

In the same month that Wellesley was advancing on Talavera, Napoleon was advancing on Vienna. He crushed the Austrians at Wagram on 4 and 5 July, three weeks before Victor's defeat in Spain. Napoleon's reaction to Talavera was a mixture of frustration and fury. 'I really ought to be everywhere,' he is reputed to have exclaimed once he had established what had happened. He had the usual glowing reports from his own commanders, anxious to please their emperor. His brother Joseph wrote, 'Yesterday, Sire, the English army was pushed back . . . the battlefield on which we are established is littered with their dead.' He even made the grotesque boast that he regretted not having taken every British soldier prisoner. The accounts Bonaparte read in the British newspapers, which he made a habit of scanning and tended to believe, told a quite different story. It took him a few more days to discover the truth and then he exploded. He sent a scathing message to Marshal Jourdan, Joseph's chief of staff, for claiming that he 'had seized the field of battle at Talavera, while subsequent reports show that we were repulsed the whole day long. Tell him that this infidelity towards the government is a regular crime . . . he has no right to disguise the truth from the government.'

But if Napoleon was beginning to register a trace of anxiety about damage the new Lord Wellington of Talavera was causing at the other end of his empire, he wasn't worried enough to think of tackling him in person. Wellington had a very small army: besides, far from advancing further into Spain, he decided to retreat. Napoleon's letters talk confidently of the prospect of the British force 'embarking' and leaving the Peninsula.

5

Damned with might and main

Retreat, 1809

I T TOOK WELLINGTON only a day or two to decide that he could go no further. Madrid was less than a hundred miles away across reasonably flat and easy country. A bigger risk-taker might have ordered a close pursuit of Joseph's army. But Wellington now faced a new threat from behind him. Soult had bounced back after his defeat at Oporto. He had gathered a large army and was racing from the north to cut Wellington off from Portugal. Wellington was not one to gamble when he didn't have to. Joseph's army was in front of him and Soult's behind. He wouldn't have won every major battle he fought if he had not always made a cool assessment of the odds against him. If the enemy had the potential strength to unite to trap him, better to avoid a battle and wait for a later opportunity. He believed that the test of a great general was 'to know when to retreat and to dare to do it'.

He knew that a retreat would give ammunition to his opponents in London. But Wellington was entirely confident of his own judge-ment and well able to cope with the loneliness of supreme command. 'I like to walk alone,' he had written to his brother Henry eight years earlier. He would pursue his campaign to weaken Napoleon's hold on the Peninsula at his own pace. Wellington's officers were by now resigned to the fact that their Commander in Chief took none of them into his confidence. He would share his plans with nobody – until he wanted them implemented. And he always haughtily rejected the idea of a second in command. He later wrote to Beresford, 'I have always felt the inutility and inconvenience of the office of second in command . . . there is no duty for the second in command to perform . . . the office is useless.' Wellington had one piece of good news the day after Talavera. His three eagerly awaited regiments of light troops arrived under the command of General 'Black Bob' Craufurd, whose skirmishers had been sorely missed at Talavera. Wellington knew of Craufurd's reputation for ruthless discipline and accomplished tactical skill on the battlefield. Black Bob's men either loved him or loathed him. They were used to his headstrong temperament, his violent fits of passion and his voice with its odd, high-pitched squeak. One quality in him they learned to value greatly was one he shared with Wellington – they were both sticklers for logistics. If soldiers were to fight, they had to be supplied. As Ned Costello recorded, 'The Caçadores particularly caused much laughter among us by shouting out in Portuguese, the moment they caught sight of him: "Long Live General Craufurd, who takes care of our bellies" . . . the General seemed highly pleased and bowed repeatedly with his hat off, as he rode down their ranks.' Someone in the commissary department once complained to Wellington that Craufurd was threatening to hang him, as he had others in the past, if supplies were not produced by a certain time. Wellington replied, 'Then I advise you to produce them, for he is quite certain to do it.'

Craufurd had force-marched his three battalions up from Portugal. On the day they arrived just too late for the battle they had marched sixty-two miles in twenty-six hours, according to William Napier, the historian, who accompanied them as a light-infantry captain. From now on they would form a critical component of Wellington's army all the way to Waterloo. First, there were the riflemen of the 1st Battalion of the 95th Regiment, the 1/95th, young officers like Jonathan Leach, George Simmons and a newcomer, Harry Smith, whose father had just bought him a commission. Among the other ranks were Ned Costello and Bugler William Green. They would share many extraordinary adventures together and tell their stories with wit and sensitivity. And there was Colonel Beckwith, the gentle, humane Sydney Beckwith, the commanding officer every last man in the 95th loved and would follow to the death. There were two other battalions in the so-called Light Brigade: the 1/52nd, which included John Dobbs, the Irishman who had joined up at fifteen only three years earlier, and the 1/43rd. This was the regiment of Thomas Garrety, another Irishman who had been bewitched by the sound of the drum and joined up at the age of fourteen. Napier developed pleurisy on the long hard march with Craufurd from Lisbon, and was lucky to survive.

'The men suffered dreadfully' on the way up from Portugal, Ned Costello remembered. Many men dropped and died by the roadside suffering from heat, excessive fatigue or fever. 'Two men of the 52nd actually put a period to their existence by shooting themselves.' Craufurd ruthlessly pressed the pace and men who were pronounced fit were given the lash if they fell out of the ranks without permission. The main hardship apart from the heat was the bivouac. Leach recalled that the best they could do for a dinner table was 'neither more nor less than the turf at the foot of a tree with a soldier's knap-sack by way of camp chair; a Japanned half pint tin cup stood for a wine glass, which with a pocket-knife, fork and spoon and a tin plate constituted the whole of our dinner service'. Then they would tuck into 'an onion or two, some rice and a mouldy ship's biscuit'. John Dobbs wrote that one hazard of bivouacking was wolves, which once attacked a dragoon and ate all of him except his feet, which were protected by boots.

Another invaluable arrival with Craufurd's brigade was the first mounted gun battery to join Wellington. 'A' Troop Royal Horse Artillery was commanded by Captain Hew Ross. It was known as the Chestnut Troop because all its 220 horses were chestnuts. To haul, prepare and fire just six guns (five that could fire six-pound balls and one 5.5-inch howitzer for lobbing shot over high walls) the battery had no fewer than 162 men. Each gun needed eight horses to drag it – a driver perched on the left-hand horse of each pair – and six more to haul along an ammunition wagon behind. There was a horse for each of the ten men loading, aiming and firing each of the six guns. Beside this, the troop had a farrier, three shoeing smiths, two collar-makers, one wheeler, one trumpeter and one acting trumpeter. There were three more wagons in the troop, a spare ammunition wagon, a baggage wagon and a forge. But, unwieldy though it sounds, the horse battery was a highly manoeuvrable weapon system that could deliver massive firepower to any part of the battlefield at a commander's nod. Ross's troop was another detachment that would fight with Wellington all the way to Waterloo.

The newcomers were shocked by the sight that met their eyes at

Talavera. As Thomas Garrety put it, 'combatants who had mingled in the fray belonging to either army lay intermingled in frightful heaps'. Harry Smith saw a battlefield 'literally covered with dead and dying . . . the stench was horrible'. But when the men tried collecting the bodies to burn them, the smell was so dreadful that they gave up. William Green noticed that on the corpses of bayoneted British soldiers 'the palms of their hands and their faces were covered with live maggots'. In one dead man's knapsack he found a letter from the soldier's wife. The man had three children and Green answered the letter 'to let the poor woman know the fate of her husband'. Fred Ponsonby, the day after his first baptism in blood and fire, was out on the battlefield with the only sergeant who had survived their charge. They found the corpse of a young lieutenant who had ridden to his death beside Ponsonby, and buried him where he lay.

August Schaumann was one of the first to see the mess a Spanish unit had made of the British quarters before they fled in panic at the start of the battle. 'Heavens! What did our quarters look like? They had been plundered by the Spanish soldiers . . . All our boxes and cases had been burst open, and their contents strewn over the floor . . . All about the floor lay broken crockery, pots, books and written records.' Schaumann and his friends found themselves a saucepan in which to prepare their usual breakfast of chocolate and water and ship's biscuits. 'We made a fire out of a few histories of the saints bound in pigskin and a number of crusty old legal authorities.'

Wellington's men didn't have to endure this harrowing scene for long. Once the Commander in Chief had judged that they were well rested, he gave the order for the withdrawal to begin. It was a mortifying moment, turning his back on the road to Madrid and ordering his men to do an about-turn. He was counting on Cuesta to stay at Talavera and ensure the safety of the British wounded. But when Victor decided to march westward again, Cuesta abandoned Talavera and 1,500 British wounded to the mercies of the French. George Simmons, who had trained as a doctor, said, 'our astonishment and vexation were beyond conception, knowing that the sick and wounded Englishmen had fallen (through the cowardice of the Spaniards) into the hands of the enemy . . .' Ned Costello was even more outspoken. He called Cuesta 'that deformed–looking lump of pride, ignorance and treachery'. Alexander Gordon, Wellington's ADC, no doubt expressing his chief's anger, wrote home to his brother: 'The Spaniards are the same lying deceitful set we found before. Cuesta is an old fool, and his army radically bad, half of them ran away at Talavera.'

And things would only get worse. Wellington now began a long retreat. He had to go through a particularly arid and barren part of Spain where food and forage were hard to find. He appealed to Cuesta to help with supplies, but without success. 'Your Excellency cannot be surprised that I should think that the British army has been neglected and ill treated . . . I shall march them back into Portugal, if they are not more regularly and more plentifully supplied with provisions and forage.' When Cuesta suffered a stroke in the middle of August, Wellington appealed to his successor, again without effect. A demoralising retreat now became a wretched ordeal for the British army. August Schaumann, who was responsible for keeping the army's meagre supplies moving on bullock carts, complained that the bullocks were being slaughtered by hungry troops and the carts abandoned in the hills. Besides, the weather got hotter every day and when they bivouacked the grass would occasionally catch fire 'owing to carelessness when cooking. Then the tumult was almost as great as when the fire alarm is rung in a town . . .' In one of these grass fires, Schaumann noted, the 23rd Dragoons, Fred Ponsonby's regiment which had suffered so severely at Talavera, lost a hundred saddles, and all their cartridge pouches were blown sky high. Soon afterwards the 23rd, sadly depleted at Talavera, was disbanded. Ponsonby was promoted lieutenant colonel and Wellington took him on to his personal staff.

Hunger was the army's main problem. 'The soldiers' wives,' wrote Schaumann, 'who as a rule went about decently clad, and were most faithful to their husbands, now rode around hungrily in rags and gave themselves to anyone who wanted them in exchange for half a loaf of bread.' By the second week of August Wellington was close to despair: 'A starving army is actually worse than none. The soldiers lose their discipline and their spirit. The officers are discontented and are almost as bad as the men.' Two weeks later he complained that it was impossible to stay in Spain. His men were starving and their horses dying in hundreds. 'More than a month has now elapsed since I informed General Cuesta if the British army were not supplied with means of transport and with provisions, not only I would not cooperate with any forward movement . . . but that I could not remain at all in Spain.' As a result he said he was now withdrawing to Portugal. Five days later, in a letter to his brother Richard, he allowed his feelings about his Spanish allies to spill over: 'It is my opinion that I ought to avoid entering into any further cooperation with the Spanish armies.' He wrote to Castlereagh in London to complain that the Spanish 'are really children in the art of war'. At the end of August Wellington's famished, dispirited men finally crossed into Portugal.

Just past the border George Simmons was to experience the hot temper of his commander, 'Black Bob' Craufurd, who had ordered him to keep an eye on the mule cart that carried his personal baggage, including a great deal of wine and food. Simmons's men were whipping the mules to try to get them moving, when suddenly the beasts took off and sped down a very steep hill: they were soon out of control and the cart was dashed to pieces. When Craufurd, who was giving a dinner party that night, heard what had happened, he roared at Simmons and told him to have the culprits lashed. Craufurd 'never forgave me', wrote Simmons in his diary for 29 August. 'I felt highly indignant at such usage for having exerted myself to serve him.' Jonathan Leach, another of Craufurd's officers, who remained an inveterate critic, remembered Craufurd's unrelenting discipline during the retreat. 'The division paraded at 6 this evening when we got volleys of abusive and blasphemous language from that infernal scoundrel Brig Gen Robert Craufurd . . . after flogging half a dozen men for some very frivolous offences committed on our harassing marches . . .'

But ordinary soldiers like Ned Costello admitted to a certain respect for Craufurd. Costello had a habit of getting himself into awkward scrapes, and one morning he went to have a drink with a friend, who was Craufurd's private servant. He went to Craufurd's room, thinking the general was out, and saw a man he thought was his friend looking out of the window. 'It entered into my head to surprise my servant friend; so . . . I stepped softly up to his rear, and with a sudden laugh, gave him a smart slap on the back. But my consternation and surprise may be better imagined than described when the gentleman in the dressing gown, starting round with a "Who the devil is that?" disclosed not the merry phiz of the valet, but the stern features of General Craufurd himself.' Costello thought he should have 'sunk through the ground at that moment, had it opened to swallow me'. He tried to mumble an explanation as he retreated towards the door. But the general 'with a good humoured smile . . . observed the fright I was in. "Well, well, you may go," said Craufurd, "but pray, sir, never again do me the honour to take me for my servant."' Craufurd's gentler side is also apparent in a touching letter he wrote to his son Charles that summer. 'Your mama tells me you want to be a soldier, but I hope you never will. When you are a man perhaps you will have a wife and children . . . and I am sure you will love them; and then, if you are obliged to leave them, it would grieve your heart as it does mine to leave your dear mama, whom I love with all my soul . . . so I hope you will never be a soldier.'

It was a grim autumn for Wellington and his men. They had won a battle but lost a campaign. In spite of the triumph of Talavera Wellesley had retained not an inch of Spanish territory. The French had the pleasure of seeing Wellington withdraw to Portugal. Napoleon's marshals also managed to defeat the Spanish in a number of encounters and in early 1810 captured all of Andalusia except Cadiz. From now on guerrilla warfare replaced pitched battles as the most telling weapon Spain could use in its revolt against France. The news the British received from the rest of Europe was glum too: the expedition to Walcheren in Holland, an attempt to get another British foothold on the continent, had been abandoned. Napoleon, fresh from his triumph over the Austrians, told his marshals to prepare 100,000 troops to remove Wellington from Portugal once and for all. He wrote to his brother Joseph in Madrid, 'There is nothing dangerous in Spain except the English; the rest cannot keep the field.' But he refrained from commanding in person. He still regarded the Peninsula as a sideshow and Wellington as a minor threat that another of his marshals should easily be able to brush away.

The new man Napoleon chose to confront Wellington was André Masséna, a sharp-minded master of campaign strategy who had fought with the young Napoleon in Italy in 1799 and helped him to win the battles of Marengo and Wagram. Masséna had a flair for the sort of independent command that the faraway war in the Peninsula demanded. Moreover Napoleon backed him up with Michel Ney, an inspiring if sometimes reckless leader in battle.

As the British army finally settled down to spend the winter on the Portuguese border, Alexander Gordon, the young ADC, expressed the pessimism that appears to have infused some of those on Wellington's top team: 'We may protract the war for a few months but it is I think impossible to hinder Portugal from eventually falling.' Gordon's view was shared by the new Tory Secretary of State for War in London, Lord Liverpool, who wrote to Wellington in early 1810: 'Your chances of successful defence are considered here by all persons military as well as civil to be improbable.' Liverpool actually asked Wellington about contingency measures for the total evacuation of the army from Portugal. Wellington, his natural self-assurance now reinforced by the conduct of his units at Talavera, replied: 'All I beg is that if I am to be responsible I may be left to the exercise of my own judgement and I ask for the fair confidence of the government upon the measures which I am to adopt.' To Colonel Torrens, the army's key staff officer, the Military Secretary in London, he wrote, 'If I am in a scrape, as appears to be the general belief in London, though certainly not my own, I will get out of it.'

It must have been an exceptionally anxious time for Wellington. Publicly he displayed that imperturbable demeanour that was now his hallmark, but if he was to pursue his campaign he knew he had to fight a long-range political battle for support. There was a constant debate between his supporters and opponents in London. Thanks to the letters and journal of Thomas Creevey, who admits he 'hated' Wellington, we have an insider's account of the bitterly hostile Whigs whom Wellington and his family – particularly his brother Richard, the former Governor General of India – had to fight. In late January Creevey described the House of Commons debate after which MPs passed a vote of thanks to the new Lord Wellington for the Battle of Talavera. The leader of the Opposition Whigs, Lord Grey, 'disputed the military, moral, and intellectual fame of Lord Wellington most capitally and called loudly upon the Marquess

[Wellington's elder brother Richard] to come forward and justify the victory'. The following day Grey sat in a coffee house with Creevey and 'damned with might and main Marquess Wellesley'. But a few days later on 1 February Creevey reported that 'all the indignation against Wellington has gone up in smoke – some of the stoutest of our crew slunk away or rather were dispersed by the indefatigable intrigues of the Wellesleys'. A little later, Creevey wrote that Wellington's career 'approaches very rapidly to a conclusion'. Wellington was not insensitive to all this. He clearly felt that his honour was being impugned and when one particularly vocal opponent of his campaign in the Peninsula, the MP Samuel Whitbread, accused him of exaggerating his achievement in the war, Wellington wrote personally to him to say that the allegations 'must have been most injurious to me'.

To add to Wellington's woes, his family was mired in worse gossip than ever. His brother Marquess Wellesley, whose standing was fast being overshadowed by his younger brother, settled down to some blatant womanising in London. 'I wish', wrote Arthur to his elder brother William, 'that Wellesley was castrated . . . it is lamentable to see talents, character and advantages such as he possesses thrown away upon whoring.'

Wellington recovered quickly from the frustration of retreat. He had set himself the task of demonstrating to his supporters in London that he could save Portugal from being overwhelmed by France. On several occasions that winter he was seen riding over the hills north of Lisbon with his chief engineer, Lieutenant Colonel Richard Fletcher. They were hills through which any French army would have to move to capture Lisbon. The contours had a shape that persuaded Wellington he could turn them into a barrier of defensive fortifications. Over the next nine months Fletcher transformed these hills into a thirty-mile-long network of 165 hillside redoubts with parapets and ditches to protect them. Called the Lines of Torres Vedras, their construction was a remarkable act of strategic foresight by Wellington, and they would prove to be worth every penny of the £100,000 they cost to build.

That autumn two other forceful and irrepressible characters joined Wellington. One, a young Irish subaltern, William Grattan, distant cousin of the great Irish statesman of the same name, arrived to help rebuild the Connaught Rangers, a feisty Irish regiment (the 88th of Foot) which had suffered badly at Talavera. The other, a general, Thomas Picton, was summoned from London to lead the 3rd Division, whose commander had died at the Battle of Talavera. Picton was a powerfully built, boisterous man with a mind of his own and a healthy disrespect for authority and convention. Like Wellington, he preferred wearing civilian clothes to uniform on the battlefield. He also had a ruthless reputation. He had narrowly escaped conviction when tried for torture: as governor of the slave island of Trinidad, he had allegedly forced a thirteen-year-old girl to stand on a spike while suspended from the ceiling. He was fiercely ambitious and determined to prove that he was the most fearsome commander in the army, to rival even 'Black Bob' Craufurd.

Grattan's Connaught Rangers, which would be one of the regiments in Picton's 3rd Division, awaited their new general's arrival 'with some anxiety'. When he first reviewed them, all went well to begin with, and Grattan remarked, 'I never saw such a perfect specimen of a soldier . . . there was manly open frankness in his appearance.' But although Picton appeared suitably impressed by the 88th on parade, when he heard that two of its members had stolen a goat on their march to join the regiment, he 'ordered an immediate drumhead court martial and had them flogged on the spot in full view of the . . . whole division'. He then addressed the men, declaring, 'You are not known in the army by the name of Connaught Rangers but by the name Connaught Footpads.' Even though Picton praised some of the regiment's later exploits, Grattan noted that throughout the Peninsular Campaign he never promoted any of the officers of the 88th. Wellington knew a rough diamond when he saw one, but he was soon to appreciate Picton's qualities. 'I found him to be a rough foul-mouthed devil as ever lived, but he always behaved extremely well, no man could do better in different services I assigned to him.' Wellington valued commanders who could inspire their men to fight with bravery and tenacity. But he was wary of officers who showed too much independent initiative. He believed passionately in his own judgement and his own need to exercise control of every part of the battlefield. Most of all he abhorred incompetence and admired officers who obeyed his orders and carried them out to the letter.

The army spent the coldest winter months quartered in towns and villages in the hills east of Oporto. Jonathan Leach encouraged the men in his company to keep fit. They had running races, held football matches and even played racquets against the tower of a church. Leach, like many others, was an enthusiast for hunting, coursing and shooting by day, 'and by night we either whiffed away cigars over some Douro wine and speculated on the campaign which was soon about to commence, or danced boleros, fandangos, and waltzes with the good looking daughters of an Israelite, in whose house I was billeted'.

6

Unpardonable butchery
The Côa and Bussaco, 1810

THERE WERE TWO ways Marshal Masséna could invade Portugal in 1810. The southern route ran past the strongholds of Badajoz in Spain and Elvas in Portugal. The northern approach was effectively controlled by the fortresses of Ciudad Rodrigo just inside Spain and Almeida twenty miles inside Portugal. No intrusion deep into Portugal would be secure without the forts on at least one of these routes being captured. In the spring of 1810 all were in the hands of Wellington and his allies. Masséna chose to advance by the northern route and duly laid siege to Ciudad Rodrigo.

Wellington had to make a strategic choice. Should he march his entire army into Spain and challenge Masséna outside Ciudad Rodrigo or wait for him at Almeida? As always he erred on the side of caution, calculating that his 55,000 men would be more judiciously placed to confront the French marshal's 60,000 in the hills around Almeida than on the flat landscape around Ciudad Rodrigo. French numbers and their superior cavalry could cause havoc on a wide, open plain. Wellington wrote to Lord Liverpool: 'The country in which I must have carried on the operations to raise the siege, or even to relieve the place, would have been highly advantageous to the enemy, on account of his superiority in cavalry.' So, in spite of his concern for the inhabitants of Ciudad Rodrigo and its 'brave' Governor, 'I have considered it my duty to refrain from an operation which it was probable would be attended by the most disastrous consequences.'

Wellington reckoned that artful use of the rolling ground inside Portugal would be more likely to thwart the French. He was also concerned that 25,000 of his men were still largely untried Portuguese troops. Craufurd's light-infantry troops, the 1/95th, 1/43rd and

1/52nd, would now be joined with two battalions of Portuguese Caçadores in a new Light Division under Craufurd's command. (Up to now Craufurd had commanded only a brigade of light troops.) The rest of the Portuguese, commanded mainly by British officers and sustained by a £1 million grant from the British government, would gradually be incorporated into Wellington's other divisions. Wellington was still uneasy about some of his senior commanders, whom he had no power to sack, but he did have at least three fine divisional commanders in the reliable Rowland Hill and the newly arrived Picton and Craufurd. 'Hill does what he is told,' the Commander in Chief told his friends. He probably would not have said the same about the other two. Relations with Picton and Craufurd were occasionally strained, but he appreciated their courage and their capacity to inspire. Other commanders, such as Major General Sir William Erskine, who Wellington complained was virtually blind, kept being foisted on him by London. He didn't hesitate to make his feelings known to his masters in Whitehall: 'When I reflect upon the characters and attainments of some of the general officers of this army . . . on whom I am to rely . . . I tremble.'

It was not just Erskine who raised eyebrows. Craufurd added to his maverick reputation by failing to go to the rescue of some British cavalry which he had ordered against a French infantry position not far from Ciudad Rodrigo. Wellington's ADC, Alexander Gordon, blamed the cavalry unit for charging foolishly against the odds: 'It was ill planned and worse executed.' But Harry Smith, one of Craufurd's own junior officers, blamed Craufurd himself for not sending some of his light infantry to the rescue of the horsemen. 'Craufurd never moved one of us . . . Our loss was very considerable. Poor Colonel Talbot of the 14th (commanding) killed and a lot of men . . . Had two companies of ours only been moved . . . the enemy would have lain down their arms.' Wellington knew that Craufurd aroused controversy, but he valued him too highly to have him removed.

Wellington sent only token forces to harry the French besieging force at Ciudad Rodrigo. By 10 July the garrison could hold out no longer and it surrendered. Masséna's next target was the fortress of Almeida. If he could storm that too, he believed the road to Lisbon would be open. But yet another of Napoleon's marshals was underestimating the resourcefulness and tactical skill of his opponent. Wellington decided to make a stand at Almeida by buttressing the defence of the fortress itself with an attempt to stop the French crossing the River Côa, which ran just behind it. Rather than place his whole army in a defensive position along the Côa, he preferred to keep most of his units in reserve behind it, leaving Craufurd's Light Division on the east bank. The plan was to delay the French without actually engaging them in a pitched battle. It was bound to be an uneven struggle. Masséna and Ney could concentrate enough troops on the east bank of the Côa to leave Craufurd massively outnumbered. They crossed the Portuguese frontier on 21 July with as many as 70,000 men. The Light Division faced gigantic odds.

What followed was one of the most heroic though controversial clashes in the Peninsular War. In spite of repeated warnings from Wellington, Robert Craufurd took the risk of fighting the French with his back to a river, which was in full flood and could be crossed only by one narrow bridge. The countryside is some of the roughest in Portugal: the Côa runs through a deep gorge with steep, rocky sides cluttered with huge boulders; any movement is severely restricted. Two weeks earlier Wellington had ordered Craufurd to withdraw to Almeida if the French threatened to attack him. 'In short,' he said, 'I do not wish to risk anything beyond the Coa.' On 16 July Wellington was more ambivalent: 'It is desirable that we should hold the other side of the Coa a little longer . . . At the same time I do not wish to risk anything in order to remain at the other side of the river.' Six days later he was more emphatic: 'I am not desirous of engaging [in] an affair beyond the Coa.' And he asked Craufurd if it wouldn't be better to pull his infantry back across the river.

Unusually for Wellington the orders were not precise, but their thrust was clear: Craufurd was to avoid being drawn into battle on the far side of the Côa where his line of retreat would be dangerously constricted. He should cross the river before he could be attacked. Craufurd did nothing of the sort. Driven by his ambition to show that he and his Light Division, which had missed Talavera, could perform outstanding feats of arms, he fought a major battle on the east bank of the Côa. It was a brave attempt, but it was against such numbers that he was bound to lose far more men than if he had moved his defensive line to the high ground the other side of the river, as Wellington had indicated. William Napier, one of Craufurd's light infantrymen, wrote in his history of the war, '[Craufurd] with headstrong ambition resolved, in defiance of reason and the reiterated orders of his General, to fight on the right bank.'

Jonathan Leach was right in the middle of the action. 'Although the left of our line was under the protection of the guns of the fortress [of Almeida] the French assailed it with great impetuosity and the right and centre also soon found itself beset with a swarm of light troops, supported by heavy columns constantly advancing, and aided by their artillery which cannonaded us warmly.' George Simmons saw the whole plain in front of him covered with advancing troops. He watched them form lines and attack: 'we repulsed them, but they came on again, yelling, with drums beating . . . French officers like mountebanks running forward and placing their hats upon their swords and, and capering about like madmen, saying as they turned to their men "Come on, children of our country. The first that advances, Napoleon will recompense him."'

Craufurd quickly woke up to the disaster he had inflicted on himself and his men and started shifting troops to the other side of the river. Many of his infantrymen were soon fighting for their lives. Ned Costello and his comrades were taken by surprise as the cry went up, 'The French cavalry are upon us!' They could do little to defend themselves against the slashing sabres of the horsemen and many were trampled underfoot. 'A French dragoon had seized me by the collar, while several others, as they passed, did me the "honour" of aiming at me with their swords. The man who had collared me had his sabre's point at my breast, when a volley was fired from our rear by the 52nd . . . which tumbled the horse of my captor.' The horse collapsed on top of its rider, who dragged Costello down with him. 'Determined to have one brief struggle for liberty, I freed myself from the dragoon and dealing him a severe blow with the butt of my rifle,' he made for the shelter of a wall behind. But his ordeal wasn't over. He felt a shot hit his right kneecap and he fell. His comrades were now all retreating fast and he was lucky to be picked up by one of them, who heaved him up on his back and ran for the bridge. His rescuer had to drop him when he too was hit by a shot, which also slammed into Costello's thigh 'where it has ever since remained'. Somehow he managed to drag himself across the bridge and 'in this crippled state and faint through loss of blood, I made a second appeal to a comrade, who assisted me to ascend a hill on the other side of the river'.

Thomas Garrety found the bridge so congested that he had to make a stand with some soldiers on the river bank. 'The conflict was tremendous: thrice we repulsed the enemy at the point of the bayonet . . . my left-hand man, one of the stoutest in the regiment, was hit by a musket shot – he threw his head back, and was instantly dead. I fired at the fellow who shot my comrade; and before I could reload, my pay-sergeant, Thomas, received a ball in the thigh and earnestly implored me to carry him away.' Somehow Garrety lugged Thomas across the bridge and was rewarded with a swig of rum from his canteen.

Craufurd struggled to prevent his Light Division's annihilation by trying to orchestrate a fighting withdrawal. Leach and a contingent of riflemen were sent to secure a small hill which commanded the approach to the bridge. 'In ascending the hill,' recalled Leach, 'a musket shot grazed the left side of my head and buried itself in the earth close by.' He struggled on up to the top and between them he and his comrades helped secure the road back to the bridge. But the French seemed to be everywhere in overwhelming numbers. The murderous fire they now brought to bear on the shrinking band of Craufurd's men on the east side of the river led to an order to abandon the hill and retreat to the bridge. It was too soon: there were hundreds still waiting to cross. The hill would have to be recaptured. The next thing Leach knew he was charging back up the hill with a bunch of skirmishers led by a Major Macleod. 'How either he or his horse escaped being blown to atoms, when, in the most daring manner, he charged on horseback, at the head of a hundred or two skirmishers . . . I am at a loss to imagine.' Scores of them were killed and injured in a few bloody minutes as their counter-attack tore into the French. It bought just enough time for the rest of Craufurd's force to reach the bridge. And then the skirmishers had to fight their way back to it themselves. Somehow the survivors ran or crawled back to Craufurd's new front line in the middle of the bridge. Some carried their wounded comrades, others dragged their own shattered limbs behind them, desperate to avoid capture. A frantic fight then followed for the bridge itself. A great cloud of smoke arose as the intense musket and artillery fire of both sides concentrated on that one narrow crossing point. Craufurd had placed Hew Ross and his Chestnut Troop of Royal Horse Artillery on the bridge and their guns gave powerful supporting fire to the retreating troops.

Once the last fugitives had managed to scramble across the bridge, Leach watched 'a few hundred French grenadiers, advancing to the tune of "Vive l'Empereur!" and "En avant, mes enfants!"' The bridge was the only place where the French could cross the Côa as the river was a fierce torrent after hours of heavy rain, and the narrow road across the bridge was now covered by three British and two Portuguese battalions. Leach was appalled by the French commander who ordered his men across the bridge into such a lethal killing zone: 'It was a piece of unpardonable and unjustifiable butchery on the part of the man who ordered those brave grenadiers to be thus wantonly sacrificed, with the most remote possibility of success.' Tom Garrety watched as 'a French surgeon coming down to the very foot of the bridge, waved his white handkerchief, and commenced dressing the wounded under the hottest fire: the appeal was heard: every musket turned from him . . .'

It had been a bloody combat for both sides. Craufurd was lucky to escape with casualties of around 400 dead, wounded or taken prisoner. But he didn't escape sharp criticism: William Grattan accused him of 'fighting a very dangerous battle – contrary to orders I believe . . . with hardihood bordering on rashness'. Jonathan Leach noted: 'we were puzzled to conjecture why General Craufurd, if he was determined to give battle . . . did not cross the Coa, without waiting to be forcibly driven over . . . and there challenge his opponent'. He accused Craufurd of making a mistake that 'the most uninstructed boy of one month's standing in the army' would not have made. He wrote home that Craufurd was even 'more abhorred' than he had been a few months earlier. Leach said Craufurd was a 'tyrant' and a 'blackguard', who had 'proved himself totally unfit to command a company much less a division.' Colonel Torrens, the influential Military Secretary in London, declared that he was 'disappointed' and that Craufurd's reputation had taken 'a knock which it will be difficult for him to recover . . . he appears to me to allow the violence of his passions and the impetuosity of his disposition to overthrow the exercise of his judgement'.

Disapproval of Craufurd's bloody encounter on the Côa was widely echoed in the rest of the army. Wellington chose not to rebuke him, but wrote a revealing letter to his brother William which suggests just how angry he was privately at his subordinate's conduct. He said he had repeatedly told Craufurd not to engage the French on the far side of the river. 'You will say, if this be the case, why not accuse Craufurd? I answer, because, if I am to be hanged for it, I cannot accuse a man who I believe meant well and whose error is one of judgment and not of intention.' Wellington was being remarkably lenient, but he was convinced that Craufurd with all his faults was too precious an asset to lose, and he was proved right over the next few months. Alexander Gordon was more blunt. 'Craufurd remained much too long before a vast superiority of the enemy. We've lost in killed or wounded 30 officers and 400 men to no purpose whatever.'

Craufurd was evidently deeply sensitive to the criticism his action at the Côa provoked. He wrote a letter to *The Times* in an attempt to justify his conduct. 'The retreat was made in a military, soldier-like manner, and without the slightest precipitation . . . we inflicted on the enemy a loss certainly double that we sustained.'

It was during the fighting on the River Côa that Craufurd and Picton had a particularly bitter row. Picton rode forward at one stage and met Craufurd, who asked him urgently for support. Picton refused it, embittered, William Napier suggests, by previous disputes between the two men. Napier says Picton was quite wrong to refuse help, as Craufurd's situation was very grave. 'Picton and Crawfurd', he observed, 'were not formed by nature to act cordially together. The stern countenance, robust frame, saturnine complexion, caustic speech, and austere demeanour of the first, promised little sympathy with the short thick figure, dark flashing eyes, quick movements, and fiery temper of the second; nor did they often meet without a quarrel.' Wellington was aware of the growing tension between Picton and Craufurd. He knew they were both highly ambitious, brave to the point of recklessness and viciously competitive. But he believed, rightly, that over time they would prove to be of inestimable value to him in fighting the French.

On the British side Harry Smith and George Simmons were among the wounded. Smith had a ball lodge in his ankle joint and was saved from being left on the east side of the bridge only by the heroic Major Macleod. He hoisted Smith up on his horse and raced him across the bridge in the nick of time. Simmons suddenly found himself plunging to the ground in the thick of the fighting. 'For a few moments I couldn't collect my ideas, and was feeling about my arms and legs for a wound, until my eye caught the stream of blood rushing through the hole in my trousers, and my leg and thigh appeared so heavy that I could not move it . . . Some men put me in a blanket and carried me off.' They passed Craufurd on the way back, who hadn't forgotten that it was Simmons who had ruined his dinner party a year earlier. Craufurd told the men it was no time to be taking away wounded officers and ordered them back. But they retorted: 'This is an officer of ours, and we must see him to safety before we leave him.' Simmons then had to suffer the discomfort and pain of being carried away with Harry Smith on a bullock cart which bounced up and down agonisingly on the bumpy roads. 'The bullocks ran away with poor George,' Smith wrote later, 'and nearly jolted him to death, for he was fearfully wounded through the thick of his thigh.'

A little later Smith, still hobbling around with a musket ball in his foot, so impressed his commanding officer, the much loved Sydney Beckwith, that the colonel asked him to become his ADC. When Smith finally got to see a doctor, 'I cocked up my leg, and said "There it is: slash away." It was five minutes, most painful indeed, before it was extracted. The ball was jagged, and the tendonous fibres had so grown into it, it was half dissected and half torn out, with most excruciating torture for a moment, the forceps breaking which had hold of the ball.' The doctors were too busy to attend to Ned Costello and maggots got into his wounds. But 'by care and syringing sweet oil into my wounds, I . . . managed to get rid of them'.

Joseph Donaldson was in no doubt which side had the best

doctors: 'The French army was much superior to ours . . . Those medical men that we had were not always ornaments of the profession. They were chiefly, I believe, composed of apothecaries' boys, who, having studied a session or two, were thrust into the army as a huge dissecting room, where they might mangle with impunity . . . and did much mischief.' As for the disposal of the bodies, James Hale was shocked by what he saw. 'As soon as a man was dead he was sewed up in an old blanket . . . and put in a coffin. But as soon as they arrived at the grave, the coffin was . . . turned over and so [they] let the corpse roll out into the grave.' The coffin was then taken back to do its job again. 'One coffin would serve a hundred men as well as one.'

Within two weeks of chasing Craufurd across the Côa the French laid siege to Almeida. It was one of the most powerfully built fortresses in the Peninsula and was well stocked with food and ammunition. There would certainly be no shortage of gunpowder or musket cartridges: a huge quantity – enough to last for months – was stored in an ancient fortified keep in the centre of the fortress. Its commander was confident and morale was high. Wellington hoped Almeida would hold out long enough to discourage Masséna from advancing deep into Portugal. What happened next was as cruel a blow as any Wellington suffered in the entire Peninsular Campaign.

By the last week in August, Masséna had sixty-five guns pounding the walls of Almeida. Its British guns roared in reply, and its walls remained intact. But it had one point of vulnerability that was to prove catastrophic. No one knows exactly what happened. It may be that in the hectic ferrying of powder and cartridges between the central fort and the gun emplacements a small trail of powder spilled from a barrel. Whatever it was, a lucky shot from a French mortar ignited some powder that led straight to the magazine in the old castle. The explosion that followed was like the eruption of a volcano, throwing up a huge cloud of smoke and a great shower of debris. Even the British guns on the battlements were tossed into the air as the entire town appeared to be blown into fragments. Stones even landed on the French trenches, killing some of the besiegers. When the smoke cleared the town was in ruins. The fort where the powder had been stored was pulverised, nothing left of it except the foundations. Almeida was defenceless and within thirty-six hours Masséna was in possession of it and planning his advance on Lisbon.

Way off to the west, more than ten miles away, Wellington's advance posts had heard the roar of the explosion. Two days later when he learned that the French had destroyed his frontier fortress, Wellington was dismayed: 'I cannot express how much I am disappointed at this fatal event.' But he soon recovered when he learned that Masséna was leading his army westward into some of the most difficult mountain country in the whole of Portugal. 'There are certainly many bad roads in Portugal,' he wrote, 'but the enemy has taken decidedly the worst in the whole kingdom.' Instead of heading south-west towards Lisbon, Masséna was struggling west along poor roads that made his progress pitifully slow. He had been badly misled by indequate maps and incompetent guides. By now autumn was setting in and for both sides the piercing wind and nightly dew made bivouacking an ordeal. The French found that the Portuguese had stripped the land of any useful crop, and even the British had a hard time: Jonathan Leach complained that the supply of wine and rum had run out, and that he had to make do with water.

Wellington, with his keen eye for terrain, saw a major opportunity in Masséna's change of route. The roads and tracks in this area all led unavoidably to a prominent mountain ridge, 1,870 feet high and seven miles long. Its steep and rocky slopes straddled Masséna's route and offered Wellington a commanding line of defence. It was called the ridge of Bussaco. 'We have an excellent position here, in which I am strongly tempted to give battle,' Wellington wrote to his cavalry commander, Sir Stapleton Cotton. He could not have chosen a more powerful defensive position. Indeed the most astonishing thing about Bussaco is that Masséna decided to attack Wellington at all. Today the entire ridge and its precipitous sides are cluttered with close-packed trees and dense undergrowth. An energetic climber could scramble up it unseen. In 1810 Bussaco was bare. Wellington and his commanders could see every move of an approaching enemy struggling up through the rocks and low brush.

Wellington placed his headquarters in a convent on the north end of the ridge and strung out his army along it, facing east. In the next

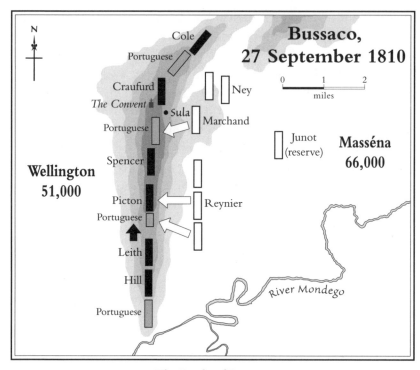

The Battle of Bussaco

two days the French appeared below and spread out along the bottom of the ridge clearly determined to attack. At dawn on 27 September, in thick mist, the Battle of Bussaco began. First Masséna threw General Reynier's troops against the British centre, where the redoubtable Thomas Picton was in command. William Grattan's Connaught Rangers were one of his battalions. Grattan couldn't see much to start with but he could tell from the firing that French light troops were leading the attack up the hill towards him. Wellington was close by 'and from the bustle amongst the staff it was manifest that the point held by Picton's division was about to be attacked . . . the fog cleared away and a bright sun enabled us to see what was passing before us. A vast crowd of *tirailleurs* were pressing onward with great ardour.' The skirmishers were followed by the main body of infantry scrambling up the rocky slope. It was vital they shouldn't break through Picton's men, seize the crest of the hill and cut Wellington's line. The fierce French fire was thinning the Connaught

Rangers, and Grattan's commanding officer, Colonel Alexander Wallace, shouted to his men: 'Now Connaught Rangers, mind what you are going to do . . . when I bring you face to face with those French rascals, drive them down the hill. Don't give them false touch but push home [your bayonets] to the muzzle.'

Grattan and his comrades followed Wallace in a counter-attack on the French. 'All was now confusion and uproar, smoke, fire and bullets, officers and soldiers, French drummers and French drums knocked down in every direction; British, French and Portuguese mixed together; while in the midst of all was to be seen Wallace, fighting – like his ancestor of old – at the head of his devoted followers and calling out to his soldiers to "press forward".' Wellington, typically, was within reach of where the fighting was hottest. A soldier quite close to him was wounded in the face. One account says that the regiment's colonel in chief, Marshal Beresford, was standing next to Wellington expressing unease that his lads faced an unequal contest. 'But when they were mixed with Reynier's men and pushing them down the hill, Lord Wellington, tapping him on the shoulder, said "Well, Beresford, look at them now!"' A few minutes later he shook Wallace's hand and said, 'Wallace, I never witnessed a more gallant charge than that made just now by your regiment.' Grattan says, 'Wallace took off his hat – but his heart was too full to speak.'

The battle was only just beginning. Another division of Reynier's launched an attack on Picton's Portuguese troops a little further along the ridge. The Portuguese were pushed aside and the French looked like winning a foothold on top of the ridge. But thanks to Wellington's foresight, General Leith's division had moved up from the south. Leith and General Hill beyond him had been told by Wellington to shift north if it became clear that the French attack was not directed at them. Leith's men raced up, keeping behind the crest of the ridge and confronted this second French onslaught as it broke through the Portuguese. James Hale was one of Leith's men, a sergeant in the 9th Regiment of Foot. He and his company were told to load their muskets but not to fire until ordered – 'so we continued moving on . . . until we got within about 100 yds of them, where we were ordered to wheel into line and give them a volley which we immediately did and saluted them with 3 cheers and a charge . . .' General Leith the brigade commander 'made the signal by taking off his hat and twirling it over his head'. Hale says the enemy stood their ground 'till we got within 20 yards of them, but seeing it was our intention to use the bayonet, they took to their heels'.

It was now the turn of Marshal Ney to try to break through the British line. He was one of Napoleon's most flamboyant commanders, recklessly brave, a great inspiration to his men but an impetuous and unreliable tactician. He fiercely disliked Masséna and the feeling was mutual. Ney's men were on the French centre right and they quickly threw British and Portuguese skirmishers out of the village of Sula, and then pursued them up the hill to where they could see Hew Ross's battery of British guns. Exhausted from the climb and struggling to keep some sort of formation among the rocks, depleted by the canister fire, Ney's men finally reached the line of guns. But Ross and his men sharply hauled the guns aside to reveal just over the crest of a ridge only twenty yards ahead two entire battalions of 'Black Bob' Craufurd's light infantry in a long line. Craufurd himself stood on a rock alongside his line of soldiers. He waited until the French column appeared over the brow just a few yards in front of him. Then William Napier recalled Craufurd's shrill voice yelling at his men to charge. 'Now, 52nd, avenge Sir John Moore,' he shouted waving his hat in the air. 'A horrid shout startled the French column, and eighteen hundred British bayonets went sparkling over the brow of the hill . . . The head of their column was violently overturned and driven upon the rear, both flanks were lapped over by the English wings, and three terrible discharges at five yards' distance completed the rout. In a few minutes a long trail of carcasses and broken arms indicated the line of retreat.'

William Napier's brother George was a yard or two in front of his men as he led them in a charge and was lucky to escape being killed: four of the nine men in the front rank just behind him were shot dead and all the rest fell wounded. George Napier was hit but managed to get on his feet immediately and chase the French down the hill 'firing and bayoneting . . . till the French were driven from the top to the bottom of the mountain like a parcel of sheep'. Jonathan Leach was one of the riflemen firing at the retreating French while the horse artillery poured on them 'a murderous fire of grape,* as they were struggling through the narrow streets of Sula, and trampling each other to death in their great haste to escape. Men, muskets, knapsacks and bayonets rolled down the side of the mountain in such a confused mass . . . it is impossible to convey a just idea of.'

Finally, in a last desperate attempt, Ney directed General Marchand's division up the hill at the Portuguese battalions a little further along the British line. The French might have expected to break them, but Marshal Beresford's painstaking training now began to show. The Portuguese fought well and turned another French attack into a rout. Wellington said later that Bussaco had inspired confidence in the Portuguese troops and gave them 'a taste for an amusement to which they were not before accustomed; and which they could not have acquired if I had not put them in a very strong position'. Ever since that day the Portuguese military have regarded Bussaco as the battle in which their army came of age. Today the ridge is ornamented with a whole forest of plaques to commemorate their victory. With the collapse of Ney's attack the French fell back and abandoned any attempt to shift Wellington from the Bussaco ridge. The British had lost 1,250 dead and wounded, the French four times as many.

Bussaco was an utter disaster for Masséna. Wellington had again demonstrated his genius for choosing the right ground on which to fight and for arranging the swift realignment of his units to concentrate strength where it was needed. The battle gave British morale a badly needed boost. Wellington's mercurial ADC, Alexander Gordon, who had, like Wellington, been deeply depressed by the destruction of Almeida only three weeks earlier, wrote: 'I have not now the least doubt of the success of this campaign and the destruction of Masséna's army. We shall give them another sound drubbing and they must retire.'

Bussaco might have been the final chapter in yet another failed French invasion of Portugal, but Masséna wasn't giving up yet.

* Grapeshot differed from the more widely used canister. A handful of iron balls were assembled and packed in a canvas bag secured with string, looking rather like a bunch of grapes. When fired from the gun, they splayed out very rapidly and were effective only at very short range.

Wellington said much later that, of all Napoleon's marshals, Masséna was the most formidable. The very night of his defeat at Bussaco Masséna's scouts revealed a canny way of turning Wellington's flank. The next morning Wellington awoke to learn that the French army had sneaked off on a minor road round the northern end of the Bussaco ridge. He had no choice but to fall back towards Lisbon in order to keep ahead of them. Fred Ponsonby noted how calmly Wellington made his decision. 'After it was made he was able to throw it entirely from his thoughts; most men would have felt anxiety; perhaps doubts till the event had taken place, but with him it was all over; at dinner that day he laughed and talked as if nothing was depending [on it] . . . it never disturbed his rest.'

Wellington's withdrawal was no forlorn retreat. He had an elaborate defensive strategy. For the past year his engineers had been working on the Lines of Torres Vedras, the network of redoubts and ramparts in the hills north of Lisbon. He withdrew his army there and in his wake he left a great zone of desolation: towns, villages, houses and fields stripped and deserted. People were told to find refuge behind the Lines. The country was left utterly barren and devoid of supplies for Masséna's army. Soon after leaving Bussaco Wellington's commissaries destroyed most of their stores so that the French couldn't lay their hands on them. They emptied kegs of rum in the streets of one village and the soldiers waded through it ankle-deep scooping up a swig or two with their cups as they marched. August Schaumann took teams of his commissaries into the territory the French army was heading for. 'My people followed . . . with mules and empty sacks. Each village we got to we'd send patrols to left and right and plunder all the houses and barns which had long been deserted . . . we would find lots of food which owners had concealed very badly.'

One newcomer to the army was John Kincaid, a twenty-two-year-old Scottish officer, with a wry sense of humour and a sparkling pen. He had seen no active service until he arrived after the Battle of Bussaco, at the height of Wellington's scorched-earth policy. All he got to eat on the retreat was a pound of beef, a mouldy biscuit and a glass of rum. And he had left his cloak with the heavy baggage miles behind. 'My only covering every night was the canopy of heaven, from whence the dews descended so refreshingly.' He slept in constant fear of scorpions, snakes and lizards crawling all over him. And come the morning, the likeliest time for an enemy attack, 'we stood to arms . . . at an hour before daylight and remained there until a grey horse could be seen a mile off (which is the military criterion by which daylight is acknowledged)'. It was cold sleeping in the open in October. 'Nothing in life can be more ridiculous than seeing a lean, lank fellow start from a profound sleep at midnight, and begin lashing away at the Highland Fling . . . but it was a measure that I very often had recourse to, as the cleverest method of producing heat.'

By October the British were quartered in and among the Lines of Torres Vedras. Masséna took one look at them and decided that his adversaries were so well prepared that it would be futile to try to press through to Lisbon. His own army had a terrible winter trying to survive in countryside the Portuguese and the British had stripped bare. Wellington was not tempted to sally out and challenge Masséna, however. His instinct was to wait for the moment when he knew he would prevail rather than to take an unnecessary risk. Revealingly he wrote to a friend: 'They won't draw me from my cautious system . . . I'll only fight them when I am pretty sure of success.' All this was enough to get the tongues wagging at home. George, Prince of Wales, one of Wellington's sharpest critics (and soon to become Prince Regent), was mean enough to say to Wellington's brother Richard, 'I condole with you heartily my dear Lord upon poor Arthur's retreat . . . Masséna has quite outgeneralled him.'

For a month the two armies faced each other with only the occasional clash. Thomas Todd and his mates of the Highland Light Infantry who had fought at Vimeiro were now back in the Peninsula. They found themselves facing a French attempt to break through the British lines. Todd was soon fighting hand to hand in a very confined space. He managed to bayonet one Frenchman and escaped being killed by another only when a random shot struck his assailant. 'I stood gasping for breath, not a shoe on my feet, my bonnet had fallen to the ground.' That didn't stop him charging off when the Frenchmen ran away. Todd then found a pair of shoes in the mud which fitted him and proceeded to plunder a dead Frenchman whose hat had fallen off. 'I struck the hat with my foot, and felt it rattle;

97

seized it in a moment and, in the lining, found a gold watch and silver crucifix. I kept them, as I had as good a right to them as any other.' William Tomkinson and his light dragoons were in and out of French lines during those days in October too. During one night of torrential rain they found shelter, by good luck, in a wine vault. One dragoon managed to fall into a wine vat where he was trapped all night.

John Kincaid and some companions were keen to make a contribution to a party a local man threw for them together with his daughter and two of her young girlfriends. The young officers mischievously stole some turkeys and a sheep. Later, when the theft was discovered and an inquiry began, 'as one of our party happened to be killed in action we, very uncharitably, put the whole of it on his shoulders'.

In places the armies were only fifty yards apart. Thomas Todd watched some Frenchmen, who were desperately short of supplies, trying to kill a bullock. But the butcher missed his blow, and the bullock ran off into the British lines. 'The French looked so foolish, we hurraed at them, secured the bullock, brought him in front, and killed him in style. Shortly after, an officer and four men came with a flag of truce and supplicated in the most humble manner for the half of the bullock, which they got for godsake.'

Masséna's plight worsened by the day. Alexander Gordon reported: 'Masséna's army now have nothing but meat alone to live upon, are very sickly and desert much . . . In about a month the rains will set in which will yet more increase his state of wretchedness.' On the morning of 16 November Jonathan Leach, like many other British front-line observers that day, found that 'the cunning rogues had played us an old trick of theirs, by placing figures of straw upright, with a soldier's cap on each, and a pole by their side to represent a musket. Their whole army had retired.'

Wellington climbed one of the most prominent hills on his defence line to see for himself. No doubt about it: Masséna had pulled out. Wellington sent his men in immediate pursuit. Many of them were horrified at the misery and brutality of the French retreat. 'We could not advance a hundred yards, without seeing dead soldiers of the enemy stretched upon the road or at a little distance from it, who had lain down to die, unable to proceed through hunger and fatigue.' But

Todd said he wasn't sorry for them: 'Their retreat resembled more that of famished wolves than men. Murder and devastation marked their way, every house was a sepulchre, a cabin of horrors . . . In a small town . . . I saw twelve dead lying in one house upon the floor! Every house contained traces of their wanton barbarity.'

Masséna withdrew about twenty miles up the north bank of the River Tagus to the town of Santarém. And there Wellington was content to leave him for the winter. Just before he called off the pursuit, he had to intervene to stop General 'Black Bob' Craufurd and his Light Division making another bid for glory. Craufurd thought he saw an opportunity for his men to destroy what looked like a French rearguard force of 2,000 or 3,000 men just ahead of him. He waved his division out into one long line and gave orders for an attack. Suddenly 'Lord Wellington arrived on the ground and stopped the attack, observing "Are you aware, General, that the whole of Junot's corps is close to the advanced body you now see, amounting to at least 23,000 men, a large portion of which is cavalry?" The attack was of course abandoned.' George Simmons had no love lost for Craufurd. Only a day later he noted that Craufurd 'over his wine, took it into his head that the enemy was moving off and he was anxious to be the first to find out'. The general nearly walked into a French picket, which opened fire on him. He had to retire, Simmons says, after he had taken 'a great chance of throwing away his life'. William Napier tells us that Craufurd 'seized a musket and, followed by a Sergeant, advanced in the night along the causeway, thus commencing a personal skirmish with the French piquets from whose fire he escaped by a miracle . . .' It certainly was a quirky and reckless action on the part of a divisional commander, but such shameless audacity was typical of the man.

Fred Ponsonby, now a lieutenant colonel, occasionally felt a pang of guilt that he was not among his constituents as MP for Kilkenny in Ireland. But the seat was more or less a Ponsonby family possession, so he was usually very relaxed about it. That autumn he was enjoying life at Wellington's headquarters. Wellington had asked him to join his team with responsibility for the cavalry. Ponsonby wrote home that he was finding life at headquarters 'very very different from the life of a regimental officer'. He spent his time hobnobbing with the other young aristocrats who made up the Commander in Chief's staff, and complaining that his family didn't write to him. He singled out his sister Caroline Lamb in a letter to his mother: 'Tell Caro she is a shabby person.' It wasn't just that Caroline wasn't a good letter-writer. Her fits of temper and violent fights with her husband, William Lamb, were a growing source of gossip. 'She stood in a corner one day and threw cups and saucers at William's head,' wrote one of her cousins. Her uncle, the Duke of Devonshire, notes that her 'oddities' prejudiced people against her, and he observed know-ingly, 'men like her a lot better than women'. Ponsonby disapproved of Caro's wayward and flirtatious character: we can only guess what he would have called her if he could have foreseen her affair with Lord Byron a year later.

7

A dangerous hour for England

Fuentes d'Oñoro, 1811

I T WAS A difficult winter for Wellington. He believed he had a strong case for continuing support from London. He had defeated another of Napoleon's marshals and stopped the French reoccupying the whole of Portugal. He could now confidently rebuild his strength behind an impregnable defence line as 1810 turned into 1811. And, come the spring, he would pounce on Masséna's wretchedly deprived army and throw it back into Spain. But that was not how it looked to many in London. To the doubters Britain's prospects in the Peninsula seemed more fragile than ever. After all, two and a half years after his first arrival in Portugal Wellington held only a tiny sliver of the country around Lisbon – less than he had controlled after the Battle of Vimeiro in August 1808. The MP William Fremantle dismissed any prospect of Wellington being able to push the French out of the Peninsula: 'Where is the man in his senses who believes that . . . we shall be able to accomplish this?' he asked. Alexander Gordon wrote home, 'People now are not satisfied because Wellington has not utterly destroyed Masséna and his army and nothing will satisfy them but a great battle being fought. Thank God Wellington is not a man to be moved by popular clamour.' Spencer Perceval's weak government was unable to give Wellington the robust support he needed and demanded. The Opposition, calling for peace with Napoleon and an end to the whole enterprise in the Peninsula, was – for the moment – supported by the Prince of Wales.

If Wellington's war was to continue, he needed to deliver a successful campaign in 1811. Gordon's main correspondent in London was his often scathing brother, Lord Aberdeen, who told him that, if the general feeling in London was 'gloomy and unfavourable', it was largely Gordon's fault for raising hopes too high. Months earlier Gordon had promised him the destruction of Masséna's army. Aberdeen now shot back: 'You taught us to expect the utter annihilation of Masséna and his army over and over again. And these expectations which you entertained so warmly were certainly in some degree countenanced by the despatches of Lord Wellington. This is the reason people are in some degree disappointed.' In reality, the most noticeable feature of Gordon's private correspondence throughout the campaign is his volatility. He swings freely between pessimism and optimism, no doubt partly reflecting the mood of the man with whom he worked so closely.

The winter break gave Wellington's men time to remember that there was more to life than war. Jonathan Leach found abundant game: 'We contrived to amuse ourselves very well . . . and often with success: hares, quails, snipes and golden plovers being abundant . . . The French cavalry pickets . . . never interfered with us, nor interrupted our sport, although we frequently coursed hares and shot quails, within half range of their carbines.' Some of the soldiers in Leach's battalion put on a play, but actors got so drunk they forgot their parts. Thomas Todd and his Highlander mates found they had not much to do during the winter: 'Having very little duty, our time was spent at football.' They were based in a convent and were poorly supplied with food until 'an accident procured us a short relief. Some of our men, amusing themselves in piercing the ceiling with their bayonets, discovered a trap door, and found a great concealed store of food and valuables. We fared well while it lasted.'

Highlanders played a pivotal role in the British army. Since the catastrophe of the Battle of Culloden half a century earlier, when the flower of Scotland's Highland clans died for Bonnie Prince Charlie in his rebellion against George II, Scotland had been the British army's most fertile recruiting ground. The Scots like the Irish were fine fighters, and in those parts of the British Isles where jobs were short the army meant work, money and adventure. But there was only one army and it was only natural that within it national feelings sometimes ran high. In Major General the Honourable Charles Colville's brigade, Joseph Donaldson and other Scots found themselves resenting their very English commander, who appeared to despise all things Scottish. 'He found means to annoy us a good deal. Perhaps he believed with many people in England that the Scots run about their native hills eating raw oats like horses with nothing but a kilt to cover their nakedness and that they had no right to receive any other treatment when they entered the army than what is usually given to any animal when caged.'

Another commander who didn't enjoy universal affection, the Light Division's Robert Craufurd, went home on leave that winter. Jonathan Leach was delighted: 'God be praised we have got rid of that vagabond.' His place was filled by Major General William Erskine. He was a near-disaster: Craufurd may have been unpredictable but he had moments of inspired brilliance; Erskine by contrast was excessively cautious and Wellington had already complained that the man was nearly blind. His poor leadership of the Light Division in 1811 made Wellington count the days to Craufurd's return.

Another officer Wellington had to part with was Fred Ponsonby, who was needed to command the cavalry protecting Cadiz 200 miles away to the south. He found himself leading a charge by German hussars at the Battle of Barrosa on 5 March 1811. A young infantry officer, Robert Blakeney, watched Ponsonby's hussars passing in front of the British line: 'We gave the Germans a cheer . . . The enemy's cavalry turned round and faced them stoutly, their commander placing himself some distance in their front. As the Germans closed on the enemy our cheers were enthusiastic. The brave French leader was instantly cut down; our cavalry charged right through them from rear to front, one red coat always conspicuous, Colonel Ponsonby.' This was Fred Ponsonby in full cry: 'The fox-hunting instinct was strong in Col Ponsonby,' said one chronicler. The British commander at Barrosa, General Graham, described Ponsonby's action as 'a brilliant and most successful charge against a squadron of French dragoons who were entirely routed'. Ponsonby was wounded in the charge and had a narrow escape. Someone lashed out at him with a sabre, but he managed 'very dexterously to turn the edge of it' so that it didn't cut through his knee. But he had a huge bruise and a slight cut across his face. He longed for the day when he would have his own regiment. He got his wish in June 1811. Wellington gave him command of the newly arrived 12th Light Dragoons.

Ponsonby was delighted, and the 12th's historian described him as the 'Beau Ideal' of a cavalry officer: 'chivalrous, modest, untouched by fear, he combined cool judgment with the utmost resolution in action . . . The 4 years in which he led the 12th light dragoons were to be numbered amongst the most brilliant in their history.'

Wellington had not been at Barrosa. He had been preoccupied with preparing his army for an early campaign. It had been a hard winter for his troops and it had been dreadful for Masséna's. By February 1811 the French around Santarém were suffering severe privation. 'The horses in Masséna's army were kept alive . . . on the stalks of the vine, bruised and mixed with corn . . . Many of the Portuguese peasantry, armed with fowling pieces, pikes etc etc aided by the militia . . . continually harassed the French, cut off their supplies, killed stragglers without mercy and in various other ways placed Masséna's army in anything but an enviable situation.'

By the beginning of March Masséna's position had become impossible. His army was on the move – northwards, away from Lisbon. Within hours the British were in Santarém seeing for themselves how the French had suffered and how they had taken it out on the local population. Jonathan Leach reported 'squalor and filth' everywhere. George Simmons found the houses 'torn and dilapidated, and the few miserable inhabitants moving skeletons'. In another village he walked into a house and found 'two young ladies . . . brutally violated . . . unable to rise from a mattress of straw . . .' The way the French 'vandals' had treated the Portuguese, he said, 'rouses the fiercest passions within us, and will make us, when we come up with the enemy, take ample vengeance upon them for their unheard of and disgusting cruelties'. August Schaumann saw the corpse of a peasant propped up in a ludicrous position in a hole in a garden wall 'to make fun of us when we came along'. The French left suffering animals in their wake too. John Kincaid, Joseph Donaldson and William Grattan found 500 donkeys left by the French hamstrung and wallowing helplessly on a river bank. 'The poor creatures looked us piteously in the face as much as to say: "Are you not ashamed to call yourselves human beings?" . . . had fate at that moment placed five hundred Frenchmen in our hands . . . I am confident that every one of them would have undergone the same operation.'

Slowly, inexorably, Wellington's Anglo-Portuguese army propelled the French back towards Spain. Wellington continued his strategy of careful exploitation of Masséna's discomfiture rather than outright confrontation. He was determined to 'force them out of Portugal by the distresses they will suffer, and do them all the mischief I can upon this retreat. Masséna is an old fox, and is as cautious as I am: he risks nothing.'

In less than a week the French pulled back seventy miles to just south of Coimbra and turned north-east apparently heading for the Spanish border. Occasionally they turned and fought. In one of these encounters Ned Costello showed what a soft-hearted fellow he was when a Frenchman sent a musket ball whizzing past his head. The Frenchman didn't then retreat with his comrades, but began to reload, so Costello promptly shot him from fifty yards away. 'In an instant I was beside him, the shot had entered his head . . . A few quick turns of the eye as it rolled its dying glances on mine turned my whole blood within me, and I reproached myself as his destroyer. An indescribable uneasiness came over me, I felt almost a criminal.' He knelt down, gave the dying man a swig of wine and wiped the foam from his lips. Then he heard a groan from another Frenchman, 'big tears suddenly gushing down his sunburst countenance, as he pointed with a finger, to my victim, "vous avez tué mon pauvre frère", he said (you have killed my poor brother)'.

Wellington took every opportunity to use the momentum of his advance to harry the French retreat. His cavalry and his lighter troops were in constant touch with Masséna's rearguard. In each clash Wellington managed to outsmart the French and force them back north and then east towards Spain. Kincaid says that at a spot called Foz de Arouce on the River Ceira, 'Lord Wellington, having a prime nose for smelling out an enemy's blunder . . . discovered Ney had left himself on the wrong side of the river.' Wellington threw in the Light Division and Picton's 3rd Division as well as the Portuguese, and the French were 'driven back across the river with great loss'. Jonathan Leach saw many Frenchmen 'drowned in the Ceira by attempting to flounder through its rapid stream. Some hundreds perished in this manner and they threw two of their eagles into the river to prevent their becoming trophies of the victors.' The eagle was a Napoleonic regiment's most prized emblem. At one stage Wellington had a lucky escape. He was, as usual, close to the action in order to maintain control. He stood on a little hill and 'some of the enemy's sharpshooters stole, unperceived, very near to him and began firing but fortunately without effect'. It was another instance of Wellington's extraordinary good luck, which persisted throughout his military career. Over the seven years between Mondego Bay and Waterloo nearly all his close aides were killed or wounded beside him.

After a day's rest Kincaid and his fellow Rifles crossed the river. 'The fords were still so deep that, as an officer with an empty haversack on my back, it was as much as I could do to flounder across it without swimming. The solders, ballasted with their knapsacks and the sixty rounds of ball cartridge, were of course in better fording trim.' When Ney and Masséna reached Celorico, the two rival French marshals clashed decisively. Masséna ordered the army to head south-east through difficult mountain country instead of along the road to Almeida and the Spanish border. Ney refused, saying it was an absurd route. Masséna dismissed him and the army's most popular marshal returned to France.

Before quitting Portugal, Masséna decided to turn and do battle with Wellington. He chose to make his stand at Sabugal on the road to Spain, where the River Côa offered him a promising line of defence against the advancing British. The fighting started in dense fog: General Erskine, in his first major test as leader of the Light Division after relieving Craufurd, ordered his men east across the Côa without being exactly sure where he was. Light-infantry troops soon found themselves outnumbered by the French and in danger of being surrounded. If it had not been for the initiative of the ever resourceful Colonel Sydney Beckwith, now a brigade commander, who concentrated his men on a small hill and fought off several attacks, the Light Division would have been severely depleted. Thomas Garrety was standing nearby when Beckwith received a nasty wound in the head. 'With the blood streaming down his face [he] rode amongst the foremost of the skirmishers, directing all with ability and praising the men in a loud cheerful voice . . . I was close to him at the time. One of our company called out: "Old Sydney is wounded."' Beckwith heard the remark and instantly replied, 'But he won't leave you: fight on my brave fellows, we shall beat them!' Garrety's musket brought down a Frenchman: 'I advanced close to the poor fellow as he lay on his side. Never shall I forget the alarm that was pictured on his countenance: he thought I was going to bayonet him, to avert which he held out his knapsack, containing most likely all his worldly substance, by way of appeasing my wrath. Unwilling to injure a fallen foe, I did not take his life . . .'

A few hours later the lifting fog allowed Wellington to send reinforcements across the river without any danger of the men losing their bearings, and the French soon retired from the battlefield. Masséna's defeat at Sabugal prompted him to withdraw from Portugal to restock in Spain. Gordon confidently wrote home that they hoped to recapture Almeida and Badajoz, the two formidable border fortresses which had just fallen to the French. 'I must say I think this has been the most brilliant campaign Great Britain has witnessed this long while, and has fully shown the superiority of British troops.' But, again no doubt echoing the sentiments of his chief, Gordon went on bitterly to attack Wellington's generals, whom he described as 'not worth anything . . . In short if Lord Wellington is not on the spot everything goes on wrong and he can place little confidence in any of them.' Erskine's command of the Light Division was certainly disappointing, and Wellington was delighted when Craufurd returned from leave in early May.

At the beginning of that month Masséna was back. He crossed the frontier with 48,000 men. Wellington had 37,000 to face him. They met just inside the Portuguese frontier at the village of Fuentes d'Oñoro. What followed was one of the fiercest battles of the Peninsular War. Once again the Irish and Scottish regiments and Bob Craufurd's Light Division played a decisive role. On the French side, Masséna had everything to lose. He had just received the news that he had been sacked by Napoleon, but his successor had not yet arrived to relieve him. He had a window of a few days in which to rescue his reputation. He seized it with his usual vigour in a last desperate attempt to throw Wellington back and rescue the French garrison in Almeida. It is astonishing that Napoleon, who now clearly recognised Wellington's qualities, still failed to come and fight him in person. He was impressed by his opponent's campaigns in the Peninsula. He said later he believed that only two people, he and Wellington, were able to display the kind of military genius that the British general had shown in his defensive campaign of 1810. But Napoleon still believed that the French armies in the Peninsula, which massively outnumbered Wellington's forces, and marshals like Masséna and Soult should be sufficient to secure his position. Besides he was preoccupied with new, warlike rumblings in central Europe. Russia and Prussia were showing signs of recovering their spirits after the shattering defeats they had suffered in 1807–8. Wellington found it hard to believe his good luck. He told Alexander Gordon that he would 'rather fight 50,000 men than Bonaparte himself'. But Wellington still believed that in Masséna he faced the 'ablest' of Napoleon's marshals. Napoleon too had been a great admirer of Masséna: his only problem was that he 'could not keep his hands

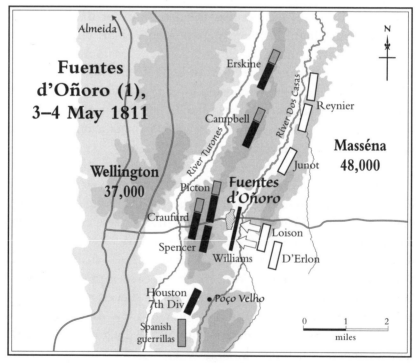

The Battle of Fuentes d'Oñoro (1)

from money . . . Had not his bright parts been soiled with the vice of avarice, he would have been a great man.'

The decisive battle of 1811, which would decide the fate of Portugal, was fought in and around the village of Fuentes d'Oñoro just over the border in Spain. It was on the main road to the great fortress town of Ciudad Rodrigo held by the French eighteen miles to the east. The British were struck by how prosperous its people and houses looked compared with those in Portugal. Joseph Donaldson called the village 'beautiful and romantic'. The ground sloped gently up westwards from a small river, called the Dos Casas, through the little cluttered houses of the village of Fuentes to a ridge 200 feet above it. Wellington had, as usual, chosen his ground well. He placed his men in the village and in an extended line northwards along the rising ground west of the river. If the French were to relieve their garrison in Almeida, eight miles off to the north-west, they would have to dislodge him. On the slopes behind the village Wellington placed Picton's division with William Grattan's Connaught Rangers and Donaldson's 94th Scots Brigade. Thomas Todd's 71st Highlanders were alongside them. A line of British guns were ranged along in front of them. In and around the village – at the front line – Wellington positioned an elite force of some 2,200 men made up of contingents from his best British and Portuguese light-infantry regiments, commanded by Lieutenant Colonel Williams. Many were armed with rifles, whose longer range would allow them to thin the ranks of the advancing French columns before they could fire their muskets.

The 3rd of May dawned a warm and cloudless day. Wellington was out early on the ridge. Through his telescope he watched the French gathering on the other side of the river, bugles blowing, drums beating, staff officers galloping from unit to unit as they shouted out orders. At 2 p.m. the French began to advance. As Williams's sharpshooters selected their targets, British guns fired at long range over the heads of the men in the village. The river was only knee-deep and no obstacle. The French came on, six battalions of them, 4,000 men, outnumbering Williams's troops. In a flash, in spite of the British rifle fire, they were in among the houses by the river. Williams sent in his men with bayonets fixed. Some of the

French withdrew but another five battalions were sent in to reinforce them, and the British and Portuguese were forced slowly back through tight little streets. Williams was wounded. From the ridge behind, Wellington watched the 4,000 French beginning to overwhelm the 2,000 allied forces, and sent in 2,000 reinforcements from Spencer's division, including two Highland battalions. One of them was Todd's 71st. Together with Williams's men, they fought from house to house. Todd noticed the contrast between the fiery French and the cool British: '[The French], each chafing each until they appear in a fury, shouting to the points of our bayonets. After the first Huzza, the British officers, restraining their men, still as death. "Steady, lads, steady" is all you hear; and that in an undertone.'

A sergeant in Donaldson's regiment had a lucky escape. With the French close on his heels he darted into a house and jumped into a large chest. He lay there 'sweating and half smothered', while the French broke the place up looking for plunder: 'they were in the act of opening the lid on his hiding place when the noise of our men cheering . . . forced them to take flight'. Wellington threw in fresh troops, gradually pressing the French back to the river. Todd received a bayonet thrust which went through between his side and his knapsack which stopped it. The Frenchman who had stabbed at him with the bayonet was shot dead by a Scottish soldier in the rank behind Todd. But then another musket ball 'took off part of my right shoulder, and killed my rear-rank man, who fell upon me'. The 71st actually managed to cross the river. But Masséna attacked again, with four fresh battalions, around 2,000 men, and regained the ground east of the river. The front lines ended that evening where they had started: the French had lost 650 men, more than twice as many as the British and their Portuguese allies. As Todd retreated with his Highlanders, he found himself standing by some wounded men. One 'pierced my heart with his cries to be lifted out of the way of the cavalry'. While his heart 'bled for them', he had no choice but to keep moving to save himself. When a wounded man's unit is in action, Kincaid observed, 'he is obliged to be left to the tender mercies of those who follow after, and they generally pay him the attention due to a mad dog . . . giving him as wide a berth as they possibly can'.

The following day, 4 May, Masséna took stock. He had hurled a

very large force directly at the village without success. He sent his
cavalry out in all directions to scout for any sign of exposed British
flanks. They reported that Wellington appeared to have over-
extended his army to the south. He had only a small detachment at
the village of Poço Velho three miles south of Fuentes d'Oñoro.
There was a group of Spanish guerrillas even further away. Masséna
saw an opportunity. He would throw a large force against these
weaker outposts in an effort to turn Wellington's right flank. More
than 20,000 would attack Poço Velho, another 14,000 would again
assault the village of Fuentes d'Oñoro in order to prevent Wellington
detaching reinforcements to his right. The French units would begin
their movements under cover of dark.

Wellington's intelligence-gathering units were busy too. In the
late afternoon of 4 May they noticed stirrings on the other side.
Wellington was aware of his weakness on the right, and sent his
newly formed 7th Division of 4,500 men to hold the line at Poço
Velho and 1,500 cavalry to support them and the Spanish guerrillas.

The evening closed in on a day which had seen no action. There
was an exchange of wounded and, as the sun set, the French were
seen dancing to music and playing football on a flat piece of ground
between the two armies. On the British side some dragoons managed
to get their hands on a stock of rum, wine and other delicacies. There
was soon a party in progress with revellers trying unsuccessfully to
keep the merriment down in order not to alert a senior officer. But
Ned Costello says a General Slade was awakened and 'with lungs that
roused the camp, as though a thirteen inch shell had exploded
amongst them, called for the Regimental Sergeant-Major Sharpe,
who on making his appearance was discovered to have partaken too
freely of the . . . strong waters and was immediately placed under
arrest'. The unfortunate RSM was stripped of his rank.

Dawn on 5 May was foggy, but one of Wellington's cavalry officers patrolling near the Spanish position at the far end of the allied
line spotted signs of movement. Could it be Spanish sentries? There
were too many of them. He realised with a shock that he was watching French cavalry mounting their horses for a general attack. Within
minutes an overwhelming force of French horsemen and infantry
was rolling up Wellington's right. The Spanish retired immediately;

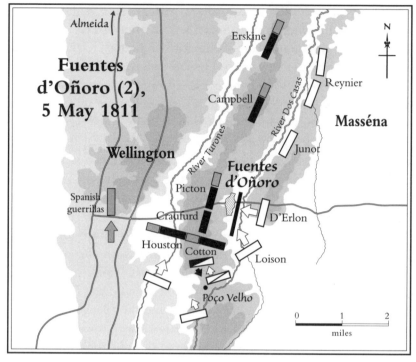

The Battle of Fuentes d'Oñoro (2)

the British cavalry had no choice but to pull back, and the 7th Division soon felt the full weight of Masséna's onslaught. They were seriously outnumbered.

Wellington, peering through the thinning fog from the top of the ridge, realised he had extended his flank too far. He was quick to rectify his mistake. Craufurd, who had returned from leave only the night before, was ordered to race his Light Division to rescue the 7th. The energetic 95th Rifles in their dark-green uniforms were the first to get there. They found the 7th Division under severe pressure, particularly the 85th Regiment who were fighting their first action in the Peninsula. 'Opposed, with their conspicuous red dresses, to the old trained French tirailleurs,' reported Ned Costello, 'it is no wonder that the gallant 85th should have suffered so severely . . . When we came up, however, our practised fellows, in their dark clothing, from the murderous nature of our arms, soon turned back the advancing French . . .' As John Kincaid ran forward, he was struck by a musket ball on his chest, 'which made me stagger a yard or two backward, and, as I felt no pain, I concluded that I was dangerously wounded; but it turned out to be owing to my not being hurt'.

While Ned Costello and his comrades were struggling to blunt the impact of Masséna's left hook, Wellington rapidly reshaped his battlefront. This reactive stroke of genius transformed the contest. His units had been stretched in a long straight line north and south, centred on the village of Fuentes d'Oñoro. He now folded back the southern part of his line to form a right angle at the village. From the point of the angle his forces would extend north as before, but the other half of his line would stretch due west from the village instead of south. But first he had to retrieve what he could of the Light Division, which was now covering the 7th's retreat to the new line. Craufurd and his men were excelling themselves. Some officers such as Simmons and Leach may have shuddered at Craufurd's return but most of the ordinary soldiers, like Costello, welcomed him back from his leave with enthusiasm: 'although a strict disciplinarian, the men knew his value in the field too well not to testify their satisfaction at his return'. Harry Smith, whom Craufurd had appointed his ADC, agreed. 'The soldiers received him with every demonstration of joy. The officers at that time execrated him . . . He was always most kind and hospitable to me.'

The Light Division consisted of fewer than 4,000 men supported by a battery of Royal Horse Artillery and 1,500 cavalry facing three or four times their number. But these men now demonstrated a mastery of fire and movement. Supported by the small force of cavalry, who charged again and again at the advancing French, they formed mobile squares to protect themselves from the massed French cavalry attacks. All the time they edged backwards towards Wellington's new line, somehow keeping at bay the continual onslaughts from French infantry and cavalry. William Napier, a Light Division officer, described in his history of the campaign how the French had attacked the squares: 'Although [the squares] were too formidable to be meddled with, there was not, during the war, a more dangerous hour for England.' Private William Wheeler was one of the 7th Division soldiers grateful for the Light Division's cover for their withdrawal. He was lucky to have a commanding officer who coolly led his men back as if they were on the drill square. 'He took advantage of the ground and led us out of a scrape without loss. I shall never forget him, he dismounted off his horse, faced us and frequently called the time "Right, Left" as he was accustomed to when drilling the regiment . . . he would now and then call out "That fellow is out of step. Keep step and they cannot hurt us."'

The guns retired at the same time, sheltering, when they could, in the squares or hoping for protection from the cavalry; otherwise they risked being captured. One section of two Royal Horse Artillery guns under Captain Norman Ramsay appeared lost in a mêlée of triumphant French soldiers. Napier was not far away:

> Men and horses there closed with confusion and tumult towards one point. A thick dust arose, and loud cries, and the sparkling of blades and the flashing of pistols indicated some extraordinary occurrence. Suddenly the multitude became violently agitated, an English shout pealed high and clear, the mass was rent asunder, and Norman Ramsay burst forth at the head of his battery, his horses breathing fire, stretched like greyhounds along the plain, the guns bounded behind them like things of no weight, and the mounted gunners followed in close career.

Moments after their flamboyant breakout Ramsay and his gunners were safely absorbed into Spencer's infantry division back at the village of Fuentes. All the retreating units including Houston's hard-pressed 7th Division rapidly consolidated on Wellington's new defence line and the French could make little impact on it. It was a triumphant end to a perilous episode in the battle: Wellington could have suffered disastrous losses but for the skill and bravery of Craufurd's men and the hard-pressed cavalry. They had allowed Wellington to extricate his right wing almost intact. Masséna now turned his attention back to the village of Fuentes d'Oñoro itself. He threw several waves of infantry into a battle that grew in intensity and butchery as more and more units were committed by each side. The Highlanders fought to hold the village. Thomas Todd noted how different French soldiers looked from the British. 'Their hats set round with feathers, their beards long and black, gave them a fierce look. Their stature was superior to ours: most of us were young. We all looked like boys, they like savages.'

French reinforcements kept advancing as the tight little streets filled with dead and wounded. After an hour and a half's fighting the struggle was going against the Highlanders. 'We were overpowered, and forced through the streets, contesting every inch.' William Grattan of the Connaught Rangers looked down from the slope above: 'Our Highlanders lay dead in heaps . . . the French grenadiers with their immense caps and gaudy plumes in piles of twenty or thirty together, some dead, others wounded with barely strength sufficient to move.' Wellington threw in more troops, and the fierce French tide ebbed a little.

But then Masséna ordered in another 10,000 French troops in an effort to push the British and Portuguese out of the village altogether. If they could reach the church at the top of the hill and consolidate in the streets and houses around it, Fuentes would be in French hands and he would be able to claim a victory. The French soldiers fought their way to a spot by the church, just short of where the Connaught Rangers and two other battalions were being held in reserve by Wellington. Grattan watched Wellington's brother-in-law Sir Edward Pakenham gallop up to the Rangers' commanding officer, Colonel Wallace, and say: 'Do you see that, Wallace?' 'I do,' replied the colonel, and he went on to say he believed he could drive the French out of the town. 'Will you?' said Pakenham. 'I shall go and tell Lord Wellington so: see, here he comes.' Wellington didn't need persuading: the time had come for a decisive stroke. In a moment Pakenham was back; waving his hat, he called out, 'He says you may go – come along, Wallace.' Off went Pakenham and Wallace leading the Irish charge down towards the church. 'The men stepped together at a smart trot, as if on a parade . . .' They had fixed bayonets. 'It so happened', wrote Grattan, 'that the command of the company which led this attack devolved upon me. When we came within sight of the French . . . I turned round to look at the men of my company: they gave me a cheer that the lapse of many years has not made me forget, and I thought that moment was the proudest of my life . . .' The struggle that followed was the most bitterly fought of the whole battle.

Every man who could lift a weapon – even the battered Highlanders – dragged himself into the struggle. Inch by inch they pressed the French out of the village and back into the river. At one stage Wallace disappeared beneath a pile of rubble when a French shell blew up a wall in the village, but he emerged unscathed. Thomas Picton, the Connaught Rangers' divisional commander, who had lambasted them in the past, exclaimed, 'Well done the brave 88th.' 'Some of them, stung by his former reproaches, cried out: "Are we the greatest blackguards in the army now?" . . . "No, No. You are brave and gallant soldiers: this day has redeemed your character."'

By 2 p.m. Masséna knew he was beaten. The French had lost nearly 2,200, the British and Portuguese fewer than 1,500. Wellington had orchestrated a masterly victory after recognising the risk he had taken in over-stretching his line, when he was faced with a superior force. He admitted later that he had made a blunder in extending his right too far. If the French had taken advantage of it, he confessed, there might have been dire consequences. 'If Boney had been there,' he remarked, 'we should have been beaten.' There were few sceptics left in Wellington's army now. Here was a general who won battles and who did his best to preserve his men's lives. Kincaid spoke for most of the army when he observed after Fuentes d'Oñoro: 'We would rather see his long nose in the fight than a reinforcement of ten thousand men any day.'

Fuentes provided Picton with another chance to criticise the man he saw as an awkward rival. He later wrote: 'The Light Division, under General Craufurd, was rather roughly handled by the enemy's cavalry, and had that arm of the French been as daring and active upon this occasion as they were when following us to the lines of Torres Vedras, they would doubtless have cut off the Light Division to a man.'

The suffering on the battlefield of Fuentes d'Oñoro went on long after the fighting was over. Kincaid spent the night manning a sentry post in the village. He found a wounded Highlander sergeant lying there. 'A ball had passed through the back part of his head, from which the brain was oozing, and his only sign of life was a convulsive hiccough every two or three seconds.' When Kincaid woke up the next morning, the sergeant was dead.

The young Arthur Wellesley, later Duke of Wellington, aged thirty-five, in 1804 at the end of a successful early career in India. The famous nose is already very prominent.

Wellesley's army lands at Mondego Bay in Portugal in August 1808. Most transport ships had to anchor well offshore and men and horses braved the surf in small boats.

Wellesley's audacious crossing of the Douro on 12 May 1809. Troops crossed in four snatched wine barges, and seized the seminary on the skyline. The French in Oporto (a mile downstream to the left) were taken by surprise and forced out of the city.

BELOW: August Schaumann, the garrulous commissary officer and observant diarist from Hanover. His innocent looks belie his mischievous and sometimes shameless character.

RIGHT: Jonathan Leach, who served with Wellington's army all the way from Portugal to Waterloo. He was a captain in the 95th Rifles, whose journal is full of the derring-do of this crack regiment so valued by Wellington.

A recruiting sergeant from the 33rd Yorkshire (West Riding) Regiment exhorts revellers at a pub to sign up for Wellington's army. The oatcake he's brandishing promises them good food, and above the pub door are the words 'Heroes', 'Wellington', 'Honor', 'Wealth' and 'Fame'.

Major General Robert Craufurd, brilliant but temperamental commander of Wellington's light troops. His ruthlessness earned him the nickname 'Black Bob', but his reckless courage cost him his life at Ciudad Rodrigo in 1812.

Lieutenant General Sir Thomas Picton, doughty commander of Wellington's 'Fighting' 3rd Division. Famously outspoken, he made an enemy of Craufurd and ignored Wellington's orders at Vitoria. In the year this was painted, 1812, he led the successful storming of Badajoz.

French infantry in columns reach the top of the Bussaco ridge on 27 September 1810 to find the British waiting for them in long red lines. Here Reynier's assault meets two of Picton's battalions – the 88th Connaught Rangers in red coats and a Portuguese regiment in blue.

BELOW: Rowland Hill, Wellington's most trusty general. He was universally adored by his troops, who called him 'Daddy'.

Fred Ponsonby was one of Wellington's favourite cavalry commanders, though his charges sometimes went too far. Behind that bland exterior he was an avid gambler and party-goer. His sister was Lord Byron's lover, Lady Caroline Lamb.

Irishman Ned Costello, son years after his boisterous career as a rifleman with th 95th. His memoirs provide one of the most vivid commentaries on life on an off the battlefield.

Wellington (left) at the Battle of Fuentes d'Oñoro on 5 May 1811 watches his Royal Horse Artillery racing back to British lines after a French attack. Note (bottom right) wounded being evacuated and treated and, beyond, a regiment sitting down for a rest.

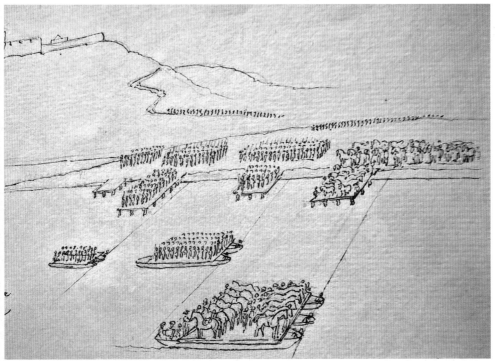

A sketch by a young cavalry officer, John Evan Luard, of his division crossing the Guadiana on 7 April 1811. On the nearest raft three men appear to be hauling a regiment's horses across by passing a rope from hand to hand.

Picton's 3rd Division crossing the River Tagus on 20 May 1811. A raft carrying a gun and its accompanying horses is being pulled across by rope. Beyond, on the left bank, large numbers of infantry have already crossed and are formed up ready to march off.

The great explosion in the breach at the siege of Ciudad Rodrigo on 19 January 1812 didn't stop the British assault troops storming the battlements. Volunteers in the so-called forlorn hope (top right) led the way to the capture of this fortress which opened the road to Madrid.

A watercolour of the morning after the storming of Ciudad Rodrigo painted by 95th Rifles officer Thomas Mitchell. The main breach is on the right. 'Black Bob' Craufurd met his death at the other breach to the left.

Picton's division storm the castle at Badajoz on 6 April 1812. They used ladders to scale the thirty-foot-high walls when all other attacks on the city had failed. After facing fierce opposition they finally seized the battlements and hoisted one of their red jackets on the castle tower.

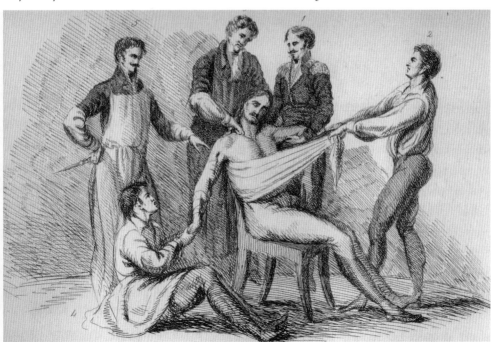

A patient about to have his arm amputated at the shoulder. The surgeon stands behind with a knife. One assistant compresses the subclavian artery in the neck to restrict the blood flow. With no anaesthetic to kill the pain, the hope was that the patient would faint.

Harry Smith, one of the brightest and most ambitious Rifles officers who went on to become a general and governor of Cape Colony. He met his fourteen-year-old wife Juana after the siege of Badajoz in 1812.

Juana María de los Dolores de León married Harry Smith soon after appealing to him to save her from marauding British soldiers during the siege of Badajoz. She accompanied him on all his campaigns, anxiously searching for him after battles. He called her his 'guardian angel'.

A caricature of Wellington's army on the march accompanied by a number of wives and other women and even children. One woman carries three babies. Wives were allowed half a man's food ration, children a quarter.

Grattan came across a makeshift hospital full of dreadfully wounded soldiers. 'Their limbs were swollen to an enormous size . . . Their ghastly countenances presented a dismal sight. The streams of gore, which had trickled down their cheeks, were quite hardened with the sun . . . their eyes were sunk and fixed . . . they sat, silent and statue-like, waiting for their turn to be carried to the amputating tables.' A little further on were the surgeons, stripped to their shirts and covered with blood. A number of doors had been ripped off their hinges to serve as amputating tables, and 'to the right and left were arms and legs, flung here and there, without distinction . . .' Grattan was asked by a doctor to hold down a man while his thigh was cut off. 'The operation was the most shocking sight I have ever witnessed: it lasted nearly half an hour but his life was saved.' Outside Grattan saw flocks of vultures hovering. He swore he would never visit such a place again.

Soon after the Battle of Fuentes d'Oñoro, Wellington was shaving when one of his officers burst in and told him that the French were leaving. The Commander in Chief removed his razor from his chin for an instant: 'Ay, I thought they meant to be off,' he said coolly, and then got back to his shave. Wellington's sangfroid was characteristic, but in truth the French retreat was scarcely unexpected. The French army, gravely mauled, had little choice but to retire to Spain. Masséna managed to get a message to the garrison commander in Almeida, General Brennier. He told him the fortress could not be saved: he should destroy it and make his escape.

But Wellington was determined that Brennier and his garrison should not be allowed to escape. The fortress was now more or less at his mercy: he gave orders for all roads and bridges leading into Spain across the River Águeda to be barred – particularly one at a spot called Barba de Puerco. This would deny the garrison supplies from Spain and block any escape. All this was to be the responsibility of General Esrkine, who had already let Wellington down badly when he was deputising for Craufurd at Sabugal. On receipt of Wellington's order to guard the bridge at Barba de Puerco, Erskine wrote out an instruction to Colonel Bevan, the battalion commander in the area, but forgot to give it to him. And when he finally did, Bevan in turn waited till he had had a good night's sleep before setting off. Brennier and his surviving men fled across the bridge in the small hours before Bevan arrived.

Wellington was apoplectic. 'I have never been so much distressed by any military event as by the escape of even a man of them,' Wellington wrote to London. In words strikingly like Napoleon's after the Battle of Talavera, he ended the letter expressing contempt for just about all his other commanders: 'I am obliged to be everywhere, and if absent from any operation, something goes wrong.' He told his brother William: 'They had about 13,000 men to watch 1,400. There they were all sleeping in their spurs even: but the French got off. I begin to be of opinion that there is nothing on earth as stupid as a gallant officer.' The unhappy Colonel Bevan was later summoned before a court martial. Overcome with shame and resentment at being made the scapegoat, he blew his brains out. As for 'drunken old' General Erskine, as Schaumann called him, he escaped formal responsibility for Almeida, but he was declared insane a year later and relieved of his command. He committed suicide in Lisbon in 1813.

Brennier's escape took some of the shine off the news of the victory at Fuentes d'Oñoro when it reached London. But it was soon recognised that Wellington had made a strategic breakthrough. Portugal was secure, provided that Wellington now moved against the two great frontier fortresses just inside Spain, Ciudad Rodrigo which commanded the northern route, and Badajoz which stood guard over the southern gateway. These two strongholds commanded the two main roads between Portugal and Madrid. As long as the French held them, Portugal would remain under threat. If Wellington could capture them, the road to Madrid would be open. He determined to tackle them both as soon as possible.

Marshal Beresford was already besieging Badajoz. On 16 May 1811 he had to fight the Battle of Albuera with Marshal Soult, who had marched up from the south to relieve the fortress. It was a victory but a bloody and expensive one: the allies lost 6,000 men, the French 7,000. When Wellington arrived from the north after the battle and visited a military hospital, he told the wounded of the 29th, whose regiment had fought so valiantly at Roliça, Vimeiro and Talavera: 'Old 29th, I am sorry to see so many of you here.' They replied, 'My lord, if you had been with us there would not have been so many of us here.' Beresford wrote a very downbeat despatch about the battle and the bloodshed. But Wellington insisted that Albuera should be represented as a victory. 'If it had not been for me,' he said, 'they would have written a whining report upon it, which would have driven the people in England mad . . . I prevented that.' Wellington still had to keep his detractors, whom he called the 'Croakers', at bay by claiming that every step was leading slowly but inevitably to final victory. What mattered was that Beresford had sent Soult packing, and Wellington could now turn to the two most critical sieges of the Peninsular War, Ciudad Rodrigo and Badajoz.

His problem was that he did not have siege artillery big enough to batter down the walls of the two great fortresses. Acquiring the necessary siege train was a massive operation. Wellington knew it was essential and planned it in meticulous detail. He would start with Ciudad Rodrigo and he ordered the guns and ammunition to be shipped from Lisbon to Oporto and then as far as possible up the River Douro; then they would be transported overland. The siege train would be hauled 'by 384 pairs of bullocks to Trancoso. The stores, that is to say, 350 rounds for each 18 pounder and 24 pounder gun, and 160 rounds for each 10 inch mortar, to be removed to Trancoso, on 892 country carts.' The core of the siege train would be thirty-four huge twenty-four-pounder guns. They and another thirty smaller guns and 1,800 barrels of powder would be lugged across country to Ciudad Rodrigo with the rest of the heavy equipment. And superintending the operation would be the man who was to earn himself an eminent place in the history of the Royal Artillery, Alexander Dickson, then a thirty-four-year-old major, soon to command all the gunners in the Peninsula. His artillerymen would be backed up by no fewer than a thousand militiamen and 300 Portuguese soldiers. Wellington reckoned the whole laborious process would take sixty-four days. It took longer. The siege did not really begin until the New Year, although there were several important skirmishes and manoeuvres before that.

Napoleon had already told Masséna he was sacked. He now appointed Auguste Marmont to succeed him. Marmont was one of

Napoleon's most trusty associates, who had campaigned with him in Italy and Germany. He did his best to foil Wellington's encirclement of Ciudad Rodrigo. The allies had a narrow escape at El Bodón, four miles south of the fortress city, on 24 September. Joseph Donaldson's Scots and other units of the 3rd Division were caught in the open by a large force of Marmont's infantry and cavalry. Only by retreating in quickly formed squares did the redoubtable Thomas Picton manage to guide them to safety. 'We were much annoyed by shot and shell from . . . French artillery . . . some of which falling on our squares did great mischief, killing and wounding several of our men, and blowing up our ammunition.' But Picton showed 'coolness and intrepidity' in steering them back to join the rest of the army. 'Never mind the French,' he said, 'mind your regiment: if the fellows come here, we will give them a warm reception.'

Wellington had actually asked Craufurd to take his Light Division to help support Picton's fighting withdrawal but Craufurd had once again sailed close to the wind, ignoring his chief's command to cover the retreat. Picton was none too pleased, nor was Wellington. Craufurd, instead of reinforcing Picton, had kept his troops out in the front line in a rather exposed position. When they next met, Wellington, with more than a hint of sarcasm, said, 'I am glad to see you safe, Craufurd.' 'Oh I was in no danger, I assure you,' responded Craufurd. To which Wellington shot back, 'But I was from your conduct.' Craufurd rode off saying, 'He is damned crusty today.'

El Bodón was a dangerous moment, but the rest of 1811 passed away without any major advance on either side. After two abortive attempts to besiege the two fortress towns, Ciudad Rodrigo and Badajoz, Wellington – with his usual strategic caution – decided to wait. Some felt he was being too circumspect. Craufurd made little secret of his view that Wellington was not ready enough to take risks for victory. And this sentiment was echoed even by the loyal Alexander Gordon, who told his brother that he was disappointed Wellington didn't have a go at the French, whose armies he would probably never find 'weaker or more dispersed than they are at present'.

But Wellington, confident as ever in his own judgement, was

determined to avoid a major move into Spain until he had the siege equipment ready. Time was on his side too: his allies, the Spanish guerrillas, were nibbling away at French strength and morale, and Napoleon's strategic ambitions were shifting again. His target now was Moscow, and he decided to recall some key units from the Peninsula for his planned invasion of Russia in 1812.

8

Now, lads, for the breach
Ciudad Rodrigo, 1812

I T WAS A bitterly cold winter. Even worse, the British army's winter quarters were in a comparatively infertile area on the Spanish–Portuguese border. In spite of Wellington's strict orders to respect the property of the local population, soldiers were soon snatching local farmers' sheep. William Grattan observed that the farmers knew very well that 'wolves were not sufficiently numerous in that part of the country to effect such havoc'. The thieves often escaped undetected and shared the tasty lamb with their companions. The ones who were caught stealing were flogged, and Picton tried to stop the thieving by insisting on a roll call of each of his companies at different times each night. 'Black Bob' Craufurd, never shy about complaining, blamed the army's lack of supplies for the large number of desertions his Light Division was suffering. This only worsened relations between Wellington and his most prickly general. Wellington prided himself on keeping his men supplied and was naturally piqued that Craufurd didn't appreciate it. Craufurd had already shown himself unscrupulously ready to go to any lengths to secure food for his men. He seized some church plate 'with a view to purchasing some corn . . . It had some effect in procuring supplies, as it convinced the priests that the distress was not feigned.'

It was a meagre Christmas that year. Lieutenant Robert Knowles, a twenty-one-year-old fusilier from Bolton in Lancashire, spent five days in one camp where they had to search a wood for acorns in place of bread. Accommodation was scarce too. 'In this starving state we had only twenty cottages to quarter seven hundred men. I say very few men in England would envy our situation.' It wasn't just hunger which wasted the army: it was disease as well. Sanitary conditions in the camps were crude, the water often polluted. Wellington reported that all the soldiers who had recently arrived from England 'and vast numbers of officers were attacked by fever, not of a very violent description, but they were rendered unable to perform any duty, and those who recovered relapsed upon making any exertions'.

But none of this stopped Wellington from devoting any free time that winter to his favourite distraction – hunting. He now had a full pack of foxhounds, and would hunt on nearly every fine day. He put a huntsman named Crane in charge of his hounds, and Crane proved so competent that Wellington kept him on after the war to manage the pack at his house at Stratfield Saye in Hampshire. The Commander in Chief would invite others to join him for the chase. John Kincaid reckoned that Wellington found these outings useful because 'it gave him an opportunity of seeing and conversing with the officers of the different departments, and other individuals . . . and the pursuits of that manly exercise too gave him a better insight into the characters of the individuals under him . . .' August Schaumann often used to meet Wellington on the hunt 'with his entourage and a magnificent pack of English hounds . . . On these occasions he is said to have been in the best of spirits, genial and *sans cérémonie*; in fact just like a genuine country squire and fox-hunter . . . how different was his demeanour on a day of battle: then he seemed like an angry God under whose threatening glance everyone trembled.'

Wellington had other ways of mixing with the men who mattered most to him. He often packed his dinner table with local dignitaries as well as his staff and other officers. If he was in jovial mood, the occasion would be marked by his loud guffaw. They would drink the best French wine, given him by Spanish guerrilla chiefs who had managed to raid a French convoy. Lieutenant Thomas Browne was a frequent guest: 'The cheerfulness or gloom of our commander's table depended much on news which he received from England, or reports from the different divisions of his army.' Browne recalled many occasions 'when scarce anyone dare open his mouth except to take his dinner, and other times when the conversation was constant and general, and Lord Wellington himself the most playful of the party'. Occasionally Wellington would throw a ball and entertain local people. If there were not enough women guests, the officers would dance with each other.

Wellington's headquarters always had an informal air to it. When he wasn't staying in quarters, his staff pitched a marquee for him big enough, according to his cook, James Thornton, to serve 'as a sitting and dining room'. Wellington's bedroom was a smaller tent inside the marquee with a sentry at the entrance. Thornton's kitchen was a tarpaulin resting on poles. They threw a mound of earth around it and cut niches where they could make fires and boil saucepans and 'a larger niche cut out for roasting'. Wellington wasn't that impressed with Thornton's cooking skills: General Lowry Cole, he reckoned, had 'the best dinners, Hill the next best, and mine are no great things and Beresford's and Picton's are very bad indeed'. Wellington rose each day at 6 a.m. He was busy writing letters, orders and despatches till nine o'clock when he had breakfast. The morning was taken up with meetings with key colleagues. He spent the afternoon riding. After dinner in the early evening, he was back at work by 9 p.m. writing and reading until he went to bed at midnight.

Wellington had no hankering for home that winter or any winter. He had a job to do and he would do it. He took not a day's home leave between the spring of 1809 and the summer of 1814. He had no urge to see Kitty, his wife, pining for him nervously in Britain, troubled by her failure to excite him and by her own feeling of inadequacy. He had little but contempt for her, and this only added to his disdain for officers who asked for home leave. Some of them had what he saw as lame excuses like a bout of rheumatism or family sickness back in England.

And for all the social life of headquarters, Wellington was always focused and ready for action. He had a small iron bedstead in his quarters, covered with Russian leather, and one pillow. If he suspected that the enemy might be on the move, Thomas Browne noted, Wellington would sleep 'in his clothes with his boots near him, ready to put on and his cloak thrown round him. His horse and that of his orderly dragoon were always ready saddled.' The boots known as Wellingtons were 'of his own invention and outside he used often to wear mudguards of strong leather'.

There was not a whiff of flamboyance about Wellington's headquarters here or anywhere else during his six years in the Peninsula. He had no time for the vain frippery and extravagance of other great commanders. The atmosphere was always serious, almost Spartan. 'There was no throng of scented staff officers with plumed hats, orders and stars, no main guard, no crowd of contractors, actors, valets, cooks, mistresses, equipages . . . as there is at French or Russian headquarters,' wrote August Schaumann, 'just a few aides de camp, who went about the streets alone and in their overcoats, a few guides, and small staff guard: that was all.' Wellington was not an approachable figure adored by his men like Rowland 'Daddy' Hill. But he commanded almost universal respect. And modest though his dress may have been, he was always recognisable. He had a 'remarkable cast of feature, which made him ever distinguishable, at an almost incredible distance'.

He also resented the fact that he was occasionally landed by the high command in London with officers whose patronage by the Prince Regent or the Duke of York gave them an arrogance he found insufferable. One of them was Colquhoun Grant, a tall black-whiskered general who wore an enormous three-cornered hat with a long fluttering feather. He was the Prince Regent's protégé. 'The commander-in-chief hated these puffed up favourites,' observed Schaumann. Wellington himself declared that he did not care too much how an officer or soldier dressed 'as long as he is forced to keep himself clean and smart as a soldier ought to be'.

One of Wellington's close-knit team, who had been good friends with Fred Ponsonby and William Tomkinson, was another light dragoon, Major Charles Cocks. He had made the effort to learn Spanish before his posting to the Peninsula and Wellington used him as his eyes and ears, absorbing information about French movements from Spanish guerrillas and local people. He was a frequent guest at Wellington's table and leaped at any chance of a party: 'I borrow two or three clarinets and a tambourine from some neighbouring infantry regiment and set the girls dancing all night.' He fell for one of them, 'a little Portuguese 16 year old with eyes black as jet, lips ripe as peaches and teeth as white as ivory and limbs for the Venus de Medici'. When she suggested marriage, he said he wasn't ready for it, but when she then left him, he was shattered: 'Her departure has aroused feelings I thought my emotions had forgot. I could kill her myself and everyone I meet.' By this time she was in the arms of that young rascal August Schaumann, who had even less intention of marrying her. His journal is full of accounts of the conquests he claims he made in many a Peninsular village.

Any uncertainty about what the French would do next vanished over Christmas. Wellington was delighted to hear that Napoleon had ordered Marmont to send part of his army to bolster French forces fighting Spanish rebels around Valencia. Typical, he thought, of Napoleon's long-distance mismanagement of the Peninsular War and just the opportunity he had been waiting for. He could now upgrade the faltering blockade of Ciudad Rodrigo into a full-scale siege. With Marmont looking east to superintend Napoleon's redeployment plan, Wellington had a chance to seize Ciudad Rodrigo before the French could rescue it, and Ciudad Rodrigo was the gateway to Spain. He ordered the army to move.

William Grattan's Connaught Rangers were alerted at 3 a.m. on 4 January 1812 and were on the march by 5 a.m. The weather was appalling. 'I scarcely remember a more disagreeable day; the rain which had fallen in the morning was succeeded by snow and sleet and some soldiers, who, sunk from cold and fatigue, fell down exhausted, soon became insensible and perished; yet, strange to say, an Irishwoman of my regiment was delivered of a child upon the road and continued the march with her infant in her arms.' By 6 January Ciudad Rodrigo was encircled by a substantial British force and the siege began. The city, whose strategic position had long marked it out as one of Spain's most prized strongholds, stood high above the east bank of the Águeda river. Its 'monasteries, convents and churches', observed light infantryman John Cooke, gave the city 'at a distance the appearance of an immense Gothic castle'.

Ciudad Rodrigo's walls looked much more formidable than they really were. Built largely of rubble they did not have the solidity of the walls of Badajoz 150 miles to the south. And 500 yards to the north of the city was a long hill, higher than the city itself, which offered Wellington's siege guns the perfect firing position. Dug in on this hill, the Grand Teson, his guns would be able to batter a breach in the city walls which his infantry could storm. But someone had to do the digging. It was an exhausting and dangerous job. British forces had not conducted a major siege for a century and a half, and

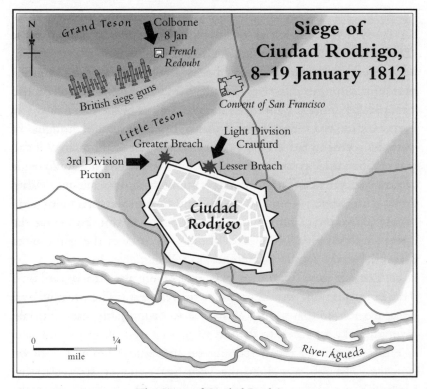

The Siege of Ciudad Rodrigo

Wellington was seriously under-equipped with trench-digging gear and the specially trained engineers to operate it. He had asked for them already, but his earnest demands had fallen on deaf ears in London. George Simmons and other riflemen had to cross the Águeda – wading through up to their shoulders – to do a day's digging, soaking wet and cold. They also had to do some sharpshooting with their rifles to keep 'Johnny François' at bay. Ned Costello found the river 'a great annoyance'. The men were so bruised by pieces of ice floating down the river that 'to obviate it, the cavalry at length were ordered to form four deep across the ford, under the lee of whom we crossed comparatively unharmed'.

Everyone was expected to do his duty digging the trenches. All resented it, believing it was a job for specialists. Wellington agreed but he had only some twenty engineers under the resourceful Richard Fletcher, who had constructed the Lines of Torres Vedras.

So most of the digging would have to be done by the infantry. Even the hardy Scots found it an ordeal. Joseph Donaldson almost froze. 'The frost was so excessive that we were almost completely benumbed, and nothing but hard working, I believe, kept us from perishing with the cold.' First they had to dig a trench, known as the 'first parallel', in line with the walls but just out of the lethal range of French guns. From the cover of this trench they would then scoop out emplacements for their first gun batteries just within range of the walls. While these batteries pounded the walls as best they could from around 500 yards, a further trench – known as a sap – would be dug at an acute angle – to avoid the enemy firing straight into it. This would allow men, guns and ammunition to be moved up under cover to another parallel within about 150 yards of the walls. This forward battery would – Fletcher and Wellington hoped – be so close that the guns would quickly shatter the walls in two places. This bombardment would create two breaches, gaps in the wall of collapsed rubble that would allow the storming parties to scramble through and gain access to the city.

First, though, a French redoubt on the Grand Teson had to be stormed. The job was done the very first night by Colonel John Colborne and men of the Light Division. 'When about fifty yards from the redoubt, I gave the word "double-quick". This movement and the rattling of canteens alarmed the garrison . . .' But the ladders were soon in place and the assault was an immediate success. According to Colborne, once they were over the wall, there was no resistance. Wellington had been watching the attack, and Colborne sent him a messenger, who ran up in great excitement and told the Commander in Chief that they had taken the fort. '"Oh, you've taken the fort have you?" he replied coolly. "Well I'm glad to hear it," and got up and rode away.' Most of the small garrison were taken prisoner, and Craufurd was not pleased when one prisoner was paraded before him who had been stripped naked by the vengeful Portuguese. Harry Smith, Craufurd's ADC, was quick to provide a large handkerchief to help the poor man cover himself. The digging could now begin in earnest. The conditions the men worked in were unimaginable. The weather was cold, the ground often frozen. The digging equipment they had was primitive, the hours they had to work almost limitless. On occasion they were on shift for twenty-four hours at a time. Speed was of the essence if Wellington was to storm the fortress before Marmont could collect an army large enough to challenge him. The trenches were under constant fire from French guns in the fort, and as they dug their way closer and closer to the walls, musket fire became a hazard too. It took a week to get all the trenches dug – to within 150 yards of the wall. Robert Knowles had the hazardous job of opening the embrasures for the guns once the trenches were dug. 'A very fine young man, a lieutenant in the Engineers, was mortally wounded standing by my side.'

With the trenches dug, the guns – massive, unwieldy monsters – were dragged into their firing positions, readied and fired, as often and as accurately as possible. By 14 January twenty-two guns in the first parallel were firing at a range of some 500 yards. It was a welcome sound to people like Simmons who had spent days digging out the trenches and the gun emplacements. 'Twenty two pieces of British cannon opened most musically against the town.' By the 19th the guns in the second parallel were firing at point-blank range only 150 yards from the walls.

The best of the gun crews had the meticulous procedure drilled to perfection. There were eight or nine men to each gun detachment. Up front was the spongeman. The moment the gun fired, he thrust his staff down the barrel, with a water-soaked sheepskin wrapped round a cylinder on the end of it to kill any remaining embers from the last shot. The loader then stuffed down the barrel a new cartridge and a sealed bag of gunpowder, followed by the cannon ball itself. While the loader was ramming in the cartridge and ball, the ventsman held his thumb down over the vent at the near end of the barrel to stop any air getting in: if it did, the cartridge could be ignited by any embers still left in the barrel. A lazy ventsman could cost a loader both his hands if the gun exploded prematurely. Once he saw cartridge and shot rammed home, the ventsman pushed a pricker into the vent to puncture the cartridge inside the barrel and draw up a small amount of powder through the hole. He then poked a little firing tube into the vent filled with very fine-grain powder, instantly combustible. The detachment commander adjusted the gun using the elevating screw behind the barrel, then shouted, 'Give fire!' A fifth man, the firer, touched the powder at the top of the vent with his slow-burning match and the cartridge exploded, propelling the ball to its target around 500 yards away. Each blast threw the gun back six feet from its firing position. So before they could fire again, the team, with the help of two or three loading assistants, had to heave the gun back to its firing position. Two rounds a minute was very fast. Twenty rounds an hour was good going.

At the height of the exchange of fire between the two sides Tom Garrety found the spectacle 'sublime'. 'The bellowing of eighty large guns shook the ground far and wide; the smoke rested in heavy columns on the battlements of the place: the walls crashed to the blow of the bullet . . . the quick clatter of musketry was heard like the pattering of hail after a peal of thunder.' By the time it was over, the five-day barrage had devoured 9,515 rounds of shot and 834 barrels of powder – each ninety pounds in weight.

By the evening of 18 January Wellington, who had been eyeing the progress of the bombardment through his telescope almost hourly, was told that two breaches in Ciudad Rodrigo's north wall were now 'practicable'. That meant they were now sufficiently battered to offer an opening to a storming party. Wellington issued detailed orders for the assault on the evening of 19 January. Men from 'Black Bob' Craufurd's Light Division would attack the Lesser Breach at the centre of the north wall, and men from Picton's division would go for the Greater Breach in the north-west corner. Each assault would be led, as usual, by a forlorn hope. This macabre expression dated from before the English Civil War and was actually derived from the Dutch *verloren hoop* – a lost troop. But in either language it aptly described the few score men at the spearhead of each storming party whose task was recognised as almost suicidal: they faced a high chance of death or dismemberment. Survival could lead to fast promotion, but the risks were high.

William Grattan's Connaught Rangers were earmarked for the Greater Breach under one of Picton's brigade commanders, General Mackinnon. While they waited for the signal Grattan watched his comrades oiling up their bayonets and adjusting their straps so that the cartridge boxes were conveniently available in front of them. The married men said goodbye to their wives: 'the women, from long habit, were accustomed to scenes of danger'. If the husband returned with plunder, recalled Grattan, that would be a cause for joy, but 'if he happened to fall, his place was sure to be supplied by some one of the company to which he belonged, so that the women . . . had little cause for alarm on this head. The worst that could happen to them was the chance of being in a state of widowhood for a week.' Grattan was more sympathetic to the plight of his male comrades almost sure to be killed in the forlorn hope. Its leader was a young lieutenant, William Mackie. Grattan noted that, when Mackie volunteered, his commanding officer had tears in his eyes. The two men came from the same town. Picton addressed his forlorn hopers and the rest of his storming force with his characteristic bluntness: 'Rangers of Connaught, it is not my intention to expend any powder this evening. We'll do this with the cold iron.'

As the light faded on 19 January, both assault parties set off. They faced the most daunting challenge any footsoldier has ever had to tackle – breaking through a heavily defended fortification in which every weapon, every booby trap, every enemy soldier is primed to repel the attackers. Craufurd gave a stirring speech, which sank deep into Ned Costello's memory: 'Soldiers! The eyes of our country are upon you. Be steady, be cool, be firm in the assault. The town must be yours this night. Once masters of the wall, let your first duty be to clear the ramparts, and in doing this keep together.' Costello 'couldn't help remarking . . . when all most probably were on the brink of being dashed into eternity, a certain solemnity and silence among the men deeper than I had ever witnessed before'. Then he and his comrades followed Craufurd across the open ground towards the outer rampart that ran around the fortress walls. 'Now lads, for the breach!' shouted Craufurd. They were quickly up and over the rampart, jumping down into the wide ditch that ran up to the walls. Some threw down bags full of grass to break their fall. Others climbed down scaling ladders. This was the most dangerous moment: a huge confused mass of men scrambled across the ditch trying to locate the Lesser Breach. Simmons was up at the front just behind the forlorn hope. 'A tremendous fire was opened upon us, and as our column was entering the ditch a . . . magazine on the ramparts near the large breach blew up and ignited a number of live shells, which also exploded and paid no sort of difference to friend or foe.' The French defenders fired everything at their disposal. Guns, grenades and muskets played havoc with the attackers in the ditch below.

Craufurd, commanding as energetically and forcefully as ever, made an obvious target. He was waving his men over the very top of the rampart, which was on the other side of the ditch below the walls. His men remember him being lit up by the glow of explosions all round him. He continued shrieking instructions in that high-pitched voice of his. This brought a great deal of enemy fire on him and a musket ball hit him, passed through his lungs and stuck near his spine. Craufurd fell and rolled down the slope. His ADC, James Shaw Kennedy, managed to drag him, desperately wounded, back to safety. Just before the siege began, on New Year's day, Robert Craufurd had written to his wife that he was longing to see her again and hoped to be reunited with her by the end of the year. He was never to see her again, but he asked his ADC to tell his wife that he was 'quite sure that they would meet in heaven'.

Most of the rest of his men were soon breaking through into the city. When it was Garrety's turn to charge in, he didn't wait for the grass bags but 'jumped down the scarp a depth of eleven feet, and rushed up the *fausse braye* [rampart], under smashing discharge of grape and musketry. The bottom of the ditch was dark and intricate, and the forlorn hope too much to their left . . . But the storming party went straight to the breach . . . when two thirds of the ascent were gained, the leading men, crushed together by the narrowness of the place, staggered under the weight of the enemy's fire.' Costello, at the top of the breach, ran slap into a French gun and fell on a wounded French officer. Another French gunner instantly seized him and 'bent double by the height and heavy person of the Frenchman I began to think that after all my escapes my game was over'. But then in the nick of time some friends came to his assistance including an 'old chum', Wilkie. They disabled the French gunner, but Wilkie suddenly staggered against the gun mortally wounded. 'Seizing me hastily by the hand, and giving it a deadly squeeze, "Ned," he articulated, "It's all up with me," and relaxing his grasp he fell back and expired.' Costello found Wilkie's body the next morning, stripped naked.

At the Greater Breach, the other assault party led by General Mackinnon swept in and had successfully scaled the walls at the top of the breach when a huge French powder magazine exploded. Mackinnon and a few others were thrown hundreds of feet into the air, and limbs and broken bodies showered down on their comrades. 'Every man on the breach at the moment of the explosion perished,' according to Grattan. 'For an instant all was confusion; the blaze of light caused by the explosion resembled a huge meteor, and presented to our sight the havoc which the enemy's fire had caused in our ranks.' The forlorn hope's leader, Lieutenant Mackie, miraculously survived. He and the other Rangers pressed on but fell prey to two French guns placed at the top of the breach. It took a charge of three men, armed with only the bayonets they had stripped off their muskets, to seize the two guns and to secure the breach. Sergeant Pat Brazil and his two companions Swan and Kelly attacked one gun. They 'engaged the French cannoniers hand to hand: a terrific but short combat was the consequence. Swan . . . was met by the two gunners on the right of the gun, but no way daunted, he engaged them and plunged his bayonet into the breast of one . . . but before he could disengage his weapon from his bleeding adversary, the second Frenchman closed upon him, and by a *coup de sabre* severed his left arm from his body a little above the elbow.' Kelly then rushed forward to help, and bayoneted two Frenchmen on the spot. That left just two of the five gunners. Swan was bleeding to death; Brazil made a lunge at one of the Frenchmen, slipped on the bloody ground and ended up bayoneting his opponent as they rolled on the ground. Kelly went for the last one, who ran away only to be killed by some other British soldiers near by.

With the gun now silenced, the attackers were soon in the streets of the town. That didn't stop some Frenchmen fighting on. Lieutenant George Faris was shot in the thigh by a Frenchman, who then tried to bayonet him. Faris sprang forward and seized the Frenchman by the collar, and they struggled desperately until Faris was able to disengage himself enough to use his sabre. 'He pushed the Frenchman from him and ere he could recover himself, he laid his head open nearly to the chin. His sword blade, a heavy, soft, ill-made Portuguese one, was doubled up with the force of the blow and retained some pieces of the skull and clotted hair.' Grattan ran up to see the dead man on the ground and his British assailant, faint from loss of blood, being applauded by his mates: 'the feeling uppermost with them was, that our man had the best of it! It was a shocking sight, but it would be a rather hazardous experiment to begin moralizing at such a moment and in such a place.'

Harry Smith wasn't far away from the explosion. He had raced along the wall after assaulting the Lesser Breach to help the stormers in the Greater Breach. The huge blast wounded Captain Uniacke at his side – they had had supper together a little earlier – and scorched Smith. 'I shall never forget the concussion when it struck me, throwing me back many feet . . . My cocked hat was blown away, my clothes all singed.' But he recovered and reached the other breach, where a great big Connaught Ranger, mistaking him for an enemy, 'seized me by the throat as if I were a kitten, crying out "You French ——." Luckily he left me room in the windpipe to d— his eyes, or the bayonet would have been through me in a moment.' Uniacke, appallingly burned, died three days later. His last words were 'Remember, I was the first man that entered the breach.'

Minutes later Lieutenant John Gurwood, a rare survivor of the forlorn hope, and the man who would later edit Wellington's despatches, sought out the French Governor and arrested him. Smith wrote later – rather snidely – that Gurwood, 'a sharp fellow', had escaped only because he was momentarily stunned and had to let the rest of the forlorn hope overtake him. Just over 1,100 allied soldiers were killed or wounded. The French suffered more than 500 dead and wounded, and another 1,360 were taken prisoner.

The assaulting troops were soon out of control, plundering, burning, abusing the local people. It was nothing to what was to happen just three months later at Badajoz, but it was an ugly episode. Groups of townspeople stood half naked in the street, stripped by the soldiers of all they had. Women went up to British officers and clung to them asking for protection. The officers tried to regain control of their troops. They even came under attack from their men for trying to restore discipline. One young light-infantry officer was appalled. 'If I had not seen, I never could have supposed that British soldiers would become so wild and furious. It was quite alarming to meet groups of them in the street, flushed as they were with drink and desperate in mischief.' Thomas Picton exploded with anger at his men's behaviour. He flew in all directions calling in a voice of thunder on the frantic soldiers to remember that they were 'men, and Englishmen – not savages!' and by exhortations and threats he contrived to bring some back to their senses. Kincaid heard Picton's voice, 'with the power of twenty trumpets . . . proclaim damnation to everybody'.

There was the odd bit of light relief: Grattan and four friends were resting in one house when they heard the crash of something falling in the apartment above. They went up and found a soldier covered in soot. He had been on a plundering expedition, but while he was surveying prospects from the roof of the house he fell down the chimney and was lucky it was large enough 'to admit an elephant to pass down it'. Picton met a band of soldiers who had been on a drinking spree: they called out, 'Well, General, we gave you a cheer last night: it's your turn now!' Picton smiled, raised his hat and replied, 'Here then, you drunken set of brave rascals, hurrah! We'll soon be in Badajoz!'

Costello saw one gang of British looters plunder a house full of giant casks of spirits. They immediately smashed in the tops of the butts, and several of them 'fell into the liquor head foremost and perished, unnoticed by the crowd'. That wasn't all: someone mistakenly dropped a light into one of the casks of spirit and the whole place went up in flames. To many of those who recorded their memories, the looting of Ciudad Rodrigo – and, later, of Badajoz – shamed the British army. But there was a more cynical view, expressed by Grattan, that part of the soldiers' reward after a successful siege was the looting of those things 'which they considered themselves entitled to by "right of conquest". I believe on a service such as the present, there is a sort of tacit acknowledgement of this "right".'

By dawn calm was restored and the shooting stopped. There were piles of bodies in and around the breaches. Ned Costello found the sight 'heartrending in the extreme. The dead lay in heaps, numbers of them stripped . . .' The remains of those who had been blown up in the explosion were 'dreadfully mangled and discoloured . . .

strewed about were dissevered arms and legs'. One corpse brought back a harrowing memory for Donaldson. He remembered a scene on the quayside back home. A crowd of wives had waited in deep anxiety while a lottery was conducted to decide which of them would accompany their husbands to the war. There would only be a handful, six to each hundred. One particular woman, known to be devoted to her husband, was shattered when she drew a blank, and Donaldson watched her tearfully but vainly imploring the ship's captain to allow her to go with Sandy, her husband. In great distress she clung to him and held out her baby for one last kiss from its dad. Convinced that she would never see him again, she bade him 'one last farewell'. That morning at Ciudad Rodrigo Donaldson saw Sandy among the dead. 'When I saw him stretched lifeless on the breach, that scene flashed full upon my memory, and I could not but remark how true his wife's forebodings had turned out.'

Craufurd was taken back to the Convent of San Francisco, where Wellington came to see him. They spent some time together and Craufurd congratulated his Commander in Chief on the successful storming of the town. To which, according to Shaw Kennedy, Wellington replied, 'Yes, a great blow, a great blow . . .', presumably referring not to the siege but to Craufurd's imminent death. Craufurd died of his wounds four days later, in what Wellington called 'the bitterest blow of the war'. He attended Craufurd's funeral when they buried him at the foot of the breach he had helped to carry. Wellington had had his differences with 'Black Bob', who had been insubordinate, reckless and often insolent, but he greatly admired his courage and flair, and recognised that the Light Division under his leadership had become one of the finest fighting forces in the world. Colborne, who was wounded twice in the final assault, rated Craufurd very highly. 'He was a fine fellow, though very stern and tyrannical, but after all, that was the way he got his division into such fine order.' When Craufurd's men were on the march and their commander saw a soldier stepping across a puddle, he would call out, 'Sit down in it, Sir, sit down in it.' Kincaid, one of his junior officers, reckoned that Craufurd's obsession with stern discipline had made him very unpopular with the Light Division 'at the commencement. And it was not until a short time before he was lost to us for ever, that we were capable of appreciating his merits and fully sensible of the incalculable advantages we derived from the perfection of his system.'

Ciudad Rodrigo transformed Wellington's image among the doubters in London. Parliament voted him another bonus of £2,000 and even the Prince Regent honoured him with a new title, Earl of Wellington. Fred Ponsonby wrote home, 'Depend upon it, we shall have Badajoz . . . and the ensuing campaign promises better than any which we have heretofore entered into.'

9

The town's our own. Hurrah!
Badajoz, 1812

WELLINGTON HAD conducted a faultless siege of one of the great frontier fortresses. He now turned his attention to the other, far more forbidding stronghold at Badajoz, 150 miles to the south. The storming of Ciudad Rodrigo had opened up the road to Salamanca and northern Spain; Badajoz commanded the road to Madrid. Wellington was now four years into his campaign. If he was to loosen Napoleon's grip on the Peninsula, he had to crack Badajoz once and for all. But it had ramparts as formidable as any in the world. And Wellington's siege trains had failed there twice before.

His first job was to assemble the artillery that would do the job properly. The year before he had abandoned a hopeless attempt to batter down the walls of Badajoz with a set of old brass guns that were no match for the city's immense stone walls. Now, in February 1812, he had a new set of iron siege guns, sixteen eighteen-pounders and eighteen massive twenty-four-pounders, shipped up from Lisbon and then towed across land to Badajoz. Portuguese militiamen were made to carry the twenty-four-pound balls, one each, a distance of twelve miles 'cursing all the way and back again'. Assembling the gunnery was a giant task, but Wellington knew he now had the men who could do it. Alexander Dickson had masterminded the bombardment of Ciudad Rodrigo. Colonel Fletcher, architect of the Lines of Torres Vedras, was his chief engineer. Even if he still hadn't the full team of dedicated engineers he needed, Wellington was confident that Badajoz could be taken.

Throughout February Wellington sent his army south towards Badajoz, as unobtrusively as he could. Unit by unit the allied army slipped away. To confuse the French, Wellington himself remained very visibly at Ciudad Rodrigo, watching the Spanish repair the

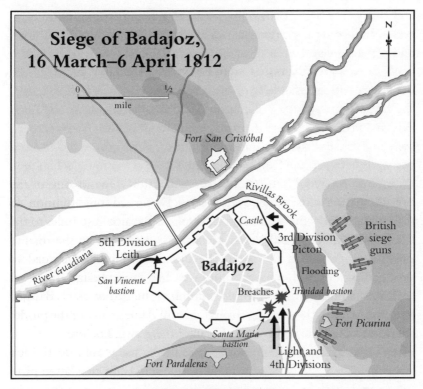

The Siege of Badajoz

breaches. All the time he kept a wary eye on intelligence reports about his enemy's moves. Once again Napoleon made his job easier. Instead of sending Marmont down to help defend Badajoz, he ordered him west towards northern Portugal. Soult, down in the south, believed Badajoz could hold out against a siege. Its commander, a resourceful and imaginative professional, Baron Armand Philippon, had a large garrison of 5,000 men behind walls he believed were virtually impregnable. A soldier for thirty-four years, Philippon had served Napoleon all over Europe and had foiled two earlier attempts by the British to storm Badajoz.

By the middle of March Wellington had quietly redeployed his army and had even managed to enjoy a few days in the saddle chasing hounds. He joined his troops in camp outside Badajoz. He knew the place well already. But he rode around it two or three times to remind himself of the defiant strength of its walls, fifteen feet thick and thirty feet high. Badajoz was one of Europe's most robust fortresses, built over the previous two centuries with five outlying forts and a main perimeter wall of spectacular thickness. Every hundred yards or so a great bastion – eight of them altogether – provided the defenders with a lethal field of fire against the flanks as well as against the front of an assault. Wellington decided to attack in three places. First he would seize Fort Picurina, a small redoubt 500 yards across a valley to the south-east of the city. From there his guns would pound the walls between the Santa María and Trinidad bastions. When they crumbled, he would throw his 4th and Light Divisions into the breach. At the same time, Picton's 3rd Division would attempt to scale with ladders the walls of the castle at the north-east corner, and the 5th Division would storm the bastion of San Vincente in the north-west corner of the walls. It would be a simultaneous three-pronged attack. He hoped the good weather would hold.

Harry Smith suddenly found himself doing what he and most infantrymen hated – digging siege trenches. At the end of his shift, he still found the time to do some hare coursing with his dog Moro, in order to keep the officers' mess supplied with soup. He had an Irish horse he called Paddy. It was, he said, 'a stupid beast of a horse', and got its foot stuck in a warren on one chase and fell on top of him. His fellow Light Division officers thought him lucky to survive. Few escaped working in the trenches, and the day after the digging began the rain came, and didn't stop. 'The elements . . . adopted the cause of the besieged . . . We never were dry the whole time,' said Kincaid. Every man did six hours' digging each day and six hours each night, ankle deep in mud. At least the sodden ground made the digging less obvious. At Ciudad Rodrigo the pickaxes had struck the hard ground with a crack. Here they made a dull thump.

There was one awkward moment when the defenders of Badajoz burst out and assaulted the British trenches. Fortunately William Grattan of the Connaught Rangers had noticed what the commanding officer had not – an unusual amount of bustle on the enemy side. Ignoring the commander, Grattan shouted at the men to drop their shovels and picks and grab their firearms. It was not a moment too soon. A ferocious struggle followed, with the British losing 120 dead and scores more wounded including Richard Fletcher, Wellington's chief engineer. The French escaped with a whole selection of the men's precious entrenching tools. After this encounter John Cooke of the Light Division came across one British soldier who had lost his leg and been left for dead. 'An adventurous Portuguese began to dis-encumber him of his clothes, when the poor soldier opened his eyes in a most imploring manner. The Portuguese had him by the belts, lifting him up, so I gave the humane Portuguese a blow with the back of my sabre, which for a time laid him prostrate by the side of the soldier he was stripping.'

The small outpost of Picurina fell on 25 March after a fierce battle. The British guns could now be hauled forward to within 300 yards of the walls of the city, and the siege proper began. For two weeks some 20,000 cannon balls – around a thousand tons in weight – were hurled at the walls of Badajoz. It took this vast weight of iron shot to produce the tell-tale signs of collapsing masonry that indicated a breach. Tom Garrety was in one of the gun trenches loading sand-bags. They were constantly exposed to French fire. A cannon ball severed the leg of a man right next to him. Moments later a comrade was loading his musket, and 'while the ramrod was in the barrel, the piece was accidentally discharged. The ramrod pierced through his body, and so firmly was the worm-end fixed near the backbone that the strongest man among us was unable to move it.'

The 5th of April was the day Wellington set for the assault on Badajoz. He was up early. No time for hunting today, not until this piece of business was out of the way. They had told him the night before that the guns had almost done their job. With the first light his guns would be pounding again, and he had to see for himself how well their work was done. The bombardment of the bastions of Trinidad and Santa María should by now be taking its toll of the city's south-east corner.

At least the weather was looking up. The ceaseless early-spring rains that had drenched the gun crews and turned their emplacements into mudslides had given way to clear skies. There was more than a hint of the summer heat that would soon burn all the green out of the Extremadura landscape. Wellington's guns had now been dragged so close that the twenty-four-pound balls were rupturing the once strong line of the stone walls. The sharp profile of the fortress which loomed over the flat and empty plain of the Guadiana was showing signs of fraying. Wellington knew the breaches his guns were making would soon be 'practicable'. They would soon offer openings through which his men could try to force their way in.

The French commander Baron Philippon knew it too. He summoned his chief engineer, Colonel Lamare, to a meeting that same morning – minutes after Lamare had toured the battlements and seen the ramparts being pulverised in several places. 'Death was dealt in every direction amongst us . . . the breaches were becoming practicable, the efforts which the workmen made nightly to clear them were ineffectual.' At the meeting Philippon gave his detailed orders for the defence of the breaches. He was well aware of the threat: he had been wounded two days earlier as he went among his men on the bastions urging them 'everywhere to make the most determined resistance' and to 'make the enemy pay with the blood of his best soldiers'. Lamare could tell that the assault was imminent: a long train of British wagons had been spotted loaded with scaling ladders.

Wellington spent some time at the gun line that morning. As usual, he was heedless of his own safety, determined to make his own personal assessment of when the breaches would be ready to assault. He was not inclined to trust the observations of his subordinates. His confidence in his own judgement and his patent contempt for any delegation of authority had long since become a fact of life for his commanders, though many still resented it. He decided that the assault on Badajoz would take place that night. The two key breaches would be tackled by the Light Division (Santa María bastion) and the 4th Division (La Trinidad). Thomas Picton, the 3rd Division commander, had the most challenging task of all. The walls of the castle which his men had to scale with ladders were thirty feet high and unbreached. Picton was nonetheless determined that his men would be first into the city.

Wellington issued a great sheaf of orders. With his usual attention to detail he was going to leave as little as he could to chance. Each unit's timetable was itemised. The men of the 4th and Light Divisions should 'not advance beyond the shelter afforded by the quarries on the left of the road, till they shall have seen the heads of the advanced guards ascend the breaches'. The men were to 'leave their knapsacks in camp'. And Picton's 3rd Division, which was to attack the castle walls, would take 'all the long ladders in the Engineers' park and must be attended by 12 carpenters with axes and six miners with crowbars'.

Wellington's men were in that mood of feverish expectation and anxiety that came before a clash in which they knew that many would die. 'Although there was a certainty', wrote John Kincaid, the wry Scots subaltern, 'of about one man in every three being knocked down . . . so great was the rage for passports into eternity . . . that even the officers' servants insisted on taking their places within the ranks.'

The men who would form the perilous forlorn hopes made the best of their last few hours before an ordeal they knew they had little chance of surviving. Bugler William Green would attack with the Light Division, and he like all forlorn hopers was given the day off. He went down to the river 'for a good bathe. I thought I would have a clean skin whether killed or wounded.' Ned Costello, the Irish corporal, whose bravado had not been dented by the two leg wounds he had suffered on the River Côa two years earlier, had volunteered for the Light Division's forlorn hope. He would remember the battle for Badajoz as 'one of the most sanguinary and awful engagements on the records of any country'. Lieutenant Harvest was to command the Light Division's forlorn hope and John Cooke watched him that afternoon 'sucking an orange . . . and very thoughtful . . . He observed "My mind is made up; I am sure to be killed." He was killed!' One of the main assault parties, which would follow behind the forlorn hope, would be commanded by an elderly Irish major, Peter O'Hare, who also knew the odds against surviving: 'A Lieutenant Colonel or cold meat within a few hours,' he confided to a fellow officer.

The air of agonised suspense was heightened at 4.00 p.m. when Wellington decided to postpone the attack until the following day. The formidable obstacles that Philippon and his staff had piled up in the breaches persuaded Wellington's engineers to create another breach between the two main ones. The breaches and the ditches in front of them were full of horrific mantraps. Sets of spikes were fixed in the ground, sometimes concealed beneath water; large wooden beams – so-called *chevaux de frise* – bristled with sword blades. Mines were laid with fuses that could be lit from behind the breaches. And on the battlements, defenders were ready with barrels of powder and what were known as carcasses – bundles of fire – which would be rolled down to ignite among the attackers. Philippon had also organised the damming of the small river, the Rivillas, that flowed past the walls, so that part of the approach to the breaches would be flooded.

The 6th of April was a dry, very still day and the night that followed was very dark. Wellington set 10 p.m. as the time for the assaults on the breaches to begin. Moments before that hour the men in the forlorn hopes began to steal forward. The longer they could retain an element of surprise, the further they would get through the ditches and up through the debris of the breaches before the enemy reacted. All they could hear above the soft pad of their own footsteps was the noise of frogs croaking. Green, ordered to carry his bugle at the head of one of the columns, had never felt such a sense of horror before, and thought to himself, 'You'll be in hell before daylight.'

The attackers crept across the ground that sloped towards the ditches without attracting attention. But the ditches were deep, and the French had made sure there was a long drop from the rim of the ditch to its bottom. The assaulting British threw down their large bags of grass to break the fall. But the French on the ramparts heard the clinking of arms as the attackers leaped down into the ditch or slid down ladders. The cry went up, 'Les voilà! There they are!' Instantly the defenders triggered their mines. They propelled fire bombs into the ditch and transformed the dark night into a blaze of light. The attackers were illuminated as they raced forward. They were now totally exposed to a fusillade from French muskets, mortars and guns firing grapeshot.

Costello was carrying a ladder with three others. They were all shot dead beside him and the full weight of the ladder fell on him. 'I fell backward with the grass bag on my breast. The remainder of the stormers rushed up, regardless of my cries or of those of the wounded around me, for by this time our men were falling fast. Many in passing were shot and fell upon me so that I was actually drenched in blood.' The ditch in front of the Trinidad bastion was flooded with water and scores of men drowned. Costello found himself up to his neck in water. But he was a good swimmer and managed to clamber out of the far side of the ditch and make for the breach. One young officer described the horrific carnage in the ditch: he heard 'shrieks uttered in wild despair as [men] vainly struggled against a watery grave with limbs convulsed'. All this time the noise was deafening: on top of the gunfire and the screams and groans of the dying and wounded the war-cries and yells of the soldiers spurred each other on. And from the ramparts the French taunted the exhausted attackers with shouts of 'Come on into Badajoz!' and 'Try again!'

William Lawrence was another forlorn hoper. He got as far as the breach and was hit three times – two shots in the leg, and one in his side, which would have killed him if it hadn't been stopped by his metal canteen. In front of him he saw *chevaux de frise*, 'from behind which the garrison opened a deadly fire on us. Vain attempts were made to remove this fearful obstacle during which my left hand was dreadfully cut by one of the blades of the chevaux de frise, but finding no success in that quarter, we were forced to retire for a time.' Lawrence, bleeding profusely, managed to crawl to the rear and fell in with Wellington, who asked him which regiment he belonged to. 'I told him the Fortieth, and that I had been one of the Forlorn Hope. He inquired as to the extent of my wounds, and if any of our troops had got into the town, and I said "No" and I did not think they ever would.' One of Wellington's staff then bound up his leg with a silk handkerchief and directed him towards the doctor.

Wellington was watching with mounting concern. He knew that Badajoz was a far tougher nut to crack than Ciudad Rodrigo, but it was quickly apparent that the depth of the ditches, the height of the walls and the skill and fury of Philippon's defenders were costing him far more than the earlier siege. But he was single-mindedly determined to press forward, no matter what the cost. Hundreds were already dead and dying, and yet the breaches were holding and the castle's walls were unscaled. The French defenders were now venturing forward from the ramparts on to the piles of rubble in the breaches. They fired their muskets at the attackers, who made easy targets caught in the cramped cauldron of fire below.

William Green, the bugler, was wounded by a ball that went through his thigh as well as through the hand that was holding the bugle. He collapsed before he had even reached the ditch, heard his bugle major sounding the advance and managed to get his bugle to his lips to repeat the sound. But an officer with a drawn sword came up beside him, shouting, 'Desist blowing that bugle: you are drawing all the fire on my men.' Green protested that he was only doing his job and managed to stagger away into the hands of a surgeon in the rear. He was in such pain that he pleaded with a surgeon to cut off his hand, but amputation was refused and Green was invalided out of the army. The wound healed but the hand remained disabled, and he was eventually awarded £15 compensation for having effectively lost the use of a limb.

Picton's 3rd Division, which had the much more challenging job of scaling the castle walls, was faring no better. The old warrior was bent on beating the other divisions into the city. So when he heard the commotion from the assaults on the breaches way over to his left, he accused his guide of losing his way and came close to striking him in anger. But the guide had brought them to the right place – just below the castle. They were soon swarming around in the ditch beneath its high walls. Their only way up was by ladder and the French defenders had the relatively simple job of dropping all manner of explosive and musket fire on the wretched attackers directly below them and bayoneting British soldiers who managed to climb to the top. Joseph Donaldson of the 94th Scots was eager to climb, but the ladders got so crowded that many of them broke and 'the poor fellows who had nearly reached the top were precipitated a height of thirty or forty feet, and were impaled on the bayonets of their comrades below'. George Hennell, the son of a ribbon-maker in Coventry, had managed to make it to the Peninsula with a letter of introduction to Picton. He was just approaching the foot of a ladder when a twenty-four-pounder shot landed very near him. 'Twelve men sank together with a groan that would have shook to the soul the nerves of the oldest soldier who ever carried a musket. I believe ten of them never rose again, the nearest was within a foot of me . . .'

Picton was quickly among his men. He reminded them that they had never been defeated and that now was the moment to 'conquer or die'. But then he was struck by a ball in the groin. One officer who was with him believed the ball had first struck the earth. But the blow was severe. He didn't fall or bleed, but in a short time became very faint and almost insensible. Picton remained in this state for nearly twenty minutes. And then, when the pain subsided a little, he refused medical aid and took command again. 'If we cannot win the castle, let's die upon the walls,' he cried. This encouraged his men to lay fresh ladders against the wall. William Grattan, whose Connaught Rangers were in Picton's assault party, wrote that although the general was not loved by his men, they respected him, 'and his appeal as well as his unshaken front, did wonders in changing the desperate state of the division'.

Back at the breaches some of the most stalwart in the assault force, including Costello and Major O'Hare, managed to battle their way beyond the ditch and place their ladders against the walls around the Light Division's breach. But that was as far as they got. O'Hare was floored by a musket shot in the chest, and Costello got a blow that sent him crashing down the ladder on to the ground below. 'Among the dead and wounded bodies around me I endeavoured to screen myself from the enemy's shot . . . The fire continued to blaze over me in all its horrors, accompanied by screams, groans and shouts, the crashing of stones and the falling of timbers. For the first time in many years I uttered something like a prayer.'

The desperate struggle went on in the dark. It was a scene of unimaginable slaughter. No night of the entire Peninsular War would be as bloody as this. Again and again waves of British soldiers threw themselves into the breaches only to be gunned down or skewered on the hideous obstructions studded with spikes and sword blades. Harry Smith, never one to miss a fight where he saw one, described the struggle as 'most murderous. We flew down the ladders and rushed at the breach. But we were broken and carried no weight with us although every soldier was a hero. The breach was covered by a breastwork from behind and ably defended at the top by chevaux de frise of sword blades, sharp as razors, chained to the ground, while the ascent to the top of the breach was covered with planks with sharp nails in them.'

The British made desperate efforts to break through. Kincaid watched officers form 'groups of fifty to a hundred men at the foot of the breach' and then try to 'carry it by desperate bravery. And fatal as it proved to each gallant band in succession, yet as fast as one dissolved another was formed.' The air was heavy with the whiff of gunpowder, and the odour of death was everywhere – overpowering even the stench of an army that had spent three weeks on the same piece of land. Uniforms, usually a striking contrast in proud bright colours, now all merged indistinguishably, spattered with blood and grime. Even Jonathan Leach's powers of description were sorely taxed by the horror of what he saw at the Light Division's breach. 'The discharge of grape shot and musketry with buck shot in addition to bullets, the hand grenades, rafters of wood and various weapons of destruction hurled from the ramparts on the heads of the assailants in the ditch . . . was of so dreadful and destructive a nature as to beggar all description and to render it a hopeless undertaking for the most gifted person to depict in true colours.'

Wellington's own account of the slaughter was lavish in its praise for his men's courage. He said the 4th and Light Divisions advanced to assault the breaches 'led by their gallant officers with the utmost intrepidity. But such was the nature of the obstacles prepared by the enemy at the top and behind the breaches and so determined their resistance that our troops could not establish themselves within the place. These efforts were repeated till after twelve at night . . .'

George Simmons, another Rifles officer, one of the most seasoned veterans of Wellington's Peninsular campaign, estimated, with under-standable exaggeration, that the breaches were assaulted 'fifty times' without effect. But then, in a picture that rings frighteningly true, he remembered that from the place he entered the ditch to near the top of the breach the ground was covered with dead and dying soldiers. 'If a man fell wounded, ten to one he never rose again, for the volleys of musketry and grape shot that were poured amongst us made our situation too horrid for description. I had seen some fighting but nothing like this . . . we could do the besieged little injury . . . we were ordered to move away . . .'

The state of Wellington's attacking force was now worse than tragic. It was pathetic. Two thousand of his best men were already lost – and still Badajoz held out. Wellington himself was standing on a small hill near the breaches. Those who were with him remember hearing the voices of the British becoming fainter and those of the

French becoming stronger, mocking their attackers, shouting at them to 'come on into Badajoz'. Officers were coming up and reporting no progress. Surgeon James McGrigor looked at Wellington's face lit up by the glare of a torch. 'I shall never forget it . . . The jaw had fallen, and the face was of unusual length, while the torchlight gave his countenance a lurid aspect: but still the expression of the face was firm.' Robert Blakeney found himself near Wellington and his staff on one occasion. They were 'screened from the enemy's direct fire, but within range of shells. One of his staff sat down by his side with a candle to enable the General to read and write all his communications and orders . . .' Blakeney wasn't near enough to know what reports Wellington was receiving, 'yet it was very evident that the information which they conveyed was far from flattering; and the recall on the bugle was again and again repeated'.

Suddenly, with hope almost extinguished, the prospects for the British attackers were transformed. Just before midnight Colonel Henry Ridge, of the 5th (Northumberland) Foot in Picton's division assaulting the castle, managed to find a spot where the walls were a little lower and succeeded in placing his ladder against the sill of an embrasure on the ramparts. The weight of the men clambering up behind him pinned the ladder against the wall in spite of all the efforts of the French to push it away. Ridge climbed to the top protected by his men's bayonets and swords. Suddenly he was on the battlements and a rush of comrades followed him. Another who was first to the top of a neighbouring ladder was William Mackie, who had led the forlorn hope at Ciudad Rodrigo, but, perhaps because he was a Connaught Ranger, was still unrewarded by Picton. Once over the wall, in a fury of revenge for all the night's bloodshed, the British scythed through the defenders and were soon pressing them back towards the castle gate that led into the town centre. Another early stormer of the castle, Lieutenant Macpherson, was struck by a musket ball as he scaled the walls but luckily it hit a Spanish dollar in his pocket and only broke two of his ribs. He managed to summon up enough strength to shin up the castle's flagstaff and tear down the French flag, substituting his own red jacket.

Lieutenant Robert Knowles was the third man up one ladder. A corporal was first but was instantly killed. 'On leaping into the place

I was knocked down by a shower of grape which broke my sword into a hundred pieces.' He seized the corporal's musket and 'with the assistance of eight or ten men, who had now got into the fort, I charged along the ramparts destroying or disarming all who opposed us.'

Minutes later an officer tore up on his horse to where Wellington's group was standing and cried, 'Where is Lord Wellington?' Wellington asked who it was, and the man replied that he was Picton's aide de camp, Lieutenant Tyler. 'Well?' said Wellington. 'General Picton has taken the castle.' 'Then the place is ours,' said the Commander in Chief, in immense relief.

Philippon, the French commander, attempted to reinforce the castle, but he was too late. Meanwhile Wellington's 5th Division way over to the north-west had managed to scale the walls of the San Vincente bastion and now advanced into the town. Philippon, in danger of being caught between them and the victorious Picton to the east, escaped across the bridge to the north bank of the River Guadiana, where he surrendered.

The moment Wellington heard of Picton's success – at midnight – he ordered the 4th and Light Divisions to retire to their start lines. But the memory of the men on the ground is that, although they were told about Picton's feat, they were soon ordered to return to the breaches and redouble their efforts to storm them. Kincaid suggests that for a time – until Picton's men actually broke into the town through the castle gate – the French defenders of the breaches fought on. Simmons, utterly spent, was lying on the grass when a staff officer rode up and told him Wellington wanted the Light Division to return immediately and attack the breaches. Harry Smith remembers Wellington's ADC, Fitzroy Somerset, riding up to him and telling him that Wellington had ordered the 4th and Light Divisions to storm again.

> 'The Devil,' says I, 'Why we have had enough. We are all kicked to pieces.'
>
> Lord Fitzroy says 'I dare say, but you must try again.'
>
> I smiled and said 'If we could not succeed with whole fresh and unscathed divisions we are likely to make a poor show of it now. But we will try with all our might.'

So again they advanced, though by the time Simmons got to the breaches 'only a few random shots were fired and we entered without opposition . . . the place was given up to be plundered and pillaged'.

The sack of Badajoz that followed was one of the worst orgies of military indiscipline in British military history. Wellington's men had lost countless comrades, and the 'Frenchies', their women and the thousands of Spanish inhabitants, who seemed to the maddened British to be indistinguishable from the French, were going to pay for it. Costello managed to drag himself through the blades of the *chevaux de frise* and into the town with the blood from his wound still dripping down his face. And there he witnessed total uproar and confusion. 'The shouts and oaths of drunken soldiers in quest of more liquor, the reports of firearms and crashing in of doors, together with the appalling shrieks of the hapless women, might have induced anyone to believe himself in the region of the damned.' At one stage Costello was on the point of shooting a French soldier who had threatened him but who was quickly disarmed. His first instinct was to avenge his own wounds and the deaths of his comrades, but as his finger was about to press the trigger the Frenchman 'fell upon his knees and implored mercy. The next moment the rifle dropped from my hand, and I felt a degree of shame that a feeling of irritation should have nearly betrayed me into the commission of a crime for which I could never have forgiven myself.' In their frantic orgy of drunkenness and plunder the British soldiers even fired on each other in order to grab booty. One nunnery was subjected to wholesale rape. George Hennell reported that 'one of our officers saw a man go among a number of women and force off all their ear-rings. Those that would not give way he broke off a bit of their ear.'

But there were flickers of humanity as well. Two young ladies approached John Kincaid and Harry Smith and appealed to them to protect them from British troops, who had just assaulted them. They had blood trickling down their necks where their ear rings had been torn off them. Kincaid remarked that the younger woman was one of 'delicate freshness . . . irresistibly attractive . . . to look at her was to love her'. But before he could do anything about it, young Smith beat him to it, proposed to the young woman, who was fourteen years old, and married her three days later in the presence of Wellington. 'Impudent fellow,' observed Kincaid. But Harry and Juana Smith were to remain happily married for a lifetime. In his own autobiography Smith confesses to being that '"impudent fellow" . . . and if any reward is due to a soldier, never was one so honoured and distinguished as I have been by this dear child . . . From that day to this she has been my guardian angel.'

The looting of Badajoz went on for three whole days. Wellington rode into the midst of it all on the evening of the day following the storming of the town, when his men were still rampaging through it. A small group of drunken soldiers gave him a cheer and fired a volley over his head. Costello saw them gathered round the general holding bottles with their tops knocked off and shouting, 'Old Boy – will you drink? The town's our own. Hurrah!' Wellington issued an order that evening for the looting to stop and had a gallows erected, presumably intended as a deterrent. But his attitude to the horrors his soldiers committed has long been the subject of debate. He did instruct the Provost Marshal 'to execute any man he may find in the act of plunder'. He expressed his revulsion at the pillage, but there was little sign that his order was promptly carried out. His men's rampage eventually petered out of its own accord. If Wellington was, in principle, opposed to and appalled by the excesses of his troops, he did occasionally betray signs of ambivalence. He was to write later that there was no denying that the sacking of a town after a siege could have the effect of encouraging less resistance when an army set out to storm another town. Costello has his own gloss on it: 'The men who besiege a town, when once they get a footing within its walls, flushed by victory, hurried on by the desire of liquor and maddened by drink, they stop at nothing. They are literally mad and hardly conscious of what they do in such a state of excitement. I do not state this in justification: I only remark on what I have observed human nature to be on these occasions.' Kincaid and Donaldson were both clearly under the impression that there was an accepted, if unspoken, right of plunder. Kincaid observed, 'the men were permitted to enjoy themselves for the remainder of the day'. And Donaldson remarked, 'we were allowed to enter the town for the purpose of plundering it'.

Whether or not Wellington believed there was some justification for the way his men behaved, the fact remains that the looting persisted for three days and no decisive action was taken by the Commander in Chief to stop it. Another indication of his thinking came in a letter to Lord Liverpool, the Secretary for War, two months later. He suggested that part of the explanation for the 'outrages committed' by British soldiers was due to the low levels of pay handed out to non-commissioned officers, which he believed made them 'as little to be depended upon as the private soldiers themselves'. He urged the government to pay the corporals and sergeants, upon whom discipline largely depended, a more generous wage.

There is further controversy about Wellington's conduct of the siege of Badajoz. Some argue that the final assault and its aftermath would not have been so fierce and bloody if he had spent several more days wearing down the defences before giving the order to attack. But Wellington was determined to make Badajoz his, and Soult's army was dangerously close to moving in to relieve it. A day or two more and Wellington's army might have had to face in two directions at the same time – fighting both Soult and Philippon. One lesson that Wellington was finally able to drive home to the government in London in his account of the battle was that the British army now deserved a proper corps of miners and sappers – a new Corps of Engineers. The particular expertise, commitment and stamina required of those who had to dig the trenches for the siege guns was something that Wellington believed was beyond the call of duty of ordinary soldiers. They had endured the misery of it in the sieges of Badajoz and Ciudad Rodrigo and he was adamant that it would not happen again. 'The truth is', he wrote to a colleague the day after the storming of Badajoz, 'that equipped as we are, the British army are not capable of carrying on a regular siege.' He made it clear that with proper engineering protection the siege guns could be brought up much nearer their targets to give closer support to the assault troops.

In taking Badajoz, Wellington had achieved one of his most important victories. The speed of his successful storming contrasted sharply with the disarray in the French high command. Two entire armies – under Soult and Marmont – had been in the area but Napoleon had ordered Marmont elsewhere, and Soult chose not to move to the immediate relief of Philippon. Wellington had proved himself yet again a master of strategic manoeuvre and logistics in moving his entire army and siege train across western Spain without being forced into battle by the French. He had captured the town that controlled access to central Spain. But it was at a huge cost – 5,000 British casualties, 3,000 of them in the actual assault. He wept openly when he visited the worst parts of the battlefield on the morning after the storming. In tears over the mangled bodies in the breaches he encountered Picton, who was limping around after his wound. 'I bit my lips and did everything I could to stop myself for I was ashamed he should see it, but I could not, and he so little entered into my feelings that he said "Good God, what is the matter?"' It was one of those rare occasions when Wellington allowed his mask of imperturbability to slip and reveal that even he could be moved by the horror of war.

Wellington knew that if he owed his triumph at Badajoz to any single man it was Thomas Picton. Picton in turn recognised his debt to the Connaught Rangers, whom he had angrily accused of misconduct back in 1809. Since then he had been impressed by their conduct at Fuentes d'Oñoro. And now during the looting of Badajoz, when one drunken private soldier shouted at him, 'Are we the Connaught Robbers now?', he replied, 'No, you are the Connaught Heroes.'

Badajoz had seen as much heroism as any siege in British history. And in a letter to Lord Liverpool Wellington wrote that the capture of Badajoz 'affords as strong an instance of the gallantry of our troops as has ever been displayed. But I greatly hope that I shall never again be the instrument of putting them to such a test as that to which they were put last night.'

10

Marmont est perdu
Salamanca, 1812

WITHIN THE SPACE of twelve weeks Wellington had swept away the two great bastions that protected Spain from attack. The way was now clear for him to stab deep into the heart of Napoleon's Iberian empire. The French Emperor remained blind to the threat from Wellington. Spain was a sideshow. His mind was on a far grander horizon. He was about to embark on his most audacious campaign of all, an invasion of Russia. One glance at the balance of forces in Spain convinced him that he had more than enough troops there. But most of them were pinned down in the north, east and south tackling the Spanish revolt. In western Spain only Marmont with 50,000 men stood between Wellington and Madrid. Wellington's task was to continue the piecemeal strategy that had so far served him well and to bring Marmont to battle without prompting all French armies in Spain to combine against him. Marmont was in Salamanca, 100 miles to the east of Ciudad Rodrigo. The magnificent old university city would be Wellington's next target. He would move against it in the summer when the fields either side of the road would be rich in grain to feed his men and horses. If he could isolate and destroy Marmont at Salamanca, he would open the way to the Spanish capital.

The only sizeable actions in the spring of 1812 were cavalry battles. In the week after Badajoz fell Fred Ponsonby helped win a major engagement at Villagarcía eighty miles south-east of Badajoz. He was in temporary command of a brigade – three regiments including his own 12th Light Dragoons. A second brigade was commanded by another up-and-coming cavalryman, John Gaspard Le Marchant. The two of them combined to surprise and trap a smaller French force. William Tomkinson was one of Ponsonby's men. He watched as Ponsonby's three regiments were suddenly joined by one of Le Marchant's heavy cavalry regiments, which 'completely upset the left flank of the enemy'. They all charged at the same time and 'success was complete. The view of the enemy from the top of the hill, the quickness of the advance on the enemy, with the spirit of the men in leaping the wall, and the charge immediately afterwards was one of the finest things, I ever saw.' The British overall cavalry commander, Lieutenant General Sir Stapleton Cotton, wrote to Wellington that Ponsonby and Le Marchant had commanded their brigades with 'much gallantry and judgment'. It was an accolade that Ponsonby relished.

Villagarcía apart, Wellington was still concerned by his cavalry commanders' tendency to overreach themselves. He hadn't forgotten Ponsonby's reckless charge at Talavera, and only two months after Villagarcía an over-ambitious cavalry charge at Manguilla ended in heavy casualties. Wellington declared that he was 'never more annoyed'. Judgement was the quality that he believed was most lacking in his cavalry commanders. He observed that British cavalry officers had acquired 'the trick of galloping at everything, and . . . galloping back as fast as they gallop at the enemy. They never consider their situation, never think of manoeuvring before an enemy – so little that one would think they cannot manoeuvre, excepting on Wimbledon Common . . .' Wellington's cavalry long resented this despatch and his continuing doubts about their conduct. But he was never to shake off his suspicion that they were incapable of self-discipline. His scepticism would become a lifelong conviction after the heroic but suicidal cavalry charges at Waterloo. It is one of the puzzles of history that Wellington, an able horseman himself, who commanded all his battles from the saddle, never managed to raise his cavalry to the same level of professionalism as his infantry.

By the middle of June Wellington was ready to advance on Salamanca. The spring rains had done their work. The rich farmland on either side of the road was bursting with fresh corn and there was plenty of food and forage for the horses. When the army arrived at Salamanca on 17 June, Marmont had moved out of the city leaving a garrison of 800 men in three forts. Over the next few days the two main armies converged north of the city – Wellington on the heights of San Cristóbal, Marmont on the plain to the east. Wellington had the stronger position and was clearly hoping that Marmont would attack him or attempt to rescue or reinforce his men in the three forts. The two armies were just 800 yards apart, and there was some skirmishing between the two sides, but no open battle. On the 21st Wellington was up early, clearly hoping to tempt Marmont to attack him. He had the advantage of higher ground and larger numbers. Even his capricious cavalry would have free range of the flat ground around the French forces. 'Damned tempting! I have a great mind to attack 'em,' he was heard to say. But he didn't. Wellington was not a man to attack unless he saw an overwhelming advantage or was faced with no alternative.

Marmont too was tempted, but that evening he agreed with those of his generals who urged him not to engage Wellington when the British commander was in a strong defensive position. He withdrew a few miles to the east of Salamanca and manoeuvred for a few days looking for an opportunity to relieve the forts. But on 27 June he heard that the forts had surrendered after ten days of resistance which had cost Wellington 500 men. He now pulled back fifty miles across the River Duero (as the Douro is called in Spain) and for the next few weeks the two armies faced each other across the river. Fred Ponsonby wrote to his mother: 'We have been looking at each other without our being able to get at them or their wishing to get at us.'

In mid-July Marmont received a letter from King Joseph, Napoleon's brother, in Madrid urging him to do battle with Wellington. In a sharp reversal of plan he ordered the French back southwards across the Duero on 15 July. The move surprised Wellington and soon both armies were heading south-west towards Salamanca. Wellington kept a constant watch on the movement of the French, anxious not to let them overtake him. At one point he and Marshal Beresford were present when some French cavalry charged Fred Ponsonby's 12th Light Dragoons and pushed them back to a ford, exposing Wellington and Beresford to attack from the French. The two commanders quickly drew their swords and John Cooke watched from only a few yards away. 'Wellington was in the thick of it, and only escaped with difficulty. He . . . crossed the ford with his straight sword drawn, at full speed, and smiling. I did not see his Lordship when the charge first took place, but he had a most narrow escape . . .' Cooke was only twenty yards from the ford when 'one of our dragoons came to the water with a frightful wound: his jaw was entirely separated from the upper part of his face, and hung on his breast: the poor fellow made an effort to drink in that wretched condition'.

The cat-and-mouse game went on for days, the two armies shadowing each other on parallel courses only a few hundred yards apart. Alexander Gordon observed: 'It was a beautiful sight seeing the 2 armies moving together . . . 100,000 men manoeuvring so near to one another that one could hardly suppose it possible they were not coming to action.' Simmons saw at not more than 500 yards' distance a 'dense mass of Frenchmen moving in the same order, horse, foot and artillery. It was quite ridiculous to see two hostile armies so close without coming to blows.' But still neither felt strong enough to attack the other. Marmont was determined to keep threatening to turn Wellington's flank and cut off his communication with Ciudad Rodrigo and Portugal. Wellington had to protect his supply line, but as he reported to London, 'I have . . . determined . . . not to fight an action, unless under very advantageous circumstances, or it should become absolutely necessary.'

On 21 July the two armies were still warily eyeing each other and sliding south-west hoping to outflank each other. Occasionally shots were exchanged. Fred Ponsonby wrote to his mother that commanding the British rearguard was 'very warm work for 15 hours. We lost a few men and horses by a cannonade and skirmish but we made a charge upon their tirailleurs and knocked most of them out.'

Both armies splashed across the Tormes river, which makes a wide curve around Salamanca. 'Luckily', said Simmons, 'we got over before the rain, which immediately afterwards came down in torrents. The night became excessively dark, the whole army groping their way, up to their knees in mud . . .' William Wheeler happened to move away from the shelter of an old oak tree for a moment to get a light for his pipe. A stroke of lightning brought the tree down on the very spot where he had been standing. 'This was a lucky pipe of tobacco,' he wrote.

By the evening of the 21st the allied army was established on a

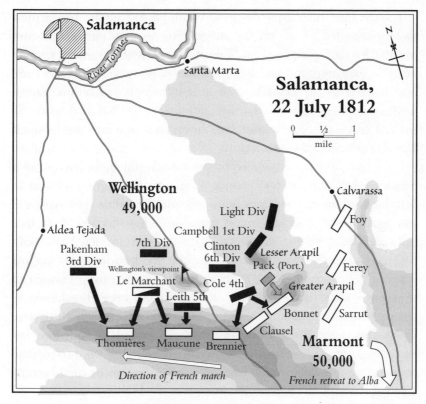

The Battle of Salamanca

ridge with its left flank at Santa Marta on the Tormes and its right on a hill called the Lesser Arapil. The French faced them – looking west across a valley from the village of Calvarassa with their left flank near a higher hill called the Greater Arapil. These two hills, called locally Los Hermanitos, the Brothers, dominated the landscape. Both Wellington, who already possessed the Lesser Arapil, and Marmont quickly saw the importance of seizing the Greater Arapil. On the morning of the 22nd they raced to occupy the hill. Marmont's men had less far to go and got there first.

It was then that Wellington displayed a rare moment of hesitation and indecision. His reaction to Marmont's seizure of the Greater Arapil was to do something he had been reluctant to do in the Peninsula so far. He decided to abandon his previous tactic of waiting for the French to attack him and ordered two of his divisions to assault the hill. But then in discussion with his staff he allowed himself to be persuaded to call off the attack. This was not the Wellington most of his staff were used to. William Tomkinson remembered him being 'a little nervous' and allowing himself to be talked out of it by Marshal Beresford. 'Lord W is so little influenced, or indeed allows any person to say a word, that his attending to the Marshal was considered singular.' But within two hours any sign of doubt in the British commander would vanish.

The two hills now became pivots round which the two armies began to deploy, each one making a right angle. Marmont began to shift his army southwards around the Greater Arapil and then towards the west. Wellington had found the ideal command post high on a hill called the Teso de San Miguel. From there he could see Marmont begin to extend his army across the hills to the south. He had to match the French marshal's every move. He shifted five of his seven divisions – each of around five or six thousand men – back behind the ridge and then swung them round to face south. One of his divisions, the 3rd, and some cavalry he moved way off to the west – to the village of Aldea Tejada, again completely out of sight of the French. He was determined to protect his access to the road back to Ciudad Rodrigo. The 3rd, now known as the Fighting Division, had successfully scaled the walls of the castle at Badajoz under Sir Thomas Picton. Picton was gravely ill with fever but had been talking of forcing himself to lead his division even though he could hardly stand. But when he heard that Wellington had given temporary command to one of the rare men Picton respected, Wellington's brother-in-law Major General Sir Edward 'Ned' Pakenham, he capitulated: 'I am glad he has to lead my brave fellows; they will have plenty of their favourite amusement with him at their head.'

At 11.30 a.m., with most of his divisions now ready to turn west around the Greater Arapil, Marmont climbed to the top and scanned the horizon. He had been told that Wellington's baggage train was already heading west. He now saw clouds of dust way off in that direction and assumed that these were British troops marching off to Ciudad Rodrigo. This prompted him to make a disastrous move. What he had seen was the dust thrown up by Pakenham's 3rd Division and its accompanying cavalry. Far from retreating to Ciudad

Rodrigo, it was now poised to defend Wellington's right flank. Marmont ordered his divisions to begin probing towards the west. But he was sending his men into a trap. Wellington – after a night sleeping out in a downpour – turned up in his blue frock coat and cocked hat for a late breakfast in a farm overlooking the landscape. He gave his telescope to one of his aides and tucked into a few mouthfuls of cold meat. He had hardly begun to chew when one of his aides said, 'The enemy are in motion, my Lord.' 'Very well, observe what they are doing,' replied Wellington. After about a minute the ADC said, 'I think they are extending to their left.' 'The devil they are,' said Wellington, springing to his feet. 'Give me the glass quickly.' He took it, and for a short time earnestly scanned the French moves. There in the sloping scrubland west of the Arapiles he could see the French forces moving west across his front. One French division, General Maucune's, halted more or less opposite the British line, but that of General Thomières did not stop but marched on west – greatly extending Marmont's line from east to west with every minute that passed. 'Come,' he exclaimed, 'I think this will do at last.' Then, to his Spanish liaison officer, General Miguel de Álava, he said, 'Mon cher Álava, Marmont est perdu [Marmont is lost].' And chucking a chicken bone over his shoulder he was off.

Leaping on his horse Wellington rode off to Aldea Tejada, the small village about three miles west of his command post where Ned Pakenham had taken up position. Wellington rode fast, ignoring the fact that his staff found it hard to keep up with him. It didn't matter because he was going to deliver his orders in person. Besides, Pakenham was only the first of his commanders he had to give orders to. Every second counted. Wellington rode in among Pakenham's troops, 'quite unruffled in his manner, and as calm as if the battle about to be fought was nothing more than an ordinary assemblage of the troops for a field day'. 'Ned,' he said, 'move on with the 3rd Division, take those heights in your front and drive everything before you.' 'I will, my Lord,' replied Pakenham – asking only to shake his brother-in-law by the hand before he set off. Wellington swung his horse round and galloped back, stopping briefly to order some cavalry units to support Pakenham's attack. Now that he had thrown Pakenham against Marmont's extreme left, he had to direct his other units at the rest of the French line. As far as he could he would exercise the tightest possible personal control over each element of the battle.

On the other side of the field Marshal Marmont had spotted the sudden weakness of his army on the left. He saw Thomières marching off west, way beyond Maucune's division, and rode off to attempt to correct the mistake. But he was unlucky. As he rode down the side of the Greater Arapil and headed west, a British shell landed right by him and severely wounded him in the arm and chest. A rumour quickly flew around that he was dead.

With the French commander incapacitated, no one warned Thomières of the impending danger. Pakenham's 3rd Division managed to approach completely unseen. The French were moving from left to right across the front of Pakenham's advancing troops. There was a gap of a few hundred yards of open ground between the marching French columns and the trees which provided cover for Pakenham's advance. First the cavalry burst out and charged across the gap, then Pakenham's three infantry brigades emerged from the trees rapidly forming into lines to bring every musket to bear as they approached. The French, taken terrifyingly by surprise, reacted quickly. They managed to shoot down a few of the charging horsemen, and Thomières shouted for his guns to move forward and hit the British infantry before they could close the gap. Joseph Donaldson, advancing with the 94th Scots, said the French 'shot and shell were now making dreadful havoc. A Portuguese cadet who was attached to our regiment received a shell in the centre of his body, which bursting at the same instant, literally blew him to pieces. Another poor fellow receiving a grape shot across his belly, his bowels protruded, and he was obliged to apply both hands to the wound to keep them in. I shall never forget the expression of agony depicted in his countenance.'

For a few moments the French fire took a heavy toll of Pakenham's advancing lines, but then the gap closed. The Connaught Rangers, the 88th, were in the front line of Pakenham's attack. Their commanding officer, Alexander Wallace, had been promoted to lead all three regiments in the front brigade, and Pakenham was beside him in the first line as they advanced. The French were on the brow of a hill and when Pakenham, Wallace and their men reached the top, 'the entire French division, with drums beating and uttering loud shouts, ran forward to meet them, and belching forth a torrent of bullets from five thousand muskets brought down almost the whole of Wallace's front rank and more than half of his officers.' But Wallace was still standing, and he urged his men on. When a French officer stepped forward and killed Major Murphy, who was leading the 88th's charge, the troops' usual drive and passion turned to fury. 'Murphy, dead and bleeding, with one foot hanging in the stirrup-iron, was dragged by his affrighted horse along the front of his regiment. The soldiers became exasperated and asked to be let forward . . . Pakenham called out to Wallace "to let them loose".' Pakenham himself was right at the front shouting, 'There they are, my lads. Let them feel the temper of your bayonets.' Such was the force of their charge that the French collapsed. Wallace's men rampaged through the French ranks, and within minutes all of Pakenham's battalions were inflicting dreadful carnage on Thomières' division. As the French turned and ran, the cavalry hacked their way in among them and completed the destruction. One regiment of 1,100 men suffered 800 casualties, another 1,500 out of 1,750. Thomières himself was one of the dead. Wellington was delighted by his brother-in-law's success: 'Pakenham may not be the brightest genius . . . but he's one of the best we have,' he wrote after the battle.

Wellington had by this time already ordered an attack on two other French divisions strung across the allied front behind Thomières. The next division along was General Maucune's. He made the mistake of forming his men into squares, as he saw Le Marchant's heavy cavalry preparing to advance towards him in support of Leith's infantry division. But the infantry arrived first in two long lines, and their volleys made havoc of Maucune's squares. John Douglas was one of Leith's soldiers and heard him shout: 'Royals . . . this shall be a glorious day for old England. If these bragadocian [sic] rascals dare but stand their ground, we will display the point of the British bayonet, and where it is properly displayed no power is able to withstand it . . . All I request of you is to be steady and obey your officers. Stand up, men!'

The squares, which might have been effective in resisting horsemen, could do little in face of the destructive power of muskets in lines. And when the cavalry did arrive, they found the French reeling back under the weight of Leith's attack. Le Marchant's dragoons were soon causing carnage with their fearsome heavy broadswords. And so great was the impact of Le Marchant's attack that it swept through much of the next French division, Brennier's, which was moving in to attempt to rescue Maucune. This division too soon crumpled before the momentum of the British assault, and Wellington, by around five o'clock, was able to watch the complete annihilation of the French left flank. The only setback was that Le Marchant himself was killed by a lucky French musket shot. Le Marchant's charge had been a spectacular success, but Wellington had been robbed of a very promising young cavalry commander. William Ponsonby, a cousin of Fred's, took over command from Le Marchant, and for once Wellington was moved to praise his cavalry. He rode up to his cavalry chief, Sir Stapleton Cotton, a thirty-eight-year-old lieutenant general who was more used to his men's efforts being disparaged. 'My God, Cotton!' shouted Wellington. 'I never saw anything so beautiful in all my life. The day is yours!'* Grattan, over with Pakenham's 3rd Division, watched 'such [Frenchmen] as got away from the sabres of the horsemen' running 'to us for protection – like men who having escaped the first shock of a wreck, will cling to any broken spar, no matter how little to be depended upon. Hundreds of beings frightfully disfigured . . . black with dust, worn down with fatigue and covered with sabre cuts and blood – threw themselves amongst us for safety.' The Anglo-Portuguese army took thousands of prisoners.

But the battle wasn't all going Wellington's way. Fifteen minutes after he had set Leith moving forward against Maucune, he launched General Cole's 4th Division against the French centre. On a slope ahead of them was General Clausel's division supported by a force on its right flank commanded by General Bonnet. Bonnet had taken over command of the army from the wounded Marmont. His troops were on the northern slopes of the Greater Arapil alongside Clausel's

---

* Cotton was always immaculately dressed in the rich uniform of a general of hussars: it earned him the nickname 'Lion d'Or' (Golden Lion). He always felt that the cavalry were undervalued in the Peninsula.

and between them they faced the assault from Cole's division and a Portuguese brigade commanded by General Pack. Pack saw that Cole would be exposed to attack from Bonnet, and he moved up to protect Cole's flank by pushing Bonnet's men off the Greater Arapil. Both these attacks ran into trouble. Pack failed to gain the top of the hill: his men hit a rocky ledge near the top and had to drop their muskets to climb over it. They ran into a devastating fire from Bonnet's men at the top and had to retire. Grattan, who reckoned no other unit matched up to the Connaught Rangers, least of all the Portuguese, wrote, 'These men totally failed in their effort.' Their retreat exposed Cole's left flank to attack from Bonnet, and Clausel's men successfully held off the thrust of Cole's main attack. Cole himself was wounded and his men, like Pack's, were forced to withdraw.

Suddenly Wellington's centre was wide open. Clausel, assuming overall command from Bonnet, who had also been severely wounded, ordered his men forward. It was after five o'clock. Clausel had his own division and Bonnet's men, who had thrown back the Portuguese. He also had three fresh cavalry regiments. He could see the chaos being wreaked by Leith and Pakenham over his left shoulder. He thought he had an opportunity to turn the battle round by plunging straight ahead after the fleeing British and Portuguese. But Wellington had more resources to commit to the struggle. The 5,500 men of General Clinton's 6th Division were in reserve, right in the path of Clausel's jubilant troops. Wellington ordered them to stop Clausel, and Beresford led one of the Portuguese brigades against Clausel's left flank. The day began to fade. The flashes of the guns, the blazing musketry and the great swathes of burning grass lit up the surface of the hill, which the British were now attacking, with a sheet of flame. The 1st Division under General Campbell was ordered to attack Clausel's other flank and a decisive struggle followed. The French in their desperation to survive fought hard. But as night fell Clausel was pushed back, Campbell captured the Greater Arapil, and Wellington still had fresh forces to throw into the battle. Fred Ponsonby's 12th Light Dragoons had heard, with some envy, of the triumph of their heavy-brigade colleagues under Le Marchant. Now Ponsonby was told to pursue the retreating French. He led one attack on a large body of 450 French infantry who lay down as his men charged over them and then rose up and loosed off their muskets at the passing horsemen. Ponsonby's sword was shattered at the hilt and his horse was wounded by several bayonet thrusts. But the battle was won. The entire French army withdrew into the forest to the south-east of the battlefield and across the River Tormes. Some fought an impressive rearguard action, most fled in panicky disorder.

Wellington decided not to order his troops to complete their victory by pursuing the French into the forest. He knew his men were exhausted. Moreover he believed that the bridge over the Tormes and the fortress of Alba beyond were held by Spanish forces. He had posted them there before the battle to deny the French any chance of crossing the river. But the Spanish were no longer there. Their commander had decided his mission was too risky and abandoned Alba without telling Wellington. Fearing Wellington's angry counter-order, he preferred to move first and explain later. Wellington was incensed hours later when he heard that the remnant of the French army had escaped across the bridge and nearby fords. But the French had suffered a decisive defeat. The battle cost the British and their allies just over 5,000 casualties, and the French as many as 14,000. 'I never saw an army get such a beating in so short a time,' Wellington wrote to his brother William. 'What havoc in little more than four hours.'

Salamanca was Wellington's masterpiece. It vindicated more than any other battle so far his grasp of the importance of terrain and his obsession with personal control. If he had his moment of hesitation in the morning, by the afternoon he was in total command of the field, delegating to no one, galloping from unit to unit, insisting on delivering his orders personally. He told no one what was going through his head until he decided what to do. Even then he told only those he needed to. He always appeared calm and confident, never under apparent strain. He took risks in riding too near the front line on many occasions, but he escaped being hit so often that he believed he had divine protection. By the end of his military career and after a number of narrow escapes, Wellington could be counted among the luckiest generals in history. Salamanca was the first major battle in the Peninsula War in which he initiated the attack. It did much to dispel the accusation made by his critics that he was prolonging the war by being too defensive and cautious. A French general at Salamanca, Maximilien Foy, one of Napoleon's most experienced soldiers, praised Wellington's victory: 'It raises Wellington's reputation almost to the level of Marlborough: he showed himself a great and able master of manoeuvres . . . kept his dispositions concealed for almost the whole day . . . a battle in the style of Frederick the Great.'

II

One step forward, two steps back

Madrid and Burgos, 1812

WELLINGTON'S VICTORY at Salamanca was a huge blow to French morale. By the time Napoleon heard he was too preoccupied with the launching of his invasion of Russia to allow himself to be distracted. But this was a severe setback. Wellington had humiliated yet another French marshal and proved that he could attack as well as defend. The remains of Marmont's army, under the command of Clausel, anxious to avoid being forced into another battle, put on all speed and escaped across the Duero. Fred Ponsonby and other light dragoons chased after the French rearguard, but Wellington did not press his infantry into any hard pursuit. 'The vigorous following of a beaten enemy', William Napier wrote, 'was never a prominent characteristic of Lord Wellington's campaigns in the Peninsula.' Even in victory Wellington was reluctant to trust his cavalry and was cautious about over-extending his infantry. Anyway the enemy were retiring, leaving Wellington scope for an orderly advance into northern Spain.

Ponsonby and forty of his best riders followed in Clausel's wake, crossed the Duero and escorted Wellington into the city of Valladolid on 30 July 1812. Ponsonby wrote to his mother that they were met everywhere by people carrying streamers, trophies and wreaths of flowers: 'women of all ranks bringing refreshments even to the privates walking by the side of our horses! – on every side were heard exclamations of "*Viva el gran capitan, Viva los heros ingleses los salvadores.*"'

Wellington now had to decide what to do with the opportunity presented by his victory. He made, as usual, a cool calculation of the strategic balance of power. However humiliated Napoleon's marshals were, the French still had at least three times the number of troops in the Peninsula that he had. But they were continually being harassed and depleted by attacks, ambushes and raids by Spanish guerrillas. And incompetent though Spain's regular forces tended to be, they pinned down tens of thousands of French troops, who would otherwise have been free to confront Wellington. If the separate French armies could link up, they could still force him to fight a battle against overwhelming odds. The trick was to keep the French forces divided and look for a chance to destroy them separately.

Wellington looked at the map. Soult and the French army of the south were fully preoccupied in the siege of Cadiz. The ever reliable General 'Daddy' Hill, with a strong force way off to the south-west, could keep an eye on them. Clausel was retreating northwards where he could hope for reinforcement from other French forces. Joseph, Napoleon's brother, was between Wellington and Madrid but with just 22,000 troops. Wellington took only a short time to decide to make Madrid his target. If he went north, he risked allowing Soult and Joseph to unite and threaten his rear. If he headed for Madrid, Joseph would be unlikely to risk a battle and would retreat to the east. Besides, the occupation of the Spanish capital would be a spectacular political coup.

It took Wellington's army a week to reach the gates of Madrid. On 12 August the Anglo-Portuguese army marched in to an ecstatic welcome from the population, who were cheering, laughing, singing, many of them in tears. People played on guitars and tambourines. Windows, decked with colourful embroidery, were full of women waving their handkerchiefs. Wellington wrote home that it was 'impossible to describe the joy manifested by the inhabitants'. George Simmons watched women throwing down their shawls and veils for Wellington's horse to walk over. 'They got hold of his legs as he sat on horseback and kissed them.' Charles Cocks said he was 'never kissed by so many pretty girls in one day in all my life'. William Wheeler was delighted by it all too. But he did draw the line at being kissed by men. 'Their breath was so highly seasoned with garlick, their huge moustaches well stiffened with sweat, dust and snuff, it was like having a hair broom pushed into one's face that had been daubed in a dirty gutter.' William Grattan and the Connaught Rangers were also mobbed by women. The officers were nearly forced from their horses, and one old friend of Grattan's, 'a remarkably plain-looking personage, was nearly suffocated in the embraces of half a dozen fair Castilians. When he recovered himself and was able to speak, he turned to me and said "How infernally fond these Madrid women must be of kissing, when they have nearly hugged to death such an ill-looking fellow as me."'

Madrid's hospitality knew no bounds, and there was entertainment for all. The liberating army was treated to free bullfights, which even some of the seasoned veterans found too bloody for their taste. Huntsmen like Jonathan Leach were soon taking pot shots at the pheasants which littered the park that Joseph Bonaparte had laid out beside his palace. There were parties and dances all over the city: Leach was given every opportunity of feasting his eyes 'on Castilian beauty which shone most resplendently'. Fred Ponsonby was in his element too. He wrote to his mother, Lady Bessborough: 'We had a grand ball . . . and what is better an excellent supper. In waltzing after supper I got a tumble by sticking my spurs into a lady's gown, and brought half Madrid down with me.' Ponsonby's mother was constantly fretting about his safety and well-being and was glad to hear that he had survived the Battle of Salamanca. She declared how delighted she was that her son 'had the advantage of being directed by the greatest general that ever lived, and the glory of being admired by him'. Harriet Bessborough had another reason to be relieved. Her daughter Caroline Lamb had just ended her torrid affair with Lord Byron. She had herself emerged from a long affair with a high-flying diplomat, Lord Granville Leveson-Gower, a liaison that had presented Fred and Caroline with a half-brother and half-sisters.

Another of Wellington's aides, Alexander Gordon, managed to get enough time off from his staff duties at Wellington's headquarters to visit some of the Old Master paintings on display in Madrid. He wrote enthusiastically to his brother Lord Aberdeen that he particularly admired some paintings he had seen by Anton Mengs, the German neo-classical portrait painter. 'I certainly think him the best of the painters of his day.' George Aberdeen was now embarking very grandly, at the age of twenty-eight, on a diplomatic career which would eventually see him prime minister. He had a rather haughty way of writing to his younger brother, who had not been to university as he had: 'Your observations are pretty judicious for so inexperienced a person with the exception of what you say about Mengs who is the most miserable dauber possible. A cartload of his works would sell for nothing in England.' If Alexander was hurt, he didn't show it. He might be looked down on by his brother, but he was now widely recognised as Wellington's favourite ADC.

In all the frivolity of the first few days in Madrid, hardly anyone seemed to notice that there were still 2,500 Frenchmen holed up in the so-called Retiro, a fort that stubbornly held out for forty-eight hours. Its garrison soon decided that they could not withstand Wellington's artillery, and, when they surrendered, the place was found to contain no fewer than 20,000 muskets and 180 guns, a sumptuous haul for Wellington's army.

Wellington's future plans depended to a great extent on the support he could expect from the Spanish armies. His problem was that, ever since the now long-departed and unlamented General Cuesta had let him down at Talavera, he had little faith in the Spanish. Although the Spanish 'cry *viva*, and are very fond of us, and hate the French', he said he did not 'expect much from their exertions'. Spanish regular forces had been defeated in nearly every encounter with the French and they appeared unwilling to respond to Wellington's call to raise, train and arm the extra forces that he badly needed to match French numbers. Wellington appreciated actions by Spanish guerrillas like Juan Martín Díaz, known as 'El Empecinado' (the Undaunted), and Julián Sánchez. They had long been doing much to harass the French and distract them from turning on his army. But he believed that, if he was to throw the French out of Spain, the Spanish had to do much more. He complained that they were ignoring his demands for a substantial increase in their regular forces. 'What can be done for this lost nation? As for raising men or supplies, or taking any one measure to enable them to carry on the war, that is out of the question. Indeed, there is nobody to excite them to exertion, or to take advantage of the enthusiasm of the people, or of their enmity against the French. Even the guerrillas are getting quietly into the large towns, and amusing themselves . . .' Wellington's frustration was understandable: central organisation was not a Spanish strength but guerrilla warfare was. It was ungracious of him not to recognise that.

Wellington now embarked on a course of action he was later to regret. He realised that his position in Madrid was vulnerable. If Soult left Andalusia, which he soon did, and joined up with Joseph he could threaten Madrid. Rather than attempt to hold Madrid against such a superior force, Wellington would go for the French army that was weaker. He decided to leave part of his army in Madrid and turn his attention back to the enemy force he had defeated at Salamanca. It was now moving south again from Burgos under General Clausel, and Wellington saw a chance to bring it to battle and defeat it or at least drive Clausel back towards France. Hill could be summoned from the south-west to guard his southern flank in case a retreat back towards Portugal became necessary. As always Wellington calculated carefully, ready to err on the side of caution, but this looked to him like an opportunity too good to miss. He left Madrid on 30 August and sent his forces north-west with the cavalry racing ahead. It was the start of a three-month campaign in which nearly everything went wrong.

Clausel had started stealing back towards the Duero river when Wellington and his forces had occupied Madrid. But when he saw Wellington was on his way back he retreated. It was all Fred Ponsonby's cavalry could do to catch up with him. He and his fellow cavalryman and friend William Tomkinson of the 16th Light Dragoons found themselves constantly in action. Ponsonby was asked by Wellington to seize a bridge across one river and secure it for his infantry to cross. But before he could canter across it the bridge was blown up by the retreating French. Clausel was taking no chances.

Five days later Ponsonby and Tomkinson were thirty miles further on, way ahead of the main force, probing up the main road towards Burgos. It was evening and the French noticed that Ponsonby and Tomkinson had only a small force with around 300 horses between them. The French decided to try and drive them back. The only way – back or forward – was along the road. The country either side was difficult for cavalry, made up of vineyards intersected by ditches. The British horsemen formed up in a block across the highway as the French made their approach. 'They came down the road at a trot, trumpeting to charge. We stood still,' wrote Tomkinson, 'and they halted within thirty yards, firing volleys at us. When we moved forward they retired, and we kept our ground till dark. Colonel Ponsonby spoke highly of our squadron, and we can with equal justice bear testimony to his conduct.' The next morning the French gave up and moved back nine miles. Clausel was not going to give Wellington a chance of attacking him, and by 18 September Wellington's army found the city of Burgos empty but for a garrison of 2,200 men, which Clausel had left in the castle there under a resourceful commander called General Dubreton. Wellington wanted to pursue Clausel beyond the Ebro if necessary, but he dared not leave Burgos behind him in French hands. He needed a secure escape route. Besides, he now heard that Marshal Soult had been ordered by Joseph to abandon Andalusia and march north to join him. The opportunity to chase Clausel was still there, but Wellington needed to capture Burgos quickly.

He settled down reluctantly to besiege the castle at Burgos. It stood on a steep knoll north of the city, and its walls had recently been rebuilt on Napoleon's orders. Wellington had only three medium eighteen-pounder siege guns and five smaller guns. He should have had at least twelve siege guns, and preferably twenty-four-pounders. Even six would have helped. Three eighteen-pounders were glaringly inadequate. Wellington knew it, but he still persisted with the siege. And he failed to make adequate arrangements to provide himself with more guns. Months of success had made him over-confident.

The first task was to seize a fortified bastion on a small hill just north-east of the castle. On the night of 20 September Charles Cocks, a young intelligence officer, whom Wellington prized greatly, led what was supposed to be a diversionary attack on the outpost, which turned into a real attack when the main attack failed on the other side. After a desperate scramble, Major Cocks and his men scaled the walls and made it into the fort. But they suffered more than 400 casualties, twice as many as the French. And they still hadn't captured the castle itself. Alexander Gordon wrote home that the 'affair was not well managed'. He also mentioned that they were attacking the main castle with 'only three 18 pounders. I am not very sanguine about the result.' His chief, Wellington, was writing home the next day: 'I am getting apprehensive that the means which I have are not sufficient to enable me to take the castle. I am informed, however, that the enemy are ill provided with water; and that their magazines of provisions are in a place exposed to be set on fire.'

But Dubreton had a resolute garrison and a few powerful guns in the castle to train on its attackers. By 2 October Wellington was reporting to Hill, 'I am afraid we shall not succeed in taking this castle . . . I have only three guns one of which was destroyed and another much damaged last night.' The attackers were now affectionately calling their damaged gun 'Nelson', after Britain's one-armed naval hero, and digging mines under the walls as a further way of forcing a breach. But it was to no avail. And on 8 October the valiant Charles Cocks was killed in an attempted storming of the breach they had made. When he was at the top of the breach, a musket ball passed between his ribs and severed an artery just above his heart. It was a severe blow to Fred Ponsonby and William Tomkinson. They had all been light dragoons together, almost inseparable. Tomkinson lost a 'sincere friend . . . He had always been so lucky in the heat of fire that I fancied he would be preserved to the army.' Wellington was to miss Cocks badly too. Ponsonby remembered the Commander in Chief walking into his room, announcing briefly that Cocks was dead and then pacing up and down silently. Wellington was close to tears. Cocks, with his easy Spanish and his superb horsemanship, had ridden many a lone mission as the army's eyes and ears: he had been a fine intelligence officer as well as lively company at Wellington's dinner table.

A few days later while the siege continued Ponsonby was galloping among his outposts on the road north-east of Burgos when he was wounded by a stray shot. 'So highly did the Duke of Wellington value this excellent officer that after his wound he had him brought to his own quarters and made him travel in his carriage until sufficiently recovered to ride.' Ponsonby's cousin, Colonel William Ponsonby, wrote to Fred's father to reassure him 'that no serious consequence is at all to be apprehended from his wound'. William said that Fred had been in a skirmish at an advanced post and received a musket ball in the thigh, 'which however was immediately extracted. The bone is certainly not injured, nor has there been any inflammation or fever, so that there is every reason to hope that he will be very shortly on his legs again.' It wasn't till two weeks later that Fred Ponsonby wrote to his sister-in-law to tell her that she could pass on to the family the news that he had 'met with a little accident . . . I hope they will not be in a great fuss about this scratch of mine.' Ponsonby was soon back in the saddle.

The siege did not last much longer. The weather was appalling. Sheets of rain were making work on the breaches well nigh impossible. But the critical turning point came when Wellington heard on 19 October that Soult was on his way from Andalusia to join up with Joseph and march on Madrid. Wellington had hoped that Soult and Joseph would be delayed by the weather or by the Spanish. He had hoped too that the Spanish would reinforce him with more than the 11,000 fresh troops they had provided over the past month. Most of all, he had hoped to be way beyond Burgos chasing Clausel across the Ebro. Only six weeks earlier he had said, 'I hope before Christmas . . . to have all the gentlemen safe on the other side of the Ebro.' But none of these things had come to pass. He decided he now had no choice but to turn round and retreat, join up with Hill and find secure winter quarters. No general likes to retreat, but Wellington was a realist, always ready to exercise judicious caution when he felt he had to. He had retreated after Talavera three years earlier. He would retreat now. He wrote to Hill telling him to abandon Madrid and march north-west to meet up with him. He also wrote to Britain's naval commander in Biscay, Commodore Sir Home Popham, telling him that he no longer needed to shift new siege guns inland from Santander, the port in northern Spain which the Royal Navy had now established as Wellington's new point of supply.

There was a lot of muttering in the ranks about Wellington's ill-conceived siege of Burgos. Occasionally the disgruntlement boiled over. While the Commander in Chief was visiting some soldiers wounded in the siege, one of them, who had lost both his legs, burst out: 'Maybe yer satisfied now, you hooky nosed vagabond!' Wellington took it in good humour and sought special treatment for the soldier, who ended up a pensioner at the Chelsea Hospital.

Nevertheless, he was deeply aware that his attack on the castle had been a mistake, and one of his gunners wrote later of the 'inadequacy of our means in artillery'. He said there wasn't the same spirit as there had been at the sieges of Ciudad Rodrigo and Badajoz. And this 'seemed to cause some discontent at the troops in the mind of the Commander in Chief'. Once again, Wellington was guilty of a certain ambivalence. Late in the siege he wrote a remarkable despatch to Lord Liverpool, now Prime Minister, saying that some people were blaming the government for the siege, but that 'it was entirely my own act'. He insisted on taking the blame for embarking on the expedition with inadequate means and inexperienced troops. But he did imply that more could have been done by the Royal Navy and by his own supply team to get some heavy guns moving faster towards Burgos. He then went on to criticise very directly an officer in charge of one attempt to storm the castle:

> He paid no attention to his orders, notwithstanding the pains I took in writing them; and in reading and explaining them to him twice over. He made none of the dispositions ordered . . . and instead of regulating the attack as he ought, he rushed on as if he had been the leader of the Forlorn Hope, and fell, together with many of those who went with him. He had my instructions in his pocket; and as the French got possession of his body, and were made acquainted with the plan, the attack could never be repeated.

That Wellington attempted – in a letter to the Prime Minister – to shift part of the blame for his failure at Burgos on to an officer who had died in the siege does him no credit. At least he had the grace to admit that he himself had made a strategic blunder in going to Burgos at all. And most of his men were in no doubt: 'I have not been in the habit much of questioning the conduct of our chief,' said one young Guards officer, John Aitchison 'even when it differed from what I expected, but . . . it appears in this instance to be extremely impolitic, not to say most wantonly reprehensible.'

Late on 21 October, under cover of darkness, Wellington set his army moving south – back towards Valladolid. What was left of his battered old siege guns was lugged across the river with straw attached to the wheels to muffle the noise. The last of the troops in the trenches didn't pull out till five o'clock the following morning.

For the next four weeks Wellington's deeply demoralised army dragged itself back the way it had advanced with such high hopes in the spring. The weather was dreadful, supplies were scarce or unobtainable, the French were constantly snapping at their heels and there were problems with their allies. Wellington sent Alexander Gordon off with two battalions of Spanish soldiers to push the French back at one river crossing. But Gordon complained that their 'state of discipline is so terrible that one can do little or nothing with them . . . One regiment who was following me pretty well, upon seeing the French run upon their right who had been attacked by us, immediately set up a sort of yell and every fellow ran forward and let fly his piece and it was quite impossible ever to get them in order again. The fact is we are in a very ticklish situation.' The French army which the British had held off during the siege of Burgos was now heavily reinforced and pressing hard on Wellington's retreating army as it recrossed the Duero. It wasn't until 31 October that Wellington, after a few anxious days, was able to say, 'I have got clear, in a handsome manner, of the worst scrape I ever was in . . .'

Hill, meanwhile, and the other half of the army were now evacuating Madrid and the surrounding cities of central Spain where they had spent the late summer. For all the fun William Grattan and his Irish companions had had there, Grattan observed that 'after a sojourn of nearly three months in the Spanish capital [the British army] knew nearly as little of its inhabitants as they did of the citizens of Pekin'. He said if the British could unbend a little and conform to the ways of their hosts, the British nation would be 'as much beloved as it is respected'. The British may not have been loved, but the people of Madrid were more than sad to see them go. They were devastated, deeply resentful that they faced renewed French occupation. They felt deserted and betrayed.

The retreat of the two armies, which reunited near Salamanca and finally arrived at Ciudad Rodrigo in mid-November, was one of the most wretched episodes of the entire Peninsular Campaign, second only to Sir John Moore's retreat to Corunna nearly four years earlier. They would start out at four o'clock in the morning, usually wet and cold after a night sleeping in the open in wind and rain. They were downhearted, exhausted and soon starving. John Kincaid and his comrades in the Light Division had seen tough marching before, but this was the worst: 'we were now walking nearly knee deep, in a stiff mud, into which no man could thrust his foot, with the certainty of having a shoe at the end of it when he pulled it out again; and, that we might not be miserable by halves, we had this evening to regale our chops with the last morsel of biscuit that they were destined to grind during the retreat.' Thomas Todd was a witness to perhaps the most horrific scene of all:

> One of our men, Thomas Caldwell, found a piece of meat, near the hospital . . . he brought it home and cooked it. A good part of it was eaten, before one of the men perceiving him, said 'What is that you are eating?' Tom said it was meat he had found. The others looked and knew it to be the fore-arm of a man; the hand was not at it; it was only a part from a little below the elbow and above the wrist. The man . . . never looked squeamish: he said it was very sweet, and was never a bit the worse.

Wellington's logistics team, the commissaries, failed to provide any food for part of the journey. Ensign George Bell said that the Commander in Chief was partly to blame. The men were reduced, he said, to scavenging for acorns off the oak trees in the woods – anything to put in their stomachs. 'Wellington supposed that the commissaries were supplying the army with their usual rations. The great commander, in whom we had the firmest reliance was unrivalled in skill, vigour, and genius, but could not see at once into the wants and necessities of 70,000 men.' Wellington was not neglecting the need for supplies: the empty fields, the scarcity of food, the scale and speed of the retreat were just too much for his commissaries.

Harry Smith had the further responsibility of looking after the fourteen-year-old wife he had rescued from Badajoz. Juana was never a burden. Her stamina and chirpy resilience constantly surprised him. He found her one evening after she had been wading through a river: 'there was this young and delicate creature, in the month of November in the north of Spain, wet as a drowned rat, with nothing to eat and no cover from the falling deluge. Not a murmur escaped her but once.'

One wife was not so lucky. She had loyally followed her husband through the war in appalling conditions, but one day's march proved too much for her. She could go no further. Her husband managed to drag her a little way but at length she stopped, quite unable to move. Her husband tried to find room for her in one of the wagons, but they were all full. The army had already had to leave large numbers of people lying on the roadside. 'The poor fellow', wrote Joseph Donaldson, 'was now in a dreadful dilemma, being necessitated either to leave her to the mercy of the French, or by remaining with her to be taken prisoner and even then perhaps unable to protect her . . . the alternative either way was heartrending.' But there was no time to lose – the French cavalry were nearly upon them. 'In despairing accents she begged him not to leave her . . . but the fear of being considered a deserter urged him to proceed, and with feelings easier imagined than described, he left her to her fate and never saw her again.'

Another young officer joined Fred Ponsonby's 12th Light Dragoons about this time. William Hay, who had been in the Peninsula earlier, was appalled by the difference he saw in the regiment within a few months. Campaigning had taken the shine off the men's once immaculate equipment. 'The men's clothes were actually in rags – some one colour, some another, some in worn out helmets, some in none; others in forage caps with handkerchiefs tied round their heads, their horses in a most woeful state, many quite unfit to carry the weight of the rider and his baggage.' Hay rode as one of the light dragoons trying to protect the army's rear. 'It was truly one of the most painful and sickening sights I ever before or afterwards witnessed.' Hundreds of British, Portuguese and German soldiers fell by the wayside, starving, sick or just exhausted. But Hay spoke warmly of Ponsonby's leadership. 'I have had the great good fortune to be commanded by one who was not only a most gallant soldier but most kind and considerate alike to men and officers.' Ponsonby's overriding anxiety at the time was to get his regiment into shape after the ordeal it had gone through, and to do so by giving as little trouble as possible. The men 'fully appreciated their colonel's kindness and gave no trouble'.

At the end of each day's march, the bedraggled army would look for what shelter it could. The soldiers would halt in a field – or, if they were lucky, in a wood – by the roadside and attempt to light a fire to cook any beef that remained. Even Joseph Donaldson and the Scots, used to fierce enough conditions in their own country, found it intolerable. 'Sometimes, indeed we managed to raise a smoke, and a number gathered around in the vain hope of getting themselves warmed, but the fire would extinguish in spite of all their efforts. Our situation was truly distressing: tormented by hunger, wet to the skin and fatigued in the extreme . . . a savage sort of desperation had taken possession of our minds.' William Grattan found himself with a dose of the ague, a form of typhus fever which could prove fatal. He was not amused when his servant remarked with a laugh: 'Don't the jaws of the boys with the ague, when they rattle so, put your honour greatly in mind of the castanet?'

Many of those who were left by the roadside, too weak to move from hunger or disease, died miserably in the bitter cold. The survivors were killed off or taken prisoner depending on the mood of the French soldiers who found them. Many who had any energy left attempted to make up for their hunger by turning to plundering the local people, action that Wellington had long preached against as a heinous crime. It was a crime now committed on a mass scale.

One further problem was that the land between Burgos and Salamanca was rich in vineyards, and there had been a good harvest. William Wheeler said that many of his fellow soldiers 'ran mad. I remember seeing a soldier, fully accoutred with his knapsack on, in a large tank he had either fell in or had been pushed in by his comrades . . . there he lay dead. I saw a dragoon fire his pistol into a large vat containing several thousands of gallons, in a few minutes we were up to our knees in wine fighting like tigers for it.' Wheeler added that the conduct of some men 'would have disgraced savages, drunkenness had prevailed to such a frightful extent that I have often wondered how it was that a great part of our army were not cut off . . . the sides of the road were strewed with soldiers as if dead, not so much by fatigue as by wine'.

But the men weren't just drowning themselves in wine. They were looting livestock as well. The most accessible were pigs which they would find looking for chestnuts and acorns in the woods. Wellington was determined to stamp out this practice, which alienated the local Spanish population. 'The commander of the forces requests the general officers commanding the divisions will take measures to prevent the shameful and unmilitary practice of soldiers shooting pigs in the woods . . . he has this day ordered two men to be hanged who were caught in the act of shooting pigs.'

One day William Hay and some hungry fellow dragoons were chasing some sheep with their sabres. One sheep had its head cut off 'from the powerful blow of my friend's sharp sword'. But then the shepherds appeared and Hay was well aware that Wellington had ordered no plundering of the inhabitants. So he grabbed the dead sheep, slung it across his friend's saddle and together they dived into the wood just as a column of British soldiers appeared. The shepherds immediately complained to the soldiers, who, fortunately for the mischief-makers, could not understand a word of the language. Hay and his mates escaped and tucked into an excellent meal. Later he and some fellow dragoons witnessed a whole British infantry division so hungry that they plundered a town and utterly destroyed it, knocking down houses for firewood and stealing food. 'I looked on with surprise and could not help reflecting upon what our tyrannical General Craufurd would have done had he been alive and witnessed the scene: at least – to be consistent – he must have hanged half the famished soldiers.'

At last the men who had survived the wretchedness of the retreat arrived in the area of Ciudad Rodrigo. Kincaid's feet were so swollen he had to cut his boots off. But at least he had arrived. Many hundreds of others never made it. The exhausted army was finally able to consolidate and find itself winter quarters in friendly territory.

Wellington, infuriated and depressed by the level of looting and plundering, decided to issue a scathing letter of disapproval to his senior officers. It was not supposed to go further than that, but its contents soon became widely known. It was dated 28 November 1812. Wellington said discipline was often hard to exercise in difficult conditions. But 'I am concerned to have to observe that the army under my command has fallen off in this respect in the late campaign to a greater degree than any army with which I have ever served, or of which I have ever read . . . from the moment the troops commenced their retreat from the neighbourhood of Burgos on the one hand, and from Madrid on the other, the officers lost all command over their men. Irregularities and outrages of all descriptions were committed with impunity, and losses have been sustained which ought never to have occurred . . .' He went on to say that there was no excuse. The army had 'suffered no privations which trifling attention on the part of the officers could not have prevented'. It was tough stuff, and its apparently blanket condemnation of everyone was unfair and ill-judged at a very demanding time when the army had been subject to weeks of severe privation. Some units had behaved disgracefully and discipline had collapsed, but others had struggled to keep their spirits up and had survived the hardships largely unscathed. Jonathan Leach observed that many thought Wellington's reprimand was 'too sweeping' and John Kincaid said it 'afforded a handle to disappointed persons, and excited a feeling against him on the part of individuals which has probably never since been obliterated'. When Fred Ponsonby received Wellington's letter, he couldn't bring himself to read out parts of it to his staff. According to his friend William Tomkinson, Ponsonby was anxious to make out that Wellington had written this rebuke to his men 'in a hasty moment when vexed with the result of the campaign'.

It was as well for Wellington that his men's resentful reaction to his message came as they entered comparatively comfortable winter quarters on and around the Portuguese frontier. His miscalculation in attacking Burgos without the right siege train and his meanness in blaming others for the consequences of his own mistake make those few weeks in the autumn of 1812 one of the low points in his career. At least one man on his staff, Alexander Gordon, believed that if Napoleon were to succeed in Russia, Britain would have to withdraw from the Peninsula. Back home the government stood loyally behind their Commander in Chief: Castlereagh, now Foreign Secretary, told the Commons that Wellington had 'accomplished all he expected . . . and gained immortal glory'. Another of Wellington's supporters, Sir Frederick Flood, said, 'Thank God we have committed our army to the care of a man of cool and deliberate judgement, one who is not foolhardy and who knows when he ought to go forward and when he ought to go backward.' But Wellington's retreat from Burgos gave his and the government's political opponents in

London their last real chance to condemn the campaign. The radical MP Francis Burdett told the Commons the retreat from Burgos was 'most disastrous' and the country was still 'deeper in a destructive and ruinous war'. Fred Ponsonby's cousin George Ponsonby, the leader of the Whig Opposition, said it had now been proved that the 'power of England is not competent to drive the French out of the peninsula'.

But, as the winter wore on, all debate about Wellington's staying power in the Peninsula came to look very different. There was startling news from the other side of Europe. Napoleon's audacious gamble in trying to add Russia to his empire had ended in total collapse. He was retreating from Moscow and his army was suffering more losses and misery than almost any other in history.

12

I saw them fall like a pack of cards
Vitoria, 1813

A S 1812 TURNED into 1813 it became clear that the gloom about Wellington's prospects in the Peninsula was misplaced. For a start his army's achievements in 1812 far overshadowed the setback of the retreat. It had secured the great frontier fortresses that now made Portugal impregnable. In Spain it had decisively demonstrated its superior fighting skill at Salamanca and the fragility of the French hold on the Peninsula by occupying Madrid.

There were two other great strategic shifts that now swung the balance in Wellington's favour. First the catastrophic defeat Napoleon had suffered in Russia. By mid-November 1812 the news was out that the Emperor was retreating from Moscow, unable to cope with the length of his supply line and the fierce Russian winter. By mid-December Marshal Ney, who had failed to blunt Wellington's defence at Bussaco two years earlier, was the last French commander to leave Russian territory. Napoleon's retreat left 400,000 men dead or disabled. The Grande Armée of more than 425,000 men was reduced to 25,000. This was welcome news to Wellington in his winter quarters on the Portuguese border.

The second great change was in France's hold on Spain. Napoleon's march to Moscow meant that he was unable to reinforce Joseph when the Spanish rebellion was hurting the French more than ever before. So severe was the pressure that Joseph had ordered Soult to abandon Andalusia in the autumn of 1812. The news that Soult had been recalled had prompted Wellington to abandon the siege of Burgos. Soult was ordered to move his army to bolster France's fragmenting position in eastern Spain. Soult was furious. He despised Joseph and he relished the power and opulence that had come his way as ruler of the south. The bitterness between the two men further weakened the French. The Spanish resistance, whose leaders had been holding out against Soult in the Andalusian city of Cadiz, invited Wellington to be commander in chief of their armies. In spite of his long-standing contempt for what he saw as the indiscipline and disorganisation of Spanish regular forces, he accepted.

All this strengthened Wellington's position back home and reduced the pressure on the government. Lord Aberdeen wrote in his usual rather grand manner to his younger brother Alexander Gordon: 'Lord Wellington's retreat gave a shake to Ministers, but people are absurdly desponding about it; for my part I expect to see you advancing very shortly into Spain.' Wellington, who followed all Napoleon's moves in meticulous detail, was in no doubt about the vast improvement in his prospects. He wrote to his brother Henry in February 1813, 'there is scarcely any French army left, except that in our front.'

He asked London for reinforcements and began to prepare for a major campaign in the spring of 1813. He made his plans in his headquarters in a long low building that still stands on the edge of the main square in the small village of Freneda just inside Portugal. Around him and as far forward as the fortress of Ciudad Rodrigo, twenty miles to the east inside Spain, his troops did their best to survive in winter quarters. The greatest threat to them, apart from the usual diseases that came with the poor sanitation, was the penetrating winter cold. Up to 500 people in the army died each week according to Seymour Larpent, who had just joined Wellington's staff as his legal adviser or judge advocate, mainly responsible for courts martial. Larpent was a well-read and thoroughly engaging character who wrote lively letters home and kept a fascinated eye on his Commander in Chief. Wellington, he noted, 'has a good stud of around eight hunters: he rides hard and only wants a good gallop, but I understand knows nothing of the sport, though very fond of it in his own way . . . He hunts almost every day, and then makes up for it by great diligence and instant decision on the intermediate days'. Larpent observed that Wellington was 'remarkably neat and most particular about his dress . . . he is well made, knows it and is willing to set off to the best what nature has bestowed'. In a word Larpent described him as 'vain'. He 'cuts the skirts of his own coats shorter, to make them look smarter: and only a short time since I found him discussing the cut of his half boots and suggesting alterations to his servant'. Larpent watched Wellington working till about four o'clock in the afternoon, and 'then for an hour or two, [he] parades with anyone whom he wants to talk to, up and down the little square in Freneda in his grey great coat'. Larpent clearly felt rather deprived at head-quarters. 'Here are no books, no women but ladies of a certain description.'

Harry Smith and Juana found themselves billeted with many of his Rifles comrades at Fuentes d'Oñoro where the battle had been fought nearly two years earlier. In spite of the weather, 'my vivacious little wife was full of animation and happiness . . . I went out cours-ing every day, and some of our regimental fellows, notwithstanding "the retreat" and its hardships, went out duck shooting, up to their middles in water, Jonathan Leach among them.' Leach shot some woodcock as well, and he also found time to get together with some others in the Rifles to stage an all-male production of *The Rivals* by Sheridan. 'It is impossible to imagine anything more truly ludicrous than to see Lydia Languish and Julia (. . . performed by two young and good looking men . . .) drinking punch and smoking cigars behind the stage at a furious rate between the acts.' They even invited the Duke of Wellington and were delighted to see that he revelled in the fun of it. Leach found himself forgiving his Commander in Chief for his reprimand a few months earlier. 'This is the right sort of man to be at the head of an army . . . he knows per-fectly well that the more the officers and soldiers enjoy themselves during winter, the more heartily will they embark in the operations of the forthcoming campaign.'

Wellington had to wait till late May to start his advance into Spain. The rains were late and his horses would go hungry without a carpet of lush green forage in the fields. But he was never idle. He super-vised constant training in battlefield drills. His campaign so far had demonstrated the superiority of his British infantry in face-to-face combat. He was determined to build on that advantage. It was, for example, essential to get his men to practise forming lines from col-umns and vice versa in no more than thirty seconds. George Bell remembered being 'very busy with parades and drills and field-days, and some little horse racing in April'. Wellington improved the men's living conditions too. To avoid the dreaded bivouacking, he managed to get tents to house everyone in the army for the coming campaign. He also provided the men with light tin kettles instead of the heavy iron ones they had carried before.

Wellington also approved plans by his Chief Medical Officer, James McGrigor, whom he greatly admired, to improve care of the wounded. McGrigor had long been concerned about the distance the wounded had to travel to hospitals often way behind the front lines. Casualties were usually transported many miles on bumpy bullock carts. The risks of further damage to their wounds and exposure to disease tended to prolong their disablement. McGrigor, with the enthusiastic support of an ever more experienced team of military surgeons, persuaded Wellington that modernising medical support would result in a much faster return of victims to active service. From now on there would be prefabricated field hospitals which would be carried forward and set up as near as possible to the front line to ensure much more rapid treatment of wounds in battle.

Wellington was always travelling. Whatever Larpent may have thought of him as a huntsman, he was second to none in the saddle. After a morning's work at his headquarters in mid-April, he thought nothing of a five-and-a-half-hour ride from his headquarters to Ciudad Rodrigo to check its fortifications. He was back for dinner. Two months earlier he had hosted a ball at Ciudad Rodrigo to celebrate the first anniversary of its storming. He rode back to headquarters afterwards in the January moonlight.

In April George Scovell, an officer who had been working hard to break Napoleon's codes, handed Wellington a message he had deciphered. Intercepted on its way from a French commander to Joseph Bonaparte, it said that a substantial part of the French army was preoccupied with chasing Spanish rebels in northern Spain. Wellington would have to face a reduced force of 80,000 rather than 100,000 French troops in any thrust he made across Spain. It was a remarkable coup by Wellington's codebreaker and by the Spanish guerrillas who were now making an almost routine habit of waylaying French messengers in any part of the country.

In mid-May Wellington had his army on the move. George Bell reported 'great hilarity, buoyant spirit and cheerfulness' among the men, although the light infantryman and future historian William Napier was said to have grumbled: 'Well, here we go again. We shall go so far and then have our arses kicked and come back again.' Wellington's strategic plan was a bold one. He would push the French back as far as he could towards their frontier at the Pyrenees. He was confident that he had enough men to risk a pitched battle with any force they could assemble. And he would attempt to roll the enemy back by splitting his force in two. He would lead the main force in a direct line north-east through Salamanca and Burgos. He would send another large force under Lieutenant General Sir Thomas Graham in a left hook through the hilly country to the north-west to exert constant pressure on the French right flank. The stratagem succeeded brilliantly. Wellington was not normally a man for theatrical gestures, but when he crossed the Spanish frontier heading east yet again, he waved his hat in the air and shouted, 'Farewell Portugal. I shall never see you again.' As he pressed on up the main road, Graham and his force in difficult country way over to the north-west conducted a series of lightning advances continually threatening to outflank the French. The combined movement of Wellington's two armies kept the French retreating for fear of being cut off. One by one the towns fell to the advancing British: Salamanca, Zamora, Valladolid and Burgos. The castle at Burgos, which had resisted Wellington so successfully just six months earlier, was blown up by the French as they pulled back. Within little more than three weeks Wellington and his army had moved further north-east than ever before. The broad River Ebro stretched across their front.

The great frontier chain of the Pyrenees and France itself were only eighty miles ahead. Wellington's staff, and even the loyal General 'Daddy' Hill, now urged him to stop. Napoleon had won two major victories in Germany in May, and Britain's hard-pressed allies Prussia, Austria and Russia had agreed to an armistice. 'All my staff', Wellington told a friend much later, '[said] we ought not to risk the army and what we had obtained, and that this armistice would enable Buonaparte* to reinforce his army in Spain, and we

---

* Wellington and a number of his men spelled Napoleon's surname Buonaparte, as a mark of contempt, to emphasise his Corsican origins.

therefore should look to a defensive system. I thought differently.' Wellington wanted to press forward in an effort to throw Napoleon's army out of Spain before he could reinforce it. He also reckoned that if Britain could score a victory it might encourage its allies to scrap the armistice and fight on in central Europe. So the order went out: 'We move on.'

Wellington's men had tramped 200 miles from where they had set off – first through the cork and olive trees of the western hills and then through the cornfields of León. In village after village they were greeted with delight by cheering crowds and pealing church bells. 'What then was our excessive delight', wrote Jonathan Leach, 'on suddenly and unexpectedly beholding an extensive valley at our feet, through which flowed the rapid Ebro, and that valley as well as the country for miles beyond teeming with fresh woods, fruit trees, beautiful villages, gardens and everything which could delight the sight . . . we procured fresh bread, fruit and vegetables – luxuries of which we had but little known for many weeks . . .' Another rifleman was struck by the colourful crowd of women who followed the army, selling butter and cheese. 'They had on generally yellow stockings, with abundance of petticoats of red, yellow and green etc etc and were all very stout made.' From then on the men were rarely short of supplies or the horses of fodder. Once beyond the Ebro the men were allowed to stuff their haversacks with fresh vegetables from fields by the roadside.

So swift was the advance and so decisively were the French outmanoeuvred that few of the men saw much action. But that was about to change. Just fifteen miles beyond the Ebro, in a great open plain surrounded by mountains, is the town of Vitoria. Joseph Bonaparte had ordered his generals, bewildered by the pace of the British advance, to gather at Vitoria for a decisive stand. Joseph had already abandoned Madrid, and then Valladolid, his next choice of capital, in a headlong retreat. He had with him a great horde of personal possessions and plundered treasures. He had to stop Wellington at Vitoria. If he failed, Wellington would be in the Pyrenees, the gateway to France.

Vitoria stands at the eastern end of a roughly rectangular patch of low country six miles wide by ten miles long – surrounded by

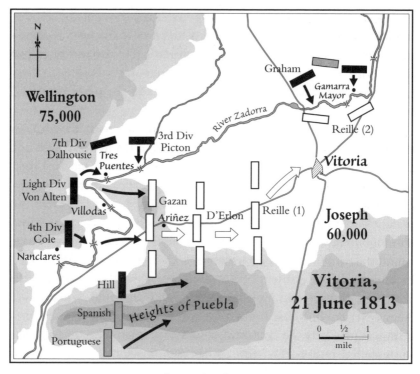

The Battle of Vitoria

mountains. The River Zadorra flows from east to west past the town, winds along the northern edge of the plain, and then curves sharply down the western side. The heights of Puebla overlook the southern side of the plain and there are mountains rising up beyond the Zadorra on the western and northern sides. Wellington arrived in the uplands to the west of the Zadorra on 20 June with just over 75,000 troops. His intelligence sources, now honed to near perfection thanks to the help of the Spanish resistance, told him that the French had around 60,000 troops, with another large force under General Clausel likely to join them soon from the south. Wellington, determined to pre-empt Clausel's arrival, conceived a bold plan of attack.

He assumed − rightly as it turned out − that the French would expect his attack to come from the west. Joseph's French forces were concentrated on the ground west of Vitoria. Wellington would attempt to strike them from no fewer than four directions. First,

Lieutenant General Sir Rowland Hill, who had never let him down, would lead his men up the heights of Puebla and then sweep down on the French lines from the south-west. Sir Thomas Graham would then attack from precisely the opposite direction – way up in the north-east corner of the plain across the Zadorra to strike at Vitoria itself and cut off the French line of retreat to the east. Sir Thomas Picton's and Lord Dalhousie's divisions would cross the Zadorra from the mountains to the north-west, and Wellington himself would attack across the river directly from the west. For a commander who had often been accused of being over-cautious and inclined to fight only defensive battles, these were highly ambitious tactics. Four such widely separated axes of attack would be very hard to co-ordinate. Timing would be everything, and Wellington's passion for speeding round the battlefield and attempting to be everywhere at once would be severely tested.

'It was a heavenly morning, bright and sunny,' observed young August Schaumann, the commissary officer, who enjoyed the luxury during battles of being able to observe rather than fight. He watched the infantry striking their flints and preparing their cartridge boxes and ADCs galloping 'in all directions carrying . . . orders to the heads of the columns that are forming. Every heart . . . stirred by the thought that for the first time we should be equal in numbers to the French.'

Early that morning Fred Ponsonby asked one of his captains, William Hay, to accompany him to a vantage point, where he could scan the French position and size up the best approach for his light dragoons. Hay had to prop up his ailing commander who was racked by fever and vomiting. Ponsonby was deeply ashamed. 'Hay, I am very ill,' he said, plunging into the undergrowth by the roadside. 'I must lie down here till the fit is over: take my orderly with you and keep a sharp look out, and if, from any movement of the enemy, we are to have anything to do, send me word immediately: but do not tell anyone I am unwell.'

Hill began the battle by assaulting the heights. 'The bright morning sunshine,' said Schaumann, 'the gloomy wooded hills, the flash of the muskets, the rolling thunder of the fire, and the wonderful shapes formed by the smoke in and out of the groups of trees covering the hills lent a picturesque grandeur to the scene.' Thomas Todd was with the Highland Light Infantry – the 71st – assaulting the heights under Hill. 'Immediately we marched up the hill, the piper playing "Hey Johnny Cope". The French had possession of the top, but we soon forced them back . . . A French officer . . . was pricking and forcing his men to stand. They heeded him not – he was very harsh – "Down with him" cried one near me; and down he fell pierced by more than one ball.' Todd and his mates got very thirsty fighting on the heights. Todd remembered one of the men finding a small spring and calling out 'that he would have a drink, let the world go as it would. He stooped to drink: a ball pierced his head: he fell with it in the well, which was discoloured by brains and blood. Thirsty as we were, we could not taste it.'

The battle on the heights swung this way and that until finally the French gave way and the badly depleted British regiments burst on to the plain and into the main French positions. Time and again they had to go through the laborious task of loading and priming their muskets. Sometimes they failed to fire. Bell watched some of his comrades trying to get 'the wretched old firelocks' to 'burn powder'. A man with a misfiring musket had to take from his pocket 'a triangle screw, to knock life into his old flint, and then clear the touchhole with a long brass picker that hung from his belt. Many a fellow was killed while performing this operation.' While Hill's force was fighting its way down the heights from the right, Wellington ordered his men in on all the other fronts. Incredibly the French had destroyed none of the bridges across the Zadorra, so there were no fewer than eleven places where the British could cross the river.

With Hill's men heavily engaged on the Heights, Wellington was among his Light Division troops at Villodas on the west side of the river. Massed around him were the crack riflemen of the 95th in their dark-green uniforms, and a bit further on the redcoats of the other light infantry, the 43rd. John Cooke stole down through the trees to look across the river at the French the other side of the bridge. 'I found myself at the edge of the wood, and within a very short distance of the enemy's guns, planted with lighted matches ready to apply them.' Cooke noticed that Wellington was glancing anxiously over towards his left where he hoped to see signs that Picton and

Dalhousie were attacking across the Zadorra. The Commander in Chief knew that Hill was now fully engaged; he wanted to be sure that the other attacks were going in before he ordered the troops on his front to attack.

Minutes later a couple of miles up the Zadorra Thomas Picton emerged from the hills with his division to meet one of Wellington's ADCs galloping up. The man skidded to a halt beside the doughty Welsh general, who was dressed as usual in civilian clothes with a wide-brimmed hat, and asked if he knew where Lord Dalhousie was. Picton was taken aback that the man was looking for a general whose division hadn't even appeared when his own division was eager to engage the enemy. 'No, sir!' said Picton. 'I have not seen his Lordship: but have you any orders for me, sir?' 'None,' came the reply. 'Then pray, sir,' asked Picton, 'what are the orders you do bring?' 'That as soon as Lord Dalhousie . . . shall commence an attack upon that bridge, the fourth and sixth are to support him.' Picton exploded with indignation that another division which wasn't even ready yet should precede his in an attack. He looked the astonished ADC in the eye and said, 'You may tell Lord Wellington from me, sir, that the third division under my command shall . . . attack the bridge and carry it, and the fourth and sixth divisions may support if they choose.' And then without waiting for Dalhousie, Picton roared, 'Come on, ye rascals, come on, ye fighting villains!' and led his men down the hill and across the Zadorra.

Back at Villodas, seeing the dust kicked up by Picton's 3rd Division, and probably before he was told about Picton's magnificent piece of insubordination, Wellington ordered the Light Division across the river. And when a local peasant offered to guide them to the bridge of Tres Puentes, undefended by the French, just around the corner, Wellington readily agreed. By lunchtime the French were being assaulted from three sides. They resisted fiercely, using their guns along their front line to fire ball and grapeshot at the advancing British. The peasant guiding the riflemen was one of the first to die, his head completely removed by a cannon ball. John Dobbs heard the sergeants behind him shouting 'Who got that?' each time a ball ploughed through a file of light infantrymen. They would then enter the names on their lists of casualties. Ned Costello was with the Rifles right at the front of the Light Division's attack. They managed to capture one enemy gun but were severely outnumbered by the French. 'A whole regiment came charging upon us, and our force . . . had to retreat with precipitation. When turning around . . . we beheld our favourite 3rd Division coming double quick down the main road to our assistance – with Picton, who was never absent in time of need, at their head.' Harry Smith was galloping from one unit to another carrying orders when his friends saw his horse collapse under him. The rumour soon got around that he was dead, and Juana was soon scouring the battlefield, not for the first time, for her husband's body. It turned out that neither Smith nor his horse was even scratched. A few moments after his horse had fallen Smith had given it a kick on the nose and it jumped up and was soon back in action.

The French forces had been deployed in three main defensive lines to protect the town of Vitoria. Their position would have been a strong one if they had faced a frontal attack from the west and had destroyed the bridges across the Zadorra to protect their flanks. But the British were now descending on them from the south off the Heights of Puebla and across the river from the north and west, with Wellington right in the middle of the fray. The Commander in Chief led a combined attack on the village of Ariñez by Picton's men, by Dalhousie's division, which had finally turned up, and by the riflemen and light infantrymen who had found their way across the undefended bridge. Costello remembered Wellington shouting, 'That's right, my lads, keep up a good fire.' John Kincaid saw Picton rampaging about swearing roundly, and at one stage heard a voice behind him, 'which I knew to be Wellington's, calling out in a tone of reproof, "Look to keeping your men together, Sir."' In the fight for the village, Kincaid reported, 'At one period, we held one side of a wall, while the French were on the other, so that any person who chose to put his head over from the other side was sure of getting a sword or a bayonet up his nostrils.' Wellington was among the riflemen when they were being hard pressed by the enemy, and he spotted the 88th, the normally fearsome Connaught Rangers, in 'extreme disorder'. So he 'halted them and made them form under the brow of the hill, the 95th [Rifles] being stopped by the fire of one or two battalions of the enemy . . . As soon as formed, the 88th advanced in good order, and attacked and drove in this body into and . . . through Arinez.'

George Bell led his men into Ariñez, where the 'clamour, the flashing of firearms, the shouts and cries of the combatants mixed with the thundering of the guns was terrible'. He heard the 'piteous cries of the wounded for water' and witnessed a sickening sight he hoped never to see again: 'The horses, distracted and torn with cannon shot, were hobbling about in painful torment, some with broken legs and others dragging their entrails after them in mad career.' Picton boasted later that his 3rd Division had 'the principal part of the action, and I may say, covered itself with glory, having contended during the whole day against five times our numbers . . . I was very fortunate, having escaped with only one shothole in my greatcoat.' William Lawrence came across a wounded Frenchman, who clearly had not more than two hours to live as a cannon ball had cut off both his thighs. He pleaded with Lawrence not to leave him to the Spanish, who would murder him. Lawrence searched him, found some food on him, which he shared, and asked if he had any money on him. 'He replied no, but not feeling quite satisfied at that, I again went through his pockets . . . I found his purse at last, which contained seven Spanish dollars and seven shillings, all of which I put in my pocket except one shilling which I returned to the poor dying man and continued on my way up the hill.'

Five miles to the north-east, way behind the main French lines, Graham's force was now trying to cross the river just north of Vitoria. Graham, at sixty-four, was a generation older than most of Wellington's senior officers, and he was not the man to hurl his force across the river like the fiery and impulsive Picton. His attack went in later than Wellington had hoped, and ran into stiff French opposition. John Aitchison, a guardsman whose letters home had been so critical of Wellington at Burgos, didn't spare Graham at Vitoria. He was a 'good deal too old . . . he displays little science and still less decision'. Fred Ponsonby, still struggling with his rebellious stomach and bowels, led his light dragoons in the fierce battle for the village of Gamarra Mayor which controlled one crossing. With all the fire and brimstone flying about, the men were quick to christen the place 'Gomorrah'. French resistance was strong and it was only after a long fight that Graham managed to get enough men across the river to cut off the main road from Vitoria to the French border.

It was 6 p.m. before Ponsonby's 12th Light Dragoons were the other side of the river. They crossed the bridge, advanced at a trot and then at a canter, and soon came within sight of what they thought were French cavalry. 'Our trumpet sounded charge,' William Hay, one of Ponsonby's officers, remembered. But as they galloped forward, they suddenly found themselves facing about 3,000 French infantry standing in squares. 'These opened such a close and well directed fire on our advance squadrons, that not only were we brought to a standstill but the ranks were broken and the leading squadrons went about.' Ponsonby's men managed to rally only when a troop of horse artillery arrived on their flanks and 'within about a hundred yards, opened such a fire of grape shot on the French infantry, that at the first round I saw the men fall like a pack of cards'.

The news of Graham's attack on the French rear had exactly the effect that Wellington had hoped for. The French swiftly withdrew some of their units facing west and weakened their lines. Word began to spread that the British were sweeping across the Zadorra and around behind Vitoria. Kincaid could see that the battle was won. The French were now fleeing 'in one confused mass'. He observed that the British cavalry had missed a golden opportunity. 'Had a single regiment of our dragoons been at hand . . . we must have taken from ten to twenty thousand prisoners . . . I have no doubt our mounted gentlemen were doing their duty . . . in another part of the field, yet it was impossible to deny ourselves the satisfaction of cursing them all, because a portion had not been there.'

Wellington deplored the performance of his cavalry. Victory at Vitoria should have led to the destruction of the French army, but much of it escaped. Besides, Graham's force failed to thrust its way as far around behind Vitoria as it might have done. The road to the strategically placed city of Pamplona remained open. William Tomkinson, another light dragoon involved in the action with Fred Ponsonby, recognised the cavalry's failure: 'Had all the cavalry been brought forward to have acted the instant the enemy passed Vitoria, I think there was a fine chance of taking a great many prisoners, but as is always the case the cavalry was not up.' Tomkinson, who had seen much of Wellington during his time at army headquarters, suggests that his excessively hands-on leadership was partly to blame for the cavalry's failure at Vitoria. 'Lord Wellington may not like to entrust officers with detachments to act according to circumstances, and I am not quite clear if he approves of much success, excepting under his own immediate eye.'

What should have been a glorious day for Wellington's men ended in disgrace. The victorious British army abandoned its pursuit of the French and turned to highway robbery. In their desperation to flee, Joseph Bonaparte, his retinue and his army's senior commanders left behind a great trail of gun carriages, coaches and wagons stuffed with their belongings. Joseph himself narrowly escaped being seized by two hussar officers who threw open the door of his coach just as he leaped out and on to the back of a horse the other side. Within minutes a chaotic convoy of abandoned vehicles littered the first few miles of the road to Pamplona. They contained all the wealth the French high command had amassed and the treasures they had plundered from the palaces of Spain in six years of occupation. Throughout the evening of 21 June whole units of the British army threw order to the winds and indulged in an orgy of looting that dwarfed what had happened at Badajoz. To many of them, after all, plunder was the reward for victory. There were also women in the convoy who did not run away, Spanish girls who had been persuaded – or forced – to join Joseph's travelling court. 'They were young and good-looking,' reported August Schaumann, and now 'all they wanted was protection and a new lover, both of which they soon obtained, and they were to be had for the asking.' There were extraordinary scenes that evening – men staggering along under the weight of boxes of gold they had seized from the carriages as well as clothes, weapons, animals, personal belongings, even documents. William Wheeler 'secured a small box of dollars'; George Bell made do with a 'big sack, a cold fowl, a few maps, and a flask of wine'.

No man could be sure he would escape with his loot: a sort of anarchy prevailed. People fought each other for the richest takings. Ned Costello spotted a man who had been working for the French carrying a heavy portmanteau. 'I compelled him to lay it down, which he did, but only after I had given him a few whacks in the ribs with my rifle.' In it were several small bags filled with gold and silver in doubloons and dollars which Costello reckoned were worth at least £1,000. He decided to keep the loot for himself as his companions had gone off somewhere else. 'All who had the opportunity were employed in reaping some personal advantage from our victory, so I determined not to be backward.' The portmanteau was too heavy to carry so he snatched one of the mules that were blocking the road, but, unable to load the bag on to the mule's back, he asked three passing soldiers to give him a hand.

'Incautiously, I rewarded them too liberally, and in giving them several handfuls of dollars they got a glimpse of the gold, half of which they demanded. Perceiving the probability of being deprived of the only prize I had made after years of hardship and suffering – and particularly to newcomers, for this regiment had newly joined from England – I inwardly resolved not to forfeit it except with my life.' Costello seized the loaded rifle he had left propped against a gun carriage and cocked it. 'Retiring three or four paces, I brought it to my shoulder and swore I would shoot dead the first man to place his hands upon my treasure. My determined air, and the ferocity of my appearance – my face was covered in perspiration and gunpowder – induced them to pause, and finally desist.' On his way back to his tent he passed Wellington, who 'to my great relief took no notice of myself and my mule, being much too occupied in securing the brilliant results of our victory'.

Much of the plunder ended up in the camp where there was soon a carnival atmosphere. The looters set up makeshift stalls to offer their spoils for sale. The whole place echoed to the clinking of coins being counted and the chatter of deals being done. 'Fifty dollars for this pipe.' 'Here is a portrait of Napoleon for a hundred dollars.' William Wheeler said he knew of nothing to compare it all with 'but an Arab camp after a successful attack on some rich caravan'. Animals like mules and goats were sold for knock-down prices. Delicacies from Joseph's royal kitchen wagon were hawked about. There was drinking and carousing in plenty too. Soldiers paraded around dressed in French uniforms they had found in vast wooden chests. And all this went on against the background of the appalling suffering that always followed a major battle. There were cartloads of wounded French,

Spanish and English soldiers, their uniforms covered with blood and dirt. Shambling queues of French prisoners waited to be locked up in churches and other temporary places of detention.

The following morning August Schaumann found the ground all around Vitoria littered with the aftermath of the looting. 'In their lust of plunder the soldiers had . . . torn the cushions and seats of vehicles and strewn their contents abroad . . . I saw huge and beautifully kept ledgers belonging to the Royal treasury, wonderful maps and expensively bound books . . . trodden underfoot and sodden with the rain which had fallen during the night.' One document was extracted from Joseph's belongings with meticulous care by codebreaker George Scovell. It was entitled 'Sa Majesté Catholique' and was the Spanish King's personal copy of the decoding table of Napoleon's Grand Cipher. Scovell had already largely broken it, but its discovery neatly capped years of work he had done to help procure Joseph's collapse. The King's silver chamber pot was spirited away by the men of the 14th Light Dragoons who had found it in Joseph's coach. Two centuries later, nicknamed 'The Emperor', it is the centrepiece of a cavalry barracks' mess silver. On mess nights it is passed round full of champagne by officers of the King's Royal Hussars, today's heirs to the young dragoons who found it in 1813. The last man to drink from it has to finish it all or have the remains poured over his head.

Wellington sent a cavalry detachment to do what it could to stop the looting. But it was too late to secure more than a few carriages. All order and discipline among his 'vagabond soldiers', he said, had been 'totally annihilated'. He expressed his fury to London with his usual hyperbole. 'We have in the service the scum of the earth as common soldiers; and of late years we have been doing every thing in our power, both by law and by publications, to relax the discipline by which alone such men can be kept in order . . . It is really a disgrace to have any thing to say to such men as some of our soldiers are.' At least Wellington had used the word 'some' to exclude others from blame, but this was a particularly furious outburst. He was clearly mortified by his failure to stop all but a fraction of the stolen coin being snatched by his soldiers. He had hoped to use it to help defray his army's expenses. He was also keenly aware of his army's failure to pursue the French effectively after such a decisive victory, a failure that allowed too many of them to fight another day. It was hardly fair of him to blame all of that on his men's behaviour when he himself might have done more to maintain the momentum of the advance. Besides those units that did ignore the temptations of the baggage train and chase after the enemy ran into strong French resistance on a difficult mountain road.

The irony is that the greatest single beneficiary of the sack of the baggage train was Wellington himself. Joseph had stashed away in his carriage a bundle of priceless Old Master canvases he had seized during his rule in Madrid. There were 165 of them altogether, including *The Waterseller of Seville* by Velázquez and Correggio's *Agony in the Garden*. A few had to be retrieved from soldiers who were using them as baggage covers. Wellington, without immediately knowing their value, had them transported to London. They still grace the walls of his home at Apsley House at Hyde Park Corner. His heirs have not been pestered by requests from the Spanish to return them: Wellington was granted permanent possession of them by a grateful Spain as a reward for its liberation.

13

The finger of God is upon me

Pyrenees, 1813

VITORIA WAS A masterly victory. Wellington had already disposed of the jibes that he only fought defensive battles by attacking and destroying Marmont at Salamanca. At Vitoria his reputation went up another notch. He had orchestrated a highly complex set of attacks from four different quarters that left his enemy completely bewildered. His determination to strike before Clausel could join Joseph gave him little time to reconnoitre the ground. Yet his instinctive eye for the terrain served him well and helped him to co-ordinate the attacks with near-perfect timing. It is true that if Graham had moved more swiftly he might have managed to cut Joseph's only remaining escape route, and some believed Wellington could have used his cavalry to more effect.

But the result was devastating for the French. Although more than 50,000 escaped, they lost 8,000 men, the British and their allies 5,000. Napoleon's hold on Spain was over. Wellington was able to boast later that he was right to ignore his staff's advice before crossing the Ebro. 'I was right in my military expectations, and I found afterwards that I was equally right in my political speculations. The victory excited a great sensation in Germany, and particularly at the head-quarters of the allies.' Alexander Gordon, one of those whose advice had been spurned, was happy to admit he was wrong: 'I never saw a large army so very soon beat and the French behave so ill . . . I have no doubt but that the army we have beaten must go back to France.'

The news of Vitoria was received with delight in Britain. It came as a very welcome boost to a Tory government which had had to work hard to explain the setbacks of the last two months of 1812. The Prime Minister Lord Liverpool wrote to Wellington, 'I trust you will be satisfied with the impression which your great and splendid victory has made upon the public in this country. I have no doubt it will produce a state of feeling not less gratifying on the continent . . .' Every effort was made to spread the news of Vitoria across Europe, and special emissaries were sent to take the detailed story to Britain's three main allies in Europe, Prussia, Russia and Austria. Wellington was appointed field marshal by a grateful Prince Regent.

He was now able to focus on the big picture, and his eyes were on the man he always saw as his main antagonist. Napoleon, with astonishing resilience, was still rampant in central Europe. He had picked himself up from the disaster of his Russian campaign in 1812, recruited another large army in 1813 and plunged into Germany. With the Austrians sitting on the sidelines, in May he won yet more victories over Britain's allies, the Prussians and Russians. The news of Vitoria shocked him. He was already aware of the danger Wellington presented to his southern flank. Only a few days before the news of Vitoria broke he had met the Austrian Foreign Minister Prince Metternich in Dresden and was reported to have told him, 'Wellington – there's a general . . . but also the only one who has ever understood me or has ever really given my marshals something to think about.'

Napoleon was now so shaken by the news of Vitoria that he immediately despatched Nicolas Soult to confront Wellington. Soult was no genius on the battlefield, but he had the administrative skills to reinvigorate and reinforce Joseph's broken army on the Spanish border. He knew as much about Spain as any of Napoleon's marshals and he relished the prospect of getting even with the man who had thrashed him at Oporto in 1809. Napoleon, now inexorably entangled in a fight for his regime's survival in central Europe, was waking up to his strategic mistake in not going to Spain himself to destroy Wellington before it was too late. 'The unfortunate war in Spain', he was to reflect years later in exile on St Helena, 'was a real affliction and the first cause of the calamities of France . . . all this effected my ruin.' Wellington had not yet met Napoleon in the field, but he studied his every move. Wellington, the aristocrat, took a typically snobbish view of Napoleon as a man: 'Buonaparte's mind was, in its details, low and ungentlemanlike. I suppose the narrowness of his early prospects and habits stuck to him; what we understand by gentleman-like feelings he knew nothing at all about.'

But Wellington was in no doubt about Napoleon's military genius. He told a friend that Napoleon's presence on a field of battle was worth 40,000 men.

If Vitoria alerted Napoleon to the critical state of his empire in the south, the battle's outcome had a powerful effect on the allies too. Prince Metternich is reported to have told Wellington later that he had been woken in the middle of the night to be told that Joseph Bonaparte had been 'screwed' in Spain, and he added that this had led to a determination among the allies to denounce the armistice and pursue the war until Napoleon himself should be 'screwed'.

For two weeks after Vitoria the British army chased the French towards the border and the formidable Pyrenees mountains, where Wellington expected his enemy to make a stand. There was little fighting, but forced marches and chilly nights in the open. George Simmons was gathering wood for the Light Division one day when he ran into Sir Thomas Picton in particularly irascible mood. The general, who had had it in for the Light Division ever since his rows with Robert Craufurd, said to Simmons: 'Well, sir, you have got enough wood for yours and my Division. I shall have it divided. Make your men throw it down. It is a damned concern to have to follow [you]. You sweep up everything before you.' Simmons promptly complained to the Light Division commander, General Alten, who happened to be near by. 'He was very much annoyed,' and Simmons left him 'to remonstrate with General Picton'.

While Fred Ponsonby's light dragoons were chasing the retreating French, he took a moment to intercede for the artillery commander Captain Norman Ramsay, who had fallen out with Wellington. Ramsay, who had made a name for himself by leading his horse artillery in a spectacular breakout at the battle of Fuentes d'Oñoro, had been arrested after Vitoria. Wellington was furious that Ramsay appeared to have disobeyed orders and taken the wrong route after the battle. Ponsonby, who greatly admired both men, felt it was a misunderstanding and successfully intervened to get Ramsay released. 'I am anxious to state how miserable he [Ramsay] is at having incurred your Lordship's displeasure,' wrote Ponsonby, 'and to express a hope that his long services in the country may induce you to pardon him.' Ramsay burst into tears when he was told he had been released and reinstated. Two years later, still commanding his troop, he was killed at Waterloo.

During this pursuit of the French, there was still time to chase the ladies. On the road to the Pyrenees August Schaumann took time off from being a commissary to perfect his skills. In one village, he claims he had no fewer than five romantic encounters. 'In the first place there were the Donnas Francisca and Stephania from Seville . . . who were very responsive . . . there was a handsome beauty who was the wife of a Spanish colonel . . . I also had a pretty girl who paid me many visits, and finally the legitimate spouse of an organist, who always availed herself of her husband's duties in the church to come to me. I therefore had plenty of variety.' George Bell and other officers of the 34th Regiment, who called themselves the Cumberland Gentlemen, had earlier spent several weeks in one Spanish town where 'there were many pretty girls . . . every fellow had his own sweetheart. The young ladies were charming, barring education . . .'

Within two weeks of Vitoria there were only three pockets of French troops between Wellington and the border – a small village called Vera in the western Pyrenees, and the towns of Pamplona and San Sebastián. Beyond them the French retired behind the border which ran along the Pyrenean mountain tops. Jonathan Leach was with the Light Division as it took up position within sight of Vera. From the heights above it they had a distant view of the ocean, which they hadn't seen for several years. 'A spontaneous and universal shout was raised by the soldiers, which must have astonished our French neighbours, who were separated from us only by a valley.' Close by, through rich green mountain country, flowed the River Bidasoa which was, for a short distance, the frontier between Spain and France, where the mountains dropped down to the sea. The main forces of either side were now concentrated on opposite banks of the Bidasoa and in the approaches to the high Pyrenean passes further east. It was wild and dramatic country, heavily forested and with steep, rocky inclines that made movement difficult. Leach was able to catch some 'uncommonly fine trout' in the Bidasoa. He and seventy-three brother officers in the three battalions of the Rifles celebrated their regimental anniversary with a huge dinner on the riverbank. They dug two trenches to sit in, leaving the ground in the middle to

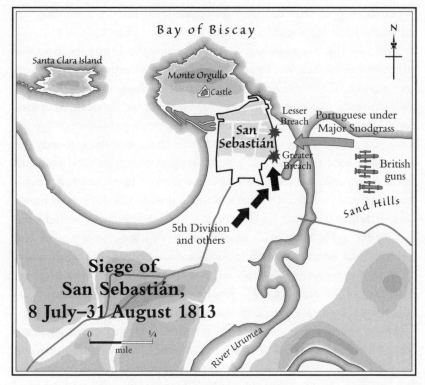

The Siege of San Sebastián

serve as a table – all within sight and earshot of the French who 'were too civil and well-behaved to disturb the harmony of so jovial a set of fellows'.

Wellington ordered Dalhousie to blockade Pamplona, while Graham began the siege of San Sebastián, the last great Spanish fortress on the main coast road into France. The siege of Pamplona would have to wait for San Sebastián to fall. The Royal Navy could now deliver guns, ammunition and food directly to the army through ports in northern Spain. The fall of San Sebastián would open up the whole of Spain's north coast. Wellington was in no hurry. Some commanders – borrowing a favorite tactic of Napoleon's – might have maintained the momentum of the advance by skirting San Sebastián and driving deep into France itself. But what if Napoleon managed to neutralise the allied threat in Germany? And what if he then swung round and threw his weight against an invasion of south-western France?

Wellington preferred to consolidate his hold on the Pyrenees and secure San Sebastián and Pamplona. Everything else could wait.

The key thing was to get the siege train, the big guns and their ammunition to San Sebastián, and Wellington ordered his artillery commander, Colonel Dickson, to have them shipped direct to a port only a mile or two east of the city. And he ordered his talented engineer, Colonel Sir Richard Fletcher, to prepare the equipment for the storming once the guns had blown a breach in the walls. It would not be easy. The city stood on a promontory with a powerfully built castle at the seaward end and massive walls and bastions protecting it from attack across the narrow isthmus that connected it to the mainland. It reminded some of Gibraltar. If well defended, it would be as formidable as Badajoz or Ciudad Rodrigo. Wellington wrote to Earl Bathurst, the Secretary of State for War, in London on 10 July 1813, 'I am in hopes that we shall obtain possession in a short time after we shall have broken ground.' He was being optimistic. The siege of San Sebastián would take him two months.

There were only two places where a realistic attack on San Sebastián could be mounted. There was the complex of bastions on the south side that faced the only approach by land and there was the eastern wall of the city which faced across the River Urumea. Wellington and Graham took the risky decision to attack the eastern wall. It was less heavily protected but it meant the storming could be mounted only at low tide when the main body of attackers would be able to wade across the river. Others who approached along the west bank would have to run under the heavily defended bastions.

The man Wellington chose to blast breaches in the wall of San Sebastián was Augustus Frazer, a Royal Horse Artilleryman whom Wellington greatly admired. He was now on Wellington's staff as senior horse artillery officer. He was put in charge of the main breaching batteries in the sand dunes east of the fortress. Firing from a distance of around 600 yards the roundshot still had the accuracy to cut – as near as they could – two straight vertical lines of holes down the wall and one horizontal line across the bottom. This was the most effective way of getting a great square slab of the wall to collapse. 'We began breaching the wall of San Sebastian at daybreak on the 20th. By midday yesterday the breach of one hundred feet long was perfectly practicable, the wall being entirely levelled. The guns have fired upwards of 300 rounds and several of them 350 daily: this is very violent.'

While his guns were blazing away, Frazer found time to have dinner with Fred Ponsonby, whose cavalry could do little but sit and wait while the siege went on. Everything now depended on Frazer and his gunners, who were themselves exposed to counter-fire from the city walls: 'I have had a scratch or two in the face and head but nothing either to spoil my good looks or spirits.' Wellington, unwisely as it turned out, had left Graham in charge of the siege and gone off to his mountain headquarters on the front line twenty-five miles away. Graham dithered. He was told by Frazer that the main breach would be practicable – open enough to assault – by 22 July. But Graham waited through the 23rd, set the date for the attack on the 24th, then postponed it when he learned that the French had started a fire in some of the nearby buildings. 'Should it not be possible to attack tomorrow, I shall be much at a loss how to proceed,' he wrote to Wellington at 5 a.m. on the 24th.

The delay allowed the gunners to open a second breach in the walls, but the penalty for waiting was that the French who were well motivated and robustly commanded by a sturdy veteran, General Emmanuel Rey, had time to improvise some nasty surprises for the men who would storm the breaches. Besides, Frazer's ammunition was running down fast, and so Graham decided that an attempt should be made to storm the city the following day, the 25th. One of Frazer's artillery officers, Richard Henegan, described how in the darkness before dawn the storming party emerged from the trenches and dashed across atrociously rough ground. They had to brave 'sharp pointed rocks and deep holes of sea water left by the receding tide' in the river. They scrambled as fast as they could along the path at the bottom of the wall towards the breach into a 'terrific fire of musketry and shells from the ramparts, while, in front, a heavy discharge of grape showered from the battery . . . which flanked the approach to the breach'. Those who made it to the breach were mown down by concentrated musket fire, and the dead and wounded soon piled up in the rubble. Others were thrown backwards into the river and swept out to sea.

The one man who made it to the top of the breach, an engineer

1813–14 Campaign

lieutenant who had offered himself as a guide, 'misled by the darkness into the belief that his footsteps would be closely followed by the stormers, bravely leapt from the breach into the town below – a distance of upwards of twelve feet.' But he was on his own, and ended 'a wounded prisoner'. Henegan blamed 'injudicious' planning for the attack, which took place in darkness rather than daylight. Augustus Frazer was close to despair: 'The assault was made but stupidly an hour before and not after daybreak . . . the enemy [commenced] a roll of musketry, the men, panic struck, turned, could never be rallied and sustained loss in running back. No man ever reached the foot of the second breach.' Both Frazer and Henegan believed that a daylight assault, in which the stormers might have drawn strength from seeing each other charging forward, would have been more successful. John Aitchison, writing home from San Sebastián, blamed Graham's 'imbecility and indecision' and the 'ignorance and indolence' of his staff for the mismanagement of the siege.

As soon as Wellington heard of the failed attack on the breach, he leaped on his horse and sped the twenty-five miles from his head-quarters on the Pyrenean border down to San Sebastián, where he found both sides removing their casualties under a truce. Soon after daybreak Frazer had ordered his battery of twenty-four-pounders to reopen their bombardment, but as he peered across at the breach he noticed a Frenchman standing – at great risk to himself – on top of the breach gesturing with his sword towards the British gunners. The officer had seen the devastating effect of the renewed gunfire on the dead and wounded British soldiers – as well as French – lying in the breach. Frazer guessed that he was calling attention to the human suffering in the breach, stopped his guns firing, and a one-hour ceasefire was agreed. When the casualties were counted, there were more than 500 British dead or wounded.

Wellington rode off deeply disappointed and determined to keep a much closer eye on the conduct of the siege from then on. But by the time he was back at his headquarters he had far more than San Sebastián to worry about. A message had reached him halfway back that a major French offensive was under way against his forces through two narrow Pyrenean passes – the pass of Maya and the pass of Roncesvalles. Marshal Soult, despatched by Napoleon from Germany two weeks earlier, had done a masterly job in rallying Joseph's demoralised army and assembling a substantial force in the mountains on the French border. Moreover he had attacked where Wellington least expected him to, not against British forces on the major coast road that led directly into France, but further south-east where he hoped he could surprise and overwhelm the troops Wellington had deployed there. In a proclamation to all his units Soult said he couldn't deny praise for what France's enemy had done in Spain. 'The dispositions and arrangements of their General have been prompt, skilful and consecutive.' But then he addressed himself to his own men: 'I have borne testimony to the Emperor of your bravery and zeal. His instructions are to drive the enemy from those lofty heights which enable him proudly to survey our fertile valleys, and chase them across the Ebro.'

The first news that reached Wellington's headquarters from the front was not good. The defenders were under immense pressure and heavily outnumbered. That evening at dinner Wellington was in one of his darker moods, scarcely speaking to anyone at table. By 10 p.m. he was writing to Graham: 'When on my road home I heard that there had been firing in the Puerto de Maya, and since my arrival I have heard that the enemy had moved in force in the morning upon Roncesvalles . . . it is impossible to know of Soult's plan yet.' Wellington went on to say that they should leave just half a dozen guns to keep up the pressure on San Sebastián and load the rest on board naval ships to be ready for action elsewhere. Wellington was now involved in a full-blown crisis and he got little sleep that night. At 4 a.m. he wrote again to Graham saying that British forces had to retire from the pass of Maya.

Soult, the Duke of Dalmatia, known mockingly in British ranks as the 'Duke of Damnation', had managed to launch 60,000 men at dawn on 25 July. Forty thousand attacked General Lowry Cole's 13,000 British, Portuguese and Spanish troops in the pass of Roncesvalles and another 20,000 men assailed the 6,000 General Hill commanded, defending the Maya Pass. Cole fought for ten hours but when a blanket of fog dropped after 4 p.m. he lost his nerve and pulled his massively outnumbered troops back down the road to Pamplona. He knew that Wellington had ordered him to hold his position at all costs, but he felt he had no choice. Fusilier John Cooper, now a sergeant, described the night withdrawal as 'horrible . . . for our path lay among rocks and bushes, and was so narrow that only one man could pass at a time . . . This was made much worse by the pitchy darkness. Many were swearing, grumbling, stumbling, tumbling. No wonder, we were worn out with fatigue and ravenous with hunger . . .' One young man killed that day was Robert Knowles, who had been one of the first to scale the walls of the castle at Badajoz in April 1812.

Hill's men fought back hard. Thomas Todd's Scottish regiment, the 71st, held on for some time, but then they were 'forced to give way . . . we had the mortification to see the French making merry in our camp, eating the dinner we had cooked for ourselves. What could we do? They were so much superior in numbers.' George Bell, with his companions in the 34th Regiment, the so-called Cumberland Gentlemen, were under less pressure than other units. He looked across to where the Gordon Highlanders, the 92nd, were facing an entire French division. 'The 92nd were in line pitching into the French like blazes, and tossing them over. They stood there like a stone wall overmatched by twenty to one, until half their blue bonnets lay beside those brave warriors.' Suddenly Bell's regiment too was swamped by an enemy attack. 'There was but one escape for us now – to run away, or be riddled to death with French lead . . . I never ran so fast in my life.' By the next morning Hill had managed to rally his men to secure a new front line at Elizondo, ten miles down the road inside Spain.

Wellington moved swiftly. He had been up all night sending despatches and receiving news. He told Graham to move enough men east to guard the main coastal road in case Soult attacked there. The following morning, 26 July, he rode twenty miles up the Bidasoa valley to see what had happened to Hill. He was pleased to find that Hill's force was effectively blocking the central route to Spain down the Baztán Valley. He spent the night in a local mountain village awaiting news from Picton and Cole, who had been hard pressed trying to defend the pass of Roncesvalles. At dawn the following morning he rode south and began to hear rumours of further withdrawals by the two generals. Wellington was incredulous: Picton of all people! He may have disapproved of the coarse Welshman's personality but he couldn't fault his fighting qualities – until this moment. Now that he had an independent command, Picton appeared to have lost that brash self-confidence. Wellington's comment on this crisis was that his generals were 'really heroes when I am on the spot to direct them, but when I am obliged to quit them they are children'.

Wellington rode furiously on. It was essential to stop the French before they could link up with their beleaguered troops in Pamplona. They were just two lone horsemen, superbly mounted, Wellington and his faithful ADC, Fitzroy Somerset, who had been by his side ever since they had landed together at Mondego Bay five years earlier. Suddenly the two men, covered in dust, their horses sweating, were in the little village of Sorauren. It took them seconds to see that they were in serious danger. The French were advancing towards them in force along the ridge to their left. British forces were taking

up position on the hillside some way ahead. With the villagers shouting, 'The French are coming, the French are coming,' Wellington
leaped off his horse, slinging his reins to Fitzroy. He sat on the bridge
scribbling out directions to his other units to make a detour to the
west to avoid the French. Fitzroy seized the note and raced off one
way while Wellington galloped through the village, just escaping the
French who were now sweeping into it. 'It was rather alarming,'
Wellington told Seymour Larpent, his judge advocate, 'and it was a
close run thing.' 'I escaped as usual unhurt,' he wrote to his brother
William. 'I begin to believe that the finger of God is upon me.'
Moments later Portuguese troops spotted a solitary rider approaching
them dressed in a simple grey coat and breeches with a familiar
cocked hat. 'Douro! Douro!' they shouted: it was the title he had
won soon after the capture of Oporto. The cheers were taken up by
the British troops as well and the French didn't take long to realise
that they would be facing Wellington himself in battle the following
day.

The Battle of Sorauren on 28 July was a fierce one. The two
armies faced each other across a valley. It was the French who moved
forward – bringing the combat to close quarters. 'The ground was
uneven, rugged and hilly,' George Bell remembered. 'Strong posts
were taken and retaken with the bayonet.' Wellington said he 'never
saw such fighting'. It was 'fair bludgeon work . . . the losses were
very severe but not of a nature to cripple us'. He was severely outnumbered, but by bringing as many muskets as he could to bear on
the French, who were attacking in columns, he was able to hold off
most of the attacks. John Cooper's fusiliers were among the hardest
pressed. Cooper found himself fighting with only one officer left
standing in his wing of the regiment. He was sent off to ask the colonel for more officers. Ignoring Cooper's request, the colonel said,
'Sergeant Cooper, go up the hill and tell the brigade major to send
down ammunition immediately or we must retire.' Cooper struggled
up the hill: 'I then dragged a Spaniard with his mule laden with ball
cartridges down to my company . . . I smashed the casks and served
out the cartridges as fast as possible while my comrades blazed away.'
The next thing he knew, 'a swarm of the enemy suddenly rushed
over the brow of the hill and swept our much reduced company

down the craggy steep behind . . . however whatever number of balls followed me, they all missed, and I had the pleasure of seeing a fresh body of red jackets coming in haste to our relief'.

When the French looked like breaking through later in the day, Wellington threw in two battalions he had carefully kept in reserve. It was decisive. Soult's attempt to smash through and relieve Pamplona had failed. Two days later, on 30 July, Soult ordered his men to withdraw before dawn. He hoped he would be able to slip away, reform and move against Wellington at another place of his own choosing. But when Wellington's pickets reported the French army on the move in two separate directions, the Commander in Chief ordered his troops to attack the retreating columns. The result was a disaster for Soult. The so-called Second Battle of Sorauren ended with Soult's men escaping to France as best they could through a number of mountain passes.

Now that he had thrown Soult's great counter-offensive back, Wellington could have seized the chance to press on into France. But again his strategic caution prevailed. The outcome of the confrontation between Napoleon and the allies in Germany was still not decided. The campaign there was to continue without resolution until mid-October. In any case Pamplona and San Sebastián remained in French hands. At least one of these had to be taken. It would be unwise to move into France leaving two great border strongholds in French hands. Wellington would first resume the siege of San Sebastián. Alexander Gordon wrote to his brother, 'there is nothing in the world to hinder our invading France as soon as one or other of these places fall'.

This time Wellington wasn't going to risk allowing Graham to make any mistakes. He ordered the guns back into the sand dunes by San Sebastián and increased their numbers. By the end of August Larpent, whose curiosity frequently took him away from his job reviewing court-martial cases, counted fifty-one guns battering away at the city. Henegan, who supervised the constant flow of ammunition wagons to the gunners, says there were no fewer than ninety-five guns altogether. These included some forty massive twenty-four-pounders, now made exclusively of iron which maximised their range and rate of fire. The old brass guns had often overheated dangerously and new technology – a product of Britain's fast-developing industrial revolution – had come to the rescue. It took eight pairs of oxen to drag just one twenty-four-pounder. Each one weighed three tons. And Henegan's ammunition wagons had to be hauled up too, running the gauntlet of enemy fire. They had to carry the powder and shot for the guns, which would devour no fewer than 43,350 cannon balls weighing nearly 500 tons during the entire siege. And that was for the twenty-four-pounders alone: over 1,160 tons of ammunition were fired altogether. In a letter to his wife, Frazer described how it sounded: 'You never heard such a row as is going on. Walls and houses falling, guns and mortars firing. The row in general almost exceeds that of the children in your drawing room.' One battery was placed in a graveyard and its gunners had the distasteful job of having to shift the bodies, which they had to dig up. These fell to pieces when they tried to lift them.

As the siege went on, Wellington was a frequent visitor. He became increasingly impatient, writing to Marshal Beresford on 27 August: 'I was yesterday in San Sebastian where I did not think matters were going exactly right.' In order not to risk another failure he asked for volunteers from other divisions to join the storming party 'and show the 5th division how to mount a breach' – a call bitterly resented by the 5th, who had tried and failed in July. All this meant that August was a quiet month for the rest of the army, particularly for the cavalry who could do little in the Pyrenean passes. Fred Ponsonby wrote home that his light dragoons were in such good spirits in their excellent quarters that he wished he could get them launched into France before the harshness of winter could change their mood.

It was not until 31 August that Graham felt ready to order the assault on two breaches the guns had opened in the walls of San Sebastián. This time the forlorn hope, the spearhead of the storming party, would move in daylight, and they would be backed up by men from the crack Light Division despatched by Wellington from their camp near the border. George Gleig, who was later to know Wellington well and write a lively biography of him, was a raw seventeen-year-old recruit when the ship carrying him to Spain arrived at San Sebastián in the middle of the siege. The 31st of August dawned dark and gloomy 'as if the elements had been aware of the approaching conflict, and were determined to add to its awfulness by their disorder. A close and oppressive heat pervaded the atmosphere.' Major Snodgrass was assigned to command a Portuguese battalion in a frontal assault on the walls – across the River Urumea. During the night he did a bold and very risky piece of personal reconnaissance. He crept forward to the river, identified a spot where he could ford it, breasted his way through the water, felt his way stealthily up the smaller, seaward of the two breaches and stood on the top of it for a moment looking over the town. 'How he managed', said Gleig, 'to elude the vigilance of the French sentinels I know not.'

By 11 a.m. Graham's men were ready. Soldiers readied their muskets, officers drew their swords. None spoke. The first casualty was Sir Richard Fletcher, Wellington's brilliant engineer who had masterminded the Lines of Torres Vedras. He was shot through the head as he carried out a last-minute survey of the state of the breaches. Then the stormers were up and scrambling through sand, water, rock and mud towards the wall. It was the first major daylight assault on a fortress in the Peninsular War. The French had a clear view of their enemy emerging from trenches they had dug for shelter a few hundred yards away. The defenders held their fire till they were closer, and then opened fire 'with the most deadly effect. Grape, canister, musketry, shells, grenades, every species of missile, in short, which modern warfare supplies, were hurled from the ramparts; beneath which our gallant fellows dropped like corn before the reaper; insomuch that, in the space of two minutes, the river was choked up with the bodies of the killed and wounded'.

Richard Henegan was standing beside Lieutenant General Graham watching the slaughter. 'As each succeeding party fell, so did another and another rush on with fearful shouts over the bodies of the slain, gaining the summit of the breach, and falling lifeless on it, as soon as gained.' Then suddenly the gaze of the spectators switched to the right where the Portuguese battalion, their dark uniforms a striking contrast to the British redcoats, surged across the sand and into the river. Led by Major Snodgrass waving his sword several yards ahead of their front rank, they waded, with the water above their waists, and threw themselves at the smaller breach. Again, the French opened up with everything in their armoury. 'An "Oh!" burst from General Graham's lips as he looked upon the murderous havoc made in the ranks of those brave men.' What made the French defence so effective was the deadly fire of a line of sharpshooters, protected by a small rampart they had built at the top of the breaches.

After two hours of slaughter Graham was faced with the prospect of utter failure. Then his chief gunner, Colonel Dickson, made a suggestion that was to sharpen the effectiveness of artillery on the battlefield from then on. He asked permission for his batteries to fire over the heads of the attacking British and Portuguese. He believed they could fire accurately enough to pick off the sharpshooters without killing their own men. He was proved right. The gunfire had an immediate effect, and one lucky howitzer shell struck a magazine just behind the rampart which exploded among the defenders with devastating effect. 'In every direction,' Henegan recalled, 'these hapless beings fell by the force of the explosion: legs and arms, heads and headless bodies, showered over the ramparts among our men, who, shouting with exultation, rushed with frenzied enthusiasm to every crevice that offered admittance.'

The garrison commander, General Rey, withdrew his troops to the castle on the end of the promontory, which they continued to defend for another week. The town itself was soon on fire and being sacked by a mob of soldiers desperate for revenge for their fallen comrades and soon maddened by drink. Casks of wine and spirits were strewn in the streets by defenders anxious to delay the attackers, but this only had the effect of driving them to further extremes. 'Fortunately there were few females in the place; but of the fate of the few which were there, I cannot even now think without a shudder. The houses were everywhere ransacked, the furniture wantonly broken, the churches profaned, the images dashed to pieces.' The British had lost 3,000 in the siege but nothing excused the atrocities that followed their victory.

All this led to a huge row between Wellington and the Spanish authorities in Cadiz. He was appalled by the behaviour of his troops in San Sebastián, but infuriated by the way his Spanish allies reacted. They claimed that his troops had set fire to the town and effectively committed war crimes against the Spanish civilian population. The

French had set fire to the houses themselves, Wellington said. He was so angry he nearly resigned his position as commander in chief of Spanish forces. He was restrained by the fact that his carefully nurtured construction of a joint Anglo-Portuguese–Spanish military coalition was producing valuable dividends. The Portuguese forces were now an essential and integral part of his army. They had had four years of training in battle, and as George Hennell remarked, after admiring the valiant Portuguese attack on the breach, 'See what our example and instruction have done. 5 years ago 100 French would have driven 1000 of these troops before them like sheep.' And Wellington had the very same day, 31 August, witnessed the Spanish 4th Division fight off an attempt by Marshal Soult to cross the Bidasoa in a belated attempt to rescue San Sebastián. At one stage the Spanish commander appealed to him for help, but he refused it, pointing out that it was better for Spain to show the world that its forces could now win victories on their own. This Spanish military success greatly encouraged Wellington, but it did little to shore up his brittle relationship with the Cortes, the republican parliament in Cadiz. The military alliance was to survive till the end of the war, but to hold it together Wellington had to display a level of tact and diplomacy that didn't come naturally.

14

Extraordinary news
Southern France, 1813–1814

T HE FRENCH THRUST across the Bidasoa on 31 August 1813
was Soult's last major attempt to claw back territory in Spain.
Harry Smith, a brigade major with the Light Division, watched
Soult's men ford the river on the 31st and attack the Spanish forces
on the other side. The Spanish fought stoutly and pushed them
back. And when the French turned back they found the river high
and the fords impassable. So they had to make for the one bridge
– at Vera, held by a small detachment of Smith's comrades. He was
infuriated when his commander, Brigadier Skerrett, would send
only a small force to hold the bridge and the cluster of houses
beside it. Smith was for posting an entire battalion of around 500
there. Skerrett said no, it was to be only a company of fifty under
the command of Smith's friend Daniel Cadoux. Smith asked
Skerrett if he really meant that to be an order. 'Yes,' said Skerrett,
'I have already told you so.' 'We shall repent this before daybreak,'
Smith fired back.

The little band at the bridge found itself facing thousands of
retreating French, desperate to cross. 'Three successive times, with
half his gallant band did he [Cadoux] charge and drive back the
enemy over the bridge, the other half remaining in the houses as support.' But then 'a melancholy shot pierced his head, and he fell lifeless
from his horse'. The French forced the bridge and escaped, and the
following morning Smith found the bridge 'almost choked with
the dead'. Cadoux and sixteen of his men had died, but they had
killed 230 French. Wellington, said Smith, was 'awfully annoyed',
and Smith was delighted when Skerrett went home sick shortly afterwards. The new brigade commander was John Colborne, a man
Smith admired as much as he loathed Skerrett.

Wellington kept his forces poised on the Bidasoa throughout September. The news from Germany was still inconclusive and the French garrison in Pamplona held out. He told the government in London that he recognised public opinion at home was growing impatient: 'I see that as usual the newspapers on all sides are raising the public expectation and that the allies are very anxious that we should enter France . . . I think I ought,' he conceded with obvious reluctance, 'and will bend a little to the views of the allies if it can be done with safety to the army, notwithstanding that I acknowledge I should prefer to turn my attention to Catalonia [in eastern Spain] as soon as I have secured this frontier.'

So with great skill and elaborate planning Wellington embarked on a surefooted but painstakingly slow winter campaign to loosen Napoleon's hold on France itself. He moved cautiously because the immediate future was uncertain. If Napoleon succeeded in subduing central Europe again, he could turn on Wellington with all that was left of his Grande Armée and challenge him to fight a decisive battle on French soil. If, on the other hand, he were defeated in Germany and forced back into France, the road could be open to Paris – with the allies forcing him back from the north-east and Wellington pressing up from the south. But Paris was 450 miles away from the border with Spain and Soult had a lot of fight left in him yet. Wellington set in motion a sequence of advances, none of them spectacular, each of them with the limited ambition of lopping off successive slices of French territory from one river line to another.

Wellington's move to establish his first foothold in France began on 7 October when he sent his men across the Bidasoa, the river that was at its seaward end the border between France and Spain. Wellington adopted the stratagem Soult had used in his abortive offensive on 24 July – in reverse. His observations, through his own telescope and from his intelligence sources, suggested that Soult appeared to be expecting an attack in the mountain passes rather than on the coast. So Wellington made as if to attack in the passes, with a feint attack at Maya, but launched his main assault at daybreak on the coast at Hendaye, and in the foothills of the Pyrenees at Vera.

The first, on the coast, was very quickly successful. The attack went across at the lowest point of the tide, but the river's flow was strong enough to sweep away a few who were killed or wounded by the first shots from the other shore. After wading through the river some of the men were faced by a battery of French guns. They managed to fire a musket volley at the gunners and then scare them away by charging with bayonets and shouting wildly. Fred Ponsonby's 12th Light Dragoons were soon across too.

There was intense competition among mounted regiments to be first into any fray, and to prove themselves in the face of Wellington's profound scepticism about their competence. Ponsonby's regimental history haughtily dismisses all the other cavalry as 'up to their bellies in fine hay and straw doing nothing . . . But Colonel Ponsonby is such a man he is never quiet unless he is in the middle of everything.' Once across on the French bank of the river Ponsonby was soon helping to push the enemy back as far as Urrugne, three miles inside France – just short of Saint-Jean-de-Luz. There Ponsonby's dragoons ran into a strong French cavalry reserve force which stopped them. Ponsonby's mother wrote a typically glowing account of her son's exploits. His light dragoons 'only had to ride quietly through with the enemy flying before them quite panic struck'.

The second attack – at Vera in the foothills of the Pyrenees ten miles to the east – was a much fiercer struggle. Wellington gave the job to the Light Division supported by the Spanish. Their objective was to clear the French out of the valley of Vera and off the mountain passes above it that led into France. But the ground was against them. The passes were dominated by the great pyramid-like massif of La Rhune. Today it is a magnificent tourist viewing-point reached by a mountain railway. In October 1813 La Rhune, the passes and the surrounding wooded slopes were alive with French earthworks and well-entrenched sharpshooters.

John Colborne's brigade had the most daunting task of all. They had no choice but to attack the French head on. Harry Smith was with Colborne and recalled the 'swarm of riflemen in skirmishing order keeping up a murderous fire. Firing up a hill is far more destructive than firing down, as the balls in the latter case fly over.' Smith and Colborne were on horseback. John Cooke was scrambling up on foot like most of the soldiers. They didn't just have to face enemy fire: 'The mountain was fearfully difficult of ascent, and it was indeed so intersected with rocks, trees, brushwood, and prickly briars that our hands and limbs were pierced with thorns and the trousers were literally torn to shreds from off our legs.'

After Colborne had captured one position, he pushed on 'rather madly' up a ravine with Smith and a small group of men. 'To my dismay,' wrote Colborne, 'I saw a body of about 400 French passing . . . below me. The only way was to put a good face on the matter.' So he coolly rode up to the French officer at the head of the column and said in French: 'You are cut off. Lay down your arms.' The officer, completely fooled, offered his sword and told his men to lay down their arms. Then Colborne turned to Harry Smith: 'Quick, Smith, get a few men together or we are yet in a scrape.' At that moment Colborne had only around fifteen men. 'I kept the French officer in play, and [Smith's reinforcement] arrived before the French had discovered their error.' 'We were called madmen for our audacity,' said Smith afterwards. 'I never witnessed such presence of mind as Colborne evinced on this occasion.'

Wellington wrote warmly of Colborne in his despatches, saying his men carried the enemy positions in a 'most gallant style'. But he was none too pleased when one of Colborne's officers blithely announced to the Commander in Chief that he had taken some pigs and poultry from a French farm. Wellington, anxious as ever to pre-vent his soldiers grabbing local produce and alienating the local population, told Colborne, 'Though your brigade have even more than usually distinguished themselves, we must respect the property of the country.' Colborne replied, 'I am fully aware of it, my lord . . . but your lordship well knows in the very heat of action a little irregu-larity will occur.' 'Ah Ah!' said Wellington. 'Stop it in future, Colborne.'

Wellington quickly tightened up discipline as he moved further into France. The Spanish, eager to avenge the French behaviour in Spain, were the worst offenders. Picton had long regarded the Spanish as hopeless fighters. Now he counted them useless allies. 'We should do much better', he said, 'without these vapouring pol-troon rascals whose irregular conduct indisposes everyone towards us.' Wellington told his generals to punish offenders with the utmost severity. August Schaumann watched Ned Pakenham,

Wellington's brother-in-law, 'riding up and down our columns like a raving lion seeking whom he might devour. His command "Let that man be hanged instantly!" was executed in a twinkling.' Schaumann saw 'the body of one Spanish muleteer, who had entered a house to steal apples, hanging from the window of that house as a warning to all marauders. In his mouth, which had fallen open in the process of strangulation, they had stuck an apple to show what he had coveted.'

The winter cold had started. One of Harry Smith's friends built a little mud hut for Harry and Juana to sleep in. It was snug and warm inside. The couple turned over their chilly tent to their servants and cuddled up to each other in their new den. 'All went well until a sudden shower of rain came on . . . In ten seconds it came down through the roof of our black-earth sods, and . . . we were drenched to the skin and as black as chimney-sweepers. The buoyant spirits of my wife and the ridiculous position we were in made her laugh herself warm.'

William Lawrence, the ploughboy from Dorset, earned promotion when he led his squad to take out a French gun that had been firing at Wellington. Lawrence and six chosen men crept up to within reach of the gun and prepared to attack. 'At last when ready, I said "Now my men, examine your flints and priming, so that all things may go right." They did so, saying "All right, Corporal, we will follow you," so I too sang out "Now for a gold chain or a wooden leg" . . . we jumped up, and giving them a volley we charged them and succeeded in gaining the cannon.' Wellington was so impressed he came up to Lawrence, asked him his name and said, 'I shall think of you another day.' A little later Lawrence heard he was a sergeant: it upped his pay by sixpence a day to one shilling and eleven pence.

One new arrival, a 'Johnny Newcome' with a keen eye and a lively pen was the dapper Welsh guardsman Rees Gronow. He soon got his first glimpse of the 'immortal Wellington' riding past with Fitzroy Somerset and the rest of his staff. 'He was very stern and grave-looking; he was in deep meditation, so long as I kept him in view, and spoke to no one. His features were bold, and I saw much decision of character in his expression. He rode a knowing-looking, thorough-bred horse, and wore a gray overcoat, Hessian boots, and a large cocked hat.' Wellington had good reason to be looking stern and grave. He was still deeply uncertain about what to do next. On 18 October he wrote to London: 'I am very doubtful indeed about the advantage of moving any farther forward here at present.' The uncertainty was being decisively resolved on that very day in central Europe. Napoleon suffered his second biggest reverse of the entire war so far. Russia had been a catastrophe for him. The Battle of Leipzig between 16 and 19 October was the beginning of the end. Defeated by Britain's three allies, Russia, Prussia and Austria, Napoleon began a retreat that was to end with his abdication in Paris in April 1814. But Wellington knew nothing of this, and Pamplona still held out against him.

For much of October, from the heights above Vera, Harry Smith and John Colborne watched the French fortifying the line of the next river beyond the Bidasoa, the Nivelle, which runs down from the Pyrenees to its mouth at Saint-Jean-de-Luz on the coast. Wellington would join them from time to time, and on 8 November he said to Colborne, 'Those fellows think themselves invulnerable, but I will beat them out, and with great ease . . . the enemy have not men to man the works and lines they occupy . . . I can pour a greater force on certain points than they can concentrate to resist me.' He then squatted down with his generals and 'it was', said Smith, 'one of the most interesting scenes I have ever witnessed'. He watched Wellington go through his plan of attack with his Quartermaster General, his chief staff officer George Murray. Then while Wellington scanned the enemy lines with his telescope Murray read back to him a summary of the orders he had issued. 'My Lord, is this your desire?' asked Murray. Wellington smiled his assent, and said the plan would win them the battle. This time, to keep Soult guessing, Wellington switched the weight of his offensive away from his left wing on the coast. The main attack would be through the mountain passes. By 10 November the army were poised to attack across the Nivelle. Harry Smith nearly forgot to say goodbye to his wife, who told him she had had a presentiment that either he or his horse would die. 'I laughed and said, ". . . I hope it may be the horse."'

Seymour Larpent dined with Wellington the night before the

attack, staying there until ten o'clock. 'He was all gaiety and spirits and only said on leaving the room: "Remember! At four in the morning."' Larpent was up early to watch it all from the top of La Rhune. 'Even the doctors and the two parsons' went off to get a ringside seat. Larpent saw it all. The day, he said, was 'beautiful', his view 'an uninterrupted panorama of battle, fire and smoke' all the way from the western seashore to the mountains over to the east. The view from La Rhune is breathtaking enough in time of peace. To the south precipitous, rocky slopes plunge sharply down to the town of Vera by the Bidasoa 3,000 feet below. To the north an elaborate pattern of hills and valleys falls gently away across the Nivelle to the plain of Bayonne and, beyond, the Biscay coast of France stretching up towards Bordeaux. On 10 November 1813, this landscape presented Larpent with a unique spectacle of death and destruction. Through gaps in the smoke he would have seen thousands of small flecks of red and blue where the footsoldiers were fighting it out. He may have spotted the odd extra flash of white and gold where light dragoons on either side cantered past the fighting looking for points of enemy weakness or carrying orders to unit commanders. Larpent may even have had a glimpse of the understated blue-grey of Wellington's jacket flitting past rocks and trees as he rode from one crisis point to another, usually with a small, colourful group of aides behind him, sometimes alone.

George Bell was with one of Hill's divisions on the far right. 'As we advanced the red-glare flash of the cannon, the bellowing of the guns and the white puff far to our left, showed us that death and destruction were extremely busy.' The French at last collapsed under the impetus of Hill's attack. 'I confess I was not sorry to see them give way, for we had enough blood and brains on the sod for one day . . . we passed on through their lines of defence . . . we found their rations uncooked and plenty of onions and other vegetables, which were transferred tout de suite into our haversacks en passant.' Bell and his mates chased the French till sundown and then sat down to rest. 'We turned out the contents of our larder – a Dutch cheese, onions, biscuit, cold ration beef and a little rum . . . it was marvellous how quick the dead and the wounded were stripped on the battlefield by the camp followers of the two great armies – an unhallowed trade.'

Further west, the Light Division swept nearly everything before them and when they came to a stop Colborne and Smith found themselves facing one last very well-defended enemy redoubt. Sydney Beckwith, who had been a highly successful and popular Rifles commander ever since he landed in Portugal just before Vimeiro five years earlier, rode up and told them that their orders were to 'move on'. 'What do you mean – attack?' asked Colborne. 'I don't know: your orders are to move on.' 'What an evasive order!' remarked Colborne. 'Oh sir,' said Smith to him, 'let's take the last of their works: it will be the operation of a few minutes.' Colborne allowed himself to be persuaded by Smith's enthusiasm. But it turned out to be a lot more difficult. The regiment lost a large number of men. Wellington said he was sorry they had attacked the strongpoint; he had not meant them to. 'Some discussion took place as to the order Colborne had received,' said Smith. 'However I think now as I did then, "move on" implied "attack".' Juana's premonition turned out to be correct. Smith's 'beautiful thoroughbred mare', called Old Chap, was hit at the Nivelle and 'she fell upon me with a crash, which I thought had squeezed me as flat as a thread-paper, her blood, like a fountain, pouring into my face.' Wellington thought Smith must have been wounded when he saw him a few minutes later, and Juana was 'horror-struck' but deeply relieved.

The Battle of the Nivelle again caught Soult on the wrong foot. As Wellington had guessed, the marshal had expected the attack on the coast where he was stronger. It came in the hills. With his forces hurled back by the force of Wellington's right hook, Soult abandoned his positions by the sea, around Saint-Jean-de-Luz, and pulled back to Bayonne, a massive fortress, strategically placed on the confluence of the Rivers Nive and Adour. Saint-Jean-de-Luz became Wellington's first headquarters in France.

Napoleon's hold on his own country was crumbling for the first time since he had come to power. Even as he heard Wellington was threatening the next riverline, the Nive, he was faced with invasion of the French homeland in the east by Prussia, Austria and Russia. But few thought the outcome inevitable. The talk on the eastern front, with varying enthusiasm on the part of each of the three powers in the alliance, was of making peace with Napoleon. They would offer the Emperor recognition within France's traditional, natural borders. Even Wellington was careful to hedge his bets. On 21 November he wrote to Bathurst in London that he was being told 'the sentiment throughout France is the same as I have found it here, an earnest desire to get rid of him [Napoleon], from a conviction that as long as he governs they will have no peace'. But Wellington's advice was 'I recommend to your Lordship to make peace with him if you can acquire all the objects which you have a right to expect . . . If Buonaparte becomes moderate, he is probably as good a Sovereign as we can desire in France . . .' As 1813 turned into 1814 and Wellington occupied more of France, his view hardened. He reported that the vast majority of French civilians he was encountering wanted Napoleon's regime replaced by the old Bourbon monarchy. But Napoleon's soldiers, for the most part, fought on and, as the Emperor himself rejected compromise, it became clear that only his defeat would end the war.

It was to take five months of occasionally very bitter fighting before the struggle ended. The first major encounter took place on and around the River Nive, which flows north-west into Bayonne from the Pyrenees. On 9 December Wellington sent part of his army across the Nive to seize the territory between it and the next river, the Adour, a little further north. Soult, with his back to Bayonne, fought back hard – first attacking the troops Wellington had left west of the Nive, then those under General Hill who had crossed it on the 9th. The pontoon bridge Wellington stretched across the river to allow his forces to support each other was swept away by a flood on the 12th. On the 13th Soult attacked Hill, who was now on his own east of the river. Soult's 35,000 French hammered into Hill's 14,000. George Bell's regiment, the 34th, was pushed back by overwhelming weight of numbers until it was rallied to make a desperate stand. 'Dead or alive, my lads, said our chief, we must hold our ground.' Bell and his men made a bayonet charge, with powerful artillery support. 'Writhing and quivering humanity lay over each other now in mortal combat, steeped in blood. The cannon shot from each side was crushing up the living with the dead and dying . . . The broken column retired.' Once again British lines were able to take a heavy toll of French columns. Bell remarked that the French always attacked in column, and he thought they were wrong to do so. 'They . . . gave us an opportunity of showing them their error, which they never acknowledged to this day.' Colborne, one of Wellington's greatest admirers, felt that on this occasion the Commander in Chief had 'committed a great error' leaving Hill quite isolated on the east bank of the Nive. It had been a risk, but Wellington wanted to keep the pressure on Soult by widening the scope of his advance. And if there was one commander he could trust to do it, it was Rowland Hill. Wellington was quick to congratulate Hill afterwards, shaking him by the hand and saying, 'Hill, the day's yours.' In spite of the odds against him Hill had inflicted 3,300 casualties on the French – almost twice the number his own side had suffered.

For much of January and February 1814 the weather made any progress impracticable. The two sides stayed in winter quarters. Jonathan Leach found plenty of time to do some shooting in January. 'The snow drove the woodcock down onto the low ground by which I profited and had some capital sport.' The brief interlude allowed the usual fraternisation to take place between some front-line pickets. One lady from Bayonne ventured as far as the front line with her pet poodle to see what the British redcoats looked like. The poodle took off and ran into the British lines. 'Without a moment's delay,' reported John Cooke, 'we sent it back by a soldier to its anxious mistress, who was highly delighted and with her own delicate hand presented a goblet of wine to the man, who . . . quaffed the delicious beverage to the dregs, touched his cap and rejoined us with a pipe in his mouth and a store of tobacco . . . presented to him by the French soldiers.'

The weather improved enough by the middle of February for Wellington to order his men forward again. Bayonne was to be encircled and besieged. Wellington did not want to leave such a formidable fortress in his wake without at least neutralising it by blockade. The treacherous mouth of the River Adour would have to be bridged to cut off the city from the north. A small British detachment managed to cross the river in small boats on 24 February and seize a position from the French on the north side of the river. A few of Fred Ponsonby's dragoons went in the boats as well, their horses swimming alongside their riders. It was now vital to construct a bridge to supply and reinforce them. What followed was an engineering feat as daring as any in the war so far. It was achieved only when the Royal Navy, inspired by the army's success, braved the wild surf at the exposed mouth of the river to ship in the heavy equipment needed to strap together a bridge of boats. Several sailors and engineers lost their lives, swept away by the waves, but the bridge was deftly built and thousands of men were soon across.

Bayonne was now surrounded and Wellington reported to London that Ponsonby and his dragoons had patrolled as far as twenty-seven miles inland before he was halted by a French outpost. Wellington remained uneasy about his cavalry and Ponsonby was one of the few cavalry officers he still felt he could trust on special operations after six years of campaigning. 'In Spain', he was to say later, 'the Germans, the 14th Light Dragoons and perhaps the 12th under Fred Ponsonby were the only regiments that knew their duty and did not get into scrapes of every description.'

Wellington's main force pressed east from the Nive leaving Bayonnne surrounded but untaken behind them. Only when they had crossed four more rivers was there serious opposition from Soult at the town of Orthez. The French marshal had taken up a formidable position on a great ridge. The only way to dislodge him was for Wellington's men to fight their way up four steep spurs. Three and a half years earlier the French had clambered up the steep slopes of the ridge at Bussaco only to be thrown back each time by the British defenders on top. Now it was the French who were defending the high ground and the British who were suffering the exhaustion of the climb and the steady fire of French skirmishers in their struggle to reach the summit. William Surtees of the Rifles watched Wellington – at his command post – looking 'extremely thoughtful and serious . . . the enemy's position proved to be exceedingly strong and difficult of access by us'. But Wellington co-ordinated his attacks with such care that his men eventually scrambled to the top from a number of different directions at the same time.

Wellington made Colborne's light infantrymen the arrowhead of the assault. 'They did it beautifully,' wrote Colborne, unashamedly claiming the glory. 'When all the rest were in confusion, the 52nd marched . . . as if on parade, accelerating their march as they approached the hill . . . I rode on to the top of the hill and waved my cap . . . and the men . . . trotted up in the finest order.' The final showdown took place at the church of Saint-Boes, which still stands above the trees on the skyline today. By the evening the French were in headlong retreat to the north, crossing the River Adour and eventually retiring to the well-fortified city of Toulouse.

Wellington wrote to his brother Richard: 'The action was for some time very warm but I never saw troops get such a beating as they did . . . and they were saved at all only by the night.' Just over 2,000 British, Portuguese and Spanish were killed or wounded at Orthez; the French lost twice as many. In recent years a stone has been erected in a small clearing just north of the town commemorating the 'English, Portuguese, French and Spanish who died in the Battle of Orthez'. It's the work of an elderly local resident, Jacques Cloup, who says the monument owes its existence to a remarkable piece of oral history. When he was a boy, he says his great-aunt told him the story of a mass burial at this spot which she had, in her turn, heard of as a young girl from her great-grandfather, who was a child at the time of the battle in 1814. He told her that the farmers of the time were so appalled by the thousands of stripped and plundered bodies of men and horses littering their fields after the battle that they clubbed together to bury them. All were moved to this spot and interred, regardless of their nationality, horses and all, in one large pit.*

Just for a moment it looked as if the 'finger of God', which Wellington had boasted about, might be pointing elsewhere. During the attack on Saint-Boes the Commander in Chief had dismounted and was standing with his Spanish liaison officer, General Álava, when a Portuguese soldier limped to the rear explaining as he passed that he was *ofendido* ('wounded' in Portuguese). 'Wellington was laughing at the expression when a grape or musket shot struck the

* To find the graveyard today, you go to Bonnut near Orthez and ask for the *cimetière des Anglais*.

hilt of his sword driving it violently against his hip. He fell to the ground, but rose to his feet immediately, smiling and saying: "By God I am ofendido this time." He was able to remount and ride slowly.'

There is another version of this story. Wellington was said to have been having a good laugh at the expense of Álava, whose bottom had just been bruised by a spent bullet. But the laugh was on Wellington moments later when he too was hit, and Álava remarked that he deserved it for laughing at him. 'It was a bad bruise and skin was broken,' Larpent observed, expressing the fervent wish that Wellington would soon make a full recovery 'as all our prospects here would vanish with that man'. It is astonishing that this was the only time Wellington was ever hurt: musket balls tore his clothing at Talavera and Salamanca, and he lost two horses under him at Assaye. Very few of his aides escaped death or severe wounding in the two dozen battles and sieges in which he and his staff spent so much time together near the front line. A cannon ball took off the head of the aide crossing the river beside him at Assaye and his second in command, Lord Uxbridge, lost a leg to a piece of canister shot from a French cannon that shaved Wellington's horse's head at Waterloo.

The campaign that Wellington and his exhausted but triumphant veterans had fought for six years was drawing to a close. Napoleon's hold on France was crumbling. In the towns and villages Wellington passed through, the white Bourbon cockade, the royalist emblem, was everywhere. Only Bayonne held out and the determined Nicolas Soult, whose army, though depleted by desertions, was still ready to fight for the Emperor. In the early months of 1814 Napoleon fought some of his most brilliant rearguard actions against the advancing Russians, Prussians and Austrians. Wellington said that Napoleon's campaign that spring was 'probably the ablest of all his performances'. Soon after the beginning of April rumours began to find their way from Paris that Napoleon had simply run out of ways to resist. But neither Wellington nor Soult knew for sure, and one final and ferocious battle in southern France was still to be fought before the shooting stopped. Soult concentrated his men in the fortified city of Toulouse, and Wellington found himself fighting more of a siege than an open battle. His plan was to conduct a multi-pronged attack on the French, who held a number of very strong positions. He made the mistake of giving his Spanish forces the task of attacking the most difficult strongpoint. Just about every-thing went wrong. Picton tried to turn what was to be a feint attack into a real one and lost 400 men, Beresford conducted his men in a long flank march which exposed them to murderous gunfire, and the Spanish were routed in an assault on the main French position at the top of a hill.

Colborne, already critical of his chief's conduct of the Battle of the Nive, called Toulouse 'the worst arranged battle that could be, noth-ing but mistakes . . . I think the Duke most deserved to have been beaten.' Wellington's loss was much greater than Soult's – 4,600 to 3,200, and it was only the fact that Soult and his army abandoned the city the night after the fighting, on 11 April, that allowed the British and their allies to claim it as a success. Wellington, making the most of the French withdrawal, described his rather dubious victory as a 'very severe affair with the enemy in which we defeated them completely'.

The loss of nearly 8,000 killed and wounded on both sides made the Battle of Toulouse one of the bloodiest as well as the most point-less in this long war. The terrible irony was that Napoleon had given up the struggle five days earlier. Fred Ponsonby brought the news from Bordeaux, where his light dragoons had been welcomed by royalists. On the way back he galloped when he could, but he had to talk his way through several French outposts. He found Wellington in his shirtsleeves pulling on his boots. 'I have extraordinary news for you,' said Ponsonby. 'Ay I thought so. I knew we should have peace: I've long expected it,' said Wellington, assuming that the allies had made peace with Napoleon. 'No,' said Ponsonby, 'Napoleon has abdicated.' 'How abdicated? Ay, 'tis time indeed. You don't say, upon my honour! Hurrah!' cried Wellington, 'turning round on his heel and snapping his fingers'.

Toulouse became a city of celebration. The white cockade appeared everywhere as if by magic. Napoleon's statue was tossed off the roof of the Town Hall and at a joyous dinner that night Wellington pronounced the toast: 'Louis XVIII!' Then Larpent watched General Álava leap to his feet and raise his glass 'with great warmth' to 'El Liberador de España'. 'There was then cheering all in confusion for nearly ten minutes! Wellington bowed, confused, and immediately called for coffee. He must have been not a little gratified with what had passed.'

In the middle of April the Bourbon King Louis XVIII whom Wellington described as a 'walking sore', racked by gout from head to toe, took back the throne his brother had lost to the guillotine in 1793.

Wellington's Peninsular War was over. It had not brought down Napoleon directly. Britain's allies in central and eastern Europe had done that. But it had helped. The sure-footed tramp of Wellington's warriors, fighting their way across the Peninsula, sometimes forward, sometimes back, never giving up, never beaten in battle, aided by the Spanish revolt, had kept a quarter of a million French troops bogged down when Napoleon badly needed them elsewhere. The Peninsula had become an open wound, sapping his strength. To the rest of Europe, desperate to see France's grip loosen, Wellington's string of successes had been a constant source of inspiration.

Wellington's men, whose occasional excesses had driven him to those famous outbursts of fury, had emerged from the campaign as the most formidable enemies of France anywhere in Europe. Wellington now had more experience of fighting the French continuously than any other general. And if his progress had been too slow and deliberate for his army to claim total victory this time, their chance would come.* Napoleon was down but not out. Just fourteen months later, Wellington and some of his Peninsular veterans – far too few for his liking – would fight the decisive battle. From commanders like Picton and Ponsonby to front-line soldiers like Wheeler and Todd, the victors of Salamanca and Vitoria would confront Napoleon on a different battlefield. And the leader few of them loved but all respected, 'that long-nosed beggar that licks the French',

---

* Wellington later admitted that at the time of Napoleon's abdication 'the British army could not have reached the scene of operations for two months' (Greville, vol. I, p. 74).

would lead them in the ultimate showdown with the man he had yet to meet in straight combat. Wellington's Peninsular Campaign had decided the fate of Spain and Portugal. His next one would decide the fate of Europe.

15

In the Elysian Fields
Paris and Vienna, 1814–1815

JUST AFTER ELEVEN o'clock on the morning of 20 April 1814, while Wellington was still in southern France, one of his Peninsular veterans, a thirty-eight-year-old Scottish colonel, supervised the departure of Napoleon from his palace at Fontainebleau. Colonel Neil Campbell had received a letter from Britain's Foreign Secretary Lord Castlereagh in Paris four days earlier: 'I have to acquaint you that you have been selected on the part of the British government to attend the late chief of the French government to the island of Elba . . .' Campbell was ordered to show 'every proper respect and attention to Napoleon, to whose secure asylum in that island it is the wish of his royal highness the Prince Regent to afford every facility and protection'. Campbell felt some sympathy for his new protégé. The man who had once ruled most of Europe had experienced 'much heartlessness and ingratitude' in his short stay at Fontainebleau. It was there that he had abdicated a week earlier, abandoned even by loyalists like Marshal Ney. In the last day or two he had been deserted even by his valet and his own personal bodyguard, an Egyptian Mameluke, who had slept at the foot of his bed with a dagger at his side.

Campbell watched Napoleon walk to a waiting carriage and then turn and say farewell to the bevy of old soldiers of the Imperial Guard who had stuck by him to the end. He told them he could have fought on, but that would have meant civil war as around a quarter of his army had now turned against him. He said, 'I embrace you,' then he raised his hand in salute and added, 'Adieu, remember me!' Some of the officers and men wept, others called out, 'Vive l'Empereur!' Napoleon was then carried away at a gallop accompanied by a great entourage of aides and attendants and more than fifty horsemen of the Imperial Guard. He was to keep the title of emperor and would be allowed to take more than a thousand soldiers with him to Elba. As his coach rattled down the road to Fréjus, he learned that he would also be allowed to retain the guns and other munitions stored on Elba. The allies had given him the island to govern. It was to be his province not his prison, and Campbell would be his manager rather than his jailer. There were few at this early stage who saw any danger in trying to contain the world's most restless military genius on a small island only 150 miles from France.

Two weeks later Wellington rode into his defeated enemy's capital on a white horse, cool and aloof as ever. Far from being in sombre mood Paris was alive with every kind of festivity – balls, parties, picnics and, at the very moment he arrived, a massive military parade. Everyone who mattered was watching the victory parade, the Tsar of Russia, the King of Prussia, the Emperor of Austria and, of course, the plump and pampered figure of the Bourbon King, Louis XVIII, who had replaced Napoleon on the throne of France. Wellington caused as much of a stir as any of them as he rode up accompanied by Lord Castlereagh. In the next few months Castlereagh would be at the peace congress in Vienna arguing with Britain's allies about how to carve up the Europe that Napoleon had left behind.

Wellington's new role was to raise eyebrows all over Europe. He was to command the allied army in the Netherlands with the task of keeping an eye on France's northern border. But, much more strikingly, the man who had crushed Napoleon's armies from Lisbon to Toulouse was to be Britain's ambassador in Paris. The Prime Minister, Lord Liverpool, apparently blissfully unaware that he had made one of the most spectacularly inappropriate appointments in history, wrote to Wellington: 'I am most happy to find by a letter from Castlereagh that you are not unhappy to accept the embassy to Paris. I am sure there is no situation in which you could be at present of more use.' Wellington's brother Henry, who was doing an effective job as Britain's ambassador to Spain, was also blind to his government's insensitivity in appointing a military victor ambassador to the people he had defeated. 'I am happy to hear you've not refused the embassy to Paris. After all you have been through you will find in diplomacy very pretty amusement.' In a letter back Wellington told his brother all the family gossip, and then added in a postscript: 'I believe I forgot to tell you I was made a duke.'

Wellington spent only a few days in Paris but he soon showed, as he had throughout the Peninsular Campaign, how much he enjoyed socialising. One of the first men he met was Marshal Blücher, the redoubtable seventy-one-year-old warhorse who had led the Prussian armies into France from the east as Wellington marched on Toulouse. The two men could do little else but shake hands and smile at each other as neither spoke the other's language. Alexander Gordon's brother, the diplomat Lord Aberdeen, threw a party at which Wellington chatted energetically about his campaigns, saying he was very glad he had never been opposed to Napoleon on a battlefield. Little did he imagine that he would meet Napoleon and Blücher in one of the greatest battles ever fought in almost exactly a year's time.

Wellington's warriors, like the new Duke himself, were convinced the fighting was over. For most of them the first few weeks of peace that spring passed in a delightful and sometimes drunken haze. George Bell, who had fought with Wellington all the way from Ciudad Rodrigo, was still little more than a teenager. 'How wonderful was the feeling of quiet. No trampling of horses nor clashing of arms, no *tirwhit* of a shell or the whop of a cannon ball splashing the mud in one's face or perhaps the brain of your camarado.' Like many of the Peninsular units, Bell's infantry regiment, the Cumberland Gentlemen, was being moved slowly up to Bordeaux through some of the best wine country in France. Many of them now had or expected the pay that was owing to them. 'An issue of six months' back pay in gold opened the eyes, and the mouths and the hands, and the hearts of the whole army.'

The men of the Rifles had stopped off at the town of Castel Sarrasin on the banks of the Garonne. It was a delightful, very friendly place, where the now close-knit team of comrades such as George Simmons, still recovering from his innumerable wounds, John Kincaid, Jonathan Leach and Ned Costello lived a charmed life. Kincaid found plenty of time 'to make love to the pretty little girls with which the place abounded'. Officers as well as other ranks like Costello found themselves liberally entertained by the French. Costello and some companions enjoyed a rumbustious evening with a crowd of French soldiers who demonstrated their determination to forget the past. When a tipsy French corporal struck up a song that attacked the British, he was bundled unceremoniously down the stairs by his fellows. Leach, invited to see some French troops parading, spotted Nicolas Soult, one of the six Napoleonic commanders Wellington had defeated in the Peninsula, presiding in his new role as one of King Louis' top generals. 'He appeared sullen and dejected,' observed Leach. 'But this was probably his natural manner.'

Harry Smith was on his way to embark at Bordeaux as well. But he was not going home. To the great distress of Juana, his devoted young Spanish wife, who had accompanied him everywhere, Smith was ordered to America. He had made such an impact as a brigade major in Spain that he was given a staff job in the British army now engaged in its third year of war against the United States. After a blissful cruise down the Garonne in a skiff, anchoring every night, Smith parted from his wife in Bordeaux when he boarded the seventy-four-gun *Royal Oak* alone for the voyage to America. 'I left her insensible and in a faint,' said Smith. He arranged for Juana to be escorted home to his father's house where she would learn to speak English. Fusilier John Cooper, who had fought with Wellington since Talavera, was posted to America too. He was discharged from the army a year later: he was to complain that he had to wait thirty years for his pension of one shilling a week.

It was time for the generals to go home too. Thomas Picton said goodbye to the men who had done him and Wellington proud, particularly at Badajoz and Vitoria. His officers clubbed together and bought him a fine service of silver plate. Notable exceptions were the officers of the Connaught Rangers, who were damned if they were going to honour the man who had regarded them as a bunch of Irish hooligans able to fight but with no idea how to behave. Picton was upset that Wellington didn't recognise his achievements with a recommendation for a peerage. He was described as full of feelings of 'silent reproach and degradation' and told his friends he now wanted to retire to a quiet farm in his beloved Wales. Many of the departing soldiers added up their regimental losses in the whole campaign, and in every case they calculated they had lost at least half their number. William Wheeler, now a corporal, still suffering from a wound he had received at the Battle of the Nivelle, reckoned he couldn't count more than a hundred men of the 900 who had left with him from England. Joseph Donaldson of the 94th Scots Brigade said he wouldn't be able to muster more than 150 of the 900 who went out to the Peninsula. Calculations of the total number of British dead in the Peninsula ranged up to 40,000. Three-quarters of the deaths were not from wounds but from disease.

When the day for departure arrived, British wives embarked with their husbands, but the women and other camp followers from Spain and Portugal were turned away from the heavily loaded ships. There were hundreds who had attached themselves to British soldiers, cared for the sick and wounded and done valuable service in the camps. Many had not even the wherewithal to return to their homes. 'These faithful and heroic women were now . . . to be seen standing on the beach, while they witnessed with bursting hearts the filling of those sails and the crowding of those ships that were to separate them for ever from those to whom they had looked for protection and support.'

Wellington made time for a special final review of his Peninsular army before it split up for the last time. He issued a General Order conveying his admiration and thanks for all the soldiers had done to push France out of Spain and Portugal. It wasn't couched in particularly warm terms – that wasn't Wellington's style. But it did end with one apparently heartfelt passage: 'The commander of forces . . . assures them that he shall never cease to feel the warmest interest in their welfare and honour, and that he will be at all times happy to be of any service to those to whose conduct, discipline and gallantry their country is so much indebted.'

It was a pledge that many felt he failed to honour. Army pensions remained at a basic minimum for a long time and the government was unable or unwilling to approve a Peninsula medal until 1847 when many of the veterans were dead. Some regiments – like the Guards – made their own arrangement to issue Peninsula medals. Fred Ponsonby's cavalrymen were granted the privilege of having the word 'Peninsula' inscribed on their pennants. Many of Wellington's soldiers felt let down and angry at what they saw as a failure to recognise their sacrifice. William Fraser, a younger contemporary of the

Duke who met him and admired him greatly, regretted that he didn't do more to press for a Peninsula medal: 'It seems a pity that when the heart of the nation was honourably and justly . . . set upon this, he did not find a greater willingness to accede to the request.' William Grattan, who had been in the heat of many a battle with the Connaught Rangers, called it 'scandalous'. Grattan's language is unusually strong. He conceded that Wellington was 'one of the most remarkable, and perhaps the greatest man of the present age', but said he felt that the Duke had 'neglected the interests and feelings of his Peninsular army . . . Were he in his grave tomorrow, hundreds of voices, that are now silent, would echo what I write.'

Most of the men who fought with Wellington, however, had come to recognise that they owed him a huge debt as a commander. He had led them from victory to victory by making a cool assessment of the odds each time and by doing all he could to ensure that they were supplied, fed and rested. His personal humanity was not in doubt: the tears in the breach at Badajoz, the grief at the loss of Cocks at Burgos, the letters he wrote to relatives of the dead proved that. He just didn't show it enough. His Chief Medical Officer James McGrigor asked him to praise the army's doctors in one of his despatches. Wellington indicated that that would be most unusual. McGrigor had to use all his powers of persuasion before the Duke finally agreed to comply. 'I have finished my despatch, but, very well, I will add something about the doctors.' One of Wellington's staff officers, Charles Napier, reckoned his leader's failure to be more lavish with praise was the product of his own arrogance. 'He repulsed the soldiers, and there are few of those who served under him who love him as much as I do. He feels that he owes all to his own abilities and he feels that justly – but he should not show it, for his soldiers stood by him manfully.'

Wellington inspired admiration rather than affection in the soldiers he led, but the British public adored him. He returned to England towards the end of June to an ecstatic welcome. Less than ten years earlier Napoleon's troops had been massing on the Channel coast awaiting his order to invade Britain. War with France had cost untold amounts of gold, to subsidise the Russians, Austrians and Prussians and to pay for the war in the Peninsula. It had cost tens of thousands of British lives. And now at last, with Napoleon apparently finally caged, people in Britain, who had lived in fear of invasion or bereavement, had the first real prospect of peace in more than twenty years. Wellington was a hero, and he hadn't been home for five years. His coach was mobbed nearly all the way from Dover to London. He had a hearty distaste for mass public emotion like this, and when in their excitement people unhitched the horses of his carriage on Westminster Bridge so that they could take the traces and haul him home themselves, his patience ran out. He climbed out of the coach and made the rest of the journey home alone, on horseback.

His wife Kitty was waiting for him. They had written to each other very little over the five years. She was tremendously proud of what he had achieved and yet felt desperately inadequate as a wife and partner. She had spent most of her time lost in shame and bewilderment that she was unable to induce him to love and value her. Her letters and other writings are devoid of hope and joy, full of pathetic self-pity. She kept – on and off – what she called her 'journal'. It makes dismal reading. Again and again she calls her life 'dull' and 'indolent'. 'Ill and idle,' reads one typical entry. 'I have nothing to say of this languid day.' And later: 'The desperate dejection, which has oppressed me thus some days passed [*sic*], will destroy me. I must pray for a calmer mind, for power to calm myself.' 'To effect a cure I know that a wound must be probed. When that wound is in the heart, how torturing is the process.' What energy Kitty had she devoted to bringing up her two boys, Arthur, who was now seven, and Charles, a year younger. She also played mother to Wellington's godson, Arthur Freese, who the gossips claimed was the result of an affair Wellington had had with an army officer's wife years earlier. Just what Kitty knew or believed about her husband's behaviour in the Peninsula she didn't say. There is no conclusive evidence that he had any love affairs there, though he enjoyed the company of women and was popular with them. Larpent, his judge advocate, who was often in his company, makes it very clear that he doubted a man of Wellington's drive could remain celibate for five whole years abroad. He records that in Toulouse the Commander in Chief chose to live in a hotel where one suite of rooms was reserved for a Spanish beauty married to the owner. 'I don't mean to be scandalous but this may perhaps have decided the choice of the house,' wrote Larpent.

Wellington's return to London did little to revive his marriage, although in anticipation of his return Kitty's spirits had lifted enough to say she would certainly like to come to Paris, and that she was confident of making a good ambassador's wife. Her husband had only a few weeks in London before he went to Paris, and he had very little time for any quiet evenings with Kitty. He had left the country a mere knight in 1809 and returned a duke. Parliament reckoned he deserved more than that and presented him with £400,000, a staggering sum worth tens of millions today. Wellington lost no time in making up for his long absence from London society. At one glittering party laid on in his honour, Fred Ponsonby's sister Lady Caroline Lamb, now long past her affair with Byron, behaved, as usual, outrageously, displaying her green pantaloons to her former lover, the poet, who was also a guest, and piling yet more embarrassment on her family. Wellington did his best to make up for lost time too, but his instinct for order and discipline sometimes got the better of him. He turned up for one soirée wrongly dressed, when the venue's management had prescribed knee breeches and a white cravat. When the manager told Britain's national hero that he was in the wrong clothes, he humbly assented and went home.

Most of Wellington's soldiers came home to a warm welcome, but for some wives the men had been away too long. Ned Costello helped one of his fellow sergeants track down the wife he hadn't seen in years. Eventually they were directed to a house where a ten-year-old girl, clearly the sergeant's daughter, opened the door. The moment the wife saw her long-lost husband she burst into hysterics. She had remarried. Seconds later a strapping carpenter walked up and held her to him. Costello's friend stood clenching his fists for some time but then drew a deep breath and said to the new husband: 'As she seems to prefer your manner of doing business, suppose you clinch the bargain with a sixpence and take her to you altogether?' The deal was done; the sergeant threw a guinea into his daughter's lap and then walked out with Costello for a long drink in the nearest pub.

On 22 August 1814 Wellington arrived in Paris to take up his duties as ambassador. With his usual foresight he had arranged for the government to purchase a fine house for its embassy. The house, more like a palace, was in the heart of Paris in the Rue Faubourg Saint-Honoré, and successive British ambassadors have had reason to be grateful to Wellington for providing them with a residence only a stone's throw from the palace of the French president. It had been the home of Napoleon's sister Pauline for eleven years. Its gardens, backing on to the Champs-Elysées, were soon nicknamed the Elysian Fields.

Wellington's prime diplomatic job in Paris was to persuade the French government to abolish the slave trade, which Britain had already determined to do. It was the first of two liberal causes this otherwise inveterate conservative would pursue with energy and enthusiasm. The other was Catholic Emancipation, which he backed as prime minister a decade and a half later. His campaign on the slave trade was an uphill task. He warned William Wilberforce, the great champion of abolition, in a letter on 8 October 1814 that it was 'impossible to get anything inserted in a French newspaper . . . in favour of the abolition, or even to show that the trade was abolished in England from motives of humanity'. One of the problems he explained was that the British press was so anti-French that 'we shall never be able to exercise the influence which we ought to have upon this question'. But in November he was able to report to Wilberforce that 'orders have at last been issued to prevent the trade in slaves by French subjects on the coast of Africa north of Cape Formoso'. He said that much still remained to be done, but France had agreed to abolish the trade completely within five years.*

Wellington ran into some of his old Peninsula opponents in Paris. He met Ney, whom he had fought and defeated at Bussaco, and Soult, whom he had outsmarted at Oporto in 1809 and pushed back from the Pyrenees to Toulouse from the summer of 1813 onwards. Both had now deftly changed sides and were working for the King. He had a friendly exchange with Masséna, whom he had always

---

* Napoleon was to act promptly to abolish the slave trade when he returned to power the following spring. He saw it as a neat way of securing the support of liberal sentiment for his restoration.

thought the most impressive of Napoleon's marshals. After a chat about the battles they had fought with each other, Masséna said: 'My Lord, you owe me a dinner – for you made me starve horribly.' Wellington burst into his well-known guffaw: 'You should give it to me, Marshal, for you prevented me from sleeping.'

As well as mixing with Napoleon's ex-marshals Wellington enjoyed a fling with the Emperor's ex-mistresses. He was frequently seen with Giuseppina Grassini, an opera diva from La Scala, who had been one of Napoleon's favourites. If Wellington wasn't having an affair with her, he did little to deny it. By this time Kitty had joined him in Paris, and even the most worldly of Britain's aristocrats found the Duke's treatment of her a bit shabby. Fred Ponsonby and his family saw a lot of Wellington that summer and Ponsonby's mother, the Countess of Bessborough, wrote that, much as she admired the Duke, 'I am afraid he is behaving very ill to that poor little woman; he is found great fault with . . . not on account of making her miserable or of the immorality of the fact, but the want of protocol and publicity of his attentions to Grassini.' Another flame of Napoleon's, Marguerite Weimer, an actress known as Mademoiselle George, was twenty-seven when she met Wellington in 1814. She later boasted that both men had been her lovers, 'Mais M. Le Duc était de beaucoup le plus fort' ('But the Duke was by far the more vigorous'). One Parisian grandee, the Duke de Broglie, said of the Duke: 'He was a true Englishman, a piece of the old rock, simple in mind, straight, solid, prudent but hard, tough and a little naive. The clumsy and pressing gallantries he permitted himself towards pretty young women he pushed as far as they would let him.'

Wellington's dalliances in Paris caused little offence to the French, who were quite used to that sort of thing, but his presence was fast becoming unpopular for more substantial reasons. King Louis and his government were seen as increasingly incompetent and ineffective. The economy, without Napoleon's vast empire to feed it, had collapsed. The Emperor may have become deeply unpopular with millions of Frenchmen, but he could lead and inspire. The flabby King Louis clearly couldn't. The army was deeply divided between royalists and Bonapartists. Both sides deplored the government's apparent neglect of the army and found it offensive and demeaning to have the commander of British forces on France's northern border doubling as ambassador in Paris. The more it looked as if the King had to rely on foreign help like Britain's to bolster his regime, the more unpopular Britain's ambassador became. In September Wellington wrote, 'Matters are going on well here,' but by the beginning of October he was reporting to Castlereagh: 'There exists a good deal of uncertainty and uneasiness in the mind of almost every individual.' By late October even the highly intelligent General Foy, a French Peninsular veteran and great admirer of Wellington's, who had been touched by a visit the Duke made to him when he was lying wounded in hospital that summer, refused to attend any more British embassy soirées. He wrote: 'Lord Wellington and the English are held in horror by everybody . . . We who were lately masters of Europe, to what servitude are we reduced. Ld Wellington is CinC of the army of occupation in Belgium . . . O Napoléon, où es tu?' ('O Napoleon, where are you?').

On Elba, Neil Campbell's relationship with Napoleon was cooling too. They had started on the best of terms, with the Emperor obviously keen to cultivate the British. Campbell noted that Napoleon admired Wellington and that he was flattered when he learned that Wellington had been deeply impressed by his campaign to keep the allies at bay in north-eastern France in the early months of 1814. But the appointment of the Duke of Wellington as ambassador to Paris, Napoleon told Campbell, was 'an open insult and injury to the feelings of the French people'.

By the end of 1814 Britain's Prime Minister Lord Liverpool had decided that Wellington should be removed – at least temporarily – from Paris. His presence there was causing too much tension, and Liverpool feared for Wellington's life, if there was serious unrest in France. There was some talk of despatching the Duke to America to take command of the so-called War of 1812 with the United States, which was not going well. But Wellington believed the war was a mistake and made it very clear he did not want to go there. Besides, he wrote to the Prime Minister, he was indispensable in Europe. 'There is nobody but myself in whom either yourselves or the country, or your allies, would feel any confidence.' Anyway, the American war – which had achieved nothing for either side in more than two years of fighting – came to an end that December with the Peace of Ghent. It was news that came too late for Wellington's brother-in-law and comrade in arms in the Peninsula, Ned Pakenham. He was killed leading the British attack on New Orleans in the first few days of January 1815.

Liverpool decided that the best place for Wellington was Vienna. Castlereagh had now spent months there trying to broker an agreement that would satisfy the allies, Prussia, Russia and Austria, that they each had a fair share of the spoils left by Napoleon's departure. Castlereagh was within reach of a deal that would see Russia absorb Poland and Prussia take a chunk of Saxony. Wellington was left to complete it. He arrived in Vienna on 3 February. Before him lay the prospect of weeks, perhaps months of horse-trading and yet more parties, balls and dazzling soirées, which he had always found a pleasant distraction from the serious and lonely business of high command.

Two weeks after Wellington had arrived in Austria, Britain's Commissioner on Elba decided to take a few days away from the island. Campbell's health was troubling him, he wrote in his journal. 'I was anxious to consult some medical man at Florence on account of the increasing deafness, supposed to arise from my wounds.' He said he was uneasy about leaving Napoleon, but the captain of the British warship that took him to Italy promised to return and make a show of cruising around Elba for a day or two. Besides, when he arrived in Florence, Campbell was met by a senior man from the Foreign Office who told him he shouldn't be uneasy about Napoleon. 'When you return to Elba,' said the British Under Secretary of State, 'you may tell Bonaparte that he is quite forgotten in Europe; no one thinks of him now.'

16

Duchess, you may give your ball
Brussels, 1815

THERE WAS HARDLY a ripple over the sea as Neil Campbell's ship, the *Partridge*, dropped anchor off Portoferraio, Elba's capital, on the morning of 28 February 1815. There was not enough wind to blow her back into harbour. Campbell had been away ten days. Sensing that something was wrong he had some seamen row him ashore in one of the ship's boats. He was back on board an hour and half later with the news that Napoleon had escaped two days earlier with a flotilla of four small vessels. He had a thousand attendants with him, including the members of his old Imperial Guard who had stayed with him throughout his exile. Campbell gave chase, but it was futile. Before he could find a breeze to help him close the gap, the Emperor was landing at Fréjus in southern France.

Napoleon was on French soil again. He headed north and reacted with panache when confronted near Grenoble by a contingent of his old Grande Armée sent to stop him at all costs with muskets at the ready. Stepping forward, alone, he asked if any of them would shoot their Emperor. For a moment there was no sound, then came the shout, 'Vive l'Empereur!' Marshal Ney and several others, who had deserted Napoleon a year earlier, changed sides yet again, Louis XVIII fled to Belgium, and on 20 March Napoleon was back in Paris.

The hapless Campbell was carpeted by Castlereagh and sent back to join the army. It wasn't long before rumours started that he had gone to Italy to see not a doctor but his mistress. Napoleon could hardly believe his good fortune that Britain's watch on him had been so lax. 'If they'd kept a frigate in the harbour and another outside it would have been impossible for me to have gone to France . . .' His mother had been one of the last to see him leave Elba, bidding him goodbye with the prophetic words: 'Go, my son. Fulfil your destiny: you were not made to die on this island.'

Wellington was told the news just before he rode off to join a crowd of grandees for a foxhunt in Vienna. He was handed a despatch that informed him Bonaparte had escaped. Wellington was in no doubt that the diplomacy and the junketing were over. The allies immediately declared Napoleon an outlaw and made it clear they would not rest until he was finally crushed. In London a few of the government's opponents declared themselves against renewing the war. Sam Whitbread, the strident successor to Charles James Fox as a leading proponent of peace with France, managed to raise seventy-two votes in the House of Commons in favour of negotiating with Napoleon. But Lord Liverpool and his cabinet were united and robust. They were well aware of Napoleon's legendary capacity to mobilise and strike before his enemies could combine. They called for immediate reinforcement of the allied army in Belgium. It was the only army likely to be ready to resist any early French military initiative. The allies agreed that Wellington should rejoin the force as soon as possible. The Russian Tsar Alexander is said to have placed his hand on Wellington's shoulder and pronounced, 'C'est pour vous encore sauver le monde' ('It is for you to save the world again').* The only issue was whether Wellington should command the army in Belgium or take on a subordinate role as chief of staff to some other allied commander. He quickly made it clear that 'subordinate' was not a word he understood. Fred Ponsonby, who now knew the Duke's mind as well as anyone, observed: 'he refused [the chief of staff job], knowing that all the responsibility would be thrown upon him without the power of enforcing his wishes'. Wellington would set off for Brussels as commander in chief.

The call went out to units all over Britain to prepare for war again.

---

* It might be wise to take this quotation with a pinch of salt: Wellington's Peninsular Campaign had hardly 'saved the world' in the eyes of the Russian Tsar, who had seen Napoleon retreat from Moscow in 1812 and whose army had helped push the French Emperor back to Paris in 1814. William Fraser, who recounts the story, is however a credible source. He was twenty-six when Wellington died. His father was on the Duke's staff at Waterloo, and Fraser himself conducted interviews with the 2nd Duke.

William Hay's squadron in Ponsonby's 12th Light Dragoons was doing some routine crowd-control work around London when the news broke about Napoleon. A man who had just travelled up from Dover burst into the pub they were drinking in: 'I have brought you news today – old Boney has broken out again and got to Paris.' Hay noted: 'We were astonished and indeed could not believe our ears.' But newspapers and letters soon confirmed the news, and there followed 'an immediate order for us to march by Canterbury, en route to Dover and then to embark for Ostend, and I must confess the news gave me the greatest satisfaction, as I had no liking for the life of a soldier in idleness'.

Some of Wellington's veterans had spent several months with their families since returning from France in the summer. But many were still in America or on their way back after the recent suspension of hostilities there. Harry Smith had served on two separate missions to the United States. He was with Ned Pakenham, 'one of the ablest Generals England ever produced', when Pakenham fell to murderous American fire at the Battle of New Orleans. As Smith's ship reached the Channel on the way home, the news from Paris was shouted to them from a passing vessel. 'Ho! Bonaparte's back again on the throne of France!' 'Such a hurrah as I set up, tossing my hat above my head!' wrote Smith. 'I will be a Lieutenant Colonel yet before the year's out!' He was delighted at the prospect of a showdown with Napoleon. His wife Juana had been warmly accepted into his family in London, and was a particular favourite of her English teacher, Smith's father. But Harry had missed her and when he received the call to head back to war in Europe, he told Juana to pack her bags. He wasn't going to leave her behind again.

Another man returning from America was Sergeant William Lawrence, who had soldiered with Wellington right through from Vimeiro to Toulouse. On his return across the Atlantic he was given no chance to visit his family at Bryant's Piddle in Dorset. His ship was simply waved straight on from Portsmouth to Flanders. William Wheeler was now a sergeant too. To the cheers of a large crowd he sailed with his regiment from Portsmouth and landed at Ostend. On 13 April they heard that Wellington was to command the army in Belgium: 'I never remember anything that caused so much joy,' said

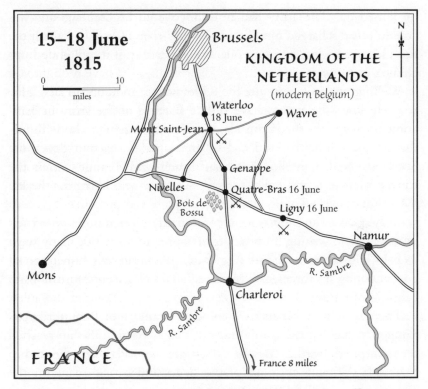

15–18 June 1815

Wheeler in his journal. 'Our men were almost frantic, every soldier you met told the joyful news. "Glorious news. Nosey has got the command: won't we give them a drubbing now."' Wheeler and his comrades got a huge welcome in every village they passed through in Belgium. The only slight hiccough was when a group of officers had a few drinks too many one evening and hauled the famous statue in Brussels of the little boy relieving himself – the Manneken Pis – off its plinth and into the fountain. But two days later it was reinstated and 'looked none the worse for the ducking'.

Not everyone looked forward to going back to war. Thomas Todd was a disappointed man. He had joined the Highland Light Infantry in a fit of despondency when he had failed to become an actor in Edinburgh and he now hoped for a discharge. He had served for nearly eight years and was due to be released after seven. The trouble was he had concealed the fact that he was only sixteen when he joined up. The army had now discovered his true age and he couldn't be discharged until he was twenty-five. He still had a year to do. He toyed with deserting but thought better of it and ended up landing in Antwerp.

Wellington made very sure the Rifles were summoned to Belgium too. He knew he would have only a fraction of the army he had come to rely on in the Peninsula, but he wasn't going to be without the 1st/95th. John Kincaid had to give up shooting woodcock in Scotland; Ned Costello, Jonathan Leach and George Simmons packed their bags and sailed to war. Simmons was horribly seasick. 'My throat swelled with vomiting to such a degree that I could scarcely speak.' But he was soon comfortably billeted in a fine house with a garden, writing his usual letters home to his family promising to help with money when he got back. 'Rumour says Bonaparte is concentrating his forces, and means to attack very soon: for my part I do not care how soon.'

There were newcomers to Wellington's ranks too. Tom Morris, a Londoner, had left the family trade of gun-making at the age of sixteen, inspired by the tales of adventure he had heard from the Peninsula. 'Stirring accounts of the sieges and battles and glorious achievements of the British troops in Spain . . . created in me an irrepressible desire for military service.' He knew his parents would disapprove, so he stole out of his house at four in the morning and joined the Highland Regiment, the 73rd Foot. Like Thomas Todd he was sixteen when he joined up but had pretended to be older to qualify for military pay. He had done some service in Holland already and was now nineteen.

William Leeke was also inspired by tales from Spain and Portugal. He was only seventeen. When he joined up, he was under-age, but he came from a prosperous family in Hampshire related to Colonel John Colborne, who had led the 52nd Light Infantry in the battles in the Pyrenees and was highly thought of by Wellington. His regiment was another valuable addition to the Duke's strength in Belgium. Leeke was thrilled when Colborne arranged for him to be admitted as an ensign, the most junior-ranking officer in the army. He had never seen a shot fired in anger. Leeke's mother 'pressed me to her and begged me with many tears not to go, saying it was not necessary that I should run into danger . . . but of course it was impossible for me to yield to her wish, dearly as I loved her'. By 11 May Leeke had bought himself a 'black horse with a long tail', and was thrilled to be part of a 'regiment of a thousand men marching down the road amongst the corn to the sound of one of those stirring tunes which are always connected with feats of arms and deeds of daring'.

A third newcomer, who was to record his adventures with Wellington in Belgium in vivid detail, was Cavalié Mercer. He was a captain, commanding a troop of Royal Horse Artillerymen. Somehow he managed to embark his complement of 200 horses and mules, six guns and their ammunition wagons, in addition to the 190 gunners, drivers, shoeing smiths, collar makers and of course the trumpeter, the farrier and the wheeler. A favourable wind blew them gently across to Ostend. But their keel had hardly touched the beach when they 'were abruptly boarded by a naval officer . . . with a gang of sailors, who, *sans cérémonie*, instantly commenced hoisting our horses out and throwing them, as well our saddlery etc overboard, without even giving time for making any disposition to receive or secure the one to the other'. Mercer protested, but he was told that the Duke of Wellington wanted the ship sent back immediately to collect more reinforcements. 'The scramble and confusion that ensued baffle all description. Bundles of harness went over the side in rapid succession, as well as horses . . .' It was a dreadful start to Mercer's campaign, but he and his troop were well received by the people of one town after another as they lugged their heavy guns inland.

Wellington arrived in Brussels on 4 April. Only a month earlier the city had been buzzing with excitement, the fashionable rendez-vous for wealthy aristocrats out to enjoy the delights of the newly liberated Europe. Now suddenly Brussels looked like the first target for the resurrected Bonaparte. The partying went on, but people started looking over their shoulders nervously for refuges a little further away from the likely path of the French army.

Napoleon had not wasted time in Paris. Within days of arriving he was assembling an army, and by the beginning of June had 124,000 ready to march north. They would be far fewer than the number his opponents could muster on one battlefield. But Napoleon's men were experienced veterans of the Grande Armée who had made their way back to France and their morale was high.

Wellington's immediate task was to secure the best men he could find to command the army of mixed nations, British, Dutch–Belgian and German, that was assembling around the Belgian capital. Sir Thomas Picton, who had been such a stalwart in the Peninsula, appeared reluctant but persuadable. He was still smarting from not being granted a peerage, and he was observed behaving rather oddly that spring. 'He had told the Duke', one raconteur reported, 'that his health was such that he did not consider himself fit to undertake the anxious task of commanding a division; and it was only at the earnest personal solicitations of the Duke that he joined the army.' Picton had a moody obsession with his own mortality. Before he left to join Wellington he jumped into a freshly dug grave in Wales and shouted, 'Why, I think this would do for me.' He took a fellow Welshman to Belgium with him, Rees Gronow, the sprightly diarist who had already spent a few months with Wellington's army in the Pyrenees. He was still only eighteen, an ambitious young blade, whose education at Eton had given him a host of well-placed contacts and an appetite for mixing with the smartest in society. Gronow had managed to talk his way into Picton's entourage. He won £600 in a gambling house, and 'made numerous purchases, amongst others two first rate horses at Tattersalls for a high figure, which were embarked for Ostend along with my groom'. Gronow's new patron Picton was still a legendary figure, cantankerous and eccentric, rarely in uniform: 'he generally wore a blue frock-coat, very tightly buttoned up to the throat, a very large black silk neckcloth . . . and a round hat'.

Picton was just one of many of Wellington's old warriors to rally to the colours. The ever reliable 'Daddy' Hill joined him, as did his closest aide Fitzroy Somerset, whose wife, Emily, Wellington's niece, gave birth to a girl in Brussels. Another of Wellington's favourite ADCs, Alexander Gordon, was there too. 'I am thicker with old Wellington than ever and of course very happy,' he wrote to his brother Robert. But if Wellington was lucky with some of his choices he was less fortunate with others imposed on him. It is extraordinary that someone of his unparalleled stature within the alliance was still unable to select his own key subordinate officers. The Duke of York, in Whitehall, remained the ultimate power in the army. His failed campaign in the Netherlands twenty years earlier had made him a mockery as the man 'who marched his men to the top of the hill and marched them down again'. But he was the second son of the King and Wellington's Commander in Chief. Promotion of officers was his prerogative and he guarded it jealously. 'The power of appointing to commissions is not vested in you,' he wrote to Wellington; 'you will be pleased to recommend to me such officers as may appear to you most deserving of promotion . . .' The most outstanding example of the Duke of York's obstinacy was in the choice of Wellington's cavalry commander. Wellington, naturally enough, wanted Sir Stapleton Cotton, who had served him well at Salamanca and elsewhere in the Peninsula. The Duke of York wanted Henry Paget, Lord Uxbridge. He had proved himself a proficient cavalry commander covering Moore's retreat to Corunna six years earlier. Uxbridge was the man who had run off with Wellington's sister-in-law a few years earlier. But that was all past and, when the Duke of York insisted, Wellington felt he had no choice. He was not to regret it: Uxbridge proved a fine cavalry commander.*

Wellington's irritation with London was about more than a restriction on his freedom of choice. The army he commanded grew in size over the next few weeks of May and June, but its quality was very uneven. By 18 June, the day of Waterloo, he would have 68,000 troops on the battlefield, but only a third of them were British and not all of these had fought with him in the Peninsula. The other two-thirds were Dutch–Belgian troops and units from the armies of other European states like Hanover, Brunswick and Nassau. Only the men of the King's German Legion, the KGL, had earned Wellington's trust through six years of tough campaigning. The other allied units consisted mainly of new recruits. And Wellington doubted the loyalty of some of the Dutch–Belgian troops, a number of whom had even fought on Napoleon's side earlier in the war. He feared that

* General Sir Stapleton Cotton, who became Lord Combermere, reckoned it was the Prince Regent who had vetoed him from the cavalry command. Combermere believed that the Prince had never forgiven him for his 'share in spreading about the story of the Prince's nocturnal visit to [his mistress] Mrs Fitzherbert' several years earlier (Combermere, vol. 1, p. 321).

while Napoleon would succeed in putting together an army of sea-soned veterans, his own army would be patently unreliable. 'It will be admitted that the army is not a very good one,' he wrote to the Secretary for War, Lord Bathurst. 'I am overloaded with people I have never seen before . . . however I'll do the best I can with the instruments which have been sent to assist me.'

Wellington's solution was to try to reduce the danger of foreign units deserting by mixing his forces up. Where possible he would have British and foreign troops fighting side by side. Each division would have at least one British brigade. That way he hoped the men who had seen little or no battle would be heartened by the courage and experience of those who had. He would fortify his uneven army by example. Throughout May and early June, as new regiments arrived, the drilling began. It was vital to instil into the mind of every footsoldier that a few seconds' delay in loading a musket or in form-ing a line or square could be the difference between life and death.

The most impressive display of military readiness was the Duke's review of his cavalry on 29 May. Uxbridge had some 6,000 of them on parade in a great blaze of colour. It was, said Mercer, a 'splendid spectacle. The scattered line of hussars in their fanciful yet pictur-esque costume; the more sober, but far more imposing line of heavy dragoons, like a wall of red brick.' Behind them were the light dra-goons, including Fred Ponsonby's 12th and William Tomkinson's 16th Regiments, in 'the third line in their blue uniforms with broad lapels of white, buff, red, yellow and orange'. On either side of the horsemen were the batteries of Royal Horse Artillery, including Mercer's own. At about 2 p.m. Wellington appeared with an 'immense cortège in which were to be seen many of the most distin-guished officers and almost every uniform in Europe'. Mercer was beside himself with pride when Wellington and Prussia's Marshal Blücher stopped to inspect his battery. Wellington referred to it as 'the beautiful battery' and Blücher announced, according to Mercer, that he had not seen anything so superb in his life, 'concluding by exclaiming "Mein Gott, dere is not von orse in dies batterie wich is not goot for Veldt Marshal"'.

In between drilling his troops, conferring with his generals and writing despatches, Wellington found plenty of time for socialising.

He gave a number of parties and lived up to the reputation he had made in Paris as a ladies' man. This time the woman he was linked with was Lady Frances Wedderburn Webster, the wife of an army officer. She was extremely attractive and, like Fred Ponsonby's sister Caroline Lamb, one of Byron's former lovers. When her husband, who was widely regarded as a bore, chose to go to London for most of the summer, Wellington was often seen in her company. He was reported as having spent one of his embassy soirées dancing with no one but her, and they were once seen descending into a hollow in a Brussels park. All this set tongues wagging. Perhaps there was an ulterior motive in Wellington's often nonchalant demeanour in early June 1815. He was anxious to keep the atmosphere in Brussels as normal as he could for as long as possible. He did not want any early sense of panic to prompt his allies to desert before he clashed with Napoleon. This led him to give the go-ahead to one of the most famous social occasions in history.

One of the many aristocratic couples to move to Brussels in pursuit of the good life after Napoleon's first abdication in 1814 was the Duke and Duchess of Richmond. They had enjoyed an energetic social life and, before a French invasion had seemed imminent, had arranged a ball for 15 June. Everyone who mattered in Brussels was invited. The Duchess was tactful enough to consult the Duke of Wellington before she sent out her invitations. 'Duke, I have no wish to pry into your secrets. I wish to give a ball,' she told him, 'and all I ask is may I give my ball? If you say, Duchess, don't give your ball, it is quite sufficient. I ask you no reason.' Wellington immediately replied, 'Duchess, you may give your ball with the greatest safety without fear of interruption.'

The strategy of the coalition of countries lined up against Napoleon was to assemble an army of some 600,000 men and invade France. But the Russians and Austrians were some way off sending their forces. Only 120,000 Prussians under Field Marshal Gebhard von Blücher and Wellington's Anglo-Dutch army of 90,000 were ready for war on France's north-eastern border. By the second week in June, it was no secret that Napoleon had around 120,000 men available to cross the Belgian frontier. Because of his overall inferiority in numbers Napoleon was thought likelier to go quickly on the offensive than remain on the defensive in France. He would attempt to pick off his opponents one by one. He would move fast to defeat Wellington and Blücher first – and then turn on the Russians and Austrians. But with the strength he had, less than half Wellington's and Blücher's combined force of 210,000, he would have to drive the two apart and crush them separately.

Wellington and Blücher met in early May and agreed to support each other in resisting any French attack on Belgium. Brussels, they believed, was sure to be Napoleon's first objective. Napoleon would have to be stopped well short of the Belgian capital. The land between it and the French border was very open, gently rolling country. The year before, in August, Wellington had spent a few days on his way to Paris exploring possible lines of defence. He made a particular note of a shallow ridge, called Mont Saint-Jean, that lay across the main road from Paris fifteen miles south of Brussels, just a couple of miles beyond the village of Waterloo.

The two field marshals agreed to keep closely in touch. Wellington would deploy his troops around Brussels. Blücher would centre on Namur. Everything now depended on getting early intelligence of any move by Napoleon. Once they knew which way he was approaching they would move sharply to confront him. The speed of their reaction would be vital. Wellington had long believed that the presence of the French Emperor on the field was worth some tens of thousands of extra troops to the French. But he and Blücher between them would comfortably outnumber any force Napoleon could deploy. He had written to London that he and Blücher could put some 150,000 men in the field, 'so that I hope we should give a good account even of Buonaparte'.

A Westminster MP, Thomas Creevey, met Wellington strolling in the park in Brussels and asked him what he thought would be the outcome of a clash with Napoleon. Wellington stopped and said, 'By God! I think Blücher and myself can do the thing.' Creevey then asked him what help he could rely on from others such as King Louis of France. 'Oh!' he said, 'don't mention such fellows! No: I think Blücher and I can do the business.' Then Wellington saw a British infantryman enter the park. He pointed at the man and said to Creevey: 'There: it all depends upon that article whether we do the business or not. Give me enough of it, and I am sure.' He may have called them the scum of the earth, but he knew they could fight. During six years of combat in the Peninsula, Wellington's infantry had delivered superbly. Now for the first time he was about to confront the greatest military commander of the age, whose massed columns of infantry had been unstoppable at battles such as Austerlitz and Jena. In the Peninsula Wellington had confronted Napoleon's marshals, whose infantry had proved inferior to his British and Portuguese veterans. Now, as he prepared to meet Napoleon himself, he had only some of those seasoned units with him. He hoped they would be enough.

In the second week of June the pace of events suddenly quickened. Napoleon had left Paris on the 12th and made all speed to the Belgian frontier. Reports began to come in to Wellington and Blücher that French forces were building up fast. Brussels was swept by fear and anxiety as people realised that a decisive confrontation was imminent. Everyone wondered how soon Wellington would order his troops on to the road. The border with France was only forty miles to the south. But Wellington appeared as cool and imperturbable as ever. He was in no particular hurry. He had to establish precisely where Napoleon would attack before he committed his men to any particular road. He also wanted to avoid panic in Brussels. The Duchess of Richmond's ball was in the last stages of preparation. Wellington could still have asked her to call it off. He didn't. He even made it clear that he would be attending himself.

At 3 p.m. on 15 June, the very day of the Duchess of Richmond's ball, Wellington was told that the French had crossed the frontier. A large French force had attacked Charleroi, and pushed the Prussians back behind the River Sambre thirty miles south of Brussels. Napoleon's men were now pouring across it on bridges which the allies had left intact. But was this Napoleon's main army? Or was this Napoleon striking one blow from the south-east when he had another to deliver from the south-west?

Wellington, with typical caution, still didn't move. He had already placed units well south and west of Brussels in a wide sweep to detect any approach from that direction. Until he had a clear indication from them, he would not send his main force anywhere. But units everywhere were alerted. The city bustled with staff officers moving to and fro. Suddenly men who had never seen action before or who had spent more than a year away from the roar of guns, were faced with the prospect of fighting for their lives. John Kincaid was strolling in the park in the early evening when he met one of the Duke's staff. The man asked him if he had his pack-saddles all prepared. Kincaid said he was nearly ready, but added, 'I suppose they won't be wanted, at all events, before tomorrow?' To which the Duke's man replied, 'If you have any preparations to make, I would recommend you not to delay too long.' Kincaid was ready when he heard the bugle blow just two hours later.

Napoleon had moved with remarkable speed. He had around 120,000 men. He knew he couldn't pitch them against the allied armies together, given that they had nearly twice his number. His aim was to destroy the Prussians, who were concentrated around Ligny, twenty-five miles south-east of Brussels, before turning on the British. If he could defeat Blücher and drive him away to the east, he would have Wellington to himself. Far from directing a second prong of his attack against Wellington, he was out to hit Blücher first.

If Wellington had known this, or guessed this, he might have moved sooner. Until he knew for sure where Napoleon was, he felt he could only alert his senior commanders to stand by to move. Rees Gronow recalls one prickly encounter with Sir Thomas Picton. Dressed in his customary civilian clothes with his great wide hat, Picton approached Wellington 'in a careless sort of way, just as he might have met an equal. The Duke bowed coldly to him, and said, "I am glad you are come, Sir Thomas; the sooner you get on horseback the better; no time is to be lost. You will take the command of the troops in advance . . ." Picton appeared not to like the Duke's manner; for, when he bowed and left, he muttered a few words which convinced those who were with him that he was not much pleased with his interview.' The old Welsh warrior was as touchy as ever, but Wellington badly needed him in any early combat with the French.

Picton may have been given his orders, but it wasn't until most senior officers were at the ball and the dancing and drinking were well advanced that Wellington finally gave them the green light to move. Before midnight he heard the news he had been waiting for: there was no French force about to strike from the south-west. Napoleon's full force was moving north from Charleroi. Wellington's suspicion that Napoleon would deliver a blow at him from further west appeared unfounded. He could now move decisively. The Prussians were across Napoleon's path at Ligny. He would try to stop Napoleon at the crossroads of Quatre-Bras, on the road to Brussels from Charleroi seven miles north-west of Ligny. That way he could block Napoleon sweeping around Blücher's right and heading for Brussels. Quatre-Bras was twenty miles away. The Anglo-Dutch army would have to move fast. Wellington gathered his senior commanders around him at the ball and told them to move their men off in the early hours. But the speed of Napoleon's advance and the earlier uncertainty about its precise direction had caught Wellington off balance. 'Napoleon has humbugged me, by God! He has gained twenty-four hours' march on me,' he told the Duke of Richmond in a chat just before he left the ball. Wellington asked Richmond if he had a map. Richmond replied that he had, and took Wellington into his dressing room to show him. As Wellington looked at it, Richmond asked him what he would do. Wellington replied that he had ordered his army to concentrate at Quatre-Bras. 'But we shall not stop him there, and if so, I must fight him here.' And Wellington 'passed his thumbnail over the position of Waterloo'. It was halfway between Brussels and Quatre-Bras.

17

Blücher has had a damn good hiding

Quatre-Bras, 16 June 1815

NOBODY GOT MUCH sleep that night. Fred Ponsonby and William Hay had both been invited to the ball. Ponsonby had accepted, Hay had wisely refused. At 3 a.m. Hay woke up when his servant walked into his bedroom, handed him his uniform and said that Ponsonby, his colonel, wanted to see him at once. He jumped out of bed, and raced over to Ponsonby's quarters. 'You were lucky not to go to the ball,' said Ponsonby, who had just ridden back from it. 'I am quite knocked up, the French are coming out in great numbers, and yesterday attacked and drove the Prussians back.' He told Hay to arrange for three days' rations and forage for the horses. As soon as that was done, the men should be ordered to march. Then Ponsonby, exhausted after a lively night on the dance floor – he was never a man to leave a party early – told Hay to leave him: 'I should like to be left quiet . . . to get some rest.' Before he set off in the morning, he managed to write a letter to Lady Georgiana Lennox, the Duke of Richmond's daughter: 'We had a great ball last night and fancy the horror of having the news in the middle of it and of seeing all one's friends fly to the right and to the left.'

Kincaid boasted that his regiment, the 1/95th Rifles, were 'to the credit of our battalion' assembled and ready to march before midnight, 'where it was nearly two o'clock in the morning before we were joined by the others'. While they waited they grabbed an hour or two's rest on the pavement. 'But we were every instant disturbed, by ladies as well as gentlemen; some stumbling over us in the dark – some shaking us out of our sleep to be told the news.' Creevey was informed of Napoleon's first clash with the Prussians when his son and daughters returned from the ball at around 2.30 a.m. They told him there had been plenty of officers at the ball

Major General Edward Pakenham, Wellington's brother-in-law. Widely popular, he led a successful early attack at Salamanca on the exposed French left. Killed at the Battle of New Orleans in 1815.

Wellington issues orders at the Battle of Salamanca, 22 July 1812. He and his staff stand on a mound with the distinctive shape of the Greater Arapil behind. British cavalry (right) played a major part in making this one of France's worst defeats.

British troops at the Battle of Vitoria, 21 June 1813, capture and ransack the French baggage train. The wagons were full of booty, amassed by Joseph Bonaparte during his six-year rule in Spain. Joseph himself narrowly escaped but a number of French wives and Spanish concubines (bottom right) were captured.

LEFT: Wellington and his ADC Fitzroy Somerset are guided into the village of Sorauren on 27 July 1813. In response to a major French offensive Wellington rode fifty miles in twenty-four hours through the passes of the Pyrenees to plan his counter-attack.

Rees Gronow, dapper Welsh socialite and lively diarist. He arrived in Spain at the age of eighteen as an ensign in the footguards, and was with them at the height of the French cavalry attacks at Waterloo.

Battle of the Nivelle, Wellington's breakthrough into France, 10 November 1813. The British (left), clearly in lines no more than two deep, bring all their muskets to bear on the French columns (right), though one French unit has managed to move into a line.

Kitty Pakenham, Wellington's wife. They married in 1806, but his burgeoning fame and her deep sense of inadequacy meant they soon grew apart. They had two children but he was openly unfaithful to her.

BELOW: Mademoiselle George, French actress, was twenty-seven in 1814 when Wellington was ambassador in Paris. She claimed she was a mistress of both Napoleon and Wellington, though Wellington was 'de beaucoup le plus fort' – 'by far the more vigorous'.

RIGHT: Harriette Wilson, celebrated London courtesan. Wellington enjoyed her charms several times – at a price. She later tried to blackmail him but his response was said to be an uncompromising 'Publish and be damned.'

Wellington was lampooned for his strong sex drive. In this cartoon one woman exclaims: 'What a spanker! I hope he won't fire it at me.' Her friend retorts: 'It can't do any harm ... he has fired it so often ... it is nearly worn out.'

Battle of Waterloo, 18 June 1815. This magnificent panorama looking south past the farmhouse of La Haye-Sainte shows Wellington (far right) on his chestnut stallion Copenhagen orchestrating resistance at the climax of the battle. On a mound just in front of him green-uniformed riflemen of the 1/95th, commanded by Jonathan Leach, pick off French cavalrymen as they attack British

squares. Napoleon (in the distance, top left) prepares his Imperial Guard for their final attack.
The painter uses considerable artistic and topographical licence but he conveys a great sense
of the dynamics of the final and decisive battle between Napoleon and Wellington.

The formidable French cuirassiers charge the wall of steel presented by British infantry in square formation, stopping short of impaling themselves on the bayonets. Note the tall rye trodden down flat.

Sergeant Charles Ewart of the Scots Greys seizes the eagle of the French 45th Regiment at Waterloo. It was one of two captured by the heavy cavalry. Eagles were the most prized trophies in battles with the French.

'Now, Maitland, now's your time!' shouts Wellington to the commander of the footguards at Waterloo as Napoleon's Imperial Guard advance to within point-blank range of the British muskets. The guards fired, then charged with their bayonets, breaking Napoleon's last and greatest challenge to the British line.

A French officer offers cognac to the gravely wounded Fred Ponsonby on the battlefield of Waterloo. Ponsonby never forgot his kindness and the two men met by chance more than a decade later.

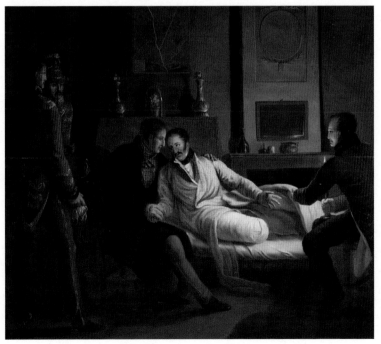

Lord Uxbridge shows Wellington the stub of his amputated leg after Waterloo. Uxbridge astonished his doctors by maintaining an unchanging heartbeat during the operation. In the battle Uxbridge exclaimed, 'By God, Sir, I've lost my leg.' 'By God, Sir, so you have,' responded the Duke.

Napoleon Bonaparte, defeated by the allies in 1814, in his palace of Fontainebleau at the time of his first abdication. Less than a year later he was back leading his army into his first ever confrontation with Wellington. After his defeat at Waterloo, Napoleon was exiled to the island of St Helena where he died in 1821.

The Waterloo banquet at Apsley House in London in 1836. Wellington, aged sixty-seven, is on his feet surrounded by his veteran commanders. King William IV sits on his right; the one-legged Lord Uxbridge, now Marquess of Anglesey, is the third on Wellington's left in a dark jacket. Sixteen years later Wellington held the last dinner here before his death in 1852.

and there were some tender scenes 'upon their ladies parting with them'.

Some of the less experienced soldiers avoided overloading their heavy packs by cutting back on provisions. Those who knew that they could be days away from their next food supply furnished themselves with three days' worth. A number of the young cavalrymen remembered to fill their horses' nosebags with corn and loaded up with a good twenty-four hours' supply of hay, but neglected to take a stock of bread and bacon for themselves.

Wellington depended for his food on his devoted chef, James Thornton, who had tried but failed to serve him a whole dinner the evening before. Before the Duke could eat his dessert, a new set of messages had him striding off to meet his staff. Thornton was warned to be ready to move at a moment's notice. Early on 16 June he sent ahead a basket of cold food in the hope that he could prepare some lunch for his commander in the field. In the event the Duke and his chef were not to meet for forty-eight hours.

Wellington managed a couple of hours' sleep before dawn, and then rode south. His infantry was already on the move, led by Picton's division which included the Rifles. They had left Brussels before dawn for Quatre-Bras, several hours' march to the south. The Duke rode past the Rifles as they halted for breakfast some miles south of Brussels. Ned Costello said his riflemen were 'merry as crickets, laughing and joking with each other . . . for even the old soldiers could not believe the enemy were so near . . . Alas! how many of our brave companions, ere that sun set, were no more!' Fred Ponsonby's light dragoons and his cousin Major General William Ponsonby's heavy cavalry were preparing for the road. Wellington's gunners also were under way. Cavalié Mercer was shaken awake by his servant in the small village west of Brussels where he and his horse artillery troop were billeted. The servant handed him a written order that had just arrived instructing him to get on the road. As Mercer pulled on his breeches, he shouted for his sergeant major and his supply officer, and within minutes three days' provisions for men and horses had been prepared, and 'the fine martial clang of "boot and saddle" resounded through the village . . . making the woods ring again and even the frogs stop to listen'.

Officers from two of Mercer's gun crews had been up late at the ball in Brussels, so it took some time to get the whole troop on the move. It was a beautiful sunny morning, but some of the tracks they had to negotiate were quite steep. They had to double the number of horses on each of their carriages, which meant that only half the troop could move at any one time.

As Mercer's horse artillery struggled on and the advanced British infantry units such as the Rifles marched down the road from Brussels, they began to pick up a 'dull, sullen sound that filled the air, somewhat resembling that of a distant water mill or still more distant thunder'. Ned Costello heard it too. It was the sound of the French and Prussian guns at Ligny twenty-five miles south-east of Brussels. By mid-afternoon this was drowned out by the much closer roar of Wellington's battle with the French at Quatre-Bras.

Wellington had ridden fast on his favourite charger, Copenhagen,* to Quatre-Bras where he arrived at about 10 a.m. He found 8,000 Dutch–Belgian troops in the woods – the Bois de Bossu – just south-west of the crossroads. They, at first, appeared confident of holding the position until they could be reinforced by Wellington's other forces, which were now moving south from Brussels and south-east from Nivelles towards the crossroads. Wellington sent a message to Blücher at Ligny seven miles away to the south-east, assuring him that he would have most of his forces in place by the middle of the day and strongly implying that he would be able to come to the aid of the Prussians if they needed him. But Wellington's forces were in fact still several hours away: he wouldn't be ready to fight till at least mid-afternoon and he decided to ride over to meet Blücher at the Brye Windmill above Ligny and tell him that he would come to his support 'provided I am not attacked'.

It was just as well he gave this proviso, because, soon after he returned, the Dutch–Belgians were fighting for their lives against a powerful attack on Quatre-Bras by Marshal Ney. It was all part of

* Copenhagen was the foal of a mare ridden at the siege of the Danish capital in 1807. Wellington bought him in Spain and rode him through most of his battles from Vitoria to Waterloo. The horse had great stamina and was steady and fearless on the battlefield. Wellington took him home to Stratfield Saye, where the horse died at the age of twenty-nine in 1836.

Napoleon's strategy: divide and destroy. He would throw most of his army against Blücher's force at Ligny. If he could destroy the Prussians or force them to wheel away and retreat to the east, he could then fall on Wellington and defeat him in turn. But his first priority was to stop Wellington reinforcing the Prussians. So Napoleon despatched Marshal Ney, the flamboyant but often reckless commander, who had faced Wellington at Bussaco five years earlier, to pin him down at Quatre-Bras. Ney had 20,000 troops, more than twice the number of Wellington's Dutch–Belgian troops, who were soon driven back from most of their positions. If the French could reach and secure the road that ran east and west through the Quatre-Bras crossroads, Wellington would be facing defeat.

But time was on his side. In the early afternoon Picton's units began pouring in from the north and took up positions along the east–west road. They were some of the best troops Wellington had. He sent the Rifles way over to his left to secure his flank. In the centre he posted his British battalions. Most of them stood in long lines to receive the French attacks with a great fusillade of musket fire. The tactic was as successful as it had been in the Peninsula. The advancing French columns suffered such high casualties that their attacks lost momentum. But still they came back for more. Wellington dashed from one battalion commander to another personally issuing orders and slowly advancing his men beyond the east–west road and across the fields beyond. This was relatively flat country. It was the only time that the Duke had been unable to deploy on a battlefield of his own choosing. He could not use the shelter of reverse slopes, and his men suffered dreadfully from superior French gunfire.

Wellington was constantly exposed to danger. At one moment he attempted and failed to rally some allied cavalry who had been forced back by the French. He was surrounded by French lancers and hussars and escaped being seized or killed only by leaping over a defensive line of Gordon Highlanders, shouting at them to lower their bayonets so that his horse could jump over their heads.

Ney could see the balance of numbers turning against him as British reinforcements moved up. So he decided to commit the most fearsome French cavalrymen of all – the cuirassiers. Few British soldiers – even in the Peninsula – had ever had to confront these men before. Only one regiment of cuirassiers, the 13th, had been deployed by Napoleon to Spain, but it served exclusively in the eastern part of the country and did not fight Wellington's Peninsular army. The cuirassiers looked like medieval knights. Their horses were massive chargers bred in Normandy. They were the armoured elite of the French cavalry, specially selected men, each at least six feet tall. Clad in helmets with their glittering steel breastplates or cuirasses edged with gilded copper rivets, they weighed over 300 pounds. These protective cuirasses strapped around their dark-blue tunics were proof against sword, lance and bayonet. Their weakness was that, although they could stop a ball fired from a pistol, they could not stop the higher velocity of a musket ball. They were far less agile in close combat than an opponent without body armour. But a charging cuirassier, leaning low over his horse's neck and stretching his sword arm forward without any bend in his elbow, was a terrifying sight to an infantryman on the ground. Nothing less than a well-aimed musket shot or the security of the infantry square offered any protection. Only men with the courage and discipline that came from years of campaigning could stand unflinching shoulder to shoulder against such a formidable foe.

This discipline was now put to serious test at Quatre-Bras as Ney launched 800 cuirassiers against the British battalions. One regiment, the South Lincolnshire, the 69th, lost 153 officers and men when it failed to form a square. Tom Morris's Highland Regiment was also attacked. He and his comrades had marched no less than twenty-seven miles through the night and then through the burning morning sun to the battlefield where they were soon immersed in a great field of rye seven feet tall. 'We were not advancing unobserved,' wrote Morris. A body of cuirassiers 'must have seen the glittering tops of our bayonets' because they 'came on us by surprise, and having no opportunity to form square, we were compelled to retire as rapidly as we could out of the cornfield'. The cuirassiers then turned their attention to the neighbouring Royal Highland Regiment, and Morris saw them causing 'great havoc in the Highland ranks'. James Anton was in one of those ranks which managed to form a square just in time to confront the cuirassiers. They charged two sides of the square and 'their heavy horses and steel armour seemed sufficient to bury us under them had they been pushed forward on our bayonets', wrote Anton. But miraculously the cuirassiers stopped short of penetrating the square and the redcoated British levelled their muskets. 'A most destructive fire was opened; riders, cased in heavy armour, fell tumbling from their horses; the horses reared, plunged and fell on the dismounted riders; steel helmets and *cuirasses* rung against unsheathed sabres, as they fell to the ground; shrieks and groans of men, the neighing of horses and the discharges of musketry rent the air, as men and horses mixed together in one heap of indiscriminate slaughter.'

Wellington was still with the Gordons (the 92nd Regiment of Foot) next door to the Highland Regiment, when the cuirassiers charged. He remained as cool as ever. A young lieutenant, Robert Winchester, watched him steadying the front line when they were particularly hard pressed. '92nd, don't fire until I tell you,' he shouted, as the cuirassiers 'under cover of their guns came charging up the fields in front of the regiment . . . and when they came within twenty or thirty paces of us, his Grace gave the order to fire, which killed and wounded an immense number of men and horses, on which they immediately faced about and galloped off'. Winchester saw one French officer, who thought his men were still following him, charge right through and beyond the Gordons. '"Damn it, 92nd," shouted Wellington. "Will you allow that fellow to escape?" Some of the men turned immediately round, fired, killed his horse and a musket ball at the same time passed through each foot of the gallant young officer.'*

A little later Tom Morris's light company of the Highlanders was detached to do some skirmishing away from the main force, but the company 'was unfortunately commanded by a Captain, 60 years of age, who had been upward of 39 years in the service but was never before in action. He knew nothing of field movements.' When a regiment of cuirassiers made for Morris's company, the officer was 'at his wits' end and there is no doubt we should all have been sacrificed had we not been seen by the adjutant of our regiment, a fine spirited fellow'. He spotted their predicament and immediately rode up and

---

* Winchester later befriended the wounded Frenchman and spent some time with his family in Paris.

exclaimed, 'Captain Robinson, what are you about? Are you going to murder your men?' He ordered Tom Morris and his comrades to rejoin the main regiment 'just in time to form square. On the cuirassiers coming up and finding us so well prepared, they wheeled off to the left receiving from us a volley as they retired.'

Tom Morris felt a growing resentment of Wellington's conduct of the Battle of Quatre-Bras as he watched one cuirassier charge after another. 'Though it's considered a sort of treason to speak against the Duke, yet I cannot help making a few observations upon the extraordinary fact that we had neither artillery nor cavalry in the field . . . fortunately for the Duke the result was successful: had it been otherwise he would have been deeply censured.' Some units suffered particularly heavy losses. Lieutenant Alex Riddock described his Essex Regiment as being 'reduced to a mere skeleton'. Particularly lethal were the French lancers: their long shafts tipped with steel blades could reach over the bayonets of the British infantry bunched in their squares and do terrible injury. As for those caught outside the squares, Riddock watched squadrons of French cuirassiers and lancers 'sweeping the field in the rear, round and round every square, showing no mercy, dashing at and sticking the helpless wounded officers and men that unfortunately lay without the protection of the square. I could compare them to nothing but a swarm of bees.'

The British cavalry and artillery was, belatedly, on its way. Cavalié Mercer moved east as fast as his horse artillerymen could drag their huge load. When they reached Nivelles they found a town in horror and fear as the dreadfully disfigured wounded and dying struggled into its streets. 'Some were staggering along unaided, the blood falling from them in large drops as they went. One man we met was wounded in the head; pale and ghastly . . . with affrighted looks and uncertain step he evidently knew little of where he was . . . At every step in short, we met numbers of more or less wounded hurrying along in search of that assistance which many would never live to receive and others receive too late.' Mercer's battery, which had been so sorely needed at Quatre-Bras, eventually arrived 'just too late to be useful'.

Fred Ponsonby's and William Tomkinson's light dragoons just missed the battle too. They had not wasted any time. As they rode through Nivelles, they threw away their forage to lighten their loads as much as possible, but they arrived on the battlefield to find the infantry had completed the task without them. William Hay accompanied Ponsonby in a tour of the field. Hay saw more men and horses lying there than anything he could have dreamed of. Ponsonby told him to look at a cuirass he had taken from one of the dead bodies. It was perforated with three holes. 'I wanted to find out', said Ponsonby, 'if these cuirasses were ball proof or not: this plainly shows that they were not.' Wellington was even more scathing about the cuirassiers. He recalled watching many of them being unhorsed and forced to the ground, and 'those that were not killed were so encumbered by their cuirasses and jackboots that they could not get up, but lay sprawling and kicking like so many turned turtles'. When the men of the Gordons gathered to cook their dinner that evening at Quatre-Bras, they found that the discarded cuirasses made excellent saucepans.

Thomas Picton had been the hero of the Battle of Quatre-Bras. Time and again he rallied his men as they faced charges by cavalry and infantry and slowly but surely shepherded the long British line forward – shouting encouragement all the time, losing a horse under him and sustaining a serious wound that broke two of his ribs. At one stage Picton found the enemy both in front of and behind his division. 'This was', as John Kincaid observed, 'a crisis in which . . . the victory was theirs, by all the rules of war, for they had superior numbers both before and behind us; but the gallant old Picton, who had been trained in a different school, did not choose to confine himself to rules in these matters; despising the forces in his rear, he advanced, charged and routed those in his front which created such a panic among the others that they galloped back through the intervals in his divisions with no other object in view than their own safety.' Picton himself told his ADC, Captain Tyler, that he had never had such a hard day's fighting and added, 'I shall begin to think that I cannot be killed after this.' Picton told no one that he was wounded and had to endure the agony of riding a borrowed horse with no saddle all through the retreat of the following day. Rees Gronow, who had persuaded Picton to let him join his entourage, was one of the few to know the old warrior was hurt. He passed by Picton's bedroom the following night: 'I heard him groan from the pain of the wound he had received at Quatre Bras, but did not of course venture to disturb him.'

The Rifles, way over on Wellington's left flank at Quatre-Bras, had a hard time of it too. It was a day of vicious fighting. Kincaid reckoned it would end with the two sides where they had started, but then to his and Jonathan Leach's delight reinforcements came up and helped them to press forward. The Rifles 'gained a considerable portion of the positions originally occupied by the enemy, when darkness obliged us to desist'. The boisterous Irishman Ned Costello had his trigger finger torn off by a musket ball and had to spend two nights in great pain on the road back to Brussels. 'To sleep was impossible with the anguish of my shattered hand and the groans of my fellow sufferers.'

Nearly every soldier saw friends killed or wounded at Quatre-Bras. One young officer, Ensign Deacon, was told by Tom Morris that he was wounded. 'God bless me – so I am,' said Deacon and rushed off to try and find his wife who was with the regiment's baggage train. Somehow they missed each other. She had already been told about his wound and was frantically trying to find him on the battlefield. She was, said Morris, 'in the last state of pregnancy'. She spent the whole night searching for him and then headed for Brussels in worsening weather 'faint, exhausted and wet to the skin, having no other clothes than a black silk dress and light shawl'. She reached Brussels two days later, found her husband and 'the next day gave birth to a fine girl which was afterwards christened Waterloo Deacon'.

The Battle of Quatre-Bras was quickly overshadowed by Waterloo, but it was one of the hardest-fought and most critical contests of the war. Both sides claimed victory. It was more like a draw. Ney's attacks made it impossible for Wellington to go to Blücher's help, as he had hoped. But the extra Anglo-allied reinforcements rolling in all day had allowed Wellington to resist Ney's attacks, and in the end to outnumber him and even force him back. The toll was high: Wellington lost 4,700 men of the 36,000 he had fielded at Quatre-Bras, Ney lost 4,300 of his 34,500. But for one massive piece of French mismanagement Wellington might well have been defeated.

A large force of 20,000 men under Count d'Erlon was sent to reinforce Ney early on. It would have given him a decisive edge over Wellington's hard-pressed units. But Napoleon suddenly switched orders to D'Erlon just before he arrived at Quatre-Bras and told him to go east to help smash Blücher. No sooner had D'Erlon and his men reached the other battlefield than Ney, desperate for reinforcement, ordered them back to rejoin him. This idiotic see-saw left D'Erlon too late to join either battle. Ney wrote later that D'Erlon's men didn't rejoin him till nine o'clock that evening. He said, with pardonable exaggeration, 'Thus twenty-five or thirty thousand men were absolutely paralysed and were idly paraded, during the whole of the battle . . . without firing a shot.' Napoleon, in his ham-fisted attempt to rewrite history in exile on St Helena, refused to accept culpability for any of this. He blamed Ney for attacking with too little too late.

· The bloodiest of the day's two battles was at Ligny, where Blücher was roundly defeated. Wellington hadn't exactly endeared himself to his Prussian ally when they met that morning. Wellington took one look at Blücher's exposed positions and observed, 'if my troops were so disposed I should expect them to be beaten'. Typical blunt Wellington. He was even more so in an aside to Sir Henry Hardinge, his liaison officer with the Prussians. 'If they fight here they will be damnably mauled.' In the event Napoleon's guns played havoc with Blücher's forces, which were posted in full view of the French on forward slopes around Ligny. French cavalry and columns of veteran infantrymen then battered the Prussians into a humiliating retreat.

Blücher himself narrowly escaped death. His horse was shot and fell on him. French cuirassiers rode past without recognising him in the failing light. Then he was nearly trampled by Prussian cavalry pushing back the French. Finally with the help of his ADC he was 'dragged out . . . bruised and half unconscious and almost fainting' and rescued from the battlefield. The doughty old field marshal was saved just in time to make the most critical strategic decision of his campaign: to stand by Wellington or to desert him? The issue was stark, the debate within the Prussian high command dramatic and emotional. Blücher later described to Henry Hardinge the row he had had with opponents on his staff. Hardinge, who was Wellington's liaison officer with the Prussians, was also a victim of Ligny. 'I passed that night with my amputated arm lying with some straw in his [Blücher's] ante-room,' he recalled. 'Next morning Blücher sent for me in, calling me *Lieber Freund*, etc., and embracing me. I perceived he smelt most strongly of gin and of rhubarb. He said to me, *Ich stinke etwas*, that he had been obliged to take medicine, having been twice rode over by the cavalry.' Blücher then went on to describe the highly charged debate in which he and his chief of staff, Count von Gneisenau, had bitterly opposed each other. The night before the Prussians had withdrawn north to the town of Wavre, nine miles east of Waterloo. Blücher wanted to stay there to be within reach of Wellington. Gneisenau was for abandoning Wellington and moving off to the east to preserve the Prussian army. He mistrusted and disliked Wellington for failing to rescue the Prussians at Ligny. Besides, if Wellington were now defeated, Gneisenau argued, they, the Prussians, would be utterly destroyed. Blücher won the argument. He was determined that Wellington would not be defeated, and he would do his damnedest to make sure he wasn't. The decision was made: Wellington would not have to face Napoleon alone. It was the first of many debts he would owe to Gebhard von Blücher.

At Quatre-Bras that morning Wellington still knew nothing of Blücher's defeat. He sent an ADC, the trusty Alexander Gordon, soon after dawn to find out what had happened at Ligny. At 7.30 Gordon was back, leaping off his sweating horse and reporting *sotto voce* to Wellington that Blücher had been battered by Napoleon and suffered up to 20,000 casualties. The field marshal had not abandoned the campaign but had withdrawn to Wavre. The Prussians were badly scarred but not destroyed.

Wellington now felt he had no choice. Quatre-Bras was a poor defensive position, as the day before had shown. If he stayed there now, several miles in advance of the Prussians, he would be exposed to attack by Napoleon and Ney on two fronts. He defined his plight with blunt realism: 'Old Blücher has had a damned good hiding and has gone back to Wavre, eighteen miles to the rear. We must do the same. I suppose they'll say in England that we have been licked. Well I can't help that.' After two nights of virtually no sleep and with much of his world collapsing around him, Wellington was acting, as always, like a man making a difficult move at chess.

At 9 a.m. on 17 June Wellington received a message from Blücher asking whether he was determined to meet Napoleon in battle. He replied: 'I still hold to the original intention of a united offensive against the French army, but now I must get back to the position at Mont St Jean where I will accept battle with Napoleon, if I am supported by one Prussian corps.'

The certainty with which Wellington pronounced his strategy that morning – to fight Napoleon at Waterloo – is perhaps the most singular example of how he was able to make a colossal decision with such cool confidence. He must have been – at least for some time that morning – racked by anxiety at the sheer scale of what was at stake. Napoleon, one of the ablest battle tacticians of all time, was determined to do battle with him with an army at least 20,000 men stronger than his. That army was all French, fortified by a core of experienced veterans utterly devoted to their Emperor. Large parts of Wellington's Anglo-allied army were of dubious loyalty and morale. Without Prussian help the odds against him would be overwhelming. He had no reason to doubt Blücher's good faith and he knew how devoted he was to the cause of destroying Napoleon. Wellington was demanding a lot of his Prussian allies who had been trounced by the French only the day before. He must have been haunted by memories of the ludicrous unreliability of General Cuesta during the Talavera campaign in Spain. But in the end he had little choice. Waterloo was the last place he could stand before Brussels and to lose the city would be a devastating setback. Napoleon would still have to face vastly superior numbers of Austrians and Russians who were preparing to crush him, but the blow to Britain's and Wellington's prestige would be disastrous.

With his mind made up, Wellington now had to orchestrate a withdrawal to Mont Saint-Jean, the ridge just south of the village of Waterloo, as discreetly as possible. A quick advance by Napoleon would catch his men exposed at Quatre-Bras or in the vulnerable first stage of withdrawal. But Wellington relied on the Emperor's long-standing habit of allowing his men a good night's rest after a major encounter. By 10 a.m. Wellington's force began to move. Mobile units like William Tomkinson's light dragoons would stay to the last and help secure the army's rear. Tomkinson had spent the night bivouacking with his squadron and slept a lot better than his brother Henry, who had never bivouacked in the open air before. When Henry awoke to the sound of men discharging and cleaning their muskets, he thought the enemy was attacking and ran for his horse. William was told of the retreat early by Fred Ponsonby, who, being a commanding officer, was often at Wellington's headquarters. Ponsonby told him he 'regretted that they were obliged to retire'. Tomkinson observed that the French did not move a man in pursuit until late in the day when only the British cavalry remained at Quatre-Bras. There were few clashes. The biggest was at the small town of Genappe, where the main street remains to this day a very narrow thoroughfare, and some French lancers blocked the road. It was the first test for Wellington's new cavalry commander Lord Uxbridge. He had the unfortunate experience of ordering his own regiment, the 7th Hussars, against the French, and watching them being beaten back. The long reach of the French lances made the hussars' sabres ineffective. To Uxbridge's shame and embarrassment he had to appeal to the superior weight and skill of the Life Guards to clear the road of the French.

Mercer and his Royal Horse Artillery battery were involved with Uxbridge in the retreat too. At one stage they found themselves caught in a narrow lane with the enemy hard on their heels. Uxbridge called out, 'Make haste, make haste! For God's sake, gallop or you will be taken!' But there was no scope for any galloping. Mercer suddenly found the narrow lane blocked by French cavalrymen, and the last he recalled of Uxbridge was a cry of 'By God we are all prisoners' before the cavalry commander made his escape, 'dashing his horse at one of the garden banks, which he cleared, and away he went, leaving us to get out of the scrape as best we could'. Mercer reckoned there was only one way out: he shouted to his men, 'Reverse by unlimbering,' and the men rapidly unhooked their guns from their carriages, and somehow manhandled the guns around so that they were facing the other way. It was hard enough to swivel a gun round, and 'the very reversing of the limber itself in so narrow a lane, with a team of eight horses, was sufficiently difficult and required first rate driving'.

By this time there was heavy rain and 'away we went helter skelter – guns, gun detachments, and hussars, all mixed *pêle-mêle*, going like mad, and covering each other with mud, to be washed off by the rain, which . . . now came down . . . in splashes instead of drops, soaking us anew to the skin, and, what was worse, extinguishing every slow-match in the brigade.'

In the course of the day Mercer came to see much of the army's so-called 'rocket' group. Its commander, Major Edward Whinyates, an enthusiast for the weapons invented by Sir William Congreve just ten years earlier, was very keen to prove their worth. Mercer watched them fire, with initial success, at some enemy gunners who were chasing them. The rocket men placed a rocket in the road on a little iron stand. 'The order to fire is given . . . the fidgety missile begins to splutter and wriggle its tail for a second or so, and then darts forth straight up the *chaussée*.' It destroyed the enemy gunners successfully, but 'the rocketeers kept shooting off rockets, none of which ever followed the course of the first. Most of them, on arriving about the middle of the ascent, took a vertical direction, whilst some actually turned back upon ourselves – and one of these, following me like a squib, actually put me in more danger than all the fire of the enemy throughout the day.' Wellington considered the rocket group little more than a joke. A few days earlier he had ordered the rockets put into store and the group's horses handed over to other units. A senior officer pleaded with Wellington: 'It will break poor Whinyates' heart to lose his rockets.' To which Wellington replied: 'Damn his heart, sir: let my order be obeyed.' Since then, the Duke had relented. Hence the absurd firework display on the road from Genappe.

As the day wore on the rain got worse, and it is astonishing that Wellington succeeded in collecting all his men on the ridge just south of Waterloo by late evening. Fred Ponsonby's horses were sinking into mud up to their fetlocks. When George Farmer and another squadron of horsemen finally arrived, the rain had 'reduced the face of the country to a state of swamp; and as our bivouac was formed in a ploughed field . . . at every step which you took, you sank to your knees and your foot, when you dragged it to the surface again, came loaded with some seventy pounds of clay . . .' Farmer and his lads were so cold and wet they raided a local village and returned with a pile of furniture they had grabbed to use for firewood.

While Mercer's troops were searching for a place to camp on the battlefield, 'a man of no very prepossessing appearance came rambling amongst our guns' and chatted to Mercer about the day. Mercer described him as dressed in a shabby, drab old greatcoat and a rusty round hat. 'Finding some of his questions rather impertinent, [I] was somewhat short in answering him and he soon left us.' Mercer was astonished to hear later that it was Sir Thomas Picton checking out the ground on which his division was taking up position on the ridge. The night that followed was dreadful. Mercer's gunners stowed themselves away beneath their gun carriages using the painted covers as additional shelter. Mercer himself and some other officers and soldiers crammed together into a small tent, 'all perfectly still and silent, the old Peninsular hands disdaining to complain before their Johnny Newcome comrades, and these fearing to do so lest they should provoke some such remarks as "What would you have done in the Pyrenees?" Or "Oho my boy! This is but child's play to what *we* saw in Spain."' Mercer and a few others found they were so wet they couldn't sleep, so they gathered round a fire under a large umbrella and lit up cigars.

Wellington had his men retire behind the ridge at Waterloo that evening so that the French wouldn't know exactly where they were. He was furious when some of his gunners – against his express orders – responded to the French artillery and gunfire echoed across the shallow valley between the two sides. Napoleon was now sure that this was where Wellington would make his stand. Many French units were slow to move up, but neither side was in any doubt that the decisive battle for Europe would be fought the next day – on Sunday 18 June.

Whatever was going on behind Wellington's calm exterior, he showed little sign of emotion in a remarkable talk with the man designated as his deputy, Lord Uxbridge. Wellington had always ignored – with typical arrogance – the duty any commander should have to provide for the possibility of his own death or incapacity in battle. The classic example of this took place that evening before the Battle of Waterloo when Uxbridge rather diffidently asked to see him.

Uxbridge had sought the advice of another senior commander, reminding him that if anything happened to the Duke he would find himself commander in chief and he would like to know how Wellington planned to go about the battle the next day. 'I have not the slightest idea what are the projects of the Duke. I would give anything in the world to know the dispositions which, I have no doubt, have been profoundly calculated.'

Uxbridge was advised to go and put his worry to the Duke himself. So off he went and explained delicately that he would like the Duke to share his plans with him. Wellington listened quietly without saying a word. Then he said calmly, 'Who will attack the first to-morrow, I or Bonaparte?' 'Bonaparte,' Uxbridge replied. 'Well,' continued the Duke in the same unemotional tone, 'Bonaparte has not given me any idea of his projects; and as my plans will depend upon his, how can you expect me to tell you what mine are?' Uxbridge bowed and made no reply. At which the Duke ended the meeting by touching Uxbridge on the shoulder in a friendly way and saying, 'There is one thing certain, Uxbridge, that is that, whatever happens, you and I will do our duty.' He then shook him warmly by the hand. Uxbridge bowed again, and then left.

18

Hard pounding

Waterloo, morning 18 June 1815

'WATERLOO, SUNDAY morning, 3 o'clock, June 18th 1815. My dear Lady Frances,' wrote the Duke of Wellington to his Brussels lover from his first-floor room at his headquarters. 'I think you ought to make your preparations . . . to remove from Brussels . . . We fought a desperate battle on Friday in which I was successful though I had but very few troops. The Prussians were very roughly handled and retired in the night which obliged me to do the same to this place yesterday.' He then pointed out that any fighting at Waterloo might expose Brussels to the French. 'I will give you the earliest intimation of any danger that may come to my knowledge; at present I know of none.' Cool and balanced as ever, Wellington recognised that the coming battle would be the greatest challenge of his life.

He had just been woken from less than three hours' sleep to be handed a message that had been rushed through wind and rain from Prussian headquarters in Wavre. It was a final and very welcome written promise from Blücher to put two Prussian corps – around 50,000 men – on the road at dawn to support Wellington at Waterloo. If Wellington had any doubts about confronting Napoleon there, they must have vanished at that moment. His trusty horse Copenhagen was saddled up in the early June dawn and the Duke rode off to inspect his men. Gronow watched him riding past that morning with his staff. 'They all seemed as gay and unconcerned as if they were riding to meet the hounds in some quiet English county.' Wellington was dressed, immaculately as ever, in civilian clothes: blue jacket and cloak, smart white leather pantaloons, white cravat and cocked hat. He might have had little sleep for the previous three nights, but at least he had had a roof over his head unlike most of his soldiers.

Most of Wellington's and Napoleon's men slept, or tried to sleep, in the open. 'I never remember a worse night in the whole of the Peninsular war,' wrote Sergeant William Lawrence, 'for the rain descended in torrents, mixed with fearful thunder and lightning . . .' It rained all night and Thomas Todd was so stiff and sore that he couldn't move freely for some time, but half an allowance of liquor was doled out, 'the most welcome thing I ever received'. William Leeke, the most junior ensign in John Colborne's 52nd, was sent off with a small party to get some straw for the troops to sleep on. They pulled some off a thatched roof in a nearby village, but it proved even soggier than lying on the ground. Tom Morris found it far too wet to lie down to sleep, so he and his companions 'collected armfuls of standing corn' to place on the ground and then sat on their knapsacks with blankets over their heads to keep dry, 'which was needless as we were so thoroughly drenched'. Sergeant William Wheeler was glad of his tobacco. 'You often blamed me for smoking when I was at home last year,' he wrote to his family. 'But I must tell you that if I had not had a good stock of tobacco this night I must have given up the Ghost.'

Morris was given the task of distributing the daily allowance of spirits to his company. He had some left over, so he had an extra swig with his friend, Sergeant Burton, who advised him to keep some for after the battle. 'I told him I thought very few of us would live to see the close of the day.' 'Tom,' he replied, 'I'll tell you what it is: there is no shot made yet for either you or me.' A thousand yards to Morris's left the Gordon Highlanders were given an allowance of gin that, one Scotsman observed, 'had the effect of infusing warmth into our almost inanimate frames'. By the middle of the day the Gordons would be in the centre of the action, just as they had been at Quatre-Bras.

When William Hay and Fred Ponsonby woke up among their horses, they found themselves 'in rather a strange plight, having sunk some 6 or 8 inches deep in the water and clay'. Spirits quickly revived when the sun came out. Most of the troops got breakfast, even if it was only a scrap of biscuit and some broth, and, as the day warmed up, they were soon in their shirtsleeves drying off their clothes and cleaning their weapons. Fred Ponsonby leaped on his horse, and rode up to the front line to look at the lie of the land, which was now, after the storm, crisply visible in the clear air.

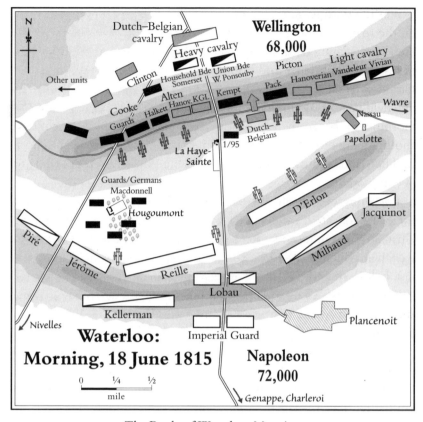

The Battle of Waterloo: Morning

Ponsonby scanned the length of the gentle ridge – about 3,500 yards from one end to the other. Behind it, on the north side, Wellington's 68,000 troops were preparing for battle, nearly all of them out of sight. In front of the ridge, to the south, fields of tall rye sloped down to a shallow valley 300 yards away. Beyond that the ground rose slowly again to where the meadows seethed with French troops parading in columns – waiting to be reviewed by Napoleon. Later that morning the unmistakable figure of the Emperor in his drab grey coat and large black hat could be seen moving through the ranks. Way beyond, on a further ridge behind the packed infantry battalions were the French cavalry, a great mass of blue, red and green uniforms, some in glinting steel helmets and body armour. Ponsonby watched squadron after squadron begin to assemble and mill around as if at the starting gate of a great race. Many French units were still on the road. Napoleon had made little effort to hurry up those of his men approaching from Ligny and Quatre-Bras. It was a further sign of his over-confidence and his faltering grip on the campaign he had started so well. Eventually there would be 72,000 French troops in the field against Wellington, but it would take them much of the morning to be ready for action. And Napoleon had despatched another 33,000 off to the east under Marshal Grouchy to pin down Blücher and prevent him from sending vital reinforcements to Wellington.

Ponsonby was on the left-hand side, the east side, of Wellington's ridge. Far off at the right-hand end, the ridge sloped down to the Château d'Hougoumont, a cluster of buildings including a barn and a chapel, which guarded Wellington's extreme right. In the centre, just below the top of the ridge, where it fell away to the valley between the opposing forces, was the farm of La Haye-Sainte, a rect-angle of robustly built farm buildings. And over to Ponsonby's left at the eastern end of the ridge, was the farm of Papelotte, the eastern edge of Wellington's front line. That was where the Prussians should show by lunchtime – if they kept their promise.

Another middle-ranking officer on horseback out early was Harry Smith. He had managed to persuade his wife Juana, unusually, to stay behind in Brussels during the fighting. He was a staff officer with a mixed force of British and German troops, and he rode for-ward to find Wellington and ask where he wanted his men posted. 'It was delightful to see his Grace on his noble horse, Copenhagen, in high spirits and very animated but so cool and clear in the issue of his orders.' One of Wellington's staff remarked in Smith's hearing, 'I don't think they will attack today.' 'Nonsense,' said the Duke, whose keen eye had already seen where the French columns were concentrating for an attack.

At Waterloo, Wellington was to employ his well-tried defensive tactic of using the dead ground – the reverse slope behind the ridge – to shelter his men from gunfire. Then, when an enemy attack came in, he would order his men to form long lines in two ranks with bayonets fixed ready to fight. Wellington knew his largely untried units, only a third of them British, would face veterans of Napoleon's old Grande Armée who had in their time vanquished every opponent they met. So he placed at least one British brigade in each division along his front line to avoid presenting Napoleon with any obvious weak points where he could break through. But just as Napoleon had weakened his main force by sending Grouchy off to secure his right, Wellington too had despatched a large force of some 17,000 men to protect his own right flank at Hal five miles to the west. He still had an uneasy feeling that Napoleon might try and deliver a blow against him from that direction. In the event both detachments proved valueless, and both commanders would deeply regret their absence.

Wellington ordered Harry Smith to take his brigade right to the centre of the British line, next to Picton. He also placed the Rifles (the 1/95th) in the middle of his position, only a hundred yards up the slope from La Haye-Sainte. 'We made a fire . . . and boiled a huge camp kettle full of tea,' recalled John Kincaid. 'All the bigwigs of the army had occasion to pass . . . I believe every one of them, from the Duke downwards, claimed a cupful.'

Wellington put Fred Ponsonby, William Hay and William Tomkinson and their light cavalry behind his far left. He posted Fred's cousin, Major General William Ponsonby, with his Union Brigade of heavy cavalry behind his centre, and all along the slope in front of his main units on the ridge he scattered skirmishers and sharpshooters – to blunt any French attack. Finally he placed the guns at intervals along his front line on top of the ridge. Mercer's battery – for the moment – was kept in reserve. Hew Ross and his battery, who had followed Wellington from the earliest days in Portugal, found themselves in the front line. Wellington posted Whinyates and his rockets well back – after the absurdity of what had happened at Genappe the day before where the rockets had done little more than treat the troops to a firework display.

All morning the Duke was riding breezily from unit to unit issuing orders. The more he was visibly seen to be exercising command and control even down to the level of the battalion, the more he reckoned he would give his men the will and confidence to win. His way of inspiring his men was to radiate cool self-confidence and to reassure them that he would make the right decisions and be in the right place at the right time, often at great personal risk. He was in no doubt of the importance of his own personal presence, and, as we have seen, believed Napoleon's appearance on a battlefield was worth several thousand extra men. But he drew the line at seizing an opportunity to decapitate the French army. At one point later in the day an artillery officer spotted Napoleon in the distance and asked Wellington for permission to fire on him. 'No! No!' replied Wellington. 'It is not the business of commanders to be firing upon each other.' It would have been unthinkable for a man of Wellington's sensibilities and against the ethos of the time to approve of what would look more like assassination than the proper conduct of warfare.

Napoleon was certainly visible early that morning reviewing his troops, but he was clearly moody and off colour. He was suffering from piles, which made riding painful. He was also disappointed that he was unable to attack Wellington at the early hour he had intended. Napoleon was now paying the penalty for failing to order his army forward quickly the day before. His guns were proving hopelessly difficult to drag through the mud after the night's downpours. Besides, the road from Genappe was cluttered with columns of foot-soldiers. But Napoleon was convinced he would win. At eight o'clock he gathered his top generals at his headquarters in a house called Le Caillou, two-and-a-half miles south of the British line. The record of the meeting, as related by the French historian Henri Houssaye, suggests that the Emperor was arrogant, testy and over-confident. 'We have ninety chances in our favour and not ten against us,' he said. Nicolas Soult, one of those who had switched sides yet again and was now Napoleon's chief of staff, was uneasy. Years of confronting Wellington had taught Soult to respect him. He advised Napoleon to recall Grouchy at once. He would need the extra men. Napoleon scoffed at him: 'Because you have been beaten by Wellington, you consider him a great general. I tell you, Wellington is a bad general, that the English are bad troops and that this affair is nothing more serious than eating one's breakfast.' 'I earnestly hope so,' replied Soult.

Napoleon then consulted Reille, who had also been worsted by Wellington at Vitoria, in the Pyrenees and in southern France. 'Well posted, as Wellington knows how to post it, and attacked from the front, I consider the English infantry to be impregnable,' Reille told him, 'owing to its calm tenacity and its superior aim in firing.' He added that the best way to attack the English was not from the front but by manoeuvre, at which the French were superior. A little later Napoleon's brother Jérôme said that he had heard rumours of Blücher and Wellington joining up. 'Nonsense,' said Napoleon, 'the Prussians and English cannot possibly link for another two days after such a battle [as Ligny]'. Napoleon then turned his attention to Grouchy. But instead of recalling him urgently, he sent him a curiously vague message: 'His Majesty desires you will head for Wavre in order to draw near to us.' It was sloppy, contradictory wording. To head for Wavre, as Grouchy continued to do when he received this order, would draw him away from, not near to, the battlefield at Waterloo.

The Battle of Waterloo finally began at 11.30 a.m. Napoleon's plan was remarkably conventional for one so adept at fast manoeuvre and surprise. It called for a series of major frontal attacks, supported massively by his guns. The Emperor had begun his career as an artillery officer and was a firm believer in using the power of heavy guns to cause chaos in enemy ranks before throwing his infantry against them. He had 246 guns at Waterloo, nowhere near the number he had fielded at Austerlitz and Leipzig, but far more than the 157 trundled out by Wellington, who in any case had far less confidence in his artillery.

Napoleon began by ordering his gunners to open up on the most critical point of Wellington's line – the Château d'Hougoumont. The well-fortified group of farm buildings with its walled gardens and orchards was chosen by Wellington as the bastion that would protect his right. As long as Wellington held it, Napoleon could not deliver a left hook at the Anglo-allied line. Without the farm Wellington's army would be exposed to attack from the flank as well as in front. Hougoumont was vital, and that was what Wellington told the man he placed in command, Lieutenant Colonel James Macdonnell of the Coldstream Guards, a giant Highlander from Invergarry in Scotland. Macdonnell had his men up early on 18 June punching loopholes in the brick wall of the garden. He commanded 1,200 defenders of Hougoumont – 200 guardsmen and 1,000 Germans.

The fight for the farm at Hougoumont was an epic struggle that lasted all day. Soon after Napoleon's guns opened up on the farm, his brother Jérôme, commanding on the French left, sent in his infantry. They cleared the woods to the south of the buildings but were soon raked by British, Dutch and German musket fire from behind the walls. There was savage face-to-face combat as the French pressed forward against Hougoumont with swords and bayonets. Muskets fired at extra-close range dealt horrific wounds and caused hundreds of deaths. Somehow, for over an hour, the defenders kept the French away from the farm's vulnerable North Gate, through which Wellington ordered a constant feed of ammunition to the besieged. First, 4,000 French infantry threw themselves at the walls, then another 3,500, then another 5,000 from General Foy's division.

The most dangerous moment for the defenders was when a huge Frenchman called Legros, nicknamed 'L'Enfonceur' (the Smasher), wielding an axe, managed to hack his way through to the North Gate and smash it open. He and a small group piled through it with wild shouts of triumph and ferocious duels soon littered the courtyard with severed limbs and bloody corpses. With his men desperately fighting the intruders, Macdonnell and four others hurled themselves at the gate in a frantic effort to close it. Somehow they managed to force it shut inch by inch and then slam down a great beam to hold it in place. Next they turned on the trapped Frenchmen. Only a small drummer boy was spared in the carnage that followed. 'The success of the battle of Waterloo', Wellington said later, 'depended on the closing of the gates of Hougoumont.'

The artillery battle over Hougoumont swung in Wellington's favour when Colonel Augustus Frazer, his Royal Horse Artillery commander, who had served him so well in the siege of San Sebastián, suggested using howitzers on the French attackers in the woods around Hougoumont. Wellington pointed out that the allies' own troops were fighting in the woods as well. 'Colonel Frazer,' Wellington said, 'you are going to do a delicate thing. Can you depend upon the force of your howitzers? Part of the wood is held by our troops, part by the enemy.' Frazer replied that his gunners could be depended upon not to kill their own troops, and he called upon his howitzers to fire at a high angle over the heads of the British and German troops. The shrapnel shells then took a severe toll of the French. Remarkably, while Wellington understood the value of using artillery in defence of Hougoumont, neither Napoleon nor any of his generals made effective use of their artillery against its walls. It seems inconceivable that the walls or wooden gates could have stood up to a properly focused bombardment. Curiously, it never happened. Napoleon missed another opportunity and thousands of foot-soldiers were sacrificed in fruitless attacks on the farm. The only French artillery that had any success were the howitzers that fired a few incendiary devices and set light to some of the buildings. 'Burning timbers crashed down on the men . . . and thick choking smoke billowed everywhere making their eyes stream . . . Through the roar of the flames came cries of help from the wounded and the wild neighing of panic-stricken horses.'

All through the day the struggle for Hougoumont continued. Wellington kept a keen eye on the action there and reinforced the garrison to 2,600 in the afternoon by adding two complete Guards battalions. By the afternoon Jérôme Bonaparte's exhausted division had been decimated and the division of General Foy, who had suffered many a beating by Wellington in the Peninsula, was gravely weakened as well. Some 3,500 British and Germans had pinned down 14,000 French troops all day. Macdonnell's dogged defence of Hougoumont tied up one-fifth of Napoleon's army and prevented it operating anywhere else on the battlefield.

Like most others in Wellington's army, Jonathan Leach spent much of the morning in a state of suspense. He was in charge of two forward companies of the Rifles posted 150 yards in front of the main British line in a sandpit just short of the farmhouse of La Haye-Sainte. He was right in the centre of the allied battlefront. He had listened to the artillery and small-arms fire from Hougoumont way over to his right till mid-morning. 'As yet all was quiet in the immediate front of our division. But after a calm comes a storm.' From about 11.30 Leach watched a line of French guns being dragged forward until they were 'staring us in the face' – around 500 yards away. He couldn't yet see the vast columns of French infantry that he, rightly, guessed were lining up behind the guns.

Napoleon moved forward to watch the build-up of 17,000 troops under Count d'Erlon. They were forming up behind the eighty guns of the new Grand Battery that Leach had seen and that were now awaiting the signal to fire. D'Erlon's infantrymen were to punch through Wellington's centre left and seize the crossroads that would put Napoleon on the road to Brussels. To maximise their firepower they would apply a lesson learned in the Peninsula. They would advance in much longer lines. Each of D'Erlon's twenty-five battalions would form into three ranks – each one of about 150 men abreast. They wouldn't be as long as Wellington's two thin red lines, but they would be a far cry from the much narrower columns that had been crushed time and again in Portugal and Spain. The battalions would follow each other in four great blocks, one battalion behind another. Count d'Erlon would lead – from the front, accompanied, some sources say, by the indomitable Marshal Ney. Then, at around one o'clock, just as the order was being given for Napoleon's newly placed guns to open fire, the Emperor himself noticed movement and a growing concentration of men four miles away to his right in the hills and woods around Château Saint-Lambert. They were coming from the direction of Wavre. His first reaction was one of relief – that Grouchy was racing to his assistance. An aide told him it was Grouchy. He put a glass to his eye and said, 'No, no. Black is black and blue is blue: those are Prussians.' A cavalry patrol was despatched and reported that it was indeed the Prussians. Napoleon found it hard to believe: 'I can . . . scarcely comprehend why it was a Prussian division and not that of Grouchy,' he said later. He had counted on the Prussians being out of the fight for at least a day or two more, and on Grouchy responding to the sound of gunfire. He immediately sent a further message to Grouchy demanding his urgent support, and then he turned to watch D'Erlon's assault on Wellington.*

---

* Napoleon had good grounds for insisting that he was poorly served that day. Soult was no substitute for his former chief of staff Alexandre Berthier, his stalwart right-hand man through two decades of campaigning, who failed to join him on his return from Elba and then mysteriously fell to his death from a window on 1 June 1815. During the day Napoleon asked Soult yet again whether he had sent for Grouchy. Soult replied that he had despatched 'un officier'. 'Un officier!' exclaimed Napoleon, and turning round to his suite he said: 'Un officier . . . ah my poor Berthier, had he been here he would have sent twenty' (Stanhope, p. 65). Three

From 1 p.m. to around 1.30 the Grand Battery fired more than 4,000 rounds at Wellington's lines. Most of them were roundshot, solid cannon balls, only a third of them shells packed with explosive. Little of Wellington's army was visible to the French gunners. The Duke had kept most of his men – except Leach's riflemen, some guns and a Dutch–Belgian battalion – hidden behind the top of the ridge. The Dutch–Belgians were hopelessly exposed and soon withdrew. Most of the roundshot ploughed harmlessly into the mud on or near the almost empty crest of the ridge: the howitzer shells which dropped behind the ridge were more lethal. With his main force sheltering well back, Wellington relied on the skirmishers on the forward slope to alert them to the arrival of the French assault. It wasn't long in coming.

John Kincaid watched from the sandpit as what looked to him like 'countless columns' of enemy infantry advanced towards him. 'We saw Buonaparte himself take post on the side of the road, immediately in our front, surrounded by a numerous staff, and each regiment as they passed him rent the air with shouts of "Vive l'Empereur!" Backed by the thunder of their artillery and carrying with them the *rubidub* of drums and the *tantarara* of trumpets . . . it looked at first as if they had some hopes of scaring us off the ground.' Leach kept Kincaid and his other sharpshooting riflemen picking off the advancing French as long as he could. But he had no choice but to retreat when D'Erlon's men tramped past them. Frenchmen tried to keep their long lines as straight as possible, but they had to struggle through the tall rye. Suddenly, as they passed over the top of the ridge, they were confronted by the men of Picton's division who had come forward to meet them. It was the first major clash of the two sides at Waterloo. The weight and momentum of the French columns initially began to force Picton's men back. This brought Sir Thomas himself up to the front roaring at his men to throw all their weight at the French. 'Charge! Hurrah! Hurrah!' he shouted. Then very abruptly, without making a sound, he slumped back on to his horse

Footnote (continued)
prominent generals mentioned in this book ended their lives by falling (or being thrown) from windows: Berthier, General Erskine in 1813 and General Junot later in the same year.

– killed instantly by a musket ball which had pierced his hat and lodged in his brain. Wellington's most tempestuous but formidable general had fulfilled his own prophecy and died fighting.

For a moment the battle hung in the balance, but then with a speed and ferocity that set the British cheering, Uxbridge's heavy cavalry – 2,600 strong – thundered in from behind the British infantry and plunged into the French ranks. 'To Paris!' shouted one exuberant cavalry colonel. 'Scotland for ever!' cried the hard-pressed Gordon Highlanders, as the Scots Greys and five other regiments of charging horsemen swept through them and set the French running for their lives. A Royal Dragoons squadron commander, Captain A. Clark Kennedy, claimed that the cavalry came to the rescue of Picton's division in the nick of time. The enemy 'had forced their way through our line . . . the crest of the height had been gained, and the charge of the cavalry at the critical moment recovered it. Had the charge been delayed two or three minutes, I feel satisfied it would probably have failed . . .'

Corporal John Dickson of the Scots Greys never forgot the strange thrill that ran through him as 'I dug my spurs into my brave old Rattler and we were off like the wind.' With the sound of the Gordons' bagpipes ringing in his ears, Dickson headed for the first Frenchman he could see. 'A young officer of Fusiliers made a slash at me with his sword, but I parried it and broke his arm: the next second we were in the thick of them. We could not see five yards ahead for the smoke.' A sergeant of the Gordons recalled the speed with which the heavy cavalry turned the battle around: 'It was fearful to see the carnage that took place. The dragoons were lopping off heads at every stroke, while the French were calling for quarter. We were also busy with the bayonet and what the cavalry did not execute we completed.' Clark Kennedy spotted an enemy colour with an eagle attached to it. 'Right shoulders forward, attack the colour,' he shouted. He ran his sword through the Frenchman holding it, and it fell across his horse's head. He attempted to break the eagle off the end of it, but one of his corporals riding close by urged him to keep it in one piece. 'Very well,' said Clark Kennedy to him, 'carry it to the rear as fast as you can. It belongs to me.' The eagle was a French regiment's most precious emblem and a prized trophy in the hands of an enemy. Another eagle was captured by Sergeant Charles Ewart of the Scots Greys.*

The great massed waves of footsoldiers that D'Erlon had led so proudly up the hill were utterly broken. Two thousand prisoners were taken and the remnants of the force fell back in disorder as Napoleon watched in dismay. Spurred on by their destruction of D'Erlon, Uxbridge's heavy cavalry now charged on with reckless abandon. Nothing was going to stop them. Dickson recalled an officer riding past him, shouting 'Charge! Charge the guns!' and although the ground was slippery with mud they spurred their horses on up the hill to where the line of the Grand Battery was, 'and we had our revenge. Such slaughtering! We sabred the gunners, lamed the horses and cut their traces and harness. I can hear the Frenchmen yet crying *"Diable!"* when I struck at them, and the long drawn hiss through their teeth as my sword went home.' At one stage Dickson's beloved Rattler went down and he had to grab a French horse. But then quite suddenly he and the other troopers realised that something had gone terribly wrong. Galloping in behind them, and between them and the British lines, came three regiments of French cavalry, and more heavy cavalry appeared ahead of them. Dickson saw lancers to his left and cuirassiers to his right. 'I shall never forget the sight. The Cuirassiers, in their sparkling steel breastplates and helmets mounted on strong black horses, with great blue rugs across the croups, were galloping towards me, tearing up the earth as they went . . .'

The British cavalry had done it again. Over-confident and driven wild by their own initial success they had rampaged out of control just as they had – to Wellington's fury – at Vimeiro and Talavera. And they had not even managed to spike the French guns they had reached. Convinced they were unstoppable, they had left themselves no avenue of escape. Now, disorganised and separated from each other, their horses breathless, they were a prey to enemy cavalrymen on fresh horses. What followed was butchery on a massive scale. The

---

* One story has it that a French eagle lost at the Battle of Borodino in 1812 was discovered inside the corpse of a dead horse on the battlefield. Its dying bearer had stuffed it up the horse's anus to conceal it from the Russians (Adkin, p. 201).

French cuirassiers – their swords six inches longer than those of the British cavalry – and a regiment of lancers – with their eight-foot-long weapons easily outreaching the sabres wielded by the exhausted British – hacked and stabbed their way through Uxbridge's six disordered regiments. Uxbridge himself was later to take much of the blame for the disaster: 'I committed a great mistake in having myself led the attack.' He had ridden with the first wave rather than with the second where he could have exercised more control. But Uxbridge, like Ney, always led from the front. Of the 2,700 horsemen who had charged minutes earlier, 589 of the Household Brigade (the Royal Horse Guards, the 1st and 2nd Life Guards and the 1st Dragoon Guards) and 612 of the Union Brigade (the Scots Greys, the Enniskilling Dragoons and the Royal Dragoons) were lost.

Fred Ponsonby's cousin William, the major general who commanded the Union Brigade, and a veteran of many a battle in the Peninsula, was one of the victims. He hadn't been able to find his horse that morning, as his groom wasn't within call, so he had had to ride a 'small bay hack'. Wading through the soft mud in a newly ploughed field William Ponsonby's weak horse slowed down, exhausted, just as some of Napoleon's much feared Polish lancers galloped up. Since his ADC was better mounted than he was, William Ponsonby was in the act of handing him his watch and a miniature of his wife for safe keeping when both of them were speared by the lancers and died immediately.

Fred Ponsonby's 12th Light Dragoons, together with the 11th and 16th, had spent a quiet morning on the extreme left of Wellington's line. But when the fighting began later in the morning, they moved across to watch the approach of D'Erlon's attack and the countercharge by the British heavy cavalry. Fred Ponsonby, like the other two regimental commanders in his brigade of light dragoons, appears to have been given some authority to act when he thought fit. He saw the broken waves of Frenchmen rolling down the hill before him. Way beyond them, he spotted the British heavy cavalry now being hard pressed by cuirassiers and lancers. He felt sure they 'were in the utmost peril unless some support were immediately afforded them'. He decided to lead his regiment against a French infantry unit in an effort to take the pressure off the beleaguered heavy dragoons.

He signalled to his men to advance in two long lines on a 260-yard front – three squadrons of around 150 men each.

Ponsonby rode out in front of the centre squadron with a bugler beside him. William Hay was the right-hand man in the left-hand squadron, about thirty yards to his colonel's left. Their attack was immediately successful and they were soon slashing with their light cavalry sabres, killing or wounding scores of French infantry who were on the ground or running for their lives. But Ponsonby's light dragoons then made the same mistake his cousin's had made earlier. They went too far and found themselves surrounded by French cavalry. They were outnumbered three to one and had to face bigger men on heavier horses. 'I know we ought not to have been there, and that we fell into the same error which we went down to correct, but I believe that this is an error almost inevitable after a successful charge.'

Hay managed to lead his squadron out of the mêlée, but as he was shepherding his men back, a shell burst under his horse and a splinter pierced its leg. The horse sat down; Hay used his spurs to try to get it up again. He failed and slid back over the horse's tail only to hear his men shouting a warning to him. Charging straight at him were two lancers 'coming full tilt at me, one instant more and both their lances would have been in the small of my back, and I have little doubt that the well directed aim of some of our noble infantry accounted for them and made them pay for their temerity by leaving their corpses where they intended mine should be left'. Fred Ponsonby was less lucky. He emerged from the fray and shouted to Hay, 'Hang it, what can detain our centre squadron? I must get back and see.' 'Those were his last words, poor fellow, he uttered that day.' Moments later Ponsonby was trapped by some lancers who thrust at him and wounded him in both arms. His horse carried him on a little but he was then struck by a blow on the head and tumbled to the ground. He tried to stagger to his feet but a lancer rode up to him shouting, 'Tu n'est pas mort, coquin?' ('You're not dead, you rascal?') and thrust his lance between Ponsonby's shoulders and through one of his lungs. The Frenchman then rode off, leaving Ponsonby for dead.

For the second time that day Wellington had succeeded in resisting Napoleon's attempt to break through his line, but this time at grave cost. He had lost around 6,000 men in half an hour. Fred Ponsonby's 12th Light Dragoons alone had lost more than a hundred of their 450 men. Wellington, who had watched his cavalry's action first with elation and then with growing horror, was heard to remark scathingly to Uxbridge when he returned with the survivors: 'Well, Paget [addressing him by his ordinary family name], I hope you are satisfied with your cavalry now.' A few days later the Duke said to a colleague: 'The cavalry of other European armies have won victories for their generals, but mine have invariably got me into scrapes.'

So far Wellington's line had held. Years of experience of fighting the French in the Peninsula were paying off. But as he squinted through his telescope at the tens of thousands of fresh troops Napoleon had not yet committed, he must have known this was the greatest challenge he had ever faced. There was a limit to the amount of this 'hard pounding', as he called it, that his unevenly mixed Anglo-allied army could stand. If the Prussians didn't join the battle soon, his men would be hard pressed to hold the ridge at Waterloo much longer. And there were still six more long hours of daylight ahead.

19

Now, Maitland, now's your time!
Waterloo, afternoon 18 June 1815

A T AROUND 4 p.m. Captain Cavalié Mercer and his battery of horse artillery found themselves right in the centre of the action in the Battle of Waterloo. 'Suddenly,' Mercer recalled, 'a dark mass of cavalry appeared for an instant on the main (French) ridge and then came sweeping down the slope in swarms, reminding me of an enormous surf bursting over the prostrate hull of a stranded vessel, and then running, hissing and foaming, up the beach.' Mercer and his guns were in Wellington's front line when it was attacked by wave after wave of French cavalry led by Marshal Ney. Once again the Duke's army faced a challenge that brought it near to breaking point.

Of all Napoleon's commanders none had a more passionate will to win than Michel Ney. It was almost a death wish. He was determined he would be in the front line of every major assault that day. Defeat at Waterloo was unthinkable. He had betrayed Napoleon in 1814. In 1815 he had betrayed the King. There would be no third chance. It was death or victory. Ney was no great strategist, but he could inspire men to fight. His flair and exemplary courage had helped Napoleon win great victories such as Jena and Friedland. He had earned the title of Prince of Moscow for his leadership at the Battle of Borodino outside the Russian capital and the nickname 'Bravest of the Brave' for his resourcefulness during the disastrous retreat from Moscow in 1812. At Waterloo that morning, according to some sources, he had accompanied D'Erlon in the first massed infantry attack. Now he was leading one of the most spectacular cavalry assaults in history. Ney was sparked into action when he noticed numbers of Anglo-allied troops withdrawing beyond the crest of the ridge. Wellington had ordered them back to the reverse slope to shield them from French gunfire. Ney thought Wellington's line was cracking. With Napoleon

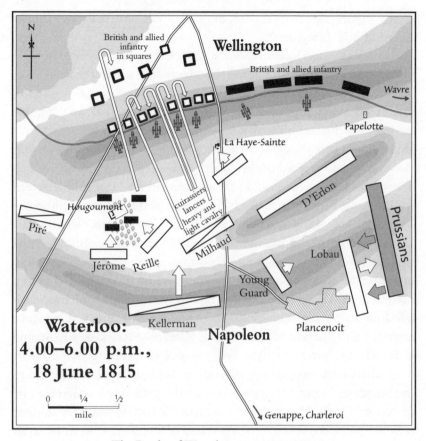

The Battle of Waterloo: 4.00–6.00 p.m.

apparently preoccupied with countering the Prussian threat from the east, Ney took it upon himself to lead a series of attacks over the next two hours with more than 9,000 horsemen on Wellington's centre right (the western half of the allied line). As he led off the first wave of cuirassiers at the trot, he shouted 'Forward! The salvation of France is at stake.'

The first Captain Mercer and his horse artillery battery knew about the great French cavalry attack was in mid-afternoon, when Sir Augustus Frazer, Wellington's horse artillery commander, galloped up to them. 'Left, limber up, and as fast as you can!' cried Frazer, whose face was 'black as a chimney-sweep's from the smoke'. He told Mercer that the French had assembled a mass of cavalry in front of the centre right of Wellington's position and that they might charge at any moment.

As they sweated up towards the top of the ridge, Mercer noticed the air growing hotter and hotter. Suddenly, as they left the protection of the dead ground behind the crest, he and his men were exposed to a massive French cannonade on Wellington's front line. 'So thick was the hail of balls and bullets that it seemed dangerous to extend the arm lest it should be torn off.' It was the prelude to Ney's cavalry assault. Wellington had spotted the build-up, and sent the alert along his line: 'Prepare to receive cavalry.' He was confident his Peninsular veterans would stand firm, but he had his doubts about regiments like the Brunswickers, which he had had to feed into his front line to allow the Guards to reinforce Hougoumont. Everything would depend on how well the officers had drilled into their men the need to kneel or stand in square formation, shoulder to shoulder, in the face of charging horsemen. Wellington's infantry rapidly formed into squares, each side four men deep with bayonets thrust out in front of them, four rows of tightly packed blades, which, if the men stayed steady, would scare off any horse. But the two squares of Brunswickers Mercer passed between were being battered by the gunfire: he saw officers and sergeants desperately trying to close the gaps in the ranks made by the cannon balls. Frazer shouted to Mercer that Wellington's orders were for all gunners, when charged by French cavalry, to seek refuge in the squares. Mercer judged that that would be fatal. The Brunswickers looked so dispirited that to seek refuge in their squares would be 'madness . . . The very moment our men ran from their guns, I was convinced, would be the signal for their disbanding.' So Mercer hurried his horse-drawn guns forward to the gap between the two Brunswicker squares, and shouted the order to load canister shot.

The first wave of some 4,500 French cavalry – stretched over a front of some 800 yards with Ney himself leading them on – were mainly cuirassiers, with their glinting steel helmets and breastplates. Behind them rode the lancers in brilliantly coloured uniforms with a banner on each lance, and the Chasseurs à Cheval, Imperial Guardsmen, decked out richly in green and gold. As they moved off, more than eighty French guns delivered a heavy bombardment on to and beyond the top of Wellington's ridge. The Duke had ordered most of his men back behind the skyline, but some of the better-aimed roundshot took a heavy toll of the closely huddled squares concealed there out of sight. And then the French guns fell silent so as not to strike their own men and the Anglo-allied guns opened up, as the French cavalry approached the top of Wellington's ridge.

'No one who was there could have forgotten the "awful grandeur" of that charge,' wrote Rees Gronow, who had been transferred from Picton's staff back to his Guards regiment, themselves now in square. He described it as 'an overwhelming, long moving line, which, ever advancing, glittered like a stormy wave of the sea when it catches the sunlight . . . the very earth seemed to vibrate beneath the thundering tramp of the mounted host. One might suppose that nothing could have resisted the shock of this terrible moving mass. In an almost incredibly short period they were within twenty yards of us, shouting "*Vive l'Empereur!*"' Tom Morris of the 73rd, thought the approaching cuirassiers – tall, powerfully built men in every saddle – looked so formidable that 'we could not have the slightest chance with them'.

Moments after his men had dragged their guns into the front line, Mercer spotted the first French horsemen emerging out of the dense smoke straight ahead. His leading gun was unlimbered within seconds and its team loading and firing their first case shot. The effect of it, once the canister left the barrel and disintegrated, was to hurl forward forty-four three-ounce balls in an ever expanding cone. 'The effect is hardly conceivable, and to paint this scene of slaughter and confusion impossible. Every discharge was followed by the fall of numbers while the survivors struggled with each other, and I actually saw them using the pommels of their swords to fight their way out of the mêlée.' Soon all Mercer's six guns were firing, and he continued to make his men disobey Wellington's orders to take shelter in the squares: they were to stay with their guns even when the French survivors of each charge ran right past them. Better that than risk disrupting the fragile squares. Besides, the Brunswickers' resolve was stiffening, encouraged by the carnage wreaked by Mercer's guns.

Mercer had to watch his best spongeman, Private Butterworth, receive a mortal wound when he slipped in the mud as he rammed a shot down the barrel. He lost both arms when the gun went off before he could jump clear. After a time Mercer's battery and the Brunswickers had the measure of their attackers. Mercer would shout 'Fire!' when the leading Frenchman was only fifty yards away. 'The ground, already encumbered with victims of the first struggle, became now almost impassable. Still however those devoted warriors struggled on, intent only on reaching us. The discharge of every gun was followed by a fall of men and horses like that of the grass before a mower's scythe.'

Tom Morris was in the front rank of his square as it faced attack after attack by cuirassiers. He was kneeling and one Frenchman, 'reaching over his horse's head . . . made a thrust at me with his sword. I could not avoid it and immediately closed my eyes. When I opened them again, my enemy was lying just in front of me.' Fortunately for Morris a man in the rank behind him had stopped the Frenchman in his tracks. 'Whether it was anguish at the wound or the chagrin of being defeated I know not: but he endeavoured to end his existence with his own sword. But that being too long for his purpose he took one of our bayonets which was lying on the ground and raising himself up on one hand placed the point of the bayonet under his cuirass and fell upon it.' Tom Morris's square held out, but he watched the cuirassiers break into the next-door square, which was restored only when the Life Guards charged in to the rescue. Morris recalled: 'Our poor old Captain' – the one who had been so nervous at Quatre-Bras – 'was horribly frightened, and several times came to me for a drop of something to keep his spirits up. Towards the end of the day he was cut in two by a cannon shot.'

As his square dwindled in size, Sergeant William Lawrence was ordered to take the regimental colour. Each regiment carried just two colours, a Union flag and a regimental colour. Two yards square, they were a regiment's most precious possession and, like the French eagle, a prize trophy for an enemy. The colours were very heavy and very visible, and Lawrence thought twice about accepting the honour of carrying them. 'This was a job I did not at all like . . . There had been before me that day fourteen Sergeants already killed and wounded in charge of those colours . . . I had not been there more than a quarter of an hour when a cannon shot came and took the Captain's head clean off.'

Wellington was everywhere, darting about from unit to unit, apparently impervious to danger, shouting words of encouragement, constantly reassuring his men and watching for critical points of weakness in his line that would need reinforcement. 'Without his personal exertion, his continued presence wherever and whenever more than usual excitement were recognised, the day had been lost,' wrote Augustus Frazer.

It wasn't long before the alternating battering of the French cannonades and the charges of their cavalry caused the squares to present what Gronow called a 'shocking sight . . . Inside we were nearly suffocated by the smoke and smell from burnt cartridges.' He couldn't move without treading on a dead or wounded comrade. 'Our square was a perfect hospital, being full of dead and dying and mutilated soldiers.' Gronow said he actually found the cavalry charges a great relief, because that was when the French guns stopped firing at them. And when the cuirassiers came, they were beaten off. 'I never shall forget the strange noise our bullets made against the breastplates . . . I can only compare it with a somewhat homely simile to the noise of a violent hailstorm beating upon panes of glass.' The ground, recalled Gronow, was 'strewed with the fallen horses and their riders which impeded the advance of those behind and broke the shock of the charge. It was pitiable to witness the agony of the poor horses . . .', and then a little later, 'the heart sickened at the moaning tones of agony which came from men and horses as they lay in fearful agony.' At one stage Wellington entered Gronow's square at one of the corners. 'As far as I could judge, he was perfectly composed but looked very thoughtful and pale.' The only other sign of nervousness anyone noticed in the Duke was that he was constantly looking at his watch and fiddling with his telescope.

By late afternoon Wellington had no more reinforcements available to plug any gaps. When Tom Morris's brigade commander, General Halkett, appealed to the Duke for some respite or relief, saying his men were 'dreadfully cut up', Wellington replied, 'Impossible. I must have British troops in the front line.' The efforts of Mercer's gunners had persuaded the wavering Brunswickers to stand fast, but others ran for it. One entire regiment, the Hanoverian troopers of the Cumberland Hussars, never even took their position in the front line: they fled to Brussels and caused panic by shouting that the French had won the battle.*

For two hours, from four o'clock to six, the French cavalry fought on, desperate to break the stubborn resistance of the British infantry. The noise was deafening – the thunder of hooves, the roar of the guns, the yells of the charging horsemen and the screams of the wounded. And the French kept coming back for more. Wellington was to say later that the repeated French cavalry charges were the bravest action he had ever seen. But his squares stood steady. French horses were shying away from impaling themselves on the bristling ranks of bayonets. Those which, with their riders, survived the artillery and musket fire were skirting the squares and galloping round behind them and then back the way they had come. Uxbridge and what was left of his cavalry picked off any who tried to penetrate further. Many British gunners who stayed with their guns, like Mercer's, or briefly sought safety in the squares as the cavalry thundered past them, returned to their batteries and fired a shot or two after the retreating French horsemen. And Wellington was relieved that the French infantry – still preoccupied with Hougoumont – made no major effort to support Ney's cavalry against the squares, a tactic which might well have won Napoleon the day. Already some men in the squares were greeting the charging cavalry by shouting, 'Here come those fools again.' As the Anglo-allied line held firm, Wellington was overheard saying, 'The battle is mine; and if the Prussians arrive soon, there will be an end of the war.'

It wasn't long before Wellington learned that the Prussians had indeed – finally – arrived. Alexander Gordon, his ADC, cross-questioned the man who brought the news: was he sure it was the Prussians? He replied that there was no doubt: the Prussians had arrived after a difficult march. The road from Wavre was narrow in places and hopelessly boggy in the Lasne valley. General Bülow, the lead commander, with some 20,000 troops had moved as slowly as

* There was already a colourful mix of fugitives leaving Brussels for fear of French occupation, as one eyewitness recalled. 'Amidst the crash of wheels, the volley of oaths, and the confusion of tongues, the mistress of the hotel, with a countenance dressed in woe, was carrying off the most valuable plate in order to secure it, ejaculating as she went, the name of Jesus incessantly' (Eaton, p. 40).

one mile an hour at times. But he was now engaging Napoleon's extreme right and advancing on the village of Plancenoit. Napoleon sent reinforcements to the village and ordered the rumour to be spread to the rest of his army that it wasn't the Prussians who had arrived but Grouchy. In fact, far from coming to the rescue, Grouchy was still trying to pin down the remaining Prussians near Wavre. Months later in exile in St Helena, Napoleon blamed Grouchy's 'imbecility' and said he believed some of the 'staff officers whom I had sent to Grouchy betrayed me and went over to the enemy'.

Napoleon was still confident of victory. But he was to miss another major opportunity. All afternoon French infantry, artillery and cavalry kept up the pressure on Wellington's centre: their prime target was the farmhouse of La Haye-Sainte which stood a few hundred yards forward of Wellington's front line and was a major obstacle to any assault on the middle of the Anglo-allied position. A battalion of the King's German Legion, excellent fighters, many of them armed with rifles, defended it against as fierce a set of attacks as any that had hit Hougoumont. They were commanded by a British major, George Baring. Thousands of French attacked. A total of 800 Germans were sent in to defend the farm. The night before, the German garrison had foolishly dismantled one of its large wooden doors and burned it for firewood. Fortunately for the defenders, French corpses soon piled up and helped block the opening as Baring's fire brought them down. But ammunition stocks were low, and, in spite of frantic appeals from Baring, the supply ran out. It was a blunder for which Wellington personally took the blame. Baring now had no choice but to try and escape. Somehow he and his men extracted themselves from the farm. They squeezed through a passage in the farmhouse and out of the back door. One young ensign, called Franks, couldn't make it. He hid under a bed and survived – even though the French bayoneted two wounded soldiers left in the bedroom with him. The fall of La Haye-Sainte left Leach's men of the 95th Rifles, who had returned to their forward position, once again gravely exposed on their hillock. The French 'kept up a dreadful fire from loopholes and windows in the upper part of it [La Haye-Sainte], whereby they raked the hillock so as to render it untenable by our battalion'. In the earlier firefights, George Simmons, lucky to have survived his severe wound in the Peninsula, was 'laughing and joking' with another young officer when he 'received a ball, which broke two of my ribs near the backbone, went through my liver and lodged in my breast'.

Ney soon had a battery of guns alongside La Haye-Sainte pouring a destructive hail of fire into Wellington's front line only 200 yards away. In the rush to deploy reinforcements to fill the gap in Wellington's centre, two of his most trusty ADCs, Fitzroy Somerset and Alexander Gordon, both of whom had been at his side all the way from his early days in Portugal, were seriously wounded, Gordon in the leg, Somerset in the arm. Wellington said later that he and Somerset were riding together near the chaotic fighting around La Haye-Sainte when a stray musket ball shattered his aide's arm. 'The finger of providence was upon me and I escaped.' Of Wellington's staff there were now few – apart from himself – still unscathed. Frazer, who was with him most of the time, reckoned that at this moment of supreme crisis Wellington was at his best. 'Cold and indifferent, nay, apparently careless in the beginning of battles, when the moment of difficulty comes intelligence flashes from the eyes of this wonderful man . . .' At one time Wellington's Spanish liaison officer, General Álava, believed the danger to the Duke was such that he suggested they move a few paces back to get out of the line of fire. Wellington agreed but kept his telescope to his eye as usual, and while he was 'reining back his horse's head, he never for a moment took his eye off the enemy's line'.

This serious reverse for Wellington, the loss of La Haye-Sainte, at around 6.15 in the evening, prompted Ney, who had now called off the cavalry charges, to suggest to Napoleon that he could now administer the *coup de grâce*. Thirteen thousand elite grenadiers and chasseurs of the Imperial Guard, with a record of crushing all before them, were still standing in reserve in the centre of the French line. Commit these troops now, said Ney, and Wellington will be beaten. But Napoleon refused. 'Troops?' he shouted at Ney. 'Where do you expect me to get them? Do you expect me to make them?' Instead he moved 3,600 of the Imperial Guardsmen to reinforce his right, which was being pushed back by the Prussians. They were men of the Young Guard, junior guardsmen, always the first of the Imperial

Guard to go into battle. Ney was furious at the opportunity this delay gave Wellington to reinforce his line. Besides, 'What was my astonishment (I should rather say indignation) when I learned . . . that so far from Marshal Grouchy having arrived to our support, as the whole army had been assured, between thirty and forty thousand Prussians were attacking our extreme right and forcing it to retire.'

Wellington knew that the Imperial Guard could yet attack and he knew their reputation. Paid more than twice as much as their equivalents in the line regiments, they had a special status in the French army which Napoleon had done much to restore in the days since his return. The reconstituted Old Guard in particular, veterans of many of the great battles against Austria, Russia and Prussia, were unmistakable with their huge moustaches which Napoleon wouldn't allow them to wax. Wellington, some of his units down to half strength, put every reliable unit he had in the front line. He knew he faced his deepest crisis of the day, yet by all accounts he remained calm. One top divisional staff officer witnessed him reacting with 'precision and energy' to each problem that required decision. He described Wellington at this critical juncture as 'confident of his own powers of being able to guide the storm which raged around him'.

The whole Anglo-allied line was under severe pressure. Over to the right some of Wellington's best men – Colborne's 52nd Light Infantry in particular – were sheltering from direct French artillery fire just behind the ridge. Some of the roundshot aimed at the top of the ridge bounced down the slope beyond. Willam Leeke, the regiment's most recent Johnny Newcome, remembered one rolling down gently towards him ' like a cricket ball'. His colour sergeant just managed to prevent him putting out his foot to stop it. Leeke noticed the 'peculiar smell of gunpowder mixed with the downtrodden wheat'. He spotted a dead kitten lying in front of him, 'probably frightened out of Hougoumont', which wasn't far away. 'The circumstance led me to think of my friends at home.' Mercer's battery too was coming under murderous gunfire. 'Every shot almost took effect, and I certainly expected we should all be annihilated . . . One shell I saw explode under the two finest wheel-horses in the troop – down they dropped . . . The whole livelong day had cost us nothing like this . . . I sighed for my poor troop.'

At around 7 p.m. some of Colborne's men saw a French cuirassier colonel approaching, shouting 'Vive le Roi! Vive le Roi!' He explained that he had been in some of the futile cavalry charges and had decided to desert. He brought with him the news that Napoleon had finally decided to commit the Imperial Guard. It was Napoleon's final throw, a last attempt to break the resolve of Wellington's infantry. It was a brave decision. Napoleon could have retreated with the forces he had left and an intact Imperial Guard, to fight another battle. But he must have concluded that that would only have postponed his eventual defeat by the Austrians and Russians gathering in the east. He had one last window, and one last resource – his undefeated Imperial Guard – to turn Wellington's line.

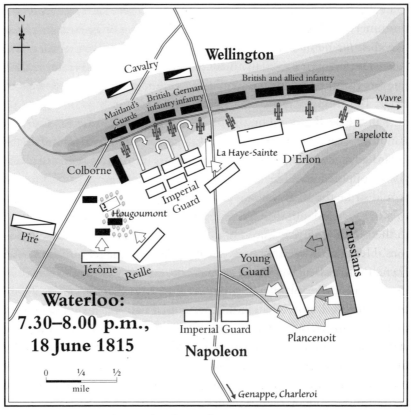

The Battle of Waterloo: 7.30–8.00 p.m.

302

Minutes later the Emperor himself led up to eight Guard battalions, around 5,000 men, forward to the start of the slope up to the British line and handed them over to Ney for the assault. The Young Guard were, temporarily at least, holding the Prussians at Plancenoit. The Middle Guard were the spearhead of this final act in the Battle of Waterloo – with the Old Guard held in reserve behind them. Slowly the Guard began to tramp up the slope. They were used to delivering the decisive stroke that usually secured victory for their Emperor. They were still fired up by the report that Grouchy had arrived. No one had told them it was false. They advanced, not in line, but in open squares, to protect themselves from cavalry attack, or in massed columns such as D'Erlon's that morning. Once again they would be unable to fire all of their weapons for fear of killing comrades in front of them.

Leeke heard 'continued shouts of "*Vive l'Empereur*" . . . and the drummers beating the *pas de charge*', which, he thought, 'sounded very like this: *the rum dum, the rum dum, the rummadum, rummadum, rum, dum*'. The Guard tramped up the slope, struggling to keep in step on the uneven ground, battered by Wellington's guns firing case shot at short range. But still they came on. Wellington's regiments were waiting in lines in the dead ground on the reverse slope, some lying down, some standing, every weapon ready and pointing straight ahead. As the Guard advanced, Colborne, towards the west end of the British line, saw an opportunity. The Guard's assault wasn't heading for his men. It would strike the British line well to his left. So Colborne told his men to move forward into the empty ground ahead of them, and then wheel to their left so that they faced the flank of the advancing Guard battalions. He then ordered them 'to make that column feel our fire'. The French guardsmen were caught in a murderous crossfire, Colborne's men firing at their flank and the main British line shooting straight at their front. Colborne's battalion was unusually strong, a thousand men in lines, nearly all of them able, unlike the French, to fire their weapons at the enemy. Assuming each musket fired a round every thirty seconds, the 52nd discharged around 2,000 balls a minute at the French guardsmen. It was too much even for Napoleon's Imperial Guard. The westernmost end of their advance was destroyed in an action that, Leeke says, 'the Duke of Wellington was . . . much pleased with'.

Wellington himself was further east behind the ranks of the main British Guards regiments under Major General Sir Peregrine Maitland. Maitland had commanded the 1st Guards Brigade with Wellington at the Nivelle in 1813 and again at the crossing of the Adour at Bayonne. Now he and his men were right at the focal point of the Imperial Guard's attack. They were lying down a few yards behind the crest of the ridge. On came the Imperial Guard over the skyline. Even after a day's fighting many British hearts must have trembled at the formidable sight of the men – with their red epaulettes, white cross-belts over their blue greatcoats and tall hairy bearskin hats – who were advancing steadily towards them.

Wellington himself controlled the timing of Maitland's order to fire. He waited until they were as little as twenty-five yards away. Then: 'Now, Maitland,' he ordered, 'now's your time!' Gronow, who was there, remembers Wellington crying, 'Guards, get up and charge!' Up sprang the 1,400 British guardsmen and fired a massive volley at such close range that it stopped the Frenchmen in their tracks. Maitland quickly followed with a bayonet charge. Gronow recalled that the French Guard appeared almost 'paralysed' as he and his comrades lunged at them. 'I witnessed several of the Imperial Guard who were run through the body apparently without any resistance on their parts. I observed a big Welshman of the name of Hughes, who was six feet seven inches in height, run through with his bayonet, and knock down with the butt end of his firelock, I should think, a dozen at least of his opponents.' The close combat lasted as little as ten minutes before the Guard fell back down the hill.

It wasn't long before Wellington – seeing the Imperial Guard in retreat and hearing the increasing roar of Prussian gunfire to the east – uttered the famous words, 'Oh dammit, in for a penny, in for a pound.' Then, raising himself in his stirrups, he waved his hat above his head and ordered a general pursuit. His soldiers everywhere gave a cheer, but as the Duke rode down past the Rifles John Kincaid heard him say, 'No cheering, my lads, but forward and complete your victory.' Kincaid, like most of the veterans, was an ardent admirer of Wellington, and he went on to write, 'I will ever maintain that Wellington's last advance would have made it the same victory had a Prussian never been seen there.'

It was remarkable then how quickly Napoleon's army collapsed. As the remnants of the Imperial Guard, who had attacked the ridge, fell back, the word swept around: 'La Garde recule [The Guard is retreating].' The story that its commander, General Cambronne, defied a British offer to surrender his men with the word 'Merde' or, more romantically, with the avowal that 'La Garde meurt mais ne se rend pas' ('The Guard dies but does not surrender') is discredited by the fact that Cambronne himself surrendered to the advancing British troops. Ney, who had five horses killed under him that day, later said, 'The brave men who have survived this terrible battle will I trust do me the justice to state that they saw me on foot with sword in hand . . . and that I was one of the last who quitted this scene of carnage.' The French were soon in headlong flight. Houssaye describes Ney in the midst of the rout as 'bareheaded, his face blackened with powder, his uniform in tatters, one of his epaulettes cut off, the hilt of his sword in his hand, shouting furiously to Count d'Erlon who was being swept past him in the swirling rout: "D'Erlon, if you and I escape, we should both be hanged."' Napoleon himself was reluctant to flee, but his guards hustled him into his carriage and they headed off to the south. Minutes later the Emperor had to take to the saddle to escape when the carriage got caught in the narrow street at Genappe. It was captured full of treasures including a hoard of diamonds and a fine gold travelling case.*

Wellington and Blücher met at La Belle Alliance, a farm on the French side of the battlefield. 'We were both on horseback,' Wellington remembered, 'but he embraced me and kissed me and called me "Mein lieber Kamarad".' It was agreed that the Prussians would conduct the immediate pursuit of the French, which finally ended with the surrender of Paris on 4 July.

One of the last shots fired on the battlefield hit Uxbridge's leg as he sat on his horse beside Wellington. The ball just missed killing Copenhagen. 'By God, Sir, I've lost my leg,' Uxbridge exclaimed. 'By God, Sir, so you have,' replied Wellington, removing the telescope from his eye for a moment. The two men's language suggests

---

* The carriage, which had bullet-proof doors, ended up in Madame Tussaud's waxwork showroom in London and was lost in a fire there in 1925.

that Uxbridge's leg was blown right off: in fact it was shattered beyond repair by a piece of canister shot. Wellington ordered his aides to move Uxbridge and Gordon, both critically ill, to his own headquarters in Waterloo village. Then, like other survivors of Waterloo, he had the heartbreaking experience of riding through the dreadful scene of carnage.

In the relatively small space in which the fighting had taken place – not more than two miles wide by a mile deep – tens of thousands lay dead or wounded, writhing, groaning and crying for help, and ten thousand horses lay dead or injured. Wellington was as deeply moved as he had been by the loss of life at Badajoz three years earlier. He was to reflect to a friend later: 'Nothing except a battle lost can be half so melancholy as a battle won.' His Anglo-allied army had lost 15,000 dead and wounded, Blücher had lost 7,000 and Napoleon in excess of 25,000. Casualties among officers were strikingly high. They had been out in front taking the lead in every action. The Royal Scots lost thirty-one out of thirty-seven officers, while the 27th Foot lost sixteen out of nineteen.

Tom Morris, another survivor wandering through the human wreckage, did what he could to help the suffering. He was shocked by the number of wounded horses with broken legs 'looking pit-eously for relief. I put several of these poor creatures out of their misery by shooting them through the head.' William Tomkinson saw local peasants begin to plunder the dead, and stopped one man pull-ing the boots off a guardsman who wasn't yet dead. He offered his help to one of Wellington's ADC's, Colonel Canning, who had only a couple of hours to live, but Canning refused his help, except to ask Tomkinson to take his sword and watch, which would no doubt have been stolen from his body later. And it wasn't only local peas-ants who robbed the dead. 'When the bloody work of the day is over, the survivor's first wish is to secure, in the shape of plunder, some recompense for the exertions he has made.' And no plunderer worried 'whether it is the dead body of a friend or of a foe from which he is seeking his booty'. The whole field was littered with other contents of the pockets of the dead – papers of every descrip-tion, love-letters, letters from mothers to sons and from children to fathers – which looters scattered in their frantic search for valuables.

Rees Gronow visited some of his comrades in hospital. Captain Robert Adair was in terrible pain. His thigh had been smashed by a cannon ball: 'The bones were sticking up near the hip in splinters. The surgeon, Mr Gilder, had much difficulty in using the knife, having blunted it and all his other instruments by amputations in the earlier part of the battle. Poor Adair during the operation had sufficient pluck to make one last ghastly joke, saying "Take your time, Mr Carver." He soon afterwards died from loss of blood.' Another Guards officer, Captain Percival, 'received a ball which carried away all his teeth and both his jaws and left nothing of his mouth but the skin of the cheeks. He had to be fed with porridge and a few spoonfuls of broth for the rest of his short life.'

Wellington finally returned to his house in Waterloo. After a pat for Copenhagen that prompted a kick which the Duke only narrowly escaped, he met his cook, James Thornton. They hadn't seen each other in three days. It was a quarter-past midnight when Wellington walked in and said, 'Let's have dinner directly.' Uxbridge had been carried in earlier. The surgeons told him he risked death if his leg wasn't amputated. 'If it is to be taken off, the sooner it is done the better,' said Uxbridge. His ADC was present at the amputation: 'He never moved or complained: no one even held his hand. He said once perfectly calmly that he thought the instrument wasn't very sharp. When it was over his nerves did not appear the least shaken and the surgeons said his pulse was not altered.'

Alexander Gordon, his leg also removed, was carried back to headquarters just after Wellington had sat down to supper in his upstairs room. The ADC was laid in a bed in the next-door room. 'I thought, as he had only lost a leg, we should save him,' Wellington recalled. 'I went to see him and said I was sorry he was so severely wounded, at the same time taking hold of his hand. "Thank God you are safe" was his reply. I then said "I have no doubt, Gordon, you will do well." He raised himself and then fell back in the manner that indicated his being completely exhausted. Poor fellow,' the Duke added, 'he probably felt there was no chance. He died the next morning at 8.' The following day Wellington wrote to Gordon's brother Lord Aberdeen, who had exchanged so many letters with Alexander during the Peninsular War. Wellington told Aberdeen of his 'extreme grief . . . The lad served me most zealously and usefully for many years and he had never distinguished himself more than in our late actions.'*

Fitzroy Somerset was luckier than Gordon: his arm was amputated successfully. When he saw it about to be thrown away, he shouted for someone to rescue the ring his wife had given him which was still on one of the fingers. Ned Costello noticed the quantity of amputations taking place after the battle and claimed that the British were braver about their suffering than the French. He said an Englishman had his arm cut off 'without betraying the slightest emotion'. But when a Frenchman next to him started 'bellowing lustily' as a surgeon probed his shoulder, the Englishman laid into the Frenchman with his severed limb telling him to 'stop your damn bellowing'.

Back on the battlefield, amid the groans of the wounded, lay one of the many heroes of Waterloo. Fred Ponsonby was critically – he thought fatally – wounded. But he was to live to tell an extraordinary story. His groom had failed to find him and returned weeping to his regiment earlier that evening. Ponsonby was still lying where he had been lanced through the lung. He found it very hard to breathe and impossible to move. 'I thought all was over . . . Not long afterwards a *tirailleur* came up to plunder me, threatening my life. I directed him to a small side pocket, in which he found three dollars.' Not satisfied with that the man tore open his waistcoat, searched him and left him lying in a most uncomfortable position. A more compassionate French officer came by and gave him a swig of brandy from his flask, placing a knapsack under his head. He then disappeared into the battle which was still going on, and Ponsonby wondered if he would ever again see the man 'to whose generosity I was indebted, as I believe, for my life'. Another French soldier came up, 'a fine young man, full of ardour'. He knelt down and fired several shots at the British, balancing his gun on Ponsonby's body, chatting gaily to him and boasting that he killed a man with every shot he fired. At last he ran off with a cheery 'Bonjour', saying the French were retreating so

* The Duke's letter is now framed on the wall of the bedroom in which Gordon died in Wellington's headquarters, now the Wellington Museum, in Waterloo. The room also contains the bed in which Gordon died and the wooden leg Uxbridge used after his amputation.

he had better go with them. At dusk two squadrons of Prussian cavalry 'passed me at full trot, lifting me from the ground and tumbling
me about most cruelly'. Ponsonby was robbed again and thought the
night would never end. At one stage a horribly wounded soldier
crawled up and lay across his legs. The man's groans and the air issuing through a wound in his side 'distressed me greatly'. Ponsonby
explained to one Prussian plunderer in his poor German that he was
a British officer, but he was robbed just the same. Finally an English
solder came up, and Ponsonby offered him money to guard him for
the rest of the night. The man arranged a cart to take him to
Wellington's headquarters, where he found himself in the bed in
which Gordon had died. Ponsonby knew he would be very lucky to
survive. He was badly wounded in seven places.

One more of Wellington's close associates was the object of an
anxious search over the next few days. Harry Smith's wife Juana,
accustomed like most wives to the wretched business of searching for
her husband after a battle, was horrified when some soldiers from the
Rifles told her that Brigade Major Smith had been killed. 'In my
agony of woe,' she recalled later, 'I approached the awful field of
Sunday's carnage in mad search of Enrique.' She saw newly dug
graves and imagined to herself that he had been buried. 'How can I
describe the horror of my sensations, my growing despair?' Suddenly
she ran into an ADC and asked, 'O where is he? Where is my
Enrique?' The officer replied that Harry was fine and not even
wounded. 'Oh why tell me this?' she cried. 'The solders tell me
Brigade Major Smith is killed.' 'Dearest Juana, believe me,' he said.
'It is poor Charlie Smyth, General Pack's Brigade Major.' He swore
to her that Harry was alive. 'Then God has heard my prayer,' she said
and finally caught up with her husband in a nearby town. 'O gracious
God, I sank into his embrace, exhausted (after riding sixty miles since
three in the morning) fatigued, happy and grateful – oh how grateful
– to God who had protected him.'

20

See the Conquering Hero Comes
Aftermath

WELLINGTON ROSE EARLY on 19 June 1815 to write his celebrated Waterloo Despatch. He made no flowery claim to a
glorious victory and was not lavish in his tributes. The letter he
wrote to Lord Bathurst, the Secretary for War in London, was the
work of a man physically exhausted and emotionally drained. He had
had little sleep and was surrounded by dead or dying comrades. He
wrote in measured tones about 'the successful result of this arduous
day' and said it gave him 'the greatest satisfaction to assure your
Lordship that the army, never upon any occasion, conducted itself
better . . . There is no officer nor description of troops that did
not behave well.' There were some notable omissions – such
as Colborne's Light Infantry – in the list of those he mentioned as
deserving the 'approbation' of the Prince Regent. But he named a
large number of units, including the artillery and the cavalry, and
thirty-seven senior officers. He made it clear how much he owed to
the 'timely assistance' of Blücher and his Prussians. It was typical
Wellington – down to earth, undramatic, understated. Back in
Brussels later that day he spoke to Creevey in the same manner 'with
the greatest gravity . . . and without the least approach to anything
like triumph or joy. "It has been a damned serious business," he said,
"Blucher and I have lost 30,000 men. It has been . . . the nearest
run thing you ever saw in your life."' And then with sublime self-
confidence he paid himself the ultimate compliment: 'By God I
don't think it would have been won if I had not been there.' 'It was
the most desperate business I ever was in,' he wrote to his brother
William. 'I was never so near being beat.'

There was no vanity in this: it was the blunt recognition of the
truth. His leadership, his grasp of the topography, his adroit dispos-

ition of his Anglo-allied battalions, his minute-by-minute control of the battlefield had been instrumental in the final destruction of Napoleon. His painstaking campaign from Portugal to Toulouse had gravely weakened and humiliated the French Emperor. At Waterloo he delivered the decisive blow that was to establish peace in Europe for the next four decades.

But for all the credit due to Wellington and Blücher for the victory, the actions of Napoleon did much to lead to his own defeat. He showed some of his old flair with his lightning advance into Belgium, his bold plan to split the two allies, his targeting of the Prussians and the blow that sent Blücher reeling back from Ligny. But then suddenly he lost imagination and momentum. He was slow to strike at Wellington after Quatre-Bras, and when he did, at Waterloo, his crude frontal attacks ignored the lessons his marshals had learned about Wellington in the Peninsula. British infantry, well drilled and motivated, could use the ground and their firepower to shatter any attack by massed columns. Besides Napoleon's choice of two of his less competent marshals, Ney and Grouchy, for key roles, and his own failure to communicate urgently enough with Grouchy, led to disastrous mismanagement of vital stages of the battle.

The 18th of June 1815 was when the myth was born that Britain's mission was to lead the world. With France out of the way and German unity still a dream, Britain was to emerge as the dominant power over the next few decades. Energised by the industrial revolution, the British economy expanded and the Royal Navy policed a huge and growing empire. The army by contrast enjoyed little innovation in the years between Waterloo and the Crimean War in the mid-1850s. Although Wellington's carefully crafted battlefield tactics had made Britain's 'thin red line' a byword, he was no moderniser. He famously argued for the continuation of flogging and the purchasing of commissions. And it was some time before merit decided promotion, as it already did at the time of Waterloo in France and Prussia. The aristocracy – for a long time yet – was to retain command. But although Wellington was no reformer he did himself prompt one important change, a change of style. With the end of the Napoleonic War the flagrant excesses of the eighteenth-century upper classes gradually shifted to the more sober demeanour of the

Victorian age. And the man who more than any other embodied this change was Arthur, Duke of Wellington.

The victor of Waterloo became, simply, the greatest living Briton. He was idolised, as was Churchill 130 years later, as the man who had saved Britain from disaster. His qualities of single-minded dedication to duty, which had seen him forgo any home leave during his campaigns, and his unemotional, understated public persona became part of the culture. He was lampooned mercilessly of course for his foibles, such as his eye for the ladies, but admiration for his military achievements lasted his whole long lifetime. He personified the stiff upper lip, the seriousness, the lack of frippery that was to become the hallmark of Victorian Britain. He remained a staunch conservative figure as politics replaced the army as his main preoccupation. He was an undistinguished prime minister for two years from 1828 to 1830 and briefly again in 1834. He was realistic enough to recognise that the country had to accept Catholic Emancipation, which would allow Catholics to stand for parliament and take senior public service jobs including commissions in the army, and he drove the reform through parliament against bitter opposition from King George IV (as the Prince Regent had become in 1820) and many in his own Tory party. But he was viscerally opposed to widening the franchise beyond men of property, and his rejection of electoral reform led to his departure from Downing Street.

His private life remained tainted by various affairs and the continuing emptiness of his marriage to Kitty. But it was touching that this man, who so seldom gave way to emotion, drew close to his wife as she succumbed to disease towards the end of her life. He was with Kitty when she died in 1831, and he later remarked that it was strange that two people could be together for so long and understand one another only at the end. Much later in life Wellington himself offered a wry comment on his unfulfilled love life, when it was put to him that he must have inspired a lot of admiration and enthusiasm from women in Britain and abroad. 'Oh yes, plenty of that! Plenty of that!' he replied. 'But no woman has ever loved me: never in my whole life.'

Wellington long outlived the other two commanders at Waterloo. Blücher lived another four years and died a national hero in Prussia at the age of seventy-six. Napoleon made an abortive bid to get the Prince Regent to grant him exile in Britain, but was promptly shipped off to the South Atlantic island of St Helena. He spent much of his time there telling his attendants how he should have won the Battle of Waterloo and why Wellington should have lost. He died, in melancholy delusion, in 1821. Many of his marshals lived to a ripe old age: Masséna died comparatively young at fifty-eight, but Grouchy lived to be eighty-one, Marmont seventy-eight, and Soult, who served as minister of war from 1830 to 1834, died at eighty-two. Ney, the greatest turncoat but the bravest of them all, was executed by French firing squad in Paris three weeks after Waterloo. He was granted his last wish – that he himself could give the order for the soldiers to fire. Wellington interceded with Louis XVIII on his behalf but was rebuffed.

Those who had served with Wellington suffered starkly contrasting fates after the war was over. Some went on to greater things. Fitzroy Somerset, without his right arm after Waterloo but with an impeccable record as Wellington's ADC, ended his career more controversially as Lord Raglan, Commander in Chief in the Crimea, who had to take much of the blame for the charge of the Light Brigade at Balaclava in 1854. He died frustrated by his failure to storm Sebastopol in 1855. Harry Smith became a general too; with Juana at his side, he fought to expand the British Empire in India and Africa. Juana outlived him by twelve years and died in 1872.

Fred Ponsonby recovered from his wounds, nursed by his mother Countess Bessborough and his sister Lady Caroline Lamb, when she could tear herself away from the parties in post-war Brussels. 'The lance pierced the lungs,' Caroline wrote to her elder brother, Lord Duncannon, 'he has been terribly trampled upon and hurt, entirely black and scratched and cut all over the body.' Somehow Ponsonby survived his wounds and married Emily, the daughter of Earl Bathurst, the Secretary of State for War. He became a major general at forty-two, and was appointed governor of Malta in 1826. He was delighted to discover that a French officer he received one day at his residence was none other than the man who had given him a tot of brandy and treated him so kindly as he lay critically wounded on the battlefield of Waterloo. Fred and Emily Ponsonby had six children, and one of them, Henry, became private secretary to Queen Victoria. Fred Ponsonby died in Dorset in the year of her accession, 1837, and from then until Lady Emily died forty years later a deputation from her husband's old regiment brought her a bouquet of flowers on each anniversary of Waterloo.

Of the riflemen, George Simmons somehow recovered from his wounds and rejoined the regiment. John Kincaid recalled Simmons's 'riddled body held together by a pair of stays'. Simmons lived long enough to be awarded the General Service Medal that was finally given to all the surviving Peninsular veterans. It was a shameful contrast to the recognition given to the survivors of Waterloo who received a commemorative medal soon after the battle. Simmons, who had survived both, died in 1858, aged seventy-two. Jonathan Leach, like William Grattan of the 88th, who accused Wellington of neglecting the men he had fought with, also highlighted the injustice done to the Peninsular veterans. 'Ere many years elapse, if the names of Vimeira, Talavera, Salamanca, Vitoria etc etc should be partially remembered, the actors in those scenes (with a few exceptions) will be entirely forgotten.'

Ned Costello, typically, didn't settle down until he had been through a whole set of extraordinary adventures. He fell for a Frenchwoman, discovered that she was betrothed to the Frenchman whose life he had spared at Badajoz, but didn't allow that to stop him running off with her. Costello's commanding officer, Jonathan Leach, helped him pay the woman's passage to England, but the couple were so badly off that she went back to her family in France. Costello rejoined the army and found himself promoted to lieutenant and posted back to Spain. He ended a yeoman warder in the Tower of London.*

William Lawrence took home a French wife to his beloved Dorset and together they managed to live on his pension of nine pence a day. Thomas Garrety got home to Ireland to find his family convinced he had died at Badajoz. Thomas Todd, back in Edinburgh,

---

* Costello's account of the depth to which his fortunes sank at one stage makes colourful reading. Desperate for money he was about to rob two men on the road to London until he discovered one was a fellow rifleman (See Costello, pp. 231–4).

was soon so broke that he set off to look for work in Spain and South America. Tom Morris was eventually discharged from the army he loved. But 'like an old warhorse I still prick up my ears at the sound of the bugle or drum and occasionally in the dark and silent hour of night would busy memory bring before me some of the horrible scenes of carnage in which I have been engaged'. The last surviving veteran of Waterloo, Private Morris O'Shea, died in Canada in 1892.

Wellington's men had nothing but praise for the way he had led them repeatedly to victory. A year after Waterloo William Wheeler wrote, 'If England should ever require the service of her army again, and I should be with it, let me have "Old Nosey" to command. Our interests would be sure to be looked into, we should never have occasion to fear an enemy.' For all his faults, which were not many – arrogance and insensitivity and a total refusal to delegate were hardly major failings – Wellington deserves to be numbered, with Marlborough a century earlier, among the greatest commanders of all time.

On 18 June 1852, thirty-seven years to the day after the Battle of Waterloo, a large crowd of people gathered outside the Duke of Wellington's mansion, Apsley House at Hyde Park Corner – its address was No. 1, London. Britain's most revered old soldier and statesman, now aged eighty-three, was to host his annual Waterloo Dinner. 'A strong body of police', reported the *Morning Chronicle*, 'were in attendance to prevent obstructions to the traffic . . . and we are happy to say that not the least confusion took place. The popular favourites received their customary ovations from the crowd. Viscount Hardinge and Sir Harry Smith were cordially welcomed, but the loudest demonstration of favour appeared to have been reserved for Field Marshal the Marquess of Anglesey [the now one-legged former Earl of Uxbridge] who was enthusiastically cheered.' At exactly half-past seven the Duke and the Prince Consort [Prince Albert] led a column of Wellington's old companions in the field into the Waterloo Chamber, still decked with the paintings taken from Joseph's coach at Vitoria. The table was laid with 'sumptuous magnificence . . . The Portuguese silver plateau, a superb piece of workmanship, with its hundreds of emblematical figures, adorned the great length of the table . . . and silver gilt statuettes of the Duke and of Napoleon . . . the chandelier that lit the gallery was a gift from Czar Alexander of Russia.'

Eighty-five diners sat around the table, nearly all of them – except Lady Emily Ponsonby, Fred Ponsonby's widow, survivors of Waterloo. Among them were Lieutenant General Lord Fitzroy Somerset, Lieutenant General Lord Seaton (formerly Colonel Colborne, who had led the 52nd against the Imperial Guard), Lieutenant General Sir George Scovell (the decoder of Napoleon's ciphers), Lieutenant General Sir Hew Dalrymple Ross (who, as a captain back in 1809, had led the first Royal Horse Artillery Troop, the Chestnut Troop, which supported Craufurd's fighting retreat across the Côa in 1810 and followed Wellington from the Peninsula to Waterloo), General Sir Peregrine Maitland (commander of the Guards at Waterloo) and Captain John Kincaid, by then a well-known diarist.

After dinner the Prince Consort rose to toast the Duke. He spoke of his 'delight and satisfaction in seeing our illustrious host in such excellent health and spirits on the present occasion'. All rose to drink Wellington's health, and the band played 'See the Conquering Hero Comes'. Wellington then invited his guests to raise their glasses 'to the memory of those who fell at the battle of Waterloo'. Then one by one he toasted each of the key units: 'the cavalry that fought at Waterloo, coupled with the name of the Marquess of Anglesey'. Anglesey thanked the Duke and to great cheers and applause praised him for all he had done. Then one by one, with responses from each of them, Wellington went on to toast 'the Foot Guards at Waterloo and Sir Peregrine Maitland', the 'artillery at Waterloo associated with the name of Sir Hew Ross', the infantry and Lord Seaton, the staff officers, the King's German Legion and the Prussians, coupled with the name of the man who had been his liaison officer with Blücher, Viscount Hardinge. Finally, Wellington singled out one 'gallant soldier and valued officer' who had 'just returned from a recent arduous and difficult service'. The man he chose to make so much of was none other than his old companion Harry Smith, by now a general and a knight, who together with his still-devoted wife Juana, had just completed a particularly taxing time as governor of Cape Colony.

They had been a hugely popular couple with the colonists, who named two towns after them – Harrismith and Ladysmith.

It was the last of Wellington's Waterloo dinners. Nearly three months later, on 14 September 1852, Arthur, Duke of Wellington died. Harry Smith was one of the pallbearers in the funeral cortège, which wound through the streets of London to St Paul's Cathedral watched by more than a million people. Not long before Wellington died someone asked him if there was anything in his long career that he could have done better. 'Yes,' he said, 'I should have given more praise.'

Author's Note

I was inspired to tell the story of Wellington and his men by the unprecedented variety of written memories of those who took part in this great military enterprise. Their clarity, honesty and wit make this 200-year-old story as real and as readable as if it had happened today. I have listed in the Bibliography all those who provide the most vivid accounts. The Notes refer to these works by their author's name. Most of them are available in the British Library, the London Library or the library of the National Army Museum, as are all the volumes of the Duke's own despatches. Many accounts have now become easily accessible in recent paperbacks from publishers such as Pen and Sword, Greenhill and Leonaur, and many have been digitised online. I have referred to these newly printed versions where they exist, and have always mentioned (in the Bibliography) the original title, publisher and date of publication of each book for those who prefer to handle the leather-bound early editions. I have satisfied myself that these modern publications are accurate reprints of the originals.

I owe a special debt to Laura Ponsonby, a direct descendant of Major General Sir Frederick Ponsonby, whose account of his breathtaking escape from death at Waterloo has always captivated me. Keen to retell his story I looked up the name Ponsonby in the London telephone directory. Laura's was the first number I tried, and I struck gold. She generously invited me to her family home, the Priory at Shulbrede in Sussex, and showed me the little red book in which Emily Ponsonby wrote down the story her husband Fred dictated to her, too disabled by his wound to write himself. Madeleine Bessborough kindly allowed me to use her picture of Fred Ponsonby being revived by a chivalrous Frenchman as he lay near death on the battlefield at Waterloo. Janet Gleason, author of *An Aristocratic Affair*, directed me to a mass of memoir and correspondence that provided a striking insight into the aristocracy that spawned so many of Wellington's officers. The fragile manuscript diaries of Rifles officer Jonathan Leach are preserved at the Royal Green Jackets Museum in Winchester, as are the letters of General 'Black Bob' Craufurd. Lieutenant General Sir Christopher Wallace, the Museum's Chairman, Curator Christine Pullen and the encyclopaedic Ken Gray have been tireless in providing material and pictures.

At Jane Luard's house in Gloucestershire I was delighted to find some sketches tucked away among the pages of her ancestor John Evan Luard's journal of his experiences in the 4th Dragoons. Special thanks too to the National Army Museum, whose staff went to great lengths to lay hands on documents and pictures that have enriched this book – in particular Michael Ball, Julian Farrance, Pip Dodd and Danu Reid. I have had prompt help in obtaining manuscripts from Alyson Stanford at the Northern Ireland Public Record Office, from Colin Gibson who looks after the Raglan Papers at the Gwent Record Office, from the National Archives in Kew and from the British Library, where Dr Arnold Hunt, Curator of Historical Manuscripts, gave me invaluable help in deciphering a letter from Lord Castlereagh. Dr Gregory Fremont-Barnes of the Department of War Studies at Sandhurst cast his expert eye over my chapters on Waterloo. The team who look after the Wellington papers at the University of Southampton were always helpful, as were Paul Evans and Mark Smith at the Royal Artillery's Firepower Museum. I had useful help from Mike Galer of the Museum of the 9th/12th Royal Lancers in Derby and from Bobby Collins, an expert on the history of the 12th Light Dragoons. Ken Timbers told me enough about Napoleonic War artillery to fill several books. Stephen Cotton lent me his bound copies of his ancestor Sir Stapleton Cotton's memoirs. Captain John Cornish helped me establish the whereabouts of Joseph Bonaparte's famous chamber pot. Nick Haynes, in Spain and Portugal, and Graeme Cooper in Belgium gave me exhaustive battlefield tours. Alyn and Lizzie Shipton, who produced a radio pro-gramme on the Peninsular War that I presented with my son Dan, were kind enough to provide me with all their research material. Andrew Green, another friend and radio producer, and a frequent visitor to the Newspaper Museum in Colindale, has unearthed many a press account of the political tussles at home over Wellington's war. I am grateful too to Frances Carver and her fellow enthusiasts in 'Waterloo 200', who are determined, like me, to remind the world of its debt to the Iron Duke and his army.

The Wellesley family have been unfailingly courteous and enthusiastic about yet another invader of their magnificent homes at Apsley House and Stratfield Saye. My thanks for their advice and hospitality to the (8th) Duke and Duchess of Wellington, to their son Charles, Marquess of Douro, and to their daughter Jane Wellesley, who has written her own history of the family. Kate Jenkins and Josephine Oxley have been tireless points of contact on Wellington memorabilia.

Among the many modern biographies of Wellington I have found Elizabeth Longford's *Wellington: The Years of the Sword*, Christopher Hibbert's *Wellington: A Personal History* and Richard Holmes's brisk but trenchant *Wellington: The Iron Duke* the most valuable commentaries on his life and personality. Holmes's *Redcoat* is a superb commentary on what a soldier's life must have been like 200 years ago. Charles Esdaile's and Jac Weller's studies of the Peninsular War are also essential reading. Dr Michael Crumplin, a medical man himself, has been a generous and authoritative source of information about the treatment of wounds and diseases in the Peninsular War, and his book *Men of Steel: Surgery in the Napoleonic Wars* is full of harrowing pictures of the injuries soldiers suffered.

The book would never have been written without the encouragement of my agent, Julian Alexander, and the enthusiasm and inspiration of Roland Philipps, my redoubtable editor and, when he had time, Managing Director of the publishers, John Murray. He and his team, in particular Victoria Murray-Browne and Anna Kenny-Ginard, provided the ultimate professional back-up to my race to meet the deadline. I am hugely grateful to them, to my cartographer Rodney Paull and to my meticulous picture researcher Juliet Brightmore, whose knack of choosing the right mix of illustrations was a priceless asset. The book's copy editor, Peter James, must be the best in the business and I was delighted to have him on board.

Finally, of course, my family. They've not only had to live with a hermit these past two years. They've read the text exhaustively and commented on it rigorously. Dan, my son, has established himself as one of the best authorities on eighteenth-century warfare with his book on Britain's battle for North America, *Death or Victory*. Nearly every conversation I've had with him has begun with a question about muskets or military discipline. My journalist wife, Ann MacMillan, managing editor of the Canadian Broadcasting Corporation in London, is the best judge I know of when a narrative goes off the rails. She and her sister, Margaret MacMillan, the historian, who is already a legend for her book *Peacemakers* and who has been a matchless editorial guide, have constantly dragged me back from the heat of battle to tell the human story of Wellington and the men who fought with him.

Notes

The authors' names refer to their alphabetical listing in the Bibliography.

I have used the following abbreviations:

NA   The National Archives, Kew, London
RGJ   Royal Green Jackets
W   Wellesley/Wellington
WD   Wellington, *Dispatches*
WO   War Office
WSD   Wellington, *Supplementary Despatches*

Introduction

1 'I don't know': Maxwell, vol. 1, p. 4
3 'The general was in the thick': WSD, vol. 4, pp. 184–6
4 'a damned fool': Arbuthnot, vol. 1, p. 168

Chapter One: First foothold

7 'caused some awful breakages': Leach, p. 33
  'exchanged for a scene': Landmann, vol. 2, pp. 76ff.
8 'Several boats were upset': Leslie, pp. 31–2
  'came running into the water': Hale, pp. 14–15
9 'I am not afraid': Croker, vol. 1, p. 12
10 'to be deployed': WD, vol. 4, p. 16, Castlereagh letter to W 30/6/1808
   'our kind, good and amiable': Bell, p. 102
   'I rejoice extremely': WD, vol. 4, p. 13, W letter to Hill 23/6/1808
   'an active and intelligent': WSD, vol. 5, p. 453, Richmond letter to W
   11/6/1808

11 'His Majesty has been pleased': WD, vol. 4, p. 30, Castlereagh letter to
W 15/7/1808
'I didn't know what': Croker, vol. 1, p. 343
'I hope I shall have': WSD, vol. 6, p. 95, W letter to Richmond
1/8/1808
'Fortunately we did not': Landmann, p. 83

12 'One punt capsized': Gleig, *Hussar*, p. 134
'and the children a quarter': WSD, vol. 6, pp. 91–2, W General Order
31/7/1808
'up to the knees in sand': Todd, p. 39
'I put a small pebble': ibid., p. 140

13 'hot enough almost': Leach, p. 34
George Landmann found himself: Landmann, p. 105
'afraid of the French': WD, vol. 4, p. 96, W letter to Castlereagh
16/8/1808
'If I had rice': Griffiths, p. 16
'a quantity, equal': WD, vol. 4, p. 57, memo for Commissary General
1/8/1808
'I have had': ibid., p. 72, W letter to Castlereagh 8/8/1808

14 'were a great many wine': Todd, p. 40
George Landmann thought: Landmann, p. 89

15 'throwing my arms': ibid., p. 161
'I remained shivering': ibid., p. 101
'Many of us': ibid., p. 128

16 'entirely new suit': ibid., p.138

18 'All was action': Harris, p. 17
'splashed thoroughly': Leach, p. 37

19 'Every mouthful of air': ibid.
'Poor Lake': Landmann, p. 144
'Few men could have': Harris, p. 16

20 'attacked with the utmost': WD, vol. 4, p. 98, W letter to Castlereagh
17/8/1808
'However acute may be': ibid., p.104, W letter to R. Borough Esq.,
18/8/1808
'She had, however': Harris, pp. 20ff.
'carefully untied': Landmann, p. 174
'one of our most important affairs': Stanhope, p. 40

Chapter Two: You must have bribed Junot

23 'for want of cavalry': WD, vol. 4, p. 103, W letter to Castlereagh
18/8/1808
24 'gave his orders': Gleig, *Hussar*, p. 143
'a cloud of light troops': Leach, p. 39
'The Rifles, as usual': Harris, p. 27
25 'No no': Landmann, p. 213
26 'I received them in line': Croker, vol. 2, p. 122
'every man throwing': Landmann, p. 214
27 'a party of the 43rd': Leslie, pp. 49–50
28 'seriously scattered': Landmann, p. 230
'particularly handsome fellow': ibid., p. 206
'Now, 20th, now!': Gleig, *Hussar*, pp. 144ff.
29 Some ran out of ammunition: Harris, p. 36
'bore himself like a hero': ibid., p. 37
'They gallop': WD, vol. 9, p. 240, Wellington letter to Hill 18/6/1812
'a breathless sensation': Todd, p. 42
30 'still playing over our heads': Lawrence, p. 38
'Sir Harry': WD, vol. 4, p. 240, proceedings of the court of inquiry
31 'turned his horse's head': Sherer, pp. 42–3
'in the midst': Hale, p. 22
'the peasantry prowling': Todd, p. 42
Harris used his bayonet: Harris, p. 39
'picked up a bill': Leslie, p. 52
'gave him a rap': Gleig, *Hussar*, p. 241
After a later battle: Harris, p. 50
32 'To several, a simple': Neale, pp. 16–21
'I don't know whether': British Library Additional MS 37415 f. 47, W
to Marquis Wellesley 5/10/1808
33 'disgorge the church plate': WSD, vol. 6, p. 123, W letter to Castlereagh 23/8/1808
'I did not think': WD, vol. 4, p. 167, proceedings of the court of
inquiry
'I feel an earnest': ibid., p.133, W letter to Castlereagh 30/8/1808
'You must have bribed': WSD, vol. 5, p. 476, Richmond letter to W
6/9/1808

Chapter Three: Scum of the earth

35 'He called to take': Blanch, pp. 122–3

36 'I had during that time': Anglesey, p. 67

37 Castlereagh briefly opposed the scheme: Castlereagh papers, letter 2/09/1809, Northern Ireland Record Office, D3030/3295

38 'The British force': WD, vol. 4, p. 262, W letter to Castlereagh 7/3/1809

39 'you have saved me': Bessborough, p. 136, F. Ponsonby letter to his mother 7/7/1805

40 'The man fell the whole': Tomkinson, p. 9
   One artful: O'Neill, p. 25

41 'sternness': Harris, p. 71
   'The affection is always there': letter to wife quoted by Craufurd, p. 263
   'a damned tyrant': Leach letter 24/7/1810, RGJ Museum, Winchester, 0028
   'long-wished-for day': Simmons, p. 5, letter home 21/5/1809

42 'duties of a war commissary': Schaumann, p. 36
   'Wherever he is': Simmons, p. 183

43 'If there is to be': WD, vol. 6, p. 325, W letter to Torrens 4/8/1810
   'I have never known': Stanhope, p. 13
   'I know from experience': Harris, p. 28
   'As seen on the far off': Farmer, p. 29

44 'What an ignorant': Wheeler, p. 49
   'in possession of a part': WD, vol. 4, p. 267, W despatch to J. Frere, Ambassador to Spanish Court, 24/4/1809
   'The weight each man': Dobbs, p. 24

46 'and began to plunder': Tomkinson, pp. 16–22
   'the dirtiest and noisiest': Costello, p. 86
   'dirty in the extreme': Simmons, p. 14
   'fighting like lions': ibid., p. 155

48 'The advancing French': Bunbury, vol. 1, pp. 32, 34

49 'splendid view': Leslie, pp. 112–13
   'retired in the utmost': WD, vol. 4, p. 324, W letter to Castlereagh 12/5/1809
   'indescribable cruelties': Schaumann, pp. 185–6

50 Tomkinson was one: Tomkinson, p. 21
   'run great risks': ibid., p. 320

'In an instant': Crumplin, p. 216

51 'I cannot say too much': WD, vol. 4, p. 325, W despatch 12/5/1809
'rabble': ibid., p. 380, W letter to Castlereagh 31/5/1809
'it is impossible': ibid., p. 432, W letter to Castlereagh 17/6/1809
'issue a proclamation': ibid., p. 374, W despatch to John Villiers 30/5/1809
On one occasion: Gleig, *Life*, p. 581

52 'composed of the scum': Stanhope, p. 14
'the stimulus of honour': O'Meara, p. 129

53 'Soldiers, I need you': Longford, *Years of the Sword*, p. 176
'The ball is now at my foot': WD, vol. 4, p. 412, W letter to John Villiers 11/6/1809

Chapter Four: The obstinate old Gentleman

54 'quite giddy': Holland papers, British Library Additional MS 51723
'I am particularly': WD, vol. 4, p. 415, W letter to Colonel Seymour 12/6/1809
'our great anxiety': Shulbrede archive, Shulbrede Priory, West Sussex, handwritten notes, dictated by F. Ponsonby to wife, pp. 1–2

55 'a brace of greyhounds': Kincaid, p. 75
'several excursions': Leach, p. 49
'sparkling black eyes': ibid., pp. 50–2

56 'I can only say': WD, vol. 4, p. 422, W letter to Frere 13/6/1809
'the General received': ibid., p. 506, W letter to Frere 13/7/1809

57 'moved forward only': Leslie, p. 137
'had fought when I': Stanhope, p. 47

58 'I find General Cuesta': WD, vol. 4, p. 526, W letter to Frere 24/7/1809

60 'are, in general, the most': WD, vol. 9, p. 366, W letter to Bathurst 18/8/1812
'motley and grotesque': Leslie, p. 135

61 'a motley crowd': Cooper, p. 21
'A battery was opened': Shulbrede archive, p. 2
'About nine o'clock': Leslie, p. 143
'It was evident': ibid., p. 144

62 'by means of': Schaumann, p. 184

63 'In the first place': Leslie, p. 146

'we were ordered': ibid., p. 148

'In we went': ibid.

64 'At about 7': ibid.

'gentlemanly to a degree': Leach, pp. 119–20

'put some coppers': Bell, p. 169

65 'An ear-splitting yell': Schaumann, p. 186

66 'Major Frederick Ponsonby': Napier, *History*, p. 218

'All we could see': Schaumann, p. 186

'We had the pleasing': Bessborough, p. 188, F. Ponsonby letter to Lady Duncannon 3/9/1809

'Good God': ibid., p. 187, Lady Caroline Lamb letter to Lady Bessborough 14/8/1809

'though it proved so fatal': Shulbrede archive, F. Ponsonby letter to Lady Duncannon 3/9/1809

67 'The thunder of the': Schaumann, p. 185

'The enemy were massing': Cooper, p. 25

68 ''Twas enough': ibid.

69 'a great and glorious': WD, vol. 5, p. 98, W to W. Huskisson 20/8/1809

'Exactly right': letters 22/8/1809 and 13/9/1809, Raglan papers, Gwent Public Record Office

'I really ought to be': Bainville, p. 293

'Yesterday, Sire': Bingham, vol. 2, p. 470

70 'had seized the field of battle': ibid., pp. 468–71

Chapter Five: Damned with might and main

71 'to know when to retreat': Fraser, p. 28

'I like to walk alone': W letter to Henry Wellesley 7/07/1801, Wellington MSS, quoted by Longford, *Years of the Sword*, p. 78

'I have always felt the inutility': WD, vol. 9, p. 584, W letter to Beresford 2/12/1812

72 'The Caçadores': Costello, p. 174

'Then I advise you': Tomkinson, p. 38; Fraser, p. 45

On the day they arrived: Napier, *History*, bk 8, p. 218

73 'The men suffered': Costello, pp. 31–2

'neither more nor less': Leach, pp. 53–4

'an onion or two': Dobbs, pp. 47–8

74 'combatants who had': Garrety, p. 72
'literally covered': Smith, p. 19
'the palms of their hands': Green, p. 36
'Heavens!': Schaumann, pp. 190–1
'our astonishment and vexation': Simmons, p. 23
'that deformed-looking lump': Costello, p. 34

75 'The Spaniards are': Gordon, p. 50, letter to Aberdeen 8/8/1809
'Your Excellency cannot': WD, vol. 5, p. 32, W letter to Cuesta 13/8/1809
'owing to carelessness': Schaumann, p. 204
'The soldiers' wives': ibid., pp. 204–5
'A starving army': WD, vol. 5, p. 15, W letter to Marquess Wellesley 8/8/1809

76 'More than a month': ibid., p. 51, W letter to Marquess Wellesley 18/8/1809
'It is my opinion': ibid., p. 80, W letter to Marquis Wellesley 24/8/1809
'are really children': ibid., p. 83, W's 'assessment of future war' 26/8/1809
'never forgave me': Simmons, p. 26
'The division paraded': Leach journal entry 12/8/09, RGJ Museum archive, Winchester, 0026, p. 4
'It entered into my head': Costello, p. 42

77 'Your mama tells me': Craufurd MS letter 15/8/1809, RGJ Museum, Winchester
'There is nothing dangerous': Bingham, p. 17, Napoleon to Joseph 31/1/1810

78 'We may protract': Gordon, p. 75, letter to Aberdeen 27/11/1809
'Your chances of': WSD, vol. 6, p. 493, Liverpool letter to W 13/3/1810
'All I beg is': WD, vol. 6, p. 10, W letter to Liverpool 2/4/1810
'If I am in a scrape': WD, vol. 5, p. 611, W letter to Torrens 31/3/1810
'disputed the military': Creevey, vol. 1, p. 123, journal entry 23/01/1810

79 'all the indignation': ibid., p. 127, journal entry 1/02/1810
'approaches very rapidly': ibid., p. 128, journal entry 17/02/1810
'must have been most': ibid., p. 105, journal entry 4/9/1809
'I wish': Brett-James, *Wellington at War*, p. 189

80 'with some anxiety': Grattan, pp. 18–20

'I found him to be': Stanhope, pp. 68–9

81 'and by night we': Leach, p. 79

Chapter Six: Unpardonable butchery

82 'The country in which': WD, vol. 6, p. 257, W letter to Liverpool 11/7/1810

83 'Hill does what he is told': Fraser, p. 182
'When I reflect': WSD, vol. 6, p. 582, W letter to Torrens 26/8/1810
'It was ill planned': Gordon, p. 94, letter to Aberdeen 12/7/1810
'Craufurd never moved': Smith, p. 29

84 'In short': WD, vol. 6, p. 259, W letter to Craufurd 11/7/1810
'It is desirable': ibid., p. 275, W letter to Craufurd 16/7/1810
'I am not desirous': ibid., p. 285, W letter to Craufurd 22/7/1810

85 '[Craufurd] with headstrong': Napier, *History*, p. 294
'Although the left': Leach, p. 95
'we repulsed them': Simmons, p. 77
'The French cavalry': Costello, pp. 50–1

86 'The conflict was tremendous': Garrety, pp. 95–6
'In ascending the hill': Leach, p. 97

87 'a few hundred': ibid., p. 98
'It was a piece of': ibid.
'a French surgeon': Garrety, p. 97
'fighting a very dangerous': Grattan, p. 25
'we were puzzled': Leach, p. 99
'more abhorred': Leach letter home 24/7/1810, RGJ Museum archive, Winchester, 0028
'disappointed': Torrens letter to Colonel Bathurst 14/8/1810, NA WO 3/597

88 'You will say': WSD, vol. 6, p. 561, W letter to W. Wellesley-Pole 31/07/1810
'Craufurd remained much too long': Gordon, p. 99, letter to Aberdeen 24/7/1810
'The retreat was made': Craufurd, pp. 139–46, quoting letter to *The Times* 21/11/1810
'Picton and Craufurd': Napier, *History*, p. 296

89 Smith had a ball: Smith, p. 31

'For a few moments': Simmons, pp. 78–81
'The bullocks ran away': Smith, p. 32
'I cocked up my leg': ibid., p. 39
'by care and syringing': Costello, p. 54
90 'The French army': Donaldson, p. 160
'As soon as a man': Hale, p. 67
91 'I cannot express': WD, vol. 5, p. 386, W letter to Hill 28/8/1810
'There are certainly': ibid., p. 453, W letter to Charles Stuart 18/9/1810
Jonathan Leach complained: Leach, p. 112
'We have an excellent': WD, vol. 5, p. 459, W letter to Cotton 21/9/1810
92 'and from the bustle': Grattan, pp. 31–5
93 'But when they were mixed': ibid., p. 37
'Wallace, I never witnessed': ibid., p. 40
'so we continued': Hale, p. 51
94 'Now, 52nd': Napier, *History*, p. 304
'firing and bayoneting': Craufurd, p. 158,
95 'a murderous fire of grape': Leach, p. 106
'a taste for an amusement': WSD, vol. 6, p. 606, W letter to W. Wellelsey-Pole 4/10/1810
'I have not now': Gordon, p. 116, letter to Aberdeen 30/9/1810
96 Wellington said much later: Stanhope, pp. 19–20
'After it was made': Shulbrede archive, p. 8
'My people followed': Schaumann, p. 269
'My only covering': Kincaid, pp. 6 and 17
97 'They won't draw me': WSD, vol. 6, p. 612, W letter to Arbuthnot 5/10/1810
'I condole with you': Buckingham, vol. 4, p. 438
'I stood gasping for breath': Todd, p. 70
98 William Tomkinson: Tomkinson, p. 61
'as one of our party': Kincaid, p. 50
'The French looked': Todd, p. 72
'Masséna's army': Gordon, p. 122, letter 27/10/1810
'the cunning rogues': Leach, p. 114
'We could not advance': Todd, pp. 72–3
99 'Lord Wellington arrived': Simmons, p. 116
'over his wine': ibid., p. 117
'seized a musket': Napier, *History*, p. 316

'very very different': Bessborough, p. 209, F. Ponsonby letter to Lady Duncannon 12/9/1810

100 'She stood in a corner': Cavendish, p. 242, letter to Lady Morpeth 12/11/1807

'men like her a lot': ibid., p. 235, letter to Lady Morpeth 6/11/1807

Chapter Seven: A dangerous hour for England

101 'Where is the man': Aldington, p. 156

'People now are not satisfied': Gordon, p. 140, letter to Aberdeen 22/12/1810

102 'You taught us to expect': ibid., p. 162, letter from Aberdeen 13/2/1811

'We contrived to amuse': Leach, p. 119

Some of the soldiers: ibid., p. 121

'Having very little duty': Todd, p. 74

103 'He found means to': Donaldson, p. 101

'God be praised': Leach, journal entry 3/2/1811, RGJ Museum archive, Winchester, 0031

'We gave the Germans a cheer': Blakeney, p. 165

'The fox-hunting': Maxwell, vol. 1, p. 164

'a brilliant and most': Royal Military Calendar, vol. 2, London, 1820, p. 157: General Thomas Graham, dispatch 6/3/1811, an account of Barrosa

Ponsonby was wounded: Bessborough, p. 214

104 'Beau Ideal': Stewart, pp. 64–5

'The horses in Masséna's army': Leach, p. 119

'squalor and filth': ibid., p. 123

'torn and dilapidated': Simmons, pp. 13–18

'to make fun of us': Schaumann, p. 290

'The poor creatures': Kincaid, p. 229

105 'force them out': WSD, vol. 7, pp. 1–2, W letter to W. Wellesley-Pole 8/10/1810

'In an instant': Costello, p. 81

'Lord Wellington': Kincaid, p. 228

'drowned in the Ceira': Leach, pp. 126–7

106 'some of the enemy's': Kincaid, p. 27

'The fords were still so': ibid., p. 229

'With the blood streaming down': Garrety, p. 133

107 'I must say I think': Gordon, p. 187, letter to Aberdeen 3/10/1811

108 only two people: Chaptal, p. 304 ('Il n'y a que Wellington et moi en Europe capable d'exécuter ces measures')

'rather fight 50,000 men': Gordon, p. 96, letter to Aberdeen 18/7/1810

'ablest': Stanhope, p. 20

'could not keep his hands': O'Meara, p. 155

109 'beautiful and romantic': Donaldson, p. 118

110 '[The French], each chafing': Todd, p. 78

'sweating and half smothered': Donaldson, p. 121

'took off my right': Todd, p. 78

'he is obliged to be left': Kincaid, p. 256

111 'with lungs that roused': Costello, p. 92

112 'Opposed, with their conspicuous': ibid., p. 94

113 'which made me stagger': Kincaid, p. 37

'although a strict': Costello, p. 92

'The soldiers received': Smith, p. 49

'Although [the squares]': Napier, *History*, p. 345

114 'He took advantage': Wheeler, p. 56

'Men and horses': Napier, *History*, p. 345

'Their hats set round': Todd, p. 79

115 'We were overpowered': ibid., p. 137

'Our Highlanders': Grattan, p. 66

'It so happened': ibid., p. 68

116 'Well done the brave 88th': Donaldson, p. 124

'If Boney had been there': WSD, vol. 7, p. 177, W letter to W. Wellesley-Pole 2/7/1811

Wellington admitted later: Larpent, vol. 1, pp. 104–5, journal entry 1/3/1813

'We would rather see his long nose': Kincaid, p. 36

'The Light Division': Craufurd, p. 178

'A ball had passed': Kincaid, p. 39

117 'Their limbs were swollen': Grattan, pp. 76–7

'Ay, I thought they meant': Larpent, vol. 1, p. 108, journal entry 6/3/1813

118 'I have never been': WD, vol. 7, p. 565, W letter to Liverpool 15/5/1811

'They had about 13,000 men': WSD, vol. 7, p. 123, W letter to W. Wellesley-Pole 23/4/1811

'drunken old': Schaumann, p. 305

'Old 29th': Leslie, p. 225

119 'If it had not been for me': WSD, vol. 7, p. 177, W letter to W. Wellesley-Pole 2/7/1811

'by 384 pairs of bullocks': WD, vol. 8, p. 122, memo 19/7/1811

His artillerymen would be: Headlam, p. 156

120 'We were much annoyed': Donaldson, p. 140

'I am glad to see you safe': Craufurd, p. 185

'weaker or more dispersed': Gordon, p. 264, letter to Aberdeen 20/11/1811

Chapter Eight: Now, lads, for the breach

122 'wolves were not': Grattan, p. 123

blamed the army's lack of supplies: Urban, *Rifles*, p. 140

'with a view to purchasing some corn': Napier, *History*, p. 292

'In this starving state': Knowles, p. 37, letter to father 3/12/1811

123 'and vast numbers of officers': W, *Selections from the Despatches*, p. 560, memo of operations in 1811, 28/12/1811

He put a huntsman named Crane: Thornton, p. 75

'it gave him an opportunity': Kincaid, p. 278

'with his entourage': Schaumann, p. 397

'The cheerfulness or gloom': Browne, p. 155

124 'as a sitting and dining room': Thornton, pp. 105–7

'the best dinners': Cole and Gwyn, p. 59

'in his clothes': Browne, p. 156

'of his own invention': Gleig, *Life*, p. 626

125 'There was no throng': Schaumann, p. 317

'remarkable cast of feature': Costello, p. 125

'The commander-in-chief': Schaumann, p. 366

'as long as he is': WD, vol. 8, pp. 378–9, W letter to Torrens 6/11/1811

'I borrow two or three': Cocks, journal entry 1/12/1811

'a little Portuguese': ibid., letter to Thomas 10/9/1811

126 'I scarcely remember': Grattan, p. 134

'monasteries, convents and churches': Cooke, p. 83

127 George Simmons: Simmons, pp. 218–19

'a great annoyance': Costello, p. 109

128 'The frost was so excessive': Donaldson, p. 144
'When about fifty yards': Colborne, pp. 161–4
Craufurd was not pleased: Costello, p. 107

129 'A very fine young man': Knowles, p. 42, letter to father 20/1/1812
'Twenty two pieces': Simmons, p. 219

130 'The bellowing of eighty': Garrety, p. 155

131 'the women, from long habit': Grattan, p. 146
'Rangers of Connaught': ibid., p. 147
'Soldiers! The eyes': Costello, p. 111
'A tremendous fire': Simmons, p. 221

132 'quite sure that they would': Craufurd, pp. 196–8, letter from General
Sir James Shaw Kennedy 1861
'jumped down the scarp': Garrety, p. 157
'bent double by the height': Costello, pp. 112–13

133 'Every man on the breach': Grattan, pp. 152–3
'engaged the French cannoniers': ibid., pp. 154–5
'He pushed the Frenchman': ibid., pp. 156–7

134 'I shall never forget': Smith, p. 58
'Remember, I was the first': Green, p. 56
'a sharp fellow': Smith, p. 58
'If I had not seen': Cooke, p. 89

135 'men, and Englishmen': Robinson, vol. 2, p. 73
'with the power of twenty trumpets': Kincaid, p. 58
'to admit an elephant': Grattan, p. 162
'Well, General': ibid., p. 166
'fell into the liquor': Costello, p. 113
'which they considered': Grattan, p. 157
'heartrending in the extreme': Costello, p. 115

136 'one last farewell': Donaldson, p. 148
'Yes, a great blow': Craufurd, pp. 196–8, letter from General Sir James
Shaw Kennedy 1861
'He was a fine fellow': Colborne, p. 166
'at the commencement': Kincaid, p. 59

137 'Depend upon it': Shulbrede archive, F. Ponsonby to his mother
21/2/1812

Chapter Nine: The town's our own. Hurrah!

138 'cursing all the way': Kincaid, p. 63

140 'a stupid beast': Smith, p. 63
'The elements': Kincaid, p. 63

141 'An adventurous Portuguese': Cooke, p. 97
'while the ramrod': Garrety, p. 166

142 'Death was dealt in every': Lamare, pp. 25, 28
'not advance beyond': WD, vol. 9, p. 37, 'memorandum for the attack on Badajoz' 6/4/1812

143 'Although there was': Kincaid, p. 63
'for a good bathe': Green, p. 58
'one of the most sanguinary': Costello, p. 129
'sucking an orange': Cooke, p. 100
'A Lieutenant Colonel': Simmons, p. 232

144 'You'll be in hell before daylight': Green, p. 58
'I fell backward': Costello, p. 131

145 'shrieks uttered': Blakeney, p. 220
'from behind which the garrison': Lawrence, p. 80
'I told him the Fortieth': ibid., p. 81

146 'Desist blowing': Green, pp. 64–74
'the poor fellows': Donaldson, p. 152
'Twelve men sank': Hennell, p. 14, letter to a friend 5/4/1812
'conquer or die': Robinson, pp. 110ff.

147 'and his appeal': Grattan, p. 200
'Among the dead and wounded': Costello, p. 132
'most murderous': Smith, p. 64
'groups of fifty to a hundred': Kincaid, p. 66

148 'The discharge of grape shot': Leach, p. 159
'led by their gallant officers': WD, vol. 9, p. 42, despatch 7/4/1812
'fifty times': Simmons, p. 229

149 'I shall never forget it': McGrigor, p. 121
'screened from the enemy's direct': Blakeney, p. 222
'On leaping into the place': Knowles, p. 48, letter to father 7/4/1812

150 '"The Devil," says I': Smith, p. 66

151 'only a few random shots': Simmons, p. 230
'The shouts and oaths': Costello, p. 134
'fell upon his knees': ibid., p. 133
'one of our officers': Hennell, p. 17, letter to a friend 5/4/1812

'delicate freshness': Kincaid, p. 287

152 '"impudent fellow"': Smith, p. 72

'Old Boy – will you drink': Costello, p. 137

'to execute any man': WSD, vol. 7, p. 311, W order 7/4/1812

'The men who besiege': Costello, p. 136

'the men were permitted': Kincaid, p. 69

'we were allowed': Donaldson, p. 153

153 'outrages committed': WD, vol. 9, p. 227, W despatch to Liverpool 10/6/1812

'The truth is': ibid., p. 49, W letter to Torrens 7/4/1812

154 'I bit my lips': Arbuthnot, vol. 1, p. 143

'Are we the Connaught': Cooke, p. 224. Picton's original rebuke is variously described by those who claimed to remember it. He is said to have called the 88th, among other things, 'blackguards', 'footpads' and 'robbers'

'affords as strong an instance': Oman, vol. 5, p. 255, quoting W letter to Liverpool 7/4/1812

Chapter Ten: *Marmont est perdu*

156 'completely upset': Tomkinson, p. 156

'much gallantry and judgment': WD, vol. 9, p. 66, Cotton letter to W 11/4/1812

'never more annoyed': ibid., W despatch 11/4/1812

'the trick of galloping': ibid., p. 240, W letter to Hill 18/6/1812

157 'Damned tempting': Fortescue, vol. 8, p. 462

'We have been looking': Shulbrede archive, 7/1812

'Wellington was in the thick': Cooke, p. 120

158 'one of our dragoons': ibid.

'It was a beautiful': Gordon, p. 298, letter to Aberdeen 25/7/1812

'dense mass of Frenchmen': Simmons, p. 239

'I have . . . determined': WD, vol. 9, p. 299, letter to Bathurst 21/7/1812

'very warm work': Granville, vol. 2, p. 450, F. Ponsonby letter to mother 25/7/1812

'Luckily we got over': Simmons, p. 241

'This was a lucky pipe': Wheeler, p. 86

160 'a little nervous': Tomkinson, p. 192

'I am glad he has': Robinson, vol. 2, p. 155

161 'The enemy are in motion': there several accounts of this episode: see
Grattan, p. 240: Fortescue, vol. 8, p. 487; Maxwell, vol. 1, p. 282
'quite unruffled in his manner': Grattan, p. 242

162 'shot and shell were': Donaldson, p. 164

163 'the entire French division': Grattan, p. 245
'Murphy, dead and bleeding': ibid., p. 246
'Pakenham may not be': WD, vol. 9, p. 395, W letter to Torrens
7/9/1812
'Royals . . . this shall be': Douglas, pp. 43–4

164 'My God, Cotton!': Combermere, vol. 1, p. 275
'such [Frenchmen] as got away': Grattan, p. 250

165 'These men totally': ibid., p. 251

166 'I never saw an army': Raglan papers, W letter to W. Wellesley-Pole
25/07/1812

167 'It raises Wellington's reputation': Girod de L'Ain, p. 178

Chapter Eleven: One step forward, two steps back

168 'The vigorous following': Napier, *History*, p. 504
'women of all ranks': Stewart, p. 75, F. Ponsonby letter to his mother
2/8/1812

169 'impossible to describe': WD, vol. 9, p. 346, letter to Clinton
13/8/1812
'They got hold of his legs': Simmons, p. 248
'never kissed by': Cocks, p. 191
'Their breath was so highly': Wheeler, p. 91

170 'a remarkably plain-looking': Grattan, p. 269
'on Castilian beauty': Leach, p. 174
'We had a grand ball': Shulbrede archive, F. Ponsonby letter to his
mother 23/8/1812
'had the advantage of': Gleason, p. 342
'I certainly think him': Gordon, p. 314, letter to Aberdeen 25/8/1812

171 'Your observations are': ibid., p. 328, letter from Aberdeen 8/10/1812
'cry *viva*, and are very fond': WD, vol. 9, p. 366, W letter to Bathurst
18/8/1812
'What can be done': ibid., pp. 369–70, W letter to Henry Wellesley
23/8/1812

172 'They came down the road': Tomkinson, p. 207

173 'affair was not well managed': Gordon, p. 321, letter to Aberdeen 21/9/1812

174 'I am getting apprehensive': WD, vol. 9, p. 437, W letter to Bathurst 21/9/1812

'I am afraid we shall': ibid., p. 458, W letter to Hill 2/10/1812

'sincere friend': Tomkinson, p. 213

'So highly did the Duke': *Royal United Services Institute Journal*, Memoir of April 1837, p. 4

'that no serious consequence': Bessborough, p. 228, W. Ponsonby letter to Lord Bessborough 18/10/1812

175 'met with a little accident': ibid., p. 229, F. Ponsonby letter to Lady Duncannon 28/10/1812

'I hope before Christmas': WD, vol. 9, p. 394, W letter to George Murray 7/9/1812

'Maybe yer satisfied': Wellington, *Anecdotes*, p. 16

176 'inadequacy of our means': Sergeant William Ingilby, journal entry 8/9/1812, Firepower Museum, Woolwich, ref MD 797

'He paid no attention': WD, vol. 9, p. 566, W letter to Liverpool 23/11/1812

'I have not been in the habit': Aitchison, p. 210, journal entry 19/10/1812

177 'state of discipline': Gordon, pp. 334–5, letter to Aberdeen 28/10/1812

'I have got clear': WD, vol. 9, p. 519, W letter to Charles Stuart 31/10/1812

'after a sojourn': Grattan, p. 273

178 'we were now walking': Kincaid, p. 92

'One of our men': Todd, p. 89

'Wellington supposed': Bell, p. 97

'there was this young': Smith, p. 86

179 'The poor fellow': Donaldson, p. 173

'The men's clothes': Hay, p. 77

'It was truly': ibid., p. 81

'I have had the great good fortune': ibid., pp. 91–2

180 'Sometimes, indeed': Donaldson, p. 174

'Don't the jaws': Grattan, p. 293

'ran mad. I remember': Wheeler, p. 106

181 'The commander of forces': WSD, vol. 7, p. 470, W General Order 16/11/1812

'from the powerful blow': Hay, pp. 70–1

'I looked on with surprise': ibid., p. 83

'I am concerned': WD, vol. 9, p. 574, W to 'Officers Commanding Divisions and Brigades' 28/11/1812

182 'too sweeping': Leach, p. 183

'afforded a handle': Kincaid, p. 96

he couldn't bring himself: Stewart, p. 78

'in a hasty moment': Tomkinson, p. 231

Britain would have to withdraw: Gordon, p. 342, letter to Aberdeen 19/11/1812

'accomplished all he expected': Hansard, vol. 24, col. 161, 3/12/1812

'Thank God we have committed': ibid., col. 168, 3/12/1812

183 'most disastrous': ibid., col. 163, 3/12/1812

'power of England is not competent': Aldington, p. 176

Chapter Twelve: I saw them fall like a pack of cards

185 'Lord Wellington's retreat': Gordon, p. 346, letter from Aberdeen 7/12/1812

'there is scarcely any French army': WD, vol. 10, p. 114, W letter to Henry Wellesley 12/2/1813

'has a good stud': Larpent, vol. 1, p. 61, journal entry 26/1/1813

'remarkably neat': ibid., vol. 3, p. 6, journal entry 22/2/1814

186 'then for an hour or two': ibid., vol. 1, p. 66, journal entry 7/2/1813

'Here are no books': ibid., p. 36, journal entry 26/11/1812

'It is impossible to imagine': Leach, p. 183

'This is the right sort of man': Leach journal entry 1/2/1813, RGJ Museum archive, Winchester, ref 0717

'very busy with parades': Bell, p. 103

187 a substantial part of the French army: Urban, *Codes*, p. 260

'great hilarity, buoyant spirit': Bell, p. 109

188 'Well here we go': Urban, *Rifles*, p. 210

'Farewell Portugal. I shall': Maxwell, vol. 1, p. 310

'All my staff': Croker, vol. 1, p. 336

189 'What then was our excessive': Leach, p. 190

'They had on generally yellow': Surtees, p. 164

191 'It was a heavenly morning': Schaumann, pp. 374–5

'Hay, I am very ill': Hay, p. 109
'The bright morning sunshine': Schaumann, p. 375

192 'Immediately we marched': Todd, p. 101
'that he would have a drink': ibid., p. 102
'the wretched old firelocks': Bell, p. 111
'I found myself': Cooke, p. 175

193 'No, sir!': Robinson, vol. 2, pp. 208–10
'Who got that?': Dobbs, p. 70

194 'A whole regiment came': Costello, p. 171
Harry Smith was galloping: Smith, pp. 97–100
'That's right, my lads': Costello, p. 174
'which I knew to be': Kincaid, pp. 108–9
'extreme disorder': WD, vol. 10, p. 530, W letter to Picton 16/7/1813

195 'clamour, the flashing': Bell, p. 112
'the principal part of the action': Robinson, vol. 1, p. 205, Picton to his brother 27/6/1813
'He replied no': Lawrence, p. 95
'good deal too old': Aitchison, p. 241, letter home 19/6/1813

196 'Our trumpet sounded': Hay, pp. 113–14
'in one confused mass': Kincaid, pp. 109–10
'Had all the cavalry': Tomkinson, p. 251

197 'Lord Wellington may not': ibid., p. 255
'They were young and good-looking': Schaumann, p. 380
'secured a small box': Wheeler, p. 118
'big sack, a cold fowl': Bell, p. 117
'I compelled him to lay it down': Costello, pp. 175–7

198 'but an Arab camp': Wheeler, p. 119

199 'In their lust of plunder': Schaumann, p. 379
One document was extracted: Urban, *Codes*, p. 274
'vagabond soldiers': WD, vol. 10, p. 473, W letter to Bathurst 29/6/1813
'We have in the service': ibid., p. 496, W letter to Bathurst 2/7/1813

Chapter Thirteen: The finger of God is upon me

201 'I was right in my military expectations': Croker, vol. 1, p. 336
'I never saw a large army': Gordon, pp. 385–6, letter to Aberdeen 23/6/1813

'I trust you will be satisfied': WSD, vol. 8, p. 64, Liverpool letter to W 7/7/1813

202 'Wellington – there's a general': Granville, vol. 2, p. 476, Lady Bessborough letter to Lord Granville Leveson-Gower, undated, probably 9/1813

'The unfortunate war': Las Cases, vol. 2, part 4, p. 185

'Buonaparte's mind': Croker, vol. 1, p. 339

203 Napoleon's presence on a field: Stanhope, p. 81

Prince Metternich is reported: Croker, vol. 1, p. 336. Croker leaves the two expletives to the imagination. I've assumed that the French word was *baisé* and translated it as 'screwed'

'Well, sir, you have got': Simmons, pp. 294–5

'I am anxious to state': Wellington MSS, Southampton University Library, 62 – 1/372f.2, F. Ponsonby letter to Wellington 13/07/1813

204 'In the first place there were': Schaumann, p. 386

'there were many pretty girls': Bell, p. 80

'uncommonly fine trout': Leach, p. 201

205 'were too civil and well-behaved': ibid., p. 205

206 'I am in hopes that': WD, vol. 10, p. 520, W letter to Bathurst 10/7/1813

'We began breaching': Frazer, letter home 23/7/1813

207 'I have had a scratch': ibid., letter home 26/7/1813

'Should it not be possible': WSD, vol. 8, p. 114, Graham letter to W 24/7/1813

'sharp pointed rocks': Henegan, p. 180

208 'The assault was made but stupidly': Frazer, letter home 26/7/1813

'imbecility and indecision': Aitchison, p. 254, letter to his father 13/7/1813

209 'The dispositions and arrangements': WD, vol. 10, p. 577, Soult speech text

210 'When on my road home': ibid., p. 566, W letter to Graham 25/7/1813

'horrible . . . for our path': Cooper, p. 84

'forced to give way': Todd, p. 104

211 'The 92nd were in line': Bell, p. 134

'really heroes when': Fortescue, vol. 9, pp. 255–6

212 'It was rather alarming': Larpent, vol. 2, p. 71, journal entry 24/8/1813

'I escaped as usual': Raglan papers, W letter to W. Wellesley-Pole 3/08/1813

'The ground was uneven': Bell, p. 139

'never saw such fighting': WD, vol. 10, p. 602, W letter to Lord Bentinck 5/8/1813

'Sergeant Cooper, go': Cooper, p. 88

213 'there is nothing in the world': Gordon, p. 392, letter to Aberdeen 22/8/1813

counted fifty-one guns: Larpent, vol. 2, p. 78, journal entry 28/8/1813

no fewer than ninety-five: Henegan, p. 189

214 They had to carry the powder: the figures come from a table published in *Royal Artillery Historical Society Proceedings*, vol. 7, no. 5, 2/10/1996

'You never heard such a row': Frazer, letter home 26/8/1813

'I was yesterday': WD, vol. 11, p. 47, W letter to Beresford 27/8/1813

'and show the 5th division': Hennell, p. 124

215 'as if the elements had been aware': Gleig, *Subaltern*, p. 48

'with the most deadly effect': ibid., p. 51

'As each succeeding party fell': Henegan, p. 189

216 'An "Oh!" burst': ibid., p. 191

'Fortunately there were few females': Gleig, *Subaltern*, p. 36

217 'See what our example': Hennell, p. 127

Chapter Fourteen: Extraordinary news

218 'Three successive times': Smith, p. 123

219 'I see that as usual': WD, vol. 11, p. 124, W letter to Bathurst 19/9/1813

220 'up to their bellies': Stewart, p. 87

'swarm of riflemen': Smith, p. 134

'The mountain was fearfully': Cooke, p. 228

221 'To my dismay': Colborne, p. 179

'We were called madmen': Smith, pp. 135-6

'most gallant style': WD, vol. 11, p. 177, W letter to Bathurst, 9/10/1813

'Though your brigade have even': Smith, pp. 136-7

'We should do much better': Robinson, vol. 2, p. 258

222 'riding up and down our columns': Schaumann, p. 395

'All went well': Smith, pp. 141-2

'At last when ready': Lawrence, p. 109

'He was very stern': Gronow, *Reminiscences*, p. 6

223 'I am very doubtful': WD, vol. 1, p. 207, W letter to Bathurst 18/10/1813

'These fellows think': Smith, pp. 142–4

224 'He was all gaiety and spirits': Larpent, vol. 2, p. 155, journal entry 10/11/1813

'As we advanced': Bell, p. 158

'We turned out the contents': ibid., p. 159

225 'What do you mean': Smith, pp. 148–50

226 'the sentiment throughout France': WD, vol. 11, pp. 303 ff., W letter to Bathurst 21/11/1813

'Dead or alive, my lads': Bell, p. 176

227 'Hill, the day's yours': ibid., p. 178

'committed a great error': Colbourne, p. 189

'The snow drove': Leach, p. 216

'Without a moment's delay': Cooke, p. 257

228 Wellington reported to London: WSD, vol. 8, p. 605, General Hope to W 27/2/1814

'In Spain': *Tradition*, vol. 3, no. 17 (1960), p. 18

'extremely thoughtful': Surtees, pp. 229–30

229 'They did it beautifully': Colborne, p. 192

'The action was for some time': WSD, vol. 8, p. 607, W to Marquis Wellesley 1/3/1814

In recent years a stone: interview with Jacques Cloup, graveyard custodian, Orthez, 12/9/2008

'Wellington was laughing': Maxwell, vol. 1, p. 366

230 There is another version: Larpent, vol. 3, p. 41, journal entry 7/3/1814, and p. 37, journal entry 5/3/1814; Gleig, *Life*, p. 494

'probably the ablest': Greville, vol. 1, p. 71

231 'the worst arranged': Colborne, p. 195

'very severe affair': WD, vol. 11, p. 629, W letter to Lord Dalhousie 12/04/1814

'I have extraordinary news for you': Broughton, journal entry 17/12/14 (as told to Lord Broughton by F. Ponsonby)

232 'with great warmth': Larpent, vol. 3, pp. 138–9, journal entry 13/4/1814

'a walking sore': Stanhope, p. 32

'that long-nosed beggar': Tomkinson, p. 123

Chapter Fifteen: In the Elysian Fields

234 'I have to acquaint you': WSD, vol. 9, p. 8, Castlereagh letter to Campbell, 16/4/1814
'much heartlessness and ingratitude': Campbell, p. 176

235 'I am most happy': WSD, vol. 9, p. 59, Liverpool letter to W 3/5/1814
'I am happy to hear': ibid., p. 74, Henry Wellesley letter to W 15/5/1814

236 'I believe I forgot to tell you': ibid., p. 100, W letter to Henry Wellesley 22/5/1814
'How wonderful was the feeling': Bell, p. 216
'An issue of six': ibid., p. 223
'to make love to the pretty': Kincaid, p.145
Costello and some companions: Costello, p. 205

237 'He appeared sullen and dejected': Leach, p. 224
'I left her insensible': Smith, pp. 186–7
He was discharged: Cooper, p. 125
'silent reproach and degradation': Robinson, vol. 2, p. 346

238 reckoned he couldn't count: Wheeler, p. 158
said he wouldn't be able to muster: Donaldson, p. 221
'These faithful and heroic women': Grattan, p. 334
'The commander of forces': WD, vol. 12, p. 62, W General Order 14/6/1814

239 'It seems a pity that': Fraser, p. 103
'scandalous': Grattan, pp. 332, 340
'I have finished my despatch': McGrigor, p. 278
'He repulsed the soldiers': Napier, *Life*, p. 306

240 'I have nothing to say of this': Wellesley, pp. 179, 186
'I don't mean to be scandalous': Larpent, vol. 3, p. 174, journal entry 29/4/1814

241 displaying her green pantaloons: Marchand, vol. 1, p. 460
When the manager told: Gronow, *Reminiscences*, p. 21
'As she seems to prefer': Costello, pp. 206f.

242 'impossible to get anything inserted': WD, vol. 12, p. 142, W letter to Wilberforce 8/10/1814
'orders have at last been issued': ibid., p. 170, W letter to Wilberforce 5/11/1814

243 'My Lord, you owe': Granville, vol. 2, p. 516, Lady Bessborough to Lord Granville 21/12/1814

'I am afraid he is behaving very ill: ibid., p. 507, Lady Bessborough to Lord Granville 13/11/1814

'Mais M. Le Duc était de beaucoup le plus fort': Delaforce, p. 74

'He was a true Englishman': ibid., p. 75

244 'Matters are going on well': WD, vol. 9, p. 146, W to Castlereagh 12/10/1814

'Lord Wellington and the English': Longford, *Years of the Sword*, p. 379 (quoting Foy MSS 26/10/1814)

'an open insult': Campbell, p. 317

'There is nobody': WSD, vol. 9, p. 425, W letter to Liverpool 9/11/1814

245 'I was anxious to consult': Campbell, p. 363

Chapter Sixteen: Duchess, you may give your ball

246 'If they'd kept a frigate': O'Meara, pp. 296–7

247 'Go, my son. Fulfil': Markham, p. 157

'C'est pour vous encore': Fraser, p. 31

'he refused [the chief of staff job]': Shulbrede archive

248 'I have brought you news': Hay, p. 158

'one of the ablest Generals': Smith, p. 247

'Ho! Bonaparte's': ibid., p. 258

'I never remember': Wheeler, pp. 161–4

250 'My throat swelled': Simmons, p. 361

'Stirring accounts of the sieges': Morris, *Recollections*, p. 3

'pressed me to her': Leeke, vol. 1, p. 3

251 'black horse with a long tail': ibid., p. 6

'were abruptly boarded': Mercer, p. 15

252 'He had told the Duke': Fraser, p. 3

'made numerous purchases': Gronow, *Reminiscences*, pp. 37–8

'he generally wore': ibid., p. 38

'whose wife, Emily, gave birth': Foulkes, p. 106

'I am thicker with old Wellington': Gordon, p. 401, letter to Robert Gordon 29/4/1815

253 'The power of appointing': WSD, vol. 10, p. 4, Duke of York letter to W 28/3/1815

254 'It will be admitted': ibid., p. 219, W letter to Bathurst 4/5/1815

'splendid spectacle': Mercer, p. 112

'concluding by exclaiming': ibid., p. 113

255 a hollow in a Brussels park: Foulkes, pp. 121–2

'Duke, I have no wish': Brett-James, *Hundred Days*, p. 39 (quoting Captain William Verner of the 7th Hussars)

256 'so that I hope we should give': WD, vol. 12, p. 346, W letter to Earl of Clancarty 3/5/1815

'By God, I think Blücher': Creevey, p. 228

258 'I suppose they won't': Kincaid, p. 153

'in a careless sort of way': Gronow, *Reminiscences*, p. 38

259 'Napoleon has humbugged': Maxwell, vol. 2, p. 14

'But we shall not stop him': Malmesbury, vol. 2, pp. 445–6

Chapter Seventeen: Blücher has had a damn good hiding

260 'You were lucky not to go': Hay, p. 159

'We had a great ball': Shulbrede archive, letter to Lady Georgiana Lennox 16/6/1815

'to the credit of our battalion': Kincaid, pp. 153–4

261 'upon their ladies parting': Creevey, p. 229

'merry as cricketers': Costello, p. 210

'the fine martial clang': Mercer, p. 121

262 'dull, sullen sound': ibid., p. 126

'provided I am not attacked': Maxwell, vol. 2, p. 44

264 'We were not advancing unobserved': Morris, *Recollections*, pp. 196–7

'their heavy horses': Anton, p. 164

265 '92nd, don't fire': Siborne, p. 386, Winchester memo 27/2/1837

'"Damn it, 92nd"': ibid., pp. 386–7

'was unfortunately commanded by': Morris, *Recollections*, p. 199

266 'Though it's considered': ibid., p. 200

'reduced to a mere skeleton': Siborne, p. 381, Riddock letter to Siborne 11/4/1837

'Some were staggering': Mercer, pp. 128–9

267 'I wanted to find out': Hay, p. 165

'those that were not killed': Croker, vol. 1, p. 330

When the men of the Gordons: Siborne, p. 387

'This was a crisis': Kincaid, p. 158

'I shall begin to think': Robinson, vol. 1, p. 377

268 'I heard him groan': Gronow, *Reminiscences and Recollections*, vol. 1, p. 185

'gained a considerable portion': Kincaid, p. 159; Leach, p. 228

'To sleep was impossible': Costello, p. 212

'God bless me – so I am': Morris, *Recollections*, p. 203

269 'Thus twenty-five or thirty': Llewellyn, p. 65, Ney letter 26/6/1815

Napoleon, in his ham-fisted: Las Cases, vol. 3, part 5, pp. 219ff.

'if my troops were so disposed': Stanhope, p. 109

'dragged out . . . bruised': Houssaye, pp. 105–6

270 'I passed that night': Stanhope, p. 110

'Old Blücher has had': Maxwell, vol. 2, pp. 37–8

271 'I still hold to the original': James, pp. 185–6

272 'regretted that they were obliged': Tomkinson, p. 284

'Make haste, make haste!': Mercer, pp. 139–40

'the very reversing of the limber': ibid., p. 140

273 'away we went': ibid., p. 141

'The order to fire is given': ibid., p. 143

'It will break': ibid., p. 88

'reduced the face of the country': Farmer, pp. 141–2

274 'a man of no very': Mercer, p. 145

'all perfectly still and silent': ibid., pp. 146–7

275 'I have not the slightest idea': Fraser, p. 2

Chapter Eighteen: Hard pounding

276 'I think you ought to make': WSD, vol. 10, p. 501

'They all seemed as gay and unconcerned': Gronow, *Reminiscences and Recollections*, vol. 1, p. 186

277 'I never remember a worse night': Lawrence, p. 141

'the most welcome thing': Todd, p. 117

sent off with a small party: Leeke, p. 15

'collected armfuls of standing corn': Morris, *Recollections*, p. 211

'You often blamed me for smoking': Wheeler, p. 170

'I told him I thought': Morris, *Recollections*, pp. 218–19

'had the effect': Llewellyn, p. 83, Sergeant Robertson

'in rather a strange plight': Hay, p. 174

279 'It was delightful to see': Smith, p. 268

280 'We made a fire': Kincaid, p. 163

281 'No! No!': Pitt Lawrence, p. 117
'We have ninety chances': Houssaye, pp. 157, 177–8, 180
282 'His Majesty desires': Chandler, p. 1067
283 'The success of the battle': Low, p. 123
'Colonel Frazer, you are going': Frazer, pp. 555f., letter 20/6/1815
284 'Burning timbers crashed down': Paget, p. 25
'As yet all was quiet': Leach, p. 235
285 'No, no. Black is black': Fraser, p. 207
'I can scarcely comprehend': O'Meara, p. 113
286 'We saw Buonaparte himself': Kincaid, pp. 165–6
287 'had forced their way through': Siborne, p. 72, Captain A. K. Clark Kennedy
'I dug my spurs': Low, pp. 142–3, Sergeant Major Dickson of the Scots Greys
'It was fearful to see': Llewellyn, p. 84, Sergeant Robertson
'Right shoulders forward': Siborne, pp. 75–6
288 'Charge! Charge the guns!': Low, p. 145, Sergeant Major Dickson of the Scots Greys
'I shall never forget the sight': ibid., pp. 145–6
289 'I committed a great mistake': Siborne, p. 9, Uxbridge letter
'were in the utmost peril': ibid., p. 112, F. Ponsonby letter
290 'I know we ought not': ibid., p. 113
'coming full tilt at me': Hay, pp. 180–1
'You're not dead, you rascal?': Shulbrede archive
291 'Well, Paget, I hope you': Anglesey, p. 135
'The cavalry of other European armies': Gronow, *Reminiscences*, p. 45
'hard pounding': Kaye, vol. 2, p. 101

Chapter Nineteen: Now, Maitland, now's your time!

292 'Suddenly a dark mass': Mercer, p. 157
293 'Forward! The salvation of France': Houssaye, p. 203
'Left, limber up': Mercer, p. 158
295 'No one who was': Gronow, *Reminiscences*, p. 40
'we could not have the slightest': Morris, *Recollections*, p. 219
'The effect is hardly': Mercer, p. 160
his best spongeman, Private Butterworth: ibid., p. 161

296 'The ground, already encumbered': ibid., p. 163

'reaching over his horse's': Morris, *Recollections*, p. 223

'Our poor old Captain': ibid.

'This was a job': Lawrence, p. 145

297 'Without his personal exertion': Frazer, p. 559

'shocking sight': Gronow, *Reminiscences and Recollections*, vol. 1, pp. 70, 190–1

'strewed with the fallen horses': Gronow, *Reminiscences*, pp. 40–1

'dreadfully cut up': Morris, *Recollections*, p. 224

298 'Here come those fools again': Creasy, p. 368 (quoting Ensign Edward Macready)

'The battle is mine': Gronow, *Reminiscences and Recollections*, vol. 1, p. 70

the Prussians had arrived: Croker, vol. 1, p. 124

299 'staff officers whom I sent to Grouchy': O'Meara, p. 249

'kept up a dreadful fire': Leach, p. 237

300 'laughing and joking': Simmons, p. 365

'The finger of providence': Stanhope, p. 184

'Cold and indifferent, nay': Frazer, p. 550

'reining back his horse's head': Pitt Lawrence, pp. 115–16

'Troops? Where do you expect': Houssaye, p. 218

301 'What was my astonishment': Llewellyn, p. 66, Ney letter 26/6/1815

'confident of his own powers': Shaw Kennedy, p. 128

'like a cricket ball': Leeke, p. 39

'Every shot almost took effect': Mercer, p. 166

303 'sounded very like this': Leeke, p. 41

'to make that column feel our fire': Siborne, p. 284

'the Duke of Wellington': Leeke, p. 45

304 'Now, Maitland': Longford, *Years of the Sword*, p. 477

'Guards, get up and charge': Gronow, *Reminiscences and Recollections*, vol. 1, p. 73

'I witnessed several': Gronow, *Reminiscences*, p. 42

'Oh dammit, in for a penny': Anglesey, p. 148; Low, p. 163

'No cheering, my lads': Kincaid, p. 171

'I will ever maintain': ibid., p. 172

305 'The brave men who have survived': Llewellyn, p. 67, Ney

'bareheaded, his face blackened': Houssaye, p. 236

'We were both on horseback': Stanhope, p. 245

'By God, Sir, I have lost my leg': Anglesey, p. 149

306 'Nothing except a battle lost': Shelley, vol. 1, p. 102
    'looking piteously for relief': Morris, *Sergeant Morris*, p. 181
    He offered his help: Tomkinson, p. 315
    'whether it is the dead body': Farmer, p. 149
307 'The bones were sticking up': Gronow, *Reminiscences and Recollections*,
    vol. 1, p. 193
    'Let's have dinner directly': Thornton, pp. 101–2
    'If it is to be taken off': Anglesey, p. 150 (quoting Uxbridge's ADC,
    Captain Wildman)
    'I thought, as he had only lost a leg': Kaye, vol. 2, p. 121
308 'extreme grief': WD, vol. 12, p. 488, W letter to Aberdeen 19/6/1815
    'without betraying the slightest emotion': Costello, p. 217
    'I thought all was over': Shulbrede archive, Ponsonby's red notebook
309 'In my agony of woe': Smith, pp. 286–8 (quoting his wife's account)

Chapter Twenty: See the Conquering Hero Comes

310 'the successful result': WD, vol. 12, p. 484, Waterloo despatch
    'the greatest satisfaction': ibid., p. 483
    'with the greatest gravity': Creevey, pp. 236–7
    'It was the most desperate business': Raglan papers, W letter to W.
    Wellesley-Pole 19/6/1815
312 he later remarked that it was strange: Longford, *Pillar of State*, p. 267
    'Oh yes, plenty of that!': Fraser, p. 73
313 'The lance pierced the lungs': Bessborough, p. 244, Lady Caroline
    Lamb letter to Lord Duncannon 7/7/1815
    He was delighted to discover: Gronow, *Reminiscences and Recollections*,
    vol. 1, p. 205
314 'riddled body held together': Kincaid, p. 285
    'Ere many years': Leach, p. 246
315 'like an old warhorse': Morris, *Sergeant Morris*, p. 232
    'If England should ever require': Wheeler, p. 196
317 'Yes, I should have': Montgomery, p. 23

Bibliography

Adkin, Mark, *The Waterloo Companion*, London, Aurum Press, 2001

Aitchison, John, *An Ensign in the Peninsular War*, ed. W. Thompson, London, Michael Joseph, 1981

Aldington, Richard, *Wellington*, London, Heinemann, 1946

Anglesey, Marquess of, *One Leg: The Life and Letters of Henry William Paget*, London, Jonathan Cape, 1961

Anton, James, *Royal Highlander*, York, Leonaur, 2007 (orig. published as *Retrospect of a Military Life*, 1841)

Arbuthnot, *Journal of Mrs Arbuthnot 1820–1832*, ed. Francis Bamford, 2 vols, London, Macmillan, 1950

Bainville, Jacques, *Napoleon*, London, Jonathan Cape, 1932

Bell, George, *Ensign Bell in the Peninsular War*, York, Leonaur, 2006 (orig. published as *Rough Notes of an Old Soldier*, 1867)

Bessborough, Earl of, *Lady Bessborough and her Family Circle*, London, John Murray, 1940

Bingham, D. A., *A Selection of the Letters and Despatches of the First Napoleon*, 3 vols, London, Chapman & Hall, 1884

Blakeney, Robert, *Light Bob*, York, Leonaur, 2006 (orig. published as *A Boy in the Peninsular War*, 1899)

Blanch, Lesley, ed., *The Game of Hearts: Harriette Wilson and her Memoirs*, London, Gryphon Books, 1957

Brett-James, Eliot, *The Hundred Days*, London, Macmillan, 1964

Brett-James, Eliot, *Wellington at War*, London, Macmillan, 1961

Broughton, Lord John, *Recollections of a Long Life*, London, John Murray, 1909

Browne, Thomas, *The Napoleonic War Journal of Captain Thomas Henry Browne 1807–16*, London, Bodley Head, 1987

Buckingham, Duke of, *Memoirs of the Court and Cabinets of George III*, 2 vols, London, Hurst & Blackett, 1855

Bunbury, Thomas, *Reminiscences of a Veteran*, London, Charles Skeet, 1861

Campbell, Neil, *Napoleon at Fontainebleau and Elba*, London, John Murray, 1869

Cavendish, Lady Harriet, *Harryo: Letters of Lady Harriet Cavendish 1796–1809*, London, John Murray, 1940

Chandler, David, *The Campaigns of Napoleon*, London, Weidenfeld & Nicolson, 1967

Chaptal, Jean Antoine, *Mes souvenirs de Bonaparte*, Paris, Plon, 1893

Cocks, Edward Charles, *Intelligence Officer in the Peninsula: Letters and Diaries of Major the Hon. Edward Charles Cocks*, ed. Julia Page, Tunbridge Wells, Spellmount, 1986

Colborne, John, *A Singular Talent for War*, York, Leonaur, 2007 (orig. published as *The Life of John Colborne, Field-Marshal Lord Seaton*, 1903)

Cole, Maud and Gwyn, Stephen, *Memoirs of Sir Lowry Cole*, London, Macmillan, 1934

Combermere, Mary, Viscountess, *Memoirs and Correspondence of Field Marshal Viscount Combermere*, 2 vols, London, Hurst & Blackett, 1866

Cooke, John, *With the Light Division*, York, Leonaur, 2007 (orig. published in 3 vols as *Memoirs of the Late War and a narrative of events in the South of France and of the attack on New Orleans in 1814 and 1815*, 1831–5)

Cooper, John, *Fusilier Cooper*, York, Leonaur, 2007 (orig. published as *Rough Notes of Seven Campaigns*, 1869)

Costello, Edward, *Rifleman Costello*, York, Leonaur, 2005 (orig. published as *Adventures of a Soldier*, 1841)

Craufurd, Alexander, *General Craufurd and his Light Division*, Uckfield, Sussex, Naval and Military Press, undated facsimile of orig. published in London by Griffith Farrar Okeden & Welsh, 1891

Creasy, Sir Edward, *Fifteen Decisive Battles of the World*, London, Richard Bentley, 1879

Creevey, Thomas, *A Selection from the Correspondence of the Late Thomas Creevey*, ed. Herbert Maxwell, London, John Murray, 1904

Croker, John Wilson, *The Croker Papers 1808–57*, 3 vols, London, John Murray, 1885

Crumplin, Michael, *Men of Steel: Surgery in the Napoleonic Wars*, Shrewsbury, Quiller Press, 2007

Delaforce, Patrick, *Wellington the Beau*, Moreton-in-Marsh, Gloucestershire, Windrush Press, 1990

Dobbs, John, *Gentlemen in Red: Recollections of an Old 52nd Man*, York, Leonaur, 2008 (orig. published 1863)

Donaldson, Joseph, *Donaldson of the 94th Scots Brigade*, York, Leonaur, 2008 (orig. published as *Recollections of the Eventful Life of a Soldier*, 1838)

Douglas, John, *Douglas's Tale of the Peninsula and Waterloo*, ed. Stanley Monick, Barnsley, Leo Cooper, 1997

Eaton, Charlotte, *Waterloo Days: The Narrative of an English Woman Resident at Brussels in June 1815*, London, George Bell, 1888

Edwards, Peter, *Talavera: Wellington's Early Peninsula Victories 1808–9*, Swindon, Crowood Press, 2005

Esdaile, Charles, *Peninsular Eyewitness*, Barnsley, Pen and Sword, 2008

Esdaile, Charles, *The Peninsular War*, London, Penguin, 2003

Farmer, George, *Adventures of a Light Dragoon in the Napoleonic Wars*, York, Leonaur, 2006 (orig. published 1844)

Fortescue, J. W., *A History of the British Army*, vols 4–10, London, Macmillan, 1906–20

Foulkes, Nick, *Dancing into Battle*, London, Phoenix, 2007

Fraser, Sir William, *Words on Wellington*, London, George Routledge, 1902 (http://www.archive.org/details/wordsonwellingtooofrasuoft)

Frazer, Sir Augustus Simon, *Letters*, London, Longman, Brown, Green, Longmans & Roberts, 1859

Garrety, Thomas, *Soldiering with the Division*, York, Leonaur, 2007 (orig. published as *Memoirs of a Late Sergeant in the 43rd*, 1835)

Girod de L'Ain, Maurice, *Vie militaire de Général Foy*, Paris, Plon, 1900

Gleason, Janet, *An Aristocratic Affair*, London, Bantam Press, 2006

Gleig, G. R., *The Hussar: The Story of Sergeant Norbert Landsheit*, Philadelphia, G. B. Ziegler, 1845 (http://books.google.com/books?id=NoQgAAAAM AAJ&oe=UTF-8)

Gleig, G. R., *Life of Wellington*, London, Longman, Green, Longman & Roberts, 1862 (http://www.archive.org/details/lifeofarthurfirsooglei)

Gleig, G. R., *The Subaltern*, Edinburgh, William Blackwood, 2nd edn, 1826

Glover, Michael, *The Peninsular War*, London, Penguin, 2001

Gordon, Alexander, *At Wellington's Right Hand: Letters of Lieutenant-Colonel Sir Alexander Gordon 1808–15*, ed. Rory Muir, Stroud, Sutton Publishing for the Army Records Society, 2003

Grattan, William, *Adventures with the Connaught Rangers 1809–14*, London, Greenhill Books, 2003

Green, William, *Bugler and Officer of the 95th Rifles*, York, Leonaur, 2005

Greville, Charles, *The Greville Memoirs: A Journal of the Reigns of King George IV and William IV*, 3 vols, London, Longmans Green, 1875

Griffiths, Major Arthur, *Wellington Memorial*, London, George Allen, 1897

Gronow, Rees, *Reminiscences*, London, Smith Elder, 1862

Gronow, Rees, *Reminiscences and Recollections*, 2 vols, London, John Nimmo, 1900 (http://www.archive.org/stream/reminiscencesreco1gron/reminis-cencesreco1gron_djvu.txt)

Hale, James, *Journal of a Late Sergeant of the 9th Regiment of Foot*, London, Longman, 1826

Harris, Benjamin, *Recollections of Rifleman Harris*, London, Cassell, 2006

Hay, Captain William, *Reminiscences 1808–15*, ed. S. Wood, London, Simpkin, Marshall, 1901

Headlam, John, *Six Centuries of RA History*, Woolwich, RA Institution, 1944

Henegan, Richard, *Campaigns with the Field Train*, York, Leonaur, 2007 (orig. published as *Seven years campaigning in the Peninsula and the Netherlands*, 1846)

Hennell, George, *A Gentleman Volunteer: Letters of George Hennell from the Peninsular War*, ed. Michael Glover, London, Heinemann, 1979

Hibbert, Christopher, *Wellington: A Personal History*, London, HarperCollins, 1997

Holmes, Richard, *Redcoat*, London, HarperCollins, 2001

Holmes, Richard, *Wellington: The Iron Duke*, London, HarperCollins, 2002

Houssaye, Henri, *1815 Waterloo*, London, A&C Black, 1900

Howarth, David, *Waterloo: A Near Run Thing*, Moreton-in-Marsh, Gloucestershire, Windrush Press, 2003

James, Colonel W. H., *The Campaign of 1815*, London, Blackwood, 1908

Kaye, J. W., *The Life and Correspondence of Major-General Sir John Malcolm*, London, Smith Elder, 1856

Keegan, John, *The Face of Battle*, London, Pimlico, 2004

Keegan, John, *The Mask of Command*, London, Jonathan Cape, 1987

Kincaid, John, *Tales from the Rifle Brigade*, Barnsley, Pen and Sword, 2005 (orig. published as *Adventures in the Rifle Brigade*, 1830, and *Random Shots from a Rifleman*, 1835)

Knowles, Robert, *The War in the Peninsula: Letters of Robert Knowles*, London, Bolton Journal and Guardian, 1909

Lamare, Jean-Baptiste-Hippolyte, *An Account of the Second Defence of the Fortress of Badajoz, by the French, in 1812*, London, T. Egerton, 1824

Landmann, George, *Recollections of my Military Life*, 2 vols, London, Hurst & Blackett, 1854

Larpent, F. Seymour, *The Journal of F. Seymour Larpent*, 3 vols, London, Richard Bentley, 1853

Las Cases, Emmanuel de, *Memorial of St Helena*, 4 vols, London, Henry Colburn, 1823

Lawrence, William, *Sergeant Lawrence*, York, Leonaur, 2007 (orig. published as *The Autobiography of Sergeant William Lawrence*, 1886)

Leach, Jonathan *Captain of the 95th Rifles*, York, Leonaur 2005 (orig. published as *Rough Sketches of an Old Soldier*, 1831)

Leeke, William, *History of Lord Seaton's 52nd Regiment*, London, Hatchards, 1866

Leslie, Charles, *Military Journal of Colonel Leslie 1807–1832*, Aberdeen, Aberdeen University Press, 1887

Leveson Gower, Lord Granville, *Private Correspondence of Lord Granville Leveson Gower, 1787 to 1821*, 2 vols, London, John Murray, 1916

Llewellyn, Frederick, ed., *Waterloo Recollections*, York, Leonaur, 2007

Longford, Elizabeth, *Wellington: Pillar of State*, London, Weidenfeld & Nicolson, 1969

Longford, Elizabeth, *Wellington: The Years of the Sword*, London, Harper & Row, 1969

Low, E. S., *With Napoleon at Waterloo and Other Unpublished Documents of the Waterloo and Peninsula Campaigns*, ed. Mackenzie Macbride, London, Francis Griffiths, 1911

McGrigor, Sir James, *The Autobiography and Services of Sir James McGrigor, Bart, Late Director General of the Army Medical Department*, London, Longman, Green, Longman & Roberts, 1861

Malmesbury, James Harris, Earl of, *Letters of the First Earl of Malmesbury*, 2 vols, London, Richard Bentley, 1870

Marchand, Leslie, *Byron*, 2 vols, London, John Murray, 1957

Markham, Felix, *The Bonapartes*, London, Weidenfeld & Nicolson, 1975

Maxwell, Sir Herbert, *The Life of Wellington*, 2 vols, London, Sampson, Low, Marston, 1899

Mercer, Alexander Cavalié, *Journal of the Campaign of 1815*, York, Leonaur, 2008 (orig. published as *Journal of the Waterloo Campaign*, 1870)

Montgomery, Viscount, *A History of Warfare*, London, Collins, 1968

Morris, Sergeant Thomas, *Recollections of Military Service*, London, James Madde, 1845

Morris, Sergeant Thomas, *Sergeant Morris of the 73rd Foot*, York, Leonaur, 2007

Muir, Rory, *Britain and the Defeat of Napoleon*, New Haven and London, Yale University Press, 1996

Napier, William, *History of the War in the Peninsula and the South of France,*

1807–14, New York, Sadlier (http://www.archive.org/details/history ofwarinpeoonapi)

Napier, William, *Life and Opinions of Charles Napier*, London, John Murray, 1857

Neale, Adam, *Letters from Portugal and Spain*, London, Richard Phillips, 1809

Oman, Sir Charles, *A History of the Peninsular War*, London, Greenhill Books, 1996

O'Meara, Barry, *Napoleon in Exile*, Philadelphia, Carey & Lea, 1822

O'Neill, Private Charles, *Private O'Neill: The Recollections of an Irish Rogue of HM 28th Regt*, York, Leonaur, 2007 (orig. published 1851)

Paget, Julian, *Second to None: The Coldstream Guards 1650–2000*, London, Leo Cooper, 2000

Pitt Lawrence, Sir William, *Three Years with the Duke of Wellington in Private Life*, London, Saunders & Otley, 1853

Roberts, Andrew, *Napoleon and Wellington*, London, Weidenfeld & Nicolson, 2001

Robinson, H. B., *Memoirs of Sir Thomas Picton*, 2 vols, London, Richard Bentley, 1836

Schaumann, August, *On the Road with Wellington: The Diary of a War Commissary*, London, Greenhill Books, 1999 (orig. published 1924)

Severn, John, *Architects of Empire: The Duke of Wellington and his Brothers*, Norman, University of Oklahoma Press, 2007

Shaw Kennedy, Sir James, *Notes on the Battle of Waterloo*, London, John Murray, 1865

Shelley, Lady Frances, *The Diary of Frances, Lady Shelley 1767–1817*, ed. Richard Edgcumbe, 2 vols, London, John Murray, 1912

Sherer, G. Moyle, *Recollections of the Peninsula*, London, Longman, Rees, Orme & Green, 5th edn, 1827

Siborne, Major General H. T., *Waterloo Letters*, London, Greenhill Books, 1993 (orig. published 1891)

Simmons, George, *A British Rifleman: Journals and Correspondence of Major George Simmons*, London, A&C Black, 1899

Smith, Harry, *Autobiography of Lieutenant-General Sir Harry Smith*, London, John Murray, 1903

Stanhope, Philip Henry, *Conversations with the Duke of Wellington*, London, Prion, 1998

Stewart, Captain P. F., *History of the 12th Royal Lancers*, London, Oxford University Press, 1950

Surtees, William, *Surtees of the 95th Rifles*, York, Leonaur, 2006 (orig. published as *Twenty-Five Years in the Rifle Brigade*, 1833)

Thornton, James, *Your Obedient Servant*, Exeter, Webb & Bower, 1985

Todd, Thomas, aka Howell, Thomas, *Bayonets, Bugles and Bonnets*, York, Leonaur, 2005 (orig. published as *Journal of a Soldier of the 71st, 1806–15*, 1828)

Tomkinson, William, *With Wellington's Light Cavalry*, York, Leonaur, 2006 (orig. published as *Diary of a Cavalry Officer*, 1894)

Urban, Mark, *The Man who Broke Napoleon's Codes*, London, Faber & Faber, 2001

Urban, Mark, *The Rifles*, London, Faber & Faber, 2004

Wellesley, Jane, *A Journey through my Family*, London, Weidenfeld & Nicolson, 2008

Weller, Jac, *Wellington at Waterloo*, New York, Thomas Crowell, 1967

Weller, Jac, *Wellington in the Peninsula*, London, Greenhill, 1962

Wellington, Duke of, *Wellington Anecdotes*, London, 1852

Wellington, Duke of, *The Dispatches of Field Marshal the Duke of Wellington*, 13 vols, ed. John Gurwood, London, John Murray, 1837–8

Wellington, Duke of, *Supplementary Despatches and Memoranda of Field Marshal Arthur, Duke of Wellington*, ed. his son the Duke of Wellington, 11 vols, London, John Murray, 1858–64

Wellington, Duke of, *Selections from the Despatches and General Orders*, London, John Murray, 1851

Wheeler, Private William, *The Letters of Private Wheeler*, ed. B. Liddell Hart, Moreton-in-Marsh, Gloucestershire, Windrush Press, 1993

Illustration credits

© Art Archive/Musée de L'Armée Paris/photo Gianni Dagli Orti: 16 above, *Napoleon at Fontainebleau* 1814, painting by Paul Delaroche. Charles Bell: 7 below, from *Illustrations of the Great Operations of Surgery* 1821, photograph courtesy of Michael Crumplin. By kind permission of Madeleine, Countess Bessborough: 15 above, *Colonel the Hon. Frederick Ponsonby, 12th Light Dragoons at the Battle of Waterloo* 1877, painting by Henri-Felix-Emmanuel Philippoteaux. © The British Library Board: 2 below, etching from George Walker's *Costume of Yorkshire* 1814. © The Trustees of the British Museum/ Department of Prints and Drawings: 11 below, *The Master of Ordnance Exercising his Hobby!* 1819 caricature by Isaac Cruikshank. © Mary Evans Picture Library: 11 above left. © Getty Images: 3 above left, 11 centre left, 11 centre right painting by Louis Courtat/Theatre de l'Odeon, Paris. Rees Gronow: 10 above right, frontispiece from *The Reminiscences and Recollections of Captain Gronow* 1889. © Philip Mould Ltd, London/Bridgeman Art Library: 16 below, study for *The Waterloo Banquet* (detail) 1836 by John William Salter. © Courtesy of the Council of the National Army Museum, London: 1 above *The Landing of the British Army at Mondego Bay 1808* watercolour by Henri L'Eveque for the series *Campaigns of the British Army in Portugal* 1812; 1 below, *Passage of the Douro by the Division under the Command of Lt Gen the Hon Edward Paget* line engraving by M. Fittler after Henri L'Eveque from the series *Campaigns of the British Army in Portugal* 1812; 3 below, *A View of the Sierra de Busaco at St. Antonio de Cantaro*, one of 16 aquatints engraved by Charles Turner after Major Thomas St Clair published 1812, from *A Series of Views of the Principal Occurrences of the Campaigns in Spain and Portugal, Peninsular War, 1810–1811*; 4 centre, *Lieutenant-General Rowland, Lord Hill* 1819 painting by George Dawe; 4 below, *Battle of Fuentes d'Onoro, taken from the right of the position occupied by the 1st, 3rd and 7th Divisions on the 5th May, 1811* aquatint engraved by Charles Turner after Major Thomas St Clair, published 1812 from *A Series of Views . . .*; 5 below, *View of the Pass of the Tagus at Villa Velha into the Alemtego by the Allied Army, on the 20th May 1811* aquatint engraved by Charles Turner after Major Thomas St Clair, published 1812 from *A Series of Views . . .*; 6 above, *The Storming of Ciudad Rodrigo 19 Jan 1813* aquatint by Thomas Sutherland after William Heath, published 1815 from *Napoleonic Wars 1799–1815: The Martial Achievements of Great Britain and Her Allies from 1799 to 1815*; 6 below, *Two officers of the Rifle Brigade examining the breaches in the walls of the city of Ciudad Rodrigo on 20th January, the day after its storming on 19th January 1812* watercolour by Cornet Thomas Livingstone Mitchell; 7 above, *The Devil's Own* watercolour en grisaille signed and dated by Richard Caton Woodville 1908; 8 below, *Soldiers on a March* 1811 coloured etching by George Moutard Woodward after Thomas Rowlandson; 9 above, *Battle of Salamanca, July 22, 1812* coloured aquatint by G. Lewis after John Augustus Atkinson published 1813; 9 below, *Victory of Vittoria, 21 June 1813* coloured aquatint by H. Moses and F. C. Lewis after J. M. Wright published 1814; 10 above, left *Wellington at Sorauren, 27 July 1813* painting by Thomas Jones Barker 1853; 10 below, *Battle of Nivelle, 10 Nov 1813* aquatint by Thomas Sutherland after William Heath, published 1815 from *Napoleonic Wars 1799–1815 . . .*; 12–13, *Centre of the British Army at La Haye Sainte, June 18th 1815* coloured etched aquatint by Thomas Sutherland after William Heath, from the series *Waterloo Scenes* published 1816; 14 left, *Attack on the British Squares by French Cavalry, Battle of Waterloo* (detail) watercolour by Denis Dighton 1815; 14 below, *The Battle of Waterloo Decided By The Duke of Wellington* aquatint by Dubourg after John Augustus Atkinson 1815 from *Historic, Military and Naval anecdotes, of personal valour, bravery and particular incidents which occurred to the armies of Great Britain, 1803–15, and her allies, in the last long-contested war terminating with the Battle of Waterloo* published 1819. © National Portrait Gallery, London: 1 above left painting by Robert Home 1804, 3 above right painting by Martin Archer Shee 1812, 9 above left painting by Thomas Heaphy 1813–14. © National Trust Photo Library/John Hammond: 15

below, *Uxbridge and Wellington After Waterloo* (detail) painting by Constantinius Fidelio Coene (Plas Newydd, the Collection of the Marquess of Anglesey on long-term loan to The National Trust). Private Collections: 4 above left, 4 above right, 5 above by kind permission of Jane Luard. The Royal Collection © 2010, Her Majesty Queen Elizabeth II: 14 above right, *The Battle of Waterloo: The Charge of the Second Brigade of Cavalry* (detail) painting c.1812–17 by Denis Dighton. © The Royal Green Jackets (Rifles) Museum: 2 above right, 8 above left. August Ludolf Friedrich Schaumann: 2 above left, frontispiece from *On the Road with Wellington* 1827, English translation of Schaumann's diary 1924. Harry Smith: 8 above right, from *The Autobiography of Lieutenant-General Sir Harry Smith* 1901.

Index

Index

NOTE: Ranks and titles are generally the highest mentioned in the text

Aberdeen, George Hamilton Gordon, 4th Earl of, 42, 101–2, 170, 185, 236, 307

Aboukir, battle of (1801), 30

Adair, Captain Robert, 307

Adour, river, 225–7, 229

Aitchison, John, 176, 195, 208

Álava, General Miguel de, 161, 229–30, 232, 300

Alba, Spain, 166

Albert, Prince Consort, 315–16

Albuera, battle of (1811), 118–19

Aldea Tejada, near Salamanca, 160–1

Alexander I, Tsar of Russia, 235, 247

Almeida, Portugal, 82–4, 90, 95, 107, 117–18

Alten, General Charles, Baron von, 203

Andalusia, 184–5

Anglesey, 1st Marquess of see Uxbridge, 2nd Earl of

Anson, General Sir George, 65

Anton, James, 264–5

artillery: types of shot, 25, 95n; Wellington acquires, 73; at siege of Ciudad Rodrigo, 119, 129; Dickson commands, 119; operation of guns, 129–30; at siege of Badajoz, 138; at siege of Burgos, 173; at siege of San Sebastián, 206–7, 213–14; development, 213–14; at Waterloo, 282, 284, 286; see also Royal Horse Artillery

Assaye, battle of (1803), 3

Austria: defeated at Wagram, 69; agrees armistice with Napoleon (1813), 188; and Napoleon's 1815 campaign, 256; see also Francis I, Emperor

Badajoz, Spain: on Masséna's route to Portugal, 82; Gordon hopes to capture, 107; Wellington advances on, 118–20; strength of fortifications, 126, 138–40, 143–4, 147; sacked by British, 134–5, 151–3; siege (1812), 138–42; assault on, 144–8; Wellington's account of battle, 153

Baker, Ezekiel: rifle design, 17

Barba de Puerco, Portugal, 117

Baring, Major George, 299

Barrosa, battle of (1811), 103–4

Bathurst, Henry, 3rd Earl, 206, 226, 254, 310

battalions: role in battle, 16–17, 58

Bayonne, 225–8, 230

Beckwith, Lt Colonel Sydney: at Vimeiro, 24; humanity, 34, 40, 72; commands 1/95th, 40, 72; appoints Smith as ADC, 89; rescues Erskine at Sabugal, 106; wounded, 106–7; at Vera, 225

Bell, Ensign George: on General Hill, 10; and hardships on retreat to Ciudad Rodrigo, 178; on training under Wellington, 186; welcomes move to Vitoria, 187; at battle of Vitoria, 192, 195; on availability of Spanish girls, 204; in Pyrenees campaign, 210–11; at battle of Sorauren, 212; at Vera, 224; at river Nive, 226–7; enjoys peace in southern France, 236

Belle Alliance, La (farm, Waterloo), 305

Beresford, General William Carr, Viscount: in Portugal, 37, 44; and Wellington's views on being second-in-command, 71; at Bussaco, 93, 95; at battle of Albuera, 118–19; besieges Badajoz, 118; opposes Marmont at Salamanca, 157, 160; letter from Wellington on siege of San Sebastián, 214; at Toulouse, 231

Berthier, Alexandre, 285n

Bessborough family, 39

Bessborough, Harriet, Countess of, 39, 54, 170, 243, 313

Bevan, Colonel Charles, 117–18

Bidasoa, river, 204, 217–19

Blakeney, Robert, 103, 149

Blücher, Marshal Prince Gebhard von: supports Wellington at Waterloo, 57, 269–71, 276; Wellington meets in Paris, 236; praises Mercer's battery, 254; and Napoleon's movements (1815), 255–8; at Ligny, 262–3, 268–9; injured, 269–70; Napoleon discounts joining up with Wellington, 282; meets Wellington after Waterloo victory, 305; Wellington praises for support at Waterloo, 310; and Napoleon's conduct of Waterloo battle, 311; death, 312–13

Bonaparte, Jérôme: at Waterloo, 282–4

Bonaparte, Joseph: as King of Spain, 10; failure in Spain, 36; commands forces at Madrid, 56, 169, 175; at Talavera, 68–9; and Napoleon's orders to remove Wellington from Portugal, 77; sends orders to Marmont at Salamanca, 157; orders Soult to abandon Andalusia, 184; defeated at Vitoria, 189–90, 203; escapes from Vitoria leaving treasure and goods, 197–200; silver chamber pot acquired by 14th Light Dragoons, 199

Bonaparte, Marie-Letizia (Napoleon's mother; 'Madame Mère'), 246–7

Bonnet, General, 164–5

Borghese, Princess Pauline (Napoleon's sister), 242

Borough, R., 20

Brazen, HMS, 23

Brazil, Sergeant Pat, 133

Brennier, General Antoine-François, 26, 30, 117–18, 164

Britain: casualties, 30, 116, 118, 134, 154, 166, 201, 209, 229, 238, 268, 291, 306; social disparity, 38–9; army officers, 43, 80–1, 125, 253; behaviour of troops, 51–2, 134–5, 180–1, 221; troops fraternise with French, 64–5, 227; food and accommodation shortages, 122; fever among troops, 123; army deaths from cold and disease in Spain, 185; inadequate honours and rewards for Peninsular veterans, 238–9, 314; as world power after Waterloo, 311

British Brigades: 94th Scots, 40, 109; Guards, 304; Light, 72

British Divisions: 3rd, 80, 83, 105, 109, 120, 140, 143, 146, 160–2, 164, 193–5, 286–7; 4th, 140, 142, 148,

150, 164, 193; 5th, 140, 150, 214;
7th, 111–14; Light, 13, 83–4,
105–7, 112–13, 116, 128, 130, 140,
142–3, 148, 150, 178, 192–4, 214,
220, 225
British Regiments: 1st Dragoon
Guards, 289; 1st Foot (Royal Scots),
306; 1st Hussars, 65; 5th Foot, 149;
7th Fusiliers, 60, 68; 7th Hussars,
272; 9th Foot, 8, 93; 11th Light
Dragoons, 289; 12th Light
Dragoons, 103–4, 155, 157, 165,
179, 196, 220, 228, 254, 266,
289–91; 14th Light Dragoons, 199,
228; 16th Light Dragoons, 172, 254,
289; 20th Light Dragoons, 14, 28–9;
23rd Light Dragoons, 39, 54, 60,
65–6, 75–80; 27th Foot, 306; 29th
Foot, 7, 16, 19, 30, 60–4, 118; 34th
(Cumberland Gentlemen), 210, 226,
236; 40th Foot, 30, 60, 145; 43rd
Light Infantry, 27, 72, 82, 192; 48th
Foot (Northamptonshire), 64, 69;
50th Foot ('Dirty Half-Hundred'),
25–6, 28; 52nd Light Infantry, 72,
83, 85, 94, 228–9, 250, 277, 301,
303, 310; 53rd Foot, 68; 69th (South
Lincolnshire), 264; 71st Foot
(Highland Light Infantry), 12, 97,
109, 115–16, 192, 210, 264; 73rd
Foot (Highland), 250, 264–6; 85th
Foot, 112; 88th Foot (Connaught
Rangers), 80, 92–3, 109, 115–16,
126, 130, 133–4, 147, 154, 162–3,
169, 194, 237; 92nd (Gordon
Highlanders), 211, 263, 265, 267,
277, 287; 95th (Rifles), 17, 24, 40,
72, 82, 112, 180, 192, 194, 250, 260,
261–3, 268, 280, 284; Cumberland
Hussars, 297; Enniskilling Dragoons,
289; Essex, 266; Guards regiments,
60, 68, 282, 284; Royal Dragoons,
287, 289; Royal Highland
Regiment, 264; Royal Horse
Guards, 289; Scots Greys, 287–8,
289
Broglie, Victor, Duc de, 243
Brotherwood, William, 29
Browne, Lieutenant Thomas, 123
Brunswickers: at Waterloo, 294–7
Brussels: British troops in, 249; as
potential target for Napoleon, 251,
256; Wellington in, 251, 254–6;
Duchess of Richmond's ball, 255,
257–8, 260; during battle of
Waterloo, 298 & n; Wellington
returns to after Waterloo, 307
Bülow, Count Friedrich Wilhelm von,
298
Bunbury, Thomas, 48
Burdett, Sir Francis, 183
Burgos: French at, 172–3; Wellington
besieges, 173–6, 182; Wellington
withdraws from, 176, 182–3; blown
up by French on retreat, 188
burials: on field, 94
Burrard, Lt General Sir Harry, 11,
23–4, 30–2
Burton, Sergeant, 277
Bussaco, battle of (1810), 91–6
Butterworth, Private, 295
Byron, George Gordon, 6th Baron:
affair with Lady Caroline Lamb, 30,
100, 170, 241; *Childe Harold*, 33

Cadiz, 169, 185
Cadoux, Daniel, 218
Caillou, Le (house, Waterloo), 281
Caldwell, Thomas, 178
Calvarassa, near Salamanca, 159
Cambronne, General Pierre-Jacques-
Etienne, 305
Campbell, Brigadier Alexander, 60,
165
Campbell, Colonel Neil, 234–5, 244–6
Canning, Colonel, 306

Canning, George: dispute with
Castlereagh over command in
Peninsula, 11; opposes Napoleon,
37
Castel Sarrasin, France, 236
Castlereagh, Robert Stewart, Viscount:
gives command in Portugal to
Wellington, 9–11; as Secretary of
State for War, 9; and Wellington's
advance in Portugal, 23; and
Wellington's negotiations for Cintra
Convention, 33; opposes Napoleon,
37; memorandum from Wellington
on strategy in Peninsula, 38; and
Wellington's view of men's
conduct, 51; and Wellington's
complaints about Spanish allies, 76;
supports Wellington in Peninsula,
182; and Napoleon's exile to Elba,
234; and Wellington's
ambassadorship in Paris, 244; and
Congress of Vienna, 245;
reprimands Neil Campbell, 246
Catholic Emancipation, 242, 312
cavalry: shortage in Portugal, 23; in
action at Vimeiro, 28; impetuosity
and rashness, 28–9, 66–7, 83, 156,
168, 288, 291; strength increased,
54; at Talavera, 65; at battle of
Fuentes d'Oñoro, 113; engagements
in 1812, 155–6; action at Waterloo,
156, 287–9, 297–8; at Salamanca,
161–2, 164; failure at Vitoria, 196,
201; in 1815 campaign, 261, 263,
272
Ceira, river (Portugal), 105
Celorico, Portugal, 106
Charleroi, Belgium, 257, 259
Cintra, Convention of (1808), 32–3
Ciudad Rodrigo, Spain: on Masséna's
route to Portugal, 82; Craufurd at,
83; French hold, 109; assault on,
130–3; Wellington awarded bonus

for conquest of, 137; Wellington
and Hill retreat to, 177, 181; troops
overwinter in (1812–13), 185–7
Clark Kennedy, Captain A., 287
Clausel, General Bertrand, comte,
164–5, 168–9, 172–3, 190, 201
Clinton, Lt General Sir Henry, 165
Cloup, Jacques, 229
Côa, river, 84–8, 106
Cobbett, William, 32
Cochan, Joseph, 20
Cocks, Major Charles, 125, 169, 173–4
Colborne, Colonel Sir John (later 1st
Baron Seaton): attacks redoubt at
Ciudad Rodrigo, 128; praises
Craufurd, 136; wounded, 136;
Smith admires as brigade
commander, 218; advance in
southern France, 220–1, 225; at
Nivelle, 223; criticises Wellington
for isolating Hill on Nive, 227, 231;
attack on Orthez, 228–9; on battle
of Toulouse, 231; and Leeke, 250,
277; Wellington admires, 250; at
Waterloo, 301–3; Wellington fails
to mention in Waterloo Despatch,
310; at 37th anniversary celebrations
of Waterloo (1852), 316
Cole, General Lowry, 124, 164–5,
210–11
Colville, Major General Charles, 102
Combermere, Viscount see Cotton, Lt
General Sir Stapleton
commissaries, 41–2
Congreve, Sir William, 273
Cooke, John, 126, 140, 143, 157–8,
192, 220, 237
Cooper, John, 60, 67–8, 210, 212
Copenhagen (Wellington's horse), 262
& n, 276, 279, 305, 307
Corunna, Spain, 37, 40, 177
Costello, Ned: enlists, 40; disparages
Portuguese, 46; force-marches with

Craufurd to reinforce Wellington, 72–3; on Cuesta, 74; accidentally slaps Craufurd, 76–7; in fight on Côa, 85–6; wounded, 89; humanity, 105; at Fuentes d'Oñoro, 111–13; at Ciudad Rodrigo, 127, 131–2, 135; in forlorn hope at Badajoz, 143–5, 147; and sack of Badajoz, 151–2; at Vitoria, 193–4; on looting after Vitoria, 197–8; in France, 236; and companion's wife's infidelity, 241; rejoins Wellington for 1815 campaign, 250; preparations for Waterloo, 261–2; loses finger at Quatre-Bras, 268; on amputations after Waterloo, 308; later career, 314

Cotton, Lt General Sir Stapleton (*later* Viscount Combermere), 91, 156, 164, 253 & n

Crane (huntsman), 123

Craufurd, Charles, 77

Craufurd, Mary (*née* Holland), 41

Craufurd, Brigadier General Robert ('Black Bob'): commands light infantry in Peninsula, 40, 55, 72, 83–4; character and harsh discipline, 41, 71, 76–7, 181; hurries towards Talavera, 60, 72–3; fails to rescue British cavalry, 83; stands and fights on Côa, 84–8; rows with Picton, 88, 116; and wounded Simmons, 89; at Bussaco, 94; recklessness, 99; home leave, 103; returns to Peninsula, 107; in battle of Fuentes d'Oñoro, 112–14; ignores Wellington's order to support Picton, 120; on desertions, 122; at Ciudad Rodrigo, 128, 130–2; shot, 132; death, 136

Creevey, Thomas, 256, 260, 310

Cuesta, General Gregorio García de la, 56–62, 74–6, 171, 271

cuirassiers (French heavy cavalry), 263–7, 288, 293–7

Dalhousie, George, 9th Earl, 191, 193–4, 205

Dalrymple, Lt General Sir Hew Whitefoord: given command in Portugal, 11; negotiates Convention of Cintra, 32

Deacon, Ensign, 268

Deacon, Waterloo, 268

Delaborde, General Henri, 15, 18, 20

D'Erlon, Jean-Baptiste Drouet, Count, 269, 285–6, 288–9, 292, 303

Devonshire, Georgiana, Duchess of, 39

Devonshire, William George Cavendish, 6th Duke of, 100

Díaz, Juan Martín ('El Empecinado'), 171

Dickson, Colonel Alexander: at sieges of Ciudad Rodrigo and Badajoz, 119, 138; at siege of San Sebastián, 206, 216

Dickson, Corporal John, 287–8

Dobbs, John, 44, 72–3, 193

Donaldson, Joseph: in Portugal, 40, 89, 102, 104; at Fuentes d'Oñoro, 109–10; narrow escape at El Bodón, 120; at Ciudad Rodrigo, 128, 136; in assault on Badajoz, 146; on plundering of Badajoz, 152; at Salamanca, 162; on soldier's abandoned wife, 178; and hardships on retreat from Madrid, 180; on loss of comrades, 238

Donegal, HMS, 9

Dos Casas, river (Spain), 109

Douglas, John, 163

Douro (Duero), river (Portugal/Spain), 46–9, 157, 172, 176

Dubreton, General Jean-Louis, 173–4

Dutch–Belgian forces: at Quatre-Bras, 262–3; at Waterloo, 286

Ebro, river, 175, 188, 201
Elba: Napoleon exiled to, 234–5, 244;
    Napoleon escapes from, 246–8
El Bodón, Spain, 120
Elizondo, Spain, 211
Elvas, Portugal, 82
Erlon see D'Erlon
Erskine, Major General Sir William,
    83, 103, 106–7, 117–18, 286n
Ewart, Sergeant Charles, 288

Faris, Lieutenant George, 133
Farmer, George, 43, 273
Fitzherbert, Maria Anne, 253n
Fletcher, Lt Colonel Richard:
    constructs Lines of Torres Vedras,
    79; as chief engineer at sieges of
    Ciudad Rodrigo and Badajoz,
    127–8, 138; wounded, 140; at
    siege of San Sebastián, 206; killed,
    215
Flood, Sir Frederick, 182
forlorn hope: at Ciudad Rodrigo,
    130–4; at Badajoz, 214; at San
    Sebastián, 214
Foy, General Maximilien, 167, 244,
    283–4
Foz de Arouce, Portugal, 105
France: treatment of Portuguese, 14,
    104; casualties, 30, 69, 110, 116,
    118, 134, 163, 166, 184, 201, 227,
    268, 306; Portuguese revenge on
    troops, 31, 49–50; occupation of
    Peninsula, 38; strength of forces in
    Spain, 54, 168–9, 187; troops
    fraternise with British, 64–5, 227;
    superior army medical care, 90;
    army retreats from Portugal, 105,
    117; codes intercepted and broken,
    187, 199; effect of Vitoria defeat,
    201; Wellington plans to enter, 219;
    and abolition of slave trade, 242;
    economic collapse and unpopularity

of Louis XVIII, 243; see also
    cuirassiers; Imperial Guard
Francis I, Emperor of Austria, 235
Franks, Ensign, 299
Fraser, William, 238–9, 247n
Frazer, Colonel Sir Augustus, 206–9,
    214, 283, 293–4, 297, 300
Frederick William III, King of Prussia,
    235
Freese, Arthur, 240
Fremantle, William, 101
Freneda, Portugal, 18
Fuentes d'Oñoro (Spain), battle of
    (1811), 107–16, 118

Gamarra Mayor (Vitoria), Spain,
    195
Garrety, Thomas: enlists, 72; on
    battlefield dead, 74; at Côa river,
    86–7, 106–7; on guns at siege of
    Ciudad Rodrigo, 130; in assault on
    Ciudad Rodrigo, 132; at Badajoz,
    141; later career, 314
Genappe, Belgium, 272–3, 281
George III, King: and Hanover, 42
George IV, King see George, Prince of
    Wales
George, Prince of Wales (later Prince
    Regent and King George IV): on
    Wellington's retreat strategy in
    Portugal, 97, 101; sends officers to
    Wellington, 125; awards earldom to
    Wellington, 137; appoints
    Wellington field marshal, 202; and
    Napoleon's exile to Elba, 234;
    liaison with Mrs Fitzherbert, 253n;
    opposes Catholic Emancipation,
    312
Ghent, Peace of (1814), 245
Gilder, Mr (surgeon), 307
Gleig, George, 214–15
Gneisenau, General August, Count
    von, 270

Gordon, Lt Colonel Sir Alexander: accompanies Wellington to Lisbon, 42; disparages Spaniards, 75; on cavalry impetuosity, 83; on Craufurd at Côa, 88; on victory at Bussaco, 95, 98; on British doubts about Wellington in Peninsula, 101–2; criticises Wellington's generals, 107; on Wellington's caution, 120; at Salamanca, 158; in Madrid, 170–1; as Wellington's favourite ADC, 171; on attack on Burgos, 173; on troops' indiscipline, 177; speculates on Napoleon's succeeding in Russia, 182; letter from Aberdeen on Wellington's position in Spain, 185; on British victory at Vitoria, 201; on invading France, 213; rejoins Wellington for 1815 campaign, 252; reports Blücher's defeat at Ligny, 270; on arrival of Prussians at Waterloo, 298; wounded at Waterloo and death, 300, 306–7

Gordon, Robert, 252

Graham, General Sir Thomas (*later* Baron Lynedoch): praises Ponsonby at Barrosa, 103; at battle of Vitoria, 191, 195–6, 201; at siege of San Sebastián, 205–8, 210, 213–16

Grant, General Colquhoun, 125

grapeshot, 95n

Grassini, Giuseppina, 243

Grattan, William: in Portugal, 79–80, 87, 92–3, 104; in battle of Fuentes d'Oñoro, 109, 115; on military hospital, 117; on British plundering of Spanish property, 122; at Ciudad Rodrigo, 126, 130, 133–5; on wives and women companions, 131; at Badajoz, 140, 147; at Salamanca, 164–5; mobbed by Spanish women, 169–70; in Madrid, 177; suffers from ague, 180; on inadequate honours for Peninsular veterans, 239, 314

Green, Bugler William, 72, 74, 143–6

Grey, Charles, 2nd Earl, 78–9

Gronow, Rees, 222, 252, 258, 267, 276, 287, 295, 304, 307

Grouchy, Marshal Emmanuel, Marquis de, 279–82, 285, 299, 301, 303, 311, 313

guerrillas *see* Spain

Gurwood, Lt John, 134

Hale, Sergeant James, 8, 31, 38, 90, 93–4

Halkett, Lt General Sir Colin, 297

Hardinge, Sir Henry, 1st Viscount, 269–70, 315–16

Harris, Rifleman Benjamin: writes account of campaigns, 4–5; at battle of Roliça, 18–19; and death of Cochan, 20; at Vimeiro, 24, 29; plunders enemy dead, 31; dislikes Craufurd, 41; on class of officers, 43

Harvest, Lieutenant, 143

Hay, William, 179, 181, 191, 196, 248, 260, 267, 277, 280, 289

Haye-Sainte, La (Waterloo), 279–80, 284, 299–300

Hendaye, Spain, 219

Henegan, Richard, 207–8, 213–16

Hennell, George, 146, 151, 217

Hill, Lt General Rowland ('Daddy'): in Portugal with Wellington, 10, 19, 83; at Vimeiro, 27; humanity, 34, 125; at Talavera, 60–1; at Bussaco, 93; watches Soult, 169; and Wellington's strategy in Spain, 172; evacuates Madrid, 175, 177; at battle of Vitoria, 191–2; Soult attacks at Maya Pass, 210–11; in attack at Vera, 224; Soult attacks on Nive, 226–7; rejoins Wellington for 1815 campaign, 252

Hougoumont, Château d' (Waterloo),
279, 282–4, 294, 298
Houssaye, Henri, 281, 305

Imperial Guard (French): at Waterloo,
300–4
India: Wellington serves in, 3

Jackson, Sergeant Thomas, 50
Jourdan, Marshal Jean-Baptiste, 70
Junot, General Jean-Andoche:
command in Portugal, 11, 14;
Wellington attacks in Lisbon, 13,
15; confidence, 21; at Vimeiro,
26–7; death by defenestration, 286n

Kellerman, General François, 27
Kelly (of Connaught Rangers), 133
Kennedy, James Shaw, 132
Kincaid, John: in Portugal, 96–8, 104;
on advance into Spain, 105–6; on
wounded in battle, 110; at Fuentes
d'Oñoro, 112–13, 116; praises
Wellington, 116; on Wellington's
hunting, 123; on Picton at Ciudad
Rodrigo, 135; on Craufurd, 136; on
weather of Badajoz, 140; in assault
on Badajoz, 143, 147, 150;
humanity after taking of Badajoz,
151–2; in retreat from Madrid to
Ciudad Rodrigo, 177–8, 181; and
Wellington's reprimand of troops'
behaviour, 182; at Vitoria, 194, 196;
in France, 236; rejoins Wellington
for 1815 campaign, 250; prepares
for Waterloo, 258, 260; on battle of
Quatre-Bras, 267–8; at Waterloo,
280, 286, 304; on Simmons's
wounds, 314; celebrates 37th
anniversary of Waterloo (1852), 316
King's German Legion: recruited in
Hanover, 42; at Talavera, 61, 68;
Wellington praises, 228; in

Netherlands campaign (1815), 253;
at Waterloo, 282, 299
Knowles, Lieutenant Robert, 122, 129,
149, 210

Lake, Lt Colonel George, 16–17, 19
Lamare, Colonel, 142
Lamb, Lady Caroline (née Ponsonby),
39, 66, 100, 170, 241, 313
Lamb, William (later 2nd Viscount
Melbourne), 100
Landmann, George: in Portugal, 7, 11,
13–16, 19, 20; at Vimeiro, 25–6, 28;
kills injured Frenchman, 31
Landsheit, Sergeant Norbert, 12, 24,
28
Larpent, Seymour, 185–7, 212–13,
223–4, 230, 232, 240–1
Lawrence, Sergeant William, 30, 60,
145, 195, 222, 248, 277, 296, 314
Leach, Jonathan: on heat in Portugal,
13, 19; at battle of Roliça, 17–19; at
Vimeiro, 24, 38; hates Craufurd, 41,
76, 87, 103, 113; returns to
Peninsula (1809), 55–6; on contact
with French, 64; on conditions in
Portugal, 73; encourages fitness
among men, 81; in battle on Côa,
85–7; on supply shortage in
Portugal, 91; at Bussaco, 94; on
French deception methods, 98;
amusements in Portugal, 102; on
conditions at Santarém, 104; and
assault on Badajoz, 148; in Madrid,
170; on Wellington's reprimand of
troops' behaviour in Spain, 182;
recreational shooting, 186, 227; on
Spanish welcome for British troops,
189; in Pyrenees, 204; in France,
236–7; rejoins Wellington for 1815
campaign, 250; at Waterloo, 284–6,
299; on neglect of Wellington's
veterans, 314

Leeke, Ensign William, 250–1, 277, 301, 303
Legros (French soldier), 283
Leipzig, battle of (1813), 223
Leith, General Sir James, 93–4, 163–5
Le Marchant, John Gaspard, 155–6, 163–5
Lennox, Lady Georgiana, 260
Leslie, Charles, 7, 27, 49, 57, 60–4
Leveson-Gower, Lord Granville (later 1st Earl Granville), 170
Ligny (Belgium), battle of (1815), 259, 262–3, 269–70
Lisbon: occupied by French, 9, 21; British plan to capture, 10–11, 13, 15; French evacuate, 32; character, 43–4, 55; Wellington in, 43; Wellington's defences, 79, 96
Liverpool, Robert Banks Jenkinson, 2nd Earl of: pessimism over Peninsular campaign, 78; letter from Wellington on resistance to Masséna, 82; and Wellington's explanation of low pay as cause of sack of Badajoz, 153; letter from Wellington on troops' gallantry at Badajoz, 154; letter from Wellington on siege of Burgos, 176; congratulates Wellington on Vitoria victory, 201–2; appoints Wellington ambassador in Paris, 235; removes Wellington from Paris ambassadorship, 244; and Wellington's attendance at Congress of Vienna, 245; determination to oppose Napoleon after escape from Elba, 247
Loison, General Louis-Henri, 14, 18
looting see plunder
Louis XVIII, King of France, 231–2, 235, 243, 256, 313

Macdonnell, Lt Colonel James, 282–4
McGrigor, Surgeon James, 149, 187, 239
Mackenzie, Major General, 69
Mackie, Lieutenant William, 131, 133, 149
Mackinnon, Major General Henry, 130, 133
Macleod, Major, 86, 89
Macpherson, Lieutenant, 149
Madrid: Joseph Bonaparte at, 56, 71, 169; Wellington advances on and occupies, 169–70, 172, 184; Retiro garrison surrenders, 171; Wellington evacuates, 175, 177
Maida (Italy), battle of (1806), 30
Maitland, Major General Sir Peregrine, 304, 316
Manguilla: cavalry charge at (1812), 156
Marathas, 3
Marchand, General Jean-Gabriel, 95
Marengo, battle of (1800), 78
Marmont, Marshal Auguste: replaces Masséna in Spain, 119–20; sends part of army to Valencia, 126; and Wellington's siege of Ciudad Rodrigo, 129; Napoleon sends to northern Iberia, 139, 153; movements and manoeuvres at Salamanca, 155–62, 201; wounded, 162; army retreats after Salamanca, 168; death, 313
Masséna, Marshal André: commands in Peninsula against Wellington, 77–8, 101, 108; advance on Portugal, 82, 84, 90–1; captures Almeida, 90–1; defeat at Bussaco, 91–6; differences with Ney, 94, 106; Wellington praises generalship, 96, 108; halts at and retreats from Torres Vedras defences, 97–9; winters in Santarém (1810–11), 104; forced back into Spain, 105, 107; dismisses Ney, 106;

Masséna, Marshal André (*cont.*)
  defeat at Sabugal, 107; dismissed by
  Napoleon, 107, 119; defeat at
  Fuentes d'Oñoro, 110–11, 113–16;
  orders Brennier to destroy fortress
  at Almeida, 117; Wellington meets
  in Paris, 242–3; death, 313
Maucune, General Antoine, 161–4
Maya, pass of (Pyrenees), 209–10, 219
medical care (of troops), 31–2, 50,
  89–90, 110, 117, 187, 307
Melbourne, 2nd Viscount *see* Lamb,
  William
Mengs, Anton, 170–1
Mercer, Captain Cavalié, 251, 254,
  261–2, 266, 272–4, 280, 292–8, 301
Metternich, Prince Clemens von,
  202–3
Mondego Bay, Portugal, 7–9, 11–13
money values, 53n
Mont Saint-Jean, Belgium, 256, 271
Moore, Lt General Sir John: Canning
  favours to command in Peninsula,
  11; as potential reinforcement for
  Wellington, 23; commands army
  against Napoleon in Peninsula,
  36–7, 40, 53; death, 37; and
  Craufurd, 41; avenged at Bussaco,
  94; retreat to Corunna, 177
Morris, Tom, 250, 264–6, 268, 277,
  295–7, 306, 315
Moscow: Napoleon aims for, 121;
  Napoleon retreats from, 183–4
Murphy, Major, 163
Murray, Lt General George, 223
muskets: description, 17

Namur, Belgium, 256
Napier, George, 88, 94, 168, 239
Napier, William, 66, 72, 85, 88, 94,
  113–14
Napoleon I (Bonaparte), Emperor of
  the French: Wellington defeats, 1,
  311; rise to power, 2–3; dismisses
  Wellington as 'sepoy general', 4;
  military successes, 8–9; infantry
  tactics, 26; leads army to Peninsula,
  36–8, 53; on conduct of British
  troops, 52; at siege of Toulon
  (1793), 63; advances on Vienna, 69;
  learns of Talavera defeat, 69–70;
  orders marshals to remove
  Wellington from Portugal, 77; fails
  to command against Wellington in
  Peninsula, 107–8, 202; invades
  Russia, 121, 182; orders Marmont
  to send forces to Valencia, 126;
  sends Marmont to northern Iberia,
  139, 153, 155; neglects Spain, 155;
  messages intercepted and codes
  broken, 187; victories in Germany
  (1813), 188, 202; praises
  Wellington's generalship, 202;
  Wellington studies and appraises,
  202–3; and Wellington's entry into
  France, 219; defeated at Leipzig
  (1813), 223; and invasion of France
  by Allies, 225–6; rearguard actions
  against Allies, 230; abdicates, 231,
  232n, 234; exiled to Elba, 234–5,
  244–5; advocates abolition of slave
  trade, 242n; Wellington enjoys
  affairs with ex-mistresses, 243;
  escapes from Elba and advances
  through France, 246–8; army
  strength in 1815 campaign, 251–2,
  258; movements before Waterloo,
  255–8; Wellington prepares to
  confront, 257, 271; orders to
  D'Erlon at Quatre-Bras, 269;
  presence at Waterloo and conduct
  of battle, 278–81, 284–6, 290,
  299–300, 302–3, 311; disparages
  Wellington before Waterloo, 281;
  Wellington refuses to fire on at
  Waterloo, 281; discounts Blücher

joining up with Wellington, 282;
and arrival of Prussians at Waterloo,
299; abandons carriage at Waterloo,
305; escapes from Waterloo, 305;
exile on St Helena and death, 313
Neale, Adam, 31–2
Ney, Marshal Michel: supports Masséna
in Peninsula, 78, 84; at Bussaco,
94–5; differences with Masséna, 94;
Wellington attacks at Foz de
Arouce, 105; Masséna dismisses,
106; leaves Russia, 184; abandons
Napoleon on abdication, 234;
Wellington meets in Paris, 242;
rejoins Napoleon after escape from
Elba, 246; commands at Quatre-
Bras, 262–3, 268–9; at Waterloo,
285, 292–4, 298, 300–1, 303, 305,
311; qualities, 292; executed, 313
Nive, river (France), 225–8
Nivelle, river (France), 223–5
Nivelles, Belgium, 266–7

O'Hare, Major Peter, 143, 147
Oporto, Portugal, 38; battle of, 45–9
Orthez, France, battle of, 228–9
O'Shea, Private Morris, 315

Pack, General Sir Denis, 165
Paget, Lt General Henry see Uxbridge,
2nd Earl of
Pakenham, Major General Sir Edward
('Ned'): status and command, 43; at
Fuentes d'Oñoro, 115; at battle of
Salamanca, 160–5; punishes
offending soldiers, 221–2; killed at
New Orleans, 245
Pakenham, Henry, 35
Pamplona, 196–7, 204–5, 211, 213,
219, 223
Papelotte (farm, Waterloo), 279
Paris: Wellington appointed ambassador
in, 235–6, 241–4

Partridge, HMS, 246
Perceval, Spencer, 101
Percival, Captain, 307
Philippon, Baron Armand, 139, 142–5,
150, 153
Picton, Lt General Sir Thomas:
character and behaviour, 80;
commands 3rd Division, 80, 83;
rows with Craufurd, 88, 116, 120; at
Bussaco, 92–3; in battle of Fuentes
d'Oñoro, 109, 116; escape at El
Bodón, 120; attempts to prevent
thieving by troops, 122; in assault
on Ciudad Rodrigo, 130–1; on
behaviour of troops in Ciudad
Rodrigo, 135, 154; in assault on
Badajoz, 142–3, 146–7, 150, 154,
160; ill with fever, 160; at battle of
Vitoria, 191–5; offends Simmons,
203; withdraws at Roncesvalles,
211; disdain for Spanish troops, 221;
at Toulouse, 231; returns home,
237; rejoins Wellington for 1815
campaign, 252; encounter with
Wellington before Waterloo, 258;
movements before Waterloo, 261;
at Quatre-Bras, 263, 267; wounded,
267–8; questions Mercer before
Waterloo, 274; killed at Waterloo,
286–7
Picurina fort, Badajoz, 140–1
Pitt, William, the Younger, 37
Plancenoit (Waterloo), 299, 303
plunder: by British troops in Portugal,
31, 51; after battle, 152, 195, 197–9,
221, 306
Poço Velho, Spain, 111
Ponsonby, Lady Emily (née Bathurst),
313, 316
Ponsonby, Major General Sir
Frederick: with 23rd Light
Dragoons, 39; in Portugal, 54; at
Talavera, 60–1, 65–7, 74; promoted,

Ponsonby, Major General Sir
Frederick (*cont.*)
75; and Wellington's retreat to
Lisbon after Bussaco, 96; at
Wellington's HQ, 99–100; at battle
of Barrosa, 103; commands 12th
Light Dragoons, 103–4; friendship
with Cocks, 125; optimism, 137;
commands brigade at Villagarcía,
155–6; at Salamanca, 157–8, 165–6;
chases French rearguard after
Salamanca, 168; in Madrid, 170;
pursues Clausel, 172–3; and death of
Cocks, 174; wounded at siege of
Burgos, 174–5; leadership in retreat
from Madrid, 179; receives
Wellington's letter reprimanding
troops' behaviour, 182; illness at
Vitoria, 191, 195–6; intercedes for
Ramsay, 203; and siege of San
Sebastián, 207; advance into France,
214, 220; at Bayonne, 228; reports
Napoleon's abdication to
Wellington, 231; regimental
Peninsular battle honour, 238;
attends Duchess of Richmond's
ball, 260; preparations for Quatre-
Bras, 261; misses Quatre-Bras battle,
266–7; and Wellington's withdrawal
to Waterloo, 272; at Waterloo, 273,
277–8, 280, 289–90; seriously
wounded at Waterloo, 290, 308–9;
later career, marriage and death,
313–14
Ponsonby, George, 183
Ponsonby, Sir Henry Frederick, 314
Ponsonby, Major General William,
164, 174, 261, 280, 289
Popham, Commodore Sir Home, 175
Portland, William Henry Cavendish
Bentinck, 3rd Duke of, 37
Portugal: Wellington's campaign in,
7–8; seeks British aid, 10; French
behaviour in, 14, 104; revenge on
French, 31, 49–50; Beresford
commands in, 37; Wellington
returns to (1809), 38, 43; conditions
and character, 44; as Wellington's
ally, 44, 46; fighting qualities, 46,
82–3, 95, 217; Wellington
withdraws to after Talavera, 76–8;
Wellington defends against
Masséna, 82–3; troops at Bussaco,
92–3, 95; troops at Fuentes
d'Oñoro, 109–10; troops in battle
of Salamanca, 165; Wellington
leaves (1813), 188; troops in assault
on San Sebastián, 215, 217; in
military alliance with Britain and
Spain, 217; casualties at Orthez, 229
Prince Regent see George, Prince of
Wales
Prussia: revives against Napoleon, 108;
agrees armistice with Napoleon
(1813), 188; in 1815 campaign
against Napoleon, 255, 260;
defeated at Ligny, 262–3, 269–70;
debates whether to support
Wellington, 270–1; and battle of
Waterloo, 291, 293, 298–9, 301,
303, 310
Pyrenees: Wellington's campaign in,
188, 203–10

Quatre-Bras, Belgium, battle of (1815),
259, 261–8

Raglan, Baron see Somerset, Lord
James Henry Fitzroy
Ramsay, Captain Norman, 114, 203–4
Reille, General Honoré, 281
Rey, General Emmanuel, 207, 216
Reynier, General Jean-Louis, 92–3
Rhune, La (Pyrenees), 220, 224
Richmond, Charles Lennox, 4th Duke
of, 10–11, 33, 255, 259

Richmond, Charlotte, Duchess of: Brussels ball (1815), 255, 257–8, 260

Riddock, Lieutenant Alex, 266

Ridge, Colonel Henry, 149

riflemen: role, 17–18

Robe, Lt Colonel William, 25, 27

Robinson, Captain (of Highland Regiment), 265–6

rockets: used by British in 1815 campaign, 273, 280

Roliça, Portugal, battle of, 15–19, 20, 23

Roncesvalles, pass of (Pyrenees), 209–11

Ross, Lt General Sir Hew Dalrymple (*earlier* Captain): commands 'A' Troop Royal Horse Artillery, 73, 87, 94; celebrates 37th anniversary of Waterloo (1852), 316

Royal Horse Artillery: 'A' Troop (Chestnut Troop), 73, 87, 95, 316; at Fuentes d'Oñoro, 113–14; in 1815 campaign, 251, 261–2, 272–3; at Quatre-Bras, 266; at Waterloo, 292–3, 301; *see also* artillery

Royal Navy: power, 9; access to Portuguese ports, 10; and supplies for Wellington, 175–6, 205; builds bridge of boats at Bayonne, 228; and British world power, 311

Russia: revives against Napoleon, 108; Napoleon invades, 121, 182; Napoleon retreats from, 183–4; agrees armistice with Napoleon (1813), 188; and Napoleon's 1815 campaign, 256

Sabugal, Portugal, battle of, 106–7

Saint-Jean-de-Luz, 220, 223, 225

Saint-Lambert, Château (Waterloo), 285

Salamanca: Marmont at, 155–7; Wellington advances on, 156–8;

manoeuvres at, 158–65; British victory, 166, 168, 184, 201

San Sebastián, siege of, 204–10, 213; assault on, 215–16; atrocities following, 216

Santander, Spain, 175

Santarém, Portugal, 99, 104

Schaumann, August: and job as commissary, 42, 49; at Talavera, 62, 66–7; on Spaniards' plundering of British quarters, 74; on Wellington's retreat after Talavera, 75; and scorched earth zone behind Torres Vedras, 96; on French atrocities in Portugal, 104; on Erskine, 118; on asceticism at Wellington's HQ, 125; womanising, 126, 204; at Vitoria, 191; on available women after Vitoria, 197; and looting after Vitoria, 199; on punishment of offending Spanish soldiers, 221–2

Scotland: supplies soldiers for British army, 102–3

Scovell, Lt General Sir George, 187, 199, 316

Seringapatam, India, 3

Seymour, Colonel, 65

Sharpe, Regimental Sergeant-Major, 111

Sherbrooke, Lt General Sir John Coape, 60

Shrapnel, William, 25

Simmons, George: writes account of campaigns, 4; praises Wellington, 42; on Portuguese, 46; complains of high prices, 53n; on Cuesta's abandoning British sick and wounded, 74; at Côa river engagement, 85; wounded, 89, 299–300; on Craufurd, 99, 113; on conditions at Santarém, 104; at siege and assault of Ciudad Rodrigo, 127, 131; on assaults on Badajoz, 148,

Simmons, George (*cont.*)
151; at Salamanca, 158; on popular
Spanish acclaim for Wellington,
169; Picton offends, 203; in France,
236; rejoins Wellington for 1815
campaign, 250; at Waterloo,
299–300; later career, 314
Skerrett, Brigadier, 218
Slade, General Sir John, 111
slave trade: abolition, 242
Smith, Lt General Harry: blames
Craufurd for inaction at Ciudad
Rodrigo, 83; wounded, 89; on
Craufurd's arrival at Fuentes
d'Oñoro, 113; at Ciudad Rodrigo,
128, 134; digs siege trenches at
Badajoz, 140; injured by horse, 140;
in assault on Badajoz, 147, 150–1;
marries young Spaniard in Badajoz,
151–2, 178; billeted at Ciudad
Rodrigo, 186; at Vitoria, 194;
watches Soult's attack on Spanish
across Bidasoa, 218; in attack at
Vera, 220–1; occupies mud hut,
222; entry into France, 223, 225;
horse killed at Nivelle, 225; sent to
America, 237, 248; returns to
Europe, 248; at Waterloo, 279–80;
survives Waterloo, 309; later career
and promotion to general, 313;
celebrates 37th anniversary of
Waterloo (1852), 315; as pallbearer
at Wellington's funeral, 317
Smith, Juana (*later* Lady), 152, 178,
186, 194, 222–3, 225, 237, 248, 279,
309, 313
Snodgrass, Major, 215
Solignac, General Jean-Baptiste, 26,
29–30
Somerset, Lord James Henry Fitzroy
(*later* Baron Raglan): as
Wellington's aide de camp in
Peninsula, 10, 42, 222; at Roliça,

19; at Badajoz, 150; in Pyrenees
with Wellington, 211–12; rejoins
Wellington for 1815 campaign, 252;
wife Emily gives birth to daughter
in Brussels, 252; wounded at
Waterloo and arm amputated, 300,
308; later career and peerage, 313
Sorauren, Spain, battles of (1813),
211–13
Soult, Marshal Nicolas: makes base in
Oporto, 38, 46–7; and British attack
on Oporto, 48–9; regroups and
attempts to cut off Wellington, 71;
position in Peninsula, 108; Beresford
defeats at Albuera, 118–19; believes
Badajoz able to withstand siege, 139;
advance on Badajoz, 153; at siege of
Cadiz, 169; as threat to Madrid, 172;
marches on Madrid, 175; abandons
Andalusia, 184; differences with
Joseph, 184–5; Napoleon sends to
confront Wellington, 202; campaign
in Pyrenees, 209–10, 213, 218;
attempts rescue of San Sebastián,
217; resists Wellington's entering
France, 219, 223, 226, 228, 230;
defeated at Nivelle, 225; retires to
Toulouse, 229; Leach sees in France
after peace, 236; Wellington meets
in Paris, 242; at Waterloo, 281,
285n; death, 313
Spain: Joseph Bonaparte imposed as
king, 10; hatred of French, 14;
strength of French forces in, 54,
168–9, 187; raises army to support
Wellington, 56; quality of army,
60–1, 171; troops at Talavera, 60–2;
troops plunder British quarters, 74;
guerrillas at Fuentes d'Oñoro, 111;
French retreat in, 117; population
welcomes Wellington's troops,
168–9; guerrillas harass French, 169,
171; military support for

Wellington, 171; guerrillas waylay French messengers, 187; Wellington's 1813 strategy, 188–9; criticises British troops for atrocities at San Sebastián, 216; in military coalition with Britain and Portugal, 217; troops' behaviour in France, 221–2; casualties at Orthez, 229; in attack on Toulouse, 231

Spencer, General Sir Brent, 13, 110, 113

surgeons: and treatment of wounds, 50, 307

Surtees, William, 228

Surveillante, HMS, 43

Swan (of Connaught Rangers), 133

Talavera, battle of (1809), 57–70, 74, 78, 156; looting in aftermath, 197

Talbot, Colonel, 83

Taylor, Colonel, 28–9, 67

Thomas, Sergeant, 86

Thomières, General Jean, 161–3

Thornton, James, 124, 261, 307

Times, The: Craufurd justifies Côa action in, 88

Tippoo Sultan, 3

Todd, Thomas: in Portugal, 12, 18, 29, 31, 97, 102; in battle of Fuentes d'Oñoro, 109–10, 114; on French soldiers, 114; witnesses act of cannibalism, 178; at Vitoria, 192; at Roncesvalles, 210; discharge deferred, 249–50; in Netherlands campaign (1815), 249–50; at Waterloo, 277; later career, 314–15

Tomkinson, Henry, 272

Tomkinson, Lt Colonel William: background, 39–40; injured at Oporto, 45–6, 50; at Bussaco, 98; friendship with Cocks, 125; at Salamanca, 155; on Wellington's hesitation at Salamanca, 160;

opposes Clausel, 172–3; and death of Cocks, 174; and Wellington's rebuke to men after Burgos, 182; in Wellington's 1815 cavalry review, 254; misses Quatre-Bras battle, 266; guards rear during Wellington's move to Waterloo, 272; at Waterloo, 280, 306

Tormes, river (Spain), 158–9, 166

Torrens, Colonel Sir Henry, 78, 87

Torres Vedras, Lines of, 79, 96–8

Toulouse, 229–31

Tyler, Captain J., 150

Uniacke, Captain, 134

United States of America: British war with (1812–14), 237

Urrugne, France, 220

Urumea, river (Spain), 206, 215

Uxbridge, Lt General Henry Paget, 2nd Earl of (*later* 1st Marquess of Anglesey): relations with Charlotte Wellesley, 36; loses leg at Waterloo, 230, 305–7; commands cavalry in 1815 campaign, 253–4, 272; questions Wellington before Waterloo, 274–5; in action at Waterloo, 287–9, 291, 298; celebrates 1852 anniversary of Waterloo, 315–16

Valladolid, Spain, 168, 176

Ventosa, Portugal, 26–7, 29–30

Vera, Spain, 204, 218–21, 223–4

Victor, Marshal Claude Perrin, 56–8, 60, 62–3, 68–9

Vienna, Congress of (1815), 235, 245

Villagarcía, battle of (1812), 155–6

Vimeiro, Portugal, battle of (1808), 20, 23–30, 33

Vitoria, battle of (1813), 189–96; looting in aftermath, 197–9; victory and effect, 201–3

Wagram, battle of (1809), 69, 78

Walcheren expedition (1809), 77

Walker, Colonel George Townshend, 25

Wallace, Colonel Alexander, 93, 115–16, 162–3

Waterloo, battle of (1815): cavalry actions, 156, 287–9, 297–8; Wellington selects as battle site, 259, 271; weather, 273, 277; Wellington's forces assemble at, 273–4; conduct of, 278–9, 282, 290–301, 304; Prussians arrive, 298–9, 310; aftermath and battlefield scenes, 306–9; casualties, 306; victory, 310–11; 37th anniversary celebrations (1852), 315–16

Waters, Colonel (later Lt General Sir) John, 48

Wavre, Belgium, 270, 276, 282, 285, 298–9

Webster, Lady Frances Wedderburn, 255, 276

Weimer, Marguerite (Mademoiselle George), 243

Wellesley, Lord Arthur Richard (later 2nd Duke of Wellington; Wellington's son), 240

Wellesley, Lord Charles (Wellington's son), 240

Wellesley, Charlotte (later Paget), 36

Wellesley, Henry, 71, 185, 235

Wellesley, Richard Colley, Marquess (Wellington's eldest brother): changes family surname, 1; promotes Wellington's career, 2; in India, 3; letter from Wellington on Spanish allies, 76; Whig hostility to, 78; womanising, 79; Wellington writes to on success at Orthez, 229

Wellesley-Pole, William (Wellington's elder brother), 79, 88, 166, 212, 310

Wellington, Arthur Wellesley, 1st Duke of: background and career, 1–4; marriage, 2, 4; writings, 4; romances and affairs, 5; lands at Mondego Bay, 8–9, 11–13; appearance, dress and manner, 9, 125, 185–6, 222–3, 276; strength of force in Peninsula, 9, 54; concern for supply, 13–14, 41, 51, 72, 122; takes Roliça, 15–16, 18, 20; lacks cavalry, 23, 28; victory at Vimeiro, 24, 26–30, 33–4; and cavalry's impetuosity, 29, 66, 156, 168, 288, 291; thwarted by Burrard, 30–1; questioned over Convention of Cintra, 32–3; returns to England from Portugal, 33; marriage relations, 35, 124, 241, 312; as Chief Secretary for Ireland, 36; returns to Portugal (1809), 38, 43, 53; commands British army in Peninsula, 40; nicknamed 'Old Nosey' by men, 42; relations with colleagues and men, 42, 80–1; Toryism and beliefs, 42–3; captures Oporto, 47–9; visits and cares for wounded, 50, 53; on conduct of own men, 51–3, 180–2, 199, 221; hunting, 54–5, 123, 139, 185; at Talavera, 58–60, 62, 66–7; battle disposition, 58, 63; escapes in battles, 59, 106, 157–8, 166, 212, 229–30, 263, 300; viscountcy, 69; withdraws in Spain after Talavera, 70–1, 74–7; on starving army, 75–6; seeks political support for Peninsular campaign, 78, 101–2; Whig hostility to, 78–9; builds Lines of Torres Vedras to protect Lisbon, 79, 96; on qualities of military commanders, 83; and Craufurd's action at river Côa, 88; and loss of Almeida, 90–1; at battle of Bussaco, 92–3; advances into Spain against Masséna, 105, 118–19; Fuentes d'Oñoro victory, 109–17; composure, 117, 265; criticises commanders after escape of Brennier, 118; and siege of Ciudad Rodrigo, 119–20, 126–30; entertaining and social life, 123–4; daily routine on campaign, 124; takes no home leave from Peninsula, 124; on losing Craufurd, 136; awarded earldom and bonus for Ciudad Rodrigo victory, 137; at siege and taking of Badajoz, 139–41, 143–5, 153; praises men's courage at Badajoz, 148; and sack of Badajoz, 152–3; advocates Corps of Engineers, 153; weeps after Badajoz victory, 154; opposes Marmont at Salamanca, 156–61; hesitation before battle of Salamanca, 159–60, 166; and conduct of battle of Salamanca, 161–4, 166–7; praises cavalry at Salamanca, 164; strategy in Spain after Salamanca, 168–9; in Madrid, 170–2; and expectations of support from Spanish, 171–2; besieges Burgos, 173–6, 182; retreats from Burgos and Madrid, 175–7, 182, 184; troops' hardships on retreat across Spain, 178–80; criticised in England for retreat from Burgos, 182–3; improved prospects in Spain after Napoleon's reverse in Russia, 184–5; supervises training in battlefield drills, 186; and troops' recreation and living conditions, 186–7; strategy in Spain (1813), 188–9; and conduct of battle of Vitoria, 190–1, 194; and looting after Vitoria, 199; acquires Joseph's Old Master paintings after Vitoria, 200; victory at Vitoria, 201; appointed field marshal, 202; studies

and appraises Napoleon, 202–3; has Ramsay arrested, 203; campaign in Pyrenees, 205–11, 219; and siege of San Sebastián, 209, 213–14; negotiates Anglo-Spanish-Portuguese military coalition, 217; enters France, 219, 221, 225–6; on proposal to negotiate peace with Napoleon, 226; hurt at Orthez, 229–30; and conduct of battle of Toulouse, 230–1; and abdication of Napoleon, 231–2; achievement in Peninsula, 232–3, 239; as British ambassador in Paris, 235, 241–4; given command of allied army in Netherlands, 235, 248–9; in Paris after Napoleon's exile, 235; dukedom, 236; fails to press for adequate recognition for Peninsular veterans, 238–9; final review of Peninsular army, 238; popular adulation for, 239–40, 312; supposed affairs on campaign, 240; awarded cash bounty, 241; dalliances and affairs in Paris and Brussels, 243, 255; attends Congress of Vienna, 245; army strength and composition in 1815 campaign, 251–6; in Brussels, 251, 254–5; battle plan in 1815 campaign, 256; and Napoleon's movements before Waterloo, 256–8; prepares to confront Napoleon, 257, 271, 276; at Quatre-Bras, 262–6, 268; troop dispositions for Waterloo, 270–1, 273–4, 279–80; writes to Lady Frances Wedderburn Webster before Waterloo, 276; conduct of battle of Waterloo, 279, 290–1, 294, 297–8, 300–1, 304, 311; refuses to fire on Napoleon at Waterloo, 281; meets Blücher at Waterloo, 305; returns to Brussels after Waterloo, 307; self-confidence, 310–11; writes

Wellington, Arthur Wellesley 1st Duke of (*cont.*)
Waterloo Despatch, 310; resists reform, 311; political career, 312; celebrates 37th anniversary of Waterloo (1852), 315–16; reputation, 315; death, 317
Wellington, Kitty, Duchess of (*née* Pakenham): marries Wellington, 2, 4; marriage relations, 35, 124, 241, 312; and Wellington's return from campaign, 240–1; joins Wellington in Paris, 243; death, 312
Wheeler, Private William: on Portugal, 44; at Fuentes d'Oñoro, 113; escapes lightning at Salamanca, 158; on popular Spanish welcome, 169; on retreat from Madrid, 180; plunder after Vitoria, 197–8; on loss of comrades, 237–8; wounded, 237; embarks for Ostend (1815), 248–9; smoking before Waterloo, 277; praises Wellington, 315
Whigs: criticise Wellington for Cintra Convention, 33; hostility to Wellington and family, 78
Whinyates, Major Edward, 273, 280
Whitbread, Samuel, 32, 79, 247
Wilberforce, William, 242
Wilkie (Costello's friend), 132–3
Williams, Lt Colonel, 109–10
Wilson, Harriette, 35
Winchester, Lieutenant Robert, 265
wolves: as danger, 73
women: accompany British army, 12, 20; hunger, 75; at siege of Ciudad Rodrigo, 131; trials on march, 178–9; troops enjoy in Spain, 204
wounded: treatment of, 31–2, 50, 89–90, 110, 117, 187, 307

York, Prince Frederick Augustus, Duke of: as Commander in Chief, 11, 252–3; sends officers to Wellington, 125, 253

Zadorra, river (Spain), 190–2, 196